NO COMMON POWER

POWER

Understanding International Relations

· THIRD EDITION ·

ROBERT J. LIEBER
Georgetown University

HarperCollinsCollegePublishers

Acquisitions Editor: Leo A.W. Wiegman
Project Coordination: Ruttle, Shaw & Wetherill, Inc.
Text Design: Nancy Sabato
Cover Designer: Kay Petronio
Electronic Production Manager: Valerie A. Sawyer
Desktop Administrator: Hilda Koparanian
Manufacturing Manager: Helene G. Landers
Electronic Page Makeup: RR Donnelley Barbados
Printer and Binder: RR Donnelley & Sons Company
Cover Printer: RR Donnelley & Sons Company

No Common Power: Understanding International Relations, Third Edition

Library of Congress Cataloging-in-Publication Data

Lieber, Robert J.
No common power: understanding international relations / Robert J. Lieber.—3rd ed.
        p. cm.
    Includes index.
    ISBN 0-673-52390-X
    1. International relations.   2. Balance of power.   3. World politics—1945–   I. Title.
JX1395.L475 1995   94-7217
327–dc20   CIP

94 95 96 97 9 8 7 6 5 4 3 2 1

Hereby it is manifest, that during the time men live without a common power to keep them in awe, they are in that condition which is called war.

—THOMAS HOBBES, *LEVIATHAN*, CHAPTER 13

CONTENTS

PREFACE

Dramatic, even revolutionary, changes have taken place in world politics. Among them have been the collapse of Soviet-dominated regimes in Eastern Europe; the end of the Cold War; the dissolution of the USSR and the initiation of an uncertain transformation toward democracy and a market economy within Russia itself; a surge toward democratization in parts of the developing world and in many countries formerly governed by Marxist-Leninist dictatorships; the ebbing of bitter regional conflicts (Central America, the Middle East, Afghanistan, southern Africa, Cambodia); widespread movement toward economic liberalization; extraordinary economic growth in China and East Asia; far-reaching trade expansion through the North American Free Trade Agreement (NAFTA) and the General Agreement on Tariffs and Trade (GATT); agreement to address global environmental dangers; the spread of instantaneous global communications as symbolized by CNN television; reinvigorated efforts toward Western European unity; and attempts at increased cooperation and peacekeeping through the United Nations.

In the immediate aftermath of the Cold War, these changes fostered optimism about the future course of international relations. Indeed, some observers even concluded that the world was on the threshold of an unprecedented period of global peace and cooperation. Yet other major events have not been so benign. They include ethnic warfare and appalling abuses of human rights throughout the former Yugoslavia; clan warfare, starvation and anarchy in Somalia; tribal massacres in Rwanda; chaos and warfare among former Soviet Republics in the Caucasus region and elsewhere along the Central Asian borders of the ex-USSR; instability in Russia and Ukraine; regimes fostering terrorism in Iraq, Iran, the Sudan, and Libya; the emergence outside the traditional East-West sphere of regional powers equipped with weapons of mass destruction (chemical and biological weapons, missiles, nuclear programs); the failure of ambitious United Nations peacekeeping efforts in Somalia and the former Yugoslavia; and outbursts of fanatical ethnic, nationalist, and religious hatreds.

Altogether, these events represent the most profound change in international relations since the emergence of the East-West conflict in the years after World War II. In responding to them, this expanded third edition of *No Common Power* devotes attention to revolutionary changes in the former Soviet Union and assesses the implications for the post–Cold War international system. Moreover, in treating problems of North-South relations, this edition provides expanded coverage of the debt crisis, economic development, the debate over dependency, ethnic conflict, and the relationship of the developing world to international politics. In addition, new attention is given to the implications of the Gulf war and to conflict in the former Yugoslavia, as well as to the problems of UN peacekeeping, arms control agreements, democracies and war, the Maastricht Treaty and European Union, the consequences of a rapid expansion in international economic relations, and the opportunities and limits of interdependence.

At the same time, this edition of *No Common Power* seeks to integrate these events with an appreciation of the underlying structural characteristics of the international system that remain resistant to fundamental change. These realities are captured in a phrase by Thomas Hobbes more than three centuries ago: Because they are "without a common power" in their international relations, states exist in a system that lacks effective authority for resolving the inevitable disputes that arise among them.

In essence, this means that states dwell in an environment of formal anarchy. Anarchy here is not synonymous with chaos. Instead the term denotes the absence of established governance above the level of the state. This fundamental characteristic shapes the relations among states and it is what sets international relations apart from domestic politics.

At the same time, the everyday realities of world affairs also display a great deal of practical order. Indeed, cooperation exists not only in the widespread observance of some rudimentary international rules, but can also be found in the extensive patterns of international economic relations and interdependence. The contrast of these two forces, the paradox of formal anarchy and practical order, conditions the manner in which world politics takes place and at the same time constrains state behavior. Attention to this interplay shapes the orientation of *No Common Power*.

Part I, Introduction: The Context of World Politics, suggests how the reader can manage the task of making sense of international relations and devotes particular attention to the anarchy concept. It also addresses the security dilemma:* the problem that in the absence of an effective international authority for resolving inevitable disputes, states need to rely on themselves for security. The result of this "self-help" system, however, is that other states face the same situation and also arm to provide their own security—as each defines it. Other things being equal, each state ultimately may become less secure. Chapter 2 goes on to assess the broad outlines of the international system in which the modern state functions. While considering the historical background, it devotes attention to the post–World War II pattern and the emergence of the post–Cold War international system.

Part II, Conflict in the Postwar and Post–Cold War Systems, treats those phenomena that made international relations in the post-1945 world unique in contrast to the previous era, and assesses the end of the bipolar system. Chapters 3 and 4 analyze the origins and development of the Cold War and East-West relations, then consider the end of the Cold War and its broader consequences for international relations. Chapter 5 then deals with the North-South conflict, ethnicity as a major source of friction, debates over dependency and development, the debt crisis, and the distinction between more and less successful developing coun-

---

* The term *security dilemma* originates with John H. Herz, *Political Realism and Political Idealism* (Chicago: University of Chicago Press, 1951). Its antecedents can be found in the writings of Thucydides, Thomas Hobbes, and Jean Jacques Rousseau. More recent important formulations and elaborations have been provided by Kenneth Waltz, Glenn Snyder, Robert Jervis, and others. The concept is discussed in more detail in Chapter 1.

tries ("third" versus "fourth" worlds). In turn, Chapter 6 addresses nuclear weapons and world politics, examining the implied penetration of the nation-state, basic concepts essential to the understanding of nuclear deterrence, arms control, proliferation, and the conduct of international relations in a nuclear world.

Part III, Watersheds in Twentieth-Century International Relations, deals with a series of international events and crises that are a common twentieth-century legacy. These events not only reflect the interplay of the forces the book is concerned with, but their impact has conditioned the contemporary understanding of international relations. Chapter 7 contrasts interpretations of the past based on 1914 (the outbreak of World War I) and 1938–1939 (appeasement of Nazi Germany and the start of World War II). Chapter 8 explores the Cuban missile crisis of October 1962 and the different interpretations that have evolved from a confrontation that brought the United States and the Soviet Union closer to the brink of nuclear war than at any time in their history. Chapters 9 and 10 consider the lessons of America's involvement in Vietnam, and then of the oil decade and the Persian Gulf crisis, with their consequences not only for the oil-importing democracies, but also for the perception of world politics held by developing countries.

Part IV, Order and the "Anarchical Society," shifts the focus away from conflict and competition and toward consideration of the ways in which states have sought to prevent war and to provide order to their relations. The section begins, in Chapter 11, by considering the causes of war. This chapter emphasizes the systemic factors that create a propensity for periodic conflicts to erupt into warfare— as exemplified in the cases of the Arab-Israeli Six-Day War of June 1967, the 1982 Falklands War between Britain and Argentina, the Gulf war, and conflict in the former Yugoslavia. It contrasts these cases with the manner in which domestic structures tend to contain conflicts and analyzes the relationship of democracies to war, including the propensity of genuinely democratic countries to refrain from going to war against one another. Chapter 12 then examines the search for order at the global level, through the League of Nations, the United Nations, and the development of international law and devotes attention to the problem of UN peacekeeping. Chapter 13 explores efforts at order undertaken at the regional level and embodied in the experience of Western Europe. It also gives attention to the Maastricht Treaty and the European Union's renewed impetus toward integration, along with the difficulties in achieving economic and monetary union as well as in foreign policy. Chapter 14 analyzes patterns of economic order. The search for economic cooperation and the pursuit of national economic interest have resulted in a pervasive interdependence and the establishment of international "regimes" to provide the framework—or rules of the game—within which much economic interaction takes place.

In Part V, Conclusion: Anarchy, Order, and Constraint, the book ends by weighing the phenomena of interdependence against power politics, including the interplay between domestic politics and foreign policy, and the contrast between systemic perspectives and the perceptions of individual states. This final chapter also reflects on the relationship between policymaking and global risk, encompassing the limits of certainty in political action, moral and collective action dilemmas, and imperatives that condition policymaking in the late twentieth-century world.

Overall, this book builds on themes foreshadowed in a number of my earlier writings. These include, *Theory and World Politics* (Winthrop and Little, Brown, 1972); *The Oil Decade* (Praeger and University Press of America, 1983 and 1986); and my contributions to *Eagle Defiant: United States Foreign Policy in the 1980s* (Little, Brown, 1983); *Eagle Resurgent? The Reagan Era in American Foreign Policy* (Little, Brown, 1987), and *Eagle in a New World* (HarperCollins, 1992). Chapter 11 here (in its discussion of game theory, Prisoner's Dilemma, and the causes of conflict) draws on parts of Chapters 2 and 5 in *Theory and World Politics;* and part of Chapter 10 draws on portions of Chapter 6 in *Eagle Resurgent?*

While the writing of this book has been an individual effort, it is a pleasure to acknowledge those to whom I am in one way or another indebted. As a student, I benefitted greatly from the teaching of Leon Epstein, John Armstrong, Walter Agard, and George Mosse at the University of Wisconsin; from Hans Morgenthau at the University of Chicago; and from Henry Kissinger, Stanley Hoffmann, Karl Deutsch, Samuel Beer, and Louis Hartz at Harvard.

In developing the approach that underlies this book, I gained valuable insights from working with my collaborators, Kenneth Oye and Donald Rothchild, in the *Eagle* books; from the realist analyses of the late Avner Yaniv vis-à-vis the harsh circumstances of the Middle East; and from the observations of Kenneth Waltz in California faculty colloquia. Others have provided valuable suggestions and comments concerning portions of the manuscript. In the end, I have gratefully incorporated many of their suggestions. They include Robert Paarlberg; Robert Art; William V. O'Brien and Anthony Arend (especially on Chapter 12); Benjamin Cohen (Chapter 13); and George Crane (Chapter 14); Richard Stites; and Nancy Lieber. Mark Lagon performed in an exemplary manner as research assistant and constructive critic, while Erik Pages and David Fite also provided helpful assistance on earlier editions. For research assistance on this third edition, I am pleased to acknowledge the help of Jeff Lord and Jacob Heilbrun. In addition, my son, Keir Lieber's critique of the manuscript has been rigorous and invaluable—by its quality the work of an accomplished colleague rather than a graduate student. I also wish to thank Gerry McCauley, Don Palm, and John Covell, all of whom encouraged me to write this book. Georgetown University, its Government Department, and its students have provided a stimulating and supportive environment in which I could undertake the writing, and subsequently the expansion and revision, of this book. I wish to express my gratitude to the reviewers of the previous edition, David Hendrickson of Colorado College and Roy Licklider of Rutgers University.

I am indebted to all of the above, though—for good or ill—responsibility for what appears in these pages remains my own.

Robert J. Lieber

ABOUT THE AUTHOR

Robert J. Lieber is Professor and Chairman of the Government Department at Georgetown University. He was born and raised in Chicago, received his undergraduate education at the University of Wisconsin and his Ph.D. at Harvard University. Previously professor and chairman in the Political Science Department at the University of California, Davis, he has also held fellowships from the Social Science Research Council, Guggenheim Foundation, Council on Foreign Relations, and the Rockefeller and Ford Foundations, among others. He has been visiting fellow or guest scholar at St. Anthony's College, Oxford; the Harvard University Center for International Affairs; Atlantic Institute, Paris; the Brookings Institution; the Woodrow Wilson International Center for Scholars; and Fudan University, Shanghai.

Professor Lieber is author of five other books: *British Politics and European Unity* (1970); *Theory and World Politics* (1972); *Oil and the Middle East War* (1976); *Contemporary Politics: Europe* (coauthor, 1976); and *The Oil Decade* (1983 and 1986). In addition, with Kenneth Oye and Donald Rothchild he is coeditor and contributing author of four volumes on American foreign policy: *Eagle Entangled: U.S. Foreign Policy in a Complex World* (1979); *Eagle Defiant: United States Foreign Policy in the 1980s* (1983); *Eagle Resurgent? The Reagan Era in American Foreign Policy* (1987); and *Eagle in a New World: American Grand Strategy in the Post–Cold War Era* (1992).

His other credits include faculty and party politics, "killer tennis," and a walk-on part in the Alfred Hitchcock film classic, *North by Northwest*.

PART 1

Introduction: The Context of World Politics

chapter 1

Understanding International Relations

Albert Einstein was once asked, "Why is it that when the mind of man has stretched so far as to discover the structure of the atom we have been unable to devise the political means to keep the atom from destroying us?" He replied, "That is simple, my friend, it is because politics is more difficult than physics."[1]

Nations dwell in perpetual anarchy, for no central authority imposes limits on the pursuit of sovereign interests. . . . At times, the absence of centralized international authority precludes attainment of common goals. . . . Yet at other times, states do realize common goals through cooperation under anarchy.

—KENNETH OYE[2]

Politics has been described as the "master science." Because it involves the authoritative allocation of values—i.e., decisions about who gets what—it encompasses almost every human action. Yet if politics holds pride of place in relations among people in their individual and national lives, there is something of particular importance in politics among nations.[3]

International relations—that is, relations among large and organized groups of peoples—have existed for several thousand years. The record of efforts to discern meaning or pattern in these relations is almost as old. Succeeding generations often consider the times in which they live to be truly unprecedented. Yet contemporary world politics is different in at least one profound respect: During the past generation, and for the first time in human history, the most powerful states have acquired the capability literally to obliterate one another. To be sure, this is an extreme possibility. It is just one of many scenarios that range from cooperation to conflict to outright war.[4]

More recently, extraordinary developments including the end of the Cold War; the dissolution of the Soviet Union; revolutionary transitions toward democracy and market economies in Eastern Europe as well as in parts of the developing world; and the spectacular economic growth of East Asia and China have seemingly ushered in a new era in international relations. These events have been accompanied by longer-term changes including a vast increase in international trade and global economic activity; the rapid international diffusion of communications and technology; the proliferation of weapons of mass destruction, such as nuclear, chemical and biological weapons and missiles to deliver them; and the growing prominence of nontraditional issues such as the environment, population, migration, and international peacekeeping.

As a consequence, it is tempting to approach world politics as though contemporary life is utterly unique. However, even though momentous changes are evident and need to be studied and understood, there are also practical realities and broader patterns which are longstanding in international politics. It is thus essential to be able to comprehend both newer and more deep-seated dimensions at the same time.

How, then, have we arrived at the present juncture? What does the record—past and present—of international relations tell us? And what are the dynamics of international relations as they shape the risks of conflict and the possibilities of cooperation?

The tasks of this book are clearly demanding. They are:

To provide a basis for understanding international relations.

To demonstrate why this understanding is quite different from mere intuition or common sense.[5]

To explain why international relations differs fundamentally from politics within states.

To analyze the dynamics of post–Cold War and post–World War II international relations, considering both the traits that set it apart from previous eras and the elements of continuity.

To examine the lessons of watershed events that have left their mark not only on international relations, but on our understanding of the subject.

To suggest why war occurs and what the principal explanations have to offer.

To assess the implications for America's role in a world that has undergone profound transformation.

This is a tall order. In seeking to carry it out, this book is organized around three basic problems: *anarchy, order,* and *constraint.*

THREE PROBLEMS OF INTERNATIONAL RELATIONS

The Problem of Anarchy and the Security Dilemma

World politics is unique and inherently different from relations within states. Domestic politics typically unfolds within a system in which some kind of central authority exists for making decisions and resolving disputes. In the best circumstances, national governments are chosen by and are somehow responsive to the will of their people. In other, often far less agreeable circumstances, the government may represent no more than the will or power of a single dominant party, ethnic group, military junta, or individual leader. Nonetheless, whether democratic or dictatorial forms prevail, most national societies exhibit some form of recognized authority. By contrast, no ultimate authority exists to govern the international system. In essence, states have no overall arbiter or institution to which they can turn for settlement of disputes, for enforcement of their rights, or even for effective protection of their basic security and survival. As a result, the existence of *formal anarchy* at the international level shapes state-to-state relations.

It is important to appreciate that formal anarchy designates the absence of central authority in the international system. It does not, however, mean the same thing as disorder or chaos. These can be consequences of anarchy, but because some restraints on conflict do exist, disorder is not necessarily present in the way that a casual understanding of "anarchy" might otherwise suggest.

Formal anarchy does describe the structural condition of the international system in which states exist. As a consequence they face a "security dilemma."[6] Because of this insecurity, and the nature of the "self-help" system in which they exist, they feel compelled to arm themselves. Yet, in doing so, they do not necessarily increase their own security, because their neighbors and rivals also resort to the same means. Indeed, this arming tends to make all states less secure, since it increases the level of potential threat to which all are exposed. This basic phenomenon was identified in the fifth century B.C. by the Greek historian Thucydides. In observing the conflict between the two foremost city-states of the era, he wrote:

What made war inevitable was the growth of Athenian power and the fear which this caused in Sparta.[7]

Recognition of the problem, and of the spiral of insecurity, thus is by no means new, but emphasizing it makes possible a better understanding of *why* rational policymakers may make seemingly irrational commitments of scarce resources to armies and weaponry while manifest human needs go unmet.

The imperatives of the security dilemma not only shape arms races; they also drive international behavior. Comprehension of this problem facilitates the understanding of why war occurs, even when foreign policymakers are not foolish, ignorant, or evil. This insight is pertinent not only to relations between the superpowers; it also bears on events in recent decades such as warfare in Bosnia and the former Yugoslavia, the Gulf crisis and war, the Falklands War between Britain and Argentina, the Iran-Iraq War, and the Arab-Israeli conflict.

As a fact of international life, the quest for and maintenance of power plays an inevitable role in the relations among nations. Indeed, a series of observers in the "realist" tradition have reminded us that an understanding of international relations and a sound approach to foreign policy must be grounded on a recognition of the realities of power.[8]

State actions, however, can have unintended consequences. While abuses of power and military aggression are not uncommon, the possession of military force can be a means to prevent or deter war rather than to cause it. The case of the Soviet-American relationship during the Cold War, in which the avoidance of a major war came to rest largely on the existence of a nuclear balance of terror, is especially compelling. The grave moral dilemmas this posed—not least that peace was maintained at the cost of living under the shadow of a nuclear apocalypse—were a pressing consequence of this reality.[9]

The Problem of Order

The above assumptions about international anarchy and the quest for security are essential to an effective understanding of international relations; nonetheless, they are not by themselves sufficient. And here it is necessary to go well beyond the older realist approach. International relations involves much more than anarchy and conflict.[10] Power politics and realist perspectives fall well short of providing a comprehensive basis for the understanding or conduct of international relations and foreign policy. Imperatives of *cooperation* and *order* are also compelling. International institutions and rules do exist, and despite their limitations, these too shape the international environment, especially in the economic realm. Indeed, the behavior of individual states is often constrained in security as well as economic realms, in ways that the anarchy model does not adequately predict.

The effort to restrain or to limit conflict and to seek cooperation has a long—albeit often unsuccessful—history. International law, efforts to create global organizations, the more limited actions of regional integration, and even alliances are examples of such behavior.

Attempts to achieve order and prevent war have been especially urgent in the aftermath of major wars. Thus, the end of the Napoleonic Wars in 1815 gave way to the Congress of Vienna, which shaped the balance of power in Europe for much of the nineteenth century. The conclusion of World War I in 1918 led to the Versailles Peace Conference and the creation of the League of Nations—which aimed to deter aggression through collective action. The Allied victory in 1945, ending World War II, brought about the establishment of the United Nations. And the end of the Cold War stimulated hopes for a "new world order" and gave rise to ambitious UN peacekeeping attempts.

Each of these efforts failed in the end to satisfy the original aspirations. Yet these and other repetitive efforts to enlarge the realm of international order suggest that it would be a mistake to conceive of all world politics strictly in terms of international anarchy and the struggle for power.

The search for international order in the aftermath of conflict can also be observed in clashes more limited than continental or world wars. For example, the 1962 Cuban missile crisis, with the glimpse of the nuclear abyss it revealed to both the United States and the USSR, gave way to a temporary easing of relations between the two superpowers and the signing in 1963 of the Limited Test Ban Treaty. The 1973 Yom Kippur War set in motion a process that ultimately led to the 1978 Camp David Agreements and the 1979 Egyptian-Israeli peace treaty. And the February 1991 victory of the American-led coalition in the Gulf War provided renewed impetus for direct Arab-Israeli, negotiations and the subsequent September 1993 agreement between Israel and the PLO.

Indeed, even in the midst of open conflict, countries often observe recognized rules of behavior, such as diplomatic immunity. The April 1984 example of the British government allowing Libyan "diplomatic" personnel to leave the country after they had fired on demonstrators and killed a policewoman outside their London embassy is a modern case in point.

Nor are attempts at order exclusively aimed at preventing military threats. The aftermath of World War II led to a comprehensive series of arrangements enhancing international economic order and cooperation. Partly in reaction to disastrous events of the 1920s and 1930s (which included severe economic depression, massive unemployment, grave political instability, and the rise of fascism), the industrial democracies succeeded in creating a series of arrangements and institutions shaping their international economic relations. These agreements, established in large part through American leadership, led to an unprecedented degree of international cooperation and to unparalleled economic growth and increases in trade and investment.

Frictions within these and other "international regimes"[11] intensified during the 1970s and 1980s, as the relative degree of American dominance (or hegemony) decreased—along with the United States' ability and willingness to pay the costs of regime maintenance. Based on historical experience, the demise of these arrangements might have been anticipated. However, member countries have thus far managed to preserve the existing international economic order and prevent their economic competition from escalating to the kind of disastrous rivalry (competitive currency devaluations, banking collapses, punitive tariff and trade barriers) that marred the 1930s and undermined the prosperity of all countries. In fact, a number of these efforts have been expanded or intensified, as in the case of the European Union, The North American Free Trade Agreement (NAFTA), and the agreement to reduce world trade barriers under the General Agreement on Tariffs and Trade (GATT).

The advanced industrial democracies have succeeded in maintaining economic cooperation, not only because of a learning experience attributable to the lessons from a half-century ago, but also because continuation of the existing institutions and rules (such as the International Monetary Fund, World Bank, the GATT, and European Union) has become a means of promoting their own national interests, and because established institutions can take on a momentum of their own.[12]

In sum, the imperative toward international order embodies compelling economic dimensions as well as security ones.[13] Together, these elements make the component of order as much a feature of international relations as the pervasive anarchic environment in which states exist.

The Problem of Constraint

Owing to the impact of modernization, a series of transformations of international relations have occurred.[14] The changes include the extension of international relations from a largely European-centered system to a global level; the increased penetration of domestic societies; the vastly expanded scope of state activity; and the growing importance of international transactions (trade, investment, technology, communications) for most societies. These and other factors impose a substantial interdependence and entangle most countries in a series of ordered relationships that they do not fully control. This leads, in turn, to the third basic problem, that of constraint.

If the simultaneous problems of anarchy and order are the dominant features of international relations at a systemic level, the problem of constraint impinges greatly on state activity at the national level. In fact, most countries do not enjoy full autonomy in either security or economic realms. It is thus vital to understand the problem their governments face in seeking to influence the external factors affecting their own societies.

International relations are molded by the interpenetration of domestic politics and foreign policy as well as by the interrelationships of politics and economics. It is important to recognize this, because analyses of these relations have often been characterized by a less subtle, "billiard ball" treatment, in which individual states are viewed as unitary, coherent actors, each moving and reacting to external forces as though it were encased within a single hard shell.[15] The reality, however, is more complex. Foreign policies often result from the pulling and hauling among divergent domestic forces within a society, as well as from the maneuvering among different bureaucracies or actors inside a government. Moreover, the interaction of states is deeply affected by the impact of international factors on domestic policy and vice versa, as well as of politics on economics and economics on politics.[16]

The contemporary realities of interdependence, and of the penetration of the state, limit the ability of national governments to fully control their own destinies. Other things being equal, these limits are usually more entangling for states that are more rather than less developed, for states that are smaller rather than larger, and for societies that are economically and politically open rather than closed.[17]

The degree of development is important because modernization means movement away from traditional and less complex forms of social organization. Among the changes involved are specialization, differentiation of function, economic growth, prosperity, longer life expectancy, and the spread of science and technology. These tend to stimulate increased contact with the outside world in trade, communications, and a wide range of matters affecting daily life.

The physical size of a country, in terms of land area and population, is also significant. Large states tend to be more self-sufficient in natural resources and in the array of goods and services they can provide for themselves than smaller ones. Thus, for example, a small industrial democracy such as the Netherlands has more than half its gross national product (GNP) accounted for by international trade, whereas the United States has imports equivalent to 11.4 percent of its GNP and exports of 10.4 percent.[18]

Finally, the nature of economic and political systems also shapes the degree of exposure to the outside world and thus to constraint. A country with a market economy and a democratic and competitive political system will be less autarkic. That is, it will be less self-contained economically. However, although autarky provides a greater degree of insulation from outside influences, it does so at an enormous price in terms of efficiency and living standards, since countries forgo the opportunity to import goods or services where these are available more cheaply elsewhere. Moreover, autarky typically entails a serious cost in terms of human liberty.

It is noteworthy that these costs of isolation and autarky, combined with the need to meet their own needs, can push even large, less-developed, and closed societies toward increased international involvement. The shift by the People's Republic of China is a case in point. There, beginning in the late 1970s and increasingly in the 1980s and early 1990s, the Communist regime sought to modernize a vast and relatively underdeveloped society by liberalizing its economy and by seeking a major increase in outside knowledge, technology, investment, and trade. Even the brutal repression by Chinese authorities at Tiananmen Square on June 4, 1989, did not lead to a fundamental reversal of the process. In the case of the Soviet Union, a set of impulses toward greater openness also became evident, especially after Mikhail Gorbachev came to power in March 1985. Beginning slowly at first, his policies of *glasnost* (openness) and *perestroika* (restructuring) became increasingly more dramatic over the remaining years of the 1980s. In turn, a radical break with the old Communist economic and political system was initiated under Russian President Boris Yeltsin in the early 1990s.

The imperatives toward international involvement are thus deep-seated—as are the limits or constraints that accompany them. This helps to explain why countries, especially developed industrial democracies, tend to support the kind of ongoing international economic cooperation cited above. Despite the difficulties of cooperation and the costs involved, continuation and even enhancement of these efforts provide a means of coping with national problems and needs for which exclusively national measures often prove inadequate.

TWENTIETH-CENTURY APPROACHES

How we think about international relations is in part shaped by the ways in which the subject has been understood in the recent past. Since the end of World War I, the study of international relations has seen a series of diverse attempts to make sense of the subject. An initial phase can be identified during the 1920s. This originated in response to the awesome destruction of "the Great War." The conflict had dealt a profound blow to Western societies after a century of remarkable progress in science, industry, improved living standards, and a pervasive sense of an upward spiral of human progress.[19] Reaction to the war stimulated efforts to prevent another such conflagration. As a result, much of the thinking about international affairs in this period rejected balances of power and alliances, which had marked European affairs in the century prior to 1914. Instead, experts focused on normative, legal, and idealistic efforts to build institutions that would outlaw war. The creation of the League of Nations, with the strong impetus of America's President Woodrow Wilson, was one early reflection of this outlook.

The legalistic and idealistic thinking of this interwar era was ill-suited to making sense of the totalitarian power of Hitler's Germany, of the menace of fascism, and the events that would culminate in World War II. Nor did it effectively address developments in Stalin's Russia. Indeed, the stress on legalism and the avoidance of war at all costs was part of a broader atmosphere in which the Allies, especially Britain and France, drifted into appeasement of aggression by Germany, Italy, and Japan. At the same time, the United States remained isolationist. Ultimately, war broke out in conditions of near-desperation for the democracies.

In response to the events of the 1930s and the horrors of World War II, the decade after 1945 saw the emergence of a "realist" school of thought, identified with the work of E. H. Carr and especially Hans Morgenthau.[20] Reacting to the traumas of appeasement and the rise of fascism in the 1930s—and later the impact of Stalin, the Soviet domination of Eastern Europe, and the initial years of the Cold War—this approach tended to focus on what international relations is, rather than what it should be. This early realism was especially critical of the legalism and pacifism of the post-World War I years (which had put too much faith in such formal agreements as the Versailles Treaty, the League of Nations, and the 1928 Kellogg-Briand Pact to outlaw war) and the wishful thinking and idealism of the 1930s (which had failed to comprehend the importance of power in countering the threat from Nazi Germany and Japan.) For Morgenthau, realism's central concept was that of national interest defined in terms of power.[21] To the extent that competing approaches existed, they often reflected "idealist" interpretations.[22]

During the latter part of the 1950s, and in the following decade, the study of international relations became increasingly marked by the emergence of behavioral or scientific approaches and a contention between these and the older traditional outlooks (including both realist and idealist variants). Behavioralism aimed to apply the concepts of social science, as had already been done in economics, psychology, and sociology, to the fields of political science and international relations. Its proponents sought observable regularities, which they often hoped to measure and quantify. Many of them also tried to maintain a strict distinction between facts and values, and were highly critical of what they considered to be the unsystematic and impressionistic approaches of their traditionalist colleagues. Nonetheless, behavioral scholars were often slow to apply their approaches to real-world policy problems.

This exchange of views generated a sometimes acrimonious confrontation. For example, a defender of traditionalism, Hedley Bull, criticized the behavioralists for omitting wisdom and intuition, which, he argued, were essential for comprehending activities involving human purpose. Bull argued that their rejection of intuitive guesses risked keeping them "as remote from the substance of international politics as the inmates of a Victorian nunnery were from the study of sex."[23] He went on to add that the proponents of science cut themselves off from history and philosophy, thus developing a view of the subject that was bound to be "callow and brash."

A prominent early advocate of behavioralism, Morton Kaplan, counterattacked by charging that traditionalists did not grasp the nature of scientific concepts, that they were confused about the methodological issues involved, and that they indulged in careless generalizations. In the end he dismissed their criticisms as "gross mistakes" and "ill-informed."[24]

In effect, each of the major orientations possessed strengths and limitations. The traditionalist approach was sometimes weak in its methods, particularly in framing nonfalsifiable propositions (i.e., assertions whose validity could not be rejected whatever the evidence revealed). Indeed, one particularly effective critic succeeded in challenging the use of Morgenthau's balance of power concept. Ernst Haas identified no fewer than eight different and sometimes contradictory meanings of the term, concluding that this made the concept too vague for effective use.[25] Moreover, while the writings of some of the leaders in the field were often powerful and incisive, many other works offered arid treatments of diplomatic history or banal collections of facts.

In turn, behavioral approaches often had their own shortcomings, especially when carried out by less sophisticated practitioners. Not only did they exhibit an exaggerated claim to being value neutral, but many of their early efforts generated theories and frameworks with too many empty boxes. That is, they produced elaborate conceptual designs with limited value or applicability. In many instances, these efforts also suffered by being too far removed from the essence of politics, both foreign and domestic.

Eventually, the contention between traditional and behavioral schools was not so much resolved as transcended. That is, less effort was expended on sterile juxtapositions of competing methodologies. Many scholars refused to define their efforts in terms that placed them squarely in one tradition or the other, and each approach tended to be enriched by insights derived from the outlook of the other. Specifically, some behavioralists devoted increasing attention to policy-relevant questions and demonstrated greater sensitivity to normative and historical concerns. Traditionalists, in turn, often became more self-conscious about the assumptions, definitions, and evidence on which their work was based. Finally, many questions with which contemporary scholars grapple (for example, strategic nuclear deterrence, foreign policy decision making, international political economy, interdependence) may lie more or less beyond the split reflected in the earlier scientific versus traditionalist division.

POWER AND NEOREALISM

If the competing imperatives of *anarchy* and *order* are dominant characteristics of the international environment, and *constraint* is the prevailing reality at the level of state activity, the role of *power* in international relations requires careful elaboration. This book is written from a perspective in which an appreciation of power in international relations is fundamental.

The folly of individual leaders or governments, the huge amounts spent on arms, and the inhumanity of war have often caused observers to long for the end of power rivalries and conflict in world affairs. If only there could be better understanding between peoples and governments, general disarmament, and a determination to avoid war, humanity's destructive pattern of conflict would become a thing of the past. Alas, though the objectives are laudable, the practicality of such proposals is severely limited.

Consider the appalling experiences that have already occurred in this century: two savage world wars; the rise and murderous reigns of Stalin and Hitler; a holocaust in which six million of Europe's Jews were systematically murdered in an experience that virtually defies human comprehension; a Soviet-American Cold War that carried the risk of a cataclysmic nuclear war; scores of local but no less cruel wars that have killed some 25 to 30 million people in the developing world since 1945; and an all-too-frequent pattern of repression, torture, and murder of people by their own governments in countries where individuals lack basic human, political, and economic rights. Finally, despite the end of the Cold War, the spread of missiles, chemical weapons, and nuclear proliferation all suggest an array of new or persistent dangers.

As a fact of life, therefore, exhortations to human understanding and to beating swords into plowshares are not a sufficient basis from which to confront the problems of international relations. An understanding of world affairs grounded in the realities of power is, above all, a response to the problem of an anarchic international environment, the accompanying security dilemma, and the resulting imperatives for self-help.

Under these circumstances of formal anarchy, in which states confront the security imperatives of the international system, differences in their capabilities become fundamental. Moreover, Kenneth Waltz has argued that different kinds of international systems can be defined in terms of the different patterns of capabilities among the states that constitute them. Thus a system marked by superpower primacy, as in the case of the Soviet-American bipolar confrontation during the height of the Cold War, would be expected to have different characteristics than one in which power is more widely diffused.

Although power does not guarantee control, Waltz notes that it does do four things. First, it offers a means to maintain autonomy in the face of force wielded by others. Second, power allows wider ranges of action even though the outcome of this action remains uncertain. Third, the more powerful have wider safety margins in dealing with the less powerful. Fourth, greater power gives those who have it a bigger stake in the system as well as the ability to act for its sake.[26]

As important as power is for international relations, the problems of defining and measuring it remain formidable. For example, Morgenthau regarded power as the essence of international politics, contending that what made politics distinct as an autonomous sphere of human action and understanding was the concept of interest defined in terms of power.[27] Yet he was criticized for the lack of rigor in his conception of power, which at various points gave the impression that power was a major goal of policy, the motivating force for political actions, a means to an end, or a relationship.[28] Nor has the problem of defining power been confined to any one author: one survey, for example, found no fewer than 17 different definitions of the concept.[29]

While raw military power is often used as an indicator of state capabilities, other dimensions are of great importance. These include economics, technology, resources, education, values and beliefs, morale, leadership, and an array of other factors. Indeed, even military power ultimately rests on the productive capacity, technology, and human and material resources a state possesses. There may even be a certain self-reversing component to military power. The expenditure of economic resources provides such power at a particular time. However, such expenditures may place a country at a long-term disadvantage vis-à-vis competitors who carry lesser defense burdens and who therefore have greater resources to allocate in the future—whether these are directed to savings, investment, or consumption.

For example, the Soviet Union maintained a level of defense spending that may have been as high as 25 percent by the mid 1980s.[30] This was a far greater burden than borne by the United States (6 percent), Germany (3–4 percent), or Japan (1 percent). Indeed, Gorbachev saw this level of spending as seriously harmful to the Soviet society and economy, as well as causing the USSR to fall farther behind the advanced countries of the world. He thus opted for major cuts in the size and cost of Soviet forces.

Military power can also have limitations in its applicability. For example, the principal use of nuclear force is to deter the use of nuclear force by other countries. A preponderance of Soviet conventional military power did not suffice to win the hearts and minds of the peoples of Eastern Europe, or to prevail against rebels in Afghanistan. For its part, the United States found its own formidable military power insufficient to bring about victory in Indochina during the years from 1965 to 1973. Nor did this power serve to secure the release of hostages—whether in Teheran after the American embassy was seized in November 1979, or later in Lebanon in the mid and late 1980s. Not only are many political issues only indirectly affected by the possession or exercise of military power, but economic issues—for example, disputes over trade policy—are often played out in a separate arena altogether.

Power thus has its limits. A balance of power between adversaries can sometimes provide an equilibrium and thus not only prevent a country from imposing itself on others but also maintain peace. Yet the balance of power that realists celebrate is not only an imprecise analytical concept, it also poses particular risks in a nuclear age. For one thing, the sometimes nostalgically invoked nineteenth-century balance of power rested on more or less accepted rules of the game.[31] Then too, the balance sometimes required limited wars as a form of adjustment. Finally, the balance became rigidified in the end. This helped to usher in World War I and even to create the conditions for another world war some twenty years later. Were a nuclear balance of power to break down and lead to a major war, the consequences would be almost unimaginable.

Power politics and realist perspectives convey useful insights, but they fail to provide a comprehensive basis for the understanding or conduct of international relations and foreign policy. It is thus essential to go beyond the understanding of international anarchy and the security dilemma. Imperatives of order are also compelling. International institutions and rules exist, and despite their limitations, these too shape the international environment, especially in the economic realm. Moreover, as considered above, the behavior of individual states is often constrained in security as well as economic realms.

With these considerations in mind, the approach of this book can be termed *neorealist.** That is, while it is anchored in an appreciation of power realities among states and the anarchic aspects of the international environment, it also incorporates the pervasive factors of order and constraint.[32]

This work assumes that it is possible to impose a considerable degree of order on the sometimes chaotic pattern of international relations. By appreciating the imperatives of the security dilemma, the dimensions of international order and interdependence, and the constraints within which states operate, we can achieve a clear and lasting comprehension of international relations. These insights thus are valuable in understanding unfolding events and problems, and their utility will remain long after intricate historical or political details have faded from memory or the latest newspaper headlines have been forgotten.

NOTES

1. Quoted in John H. Herz, *International Politics in the Atomic Age* (New York: Columbia University Press, 1962), p. 214n.
2. "Explaining Cooperation Under Anarchy: Hypotheses and Strategies," *World Politics* 38 (October 1985): 1.
3. *Politics Among Nations* was the title of Hans Morgenthau's pioneering text. (New York: Knopf, first edition 1948.) The phrase, "politics: who gets what," gained emphasis in political science with the book by Harold D. Lasswell, *Politics: Who Gets What, When, How* (New York: Whittlesey, 1936 and Meridian Books, 1958).
4. Note that war can take many forms, including small- or large-scale conventional (i.e., nonnuclear) war, as well as hypothetical variants of limited and general nuclear war. See, for example, Herman Kahn, *On Escalation: Metaphors and Scenarios* (New York: Prager, 1965).
5. William Clark, who became national security advisor to President Reagan without having had prior training or professional experience in the field, once observed: "I've never felt inhibited by a lack of background, because I feel the process is no different here from what it was on the Court." Quoted in Steven R. Weisman, "The Influence of William Clark," *New York Times Magazine,* 14 August 1983, p. 18.
6. The idea of the security dilemma originates with John H. Herz, *Political Realism and Political Idealism* (Chicago: University of Chicago Press, 1951); also see Robert Jervis, "Cooperation Under the Security Dilemma," *World Politics* (January 1978): 167–214. For a broader view on the problem of anarchy, see Herbert Butterfield, *History and Human Relations* (London: Collins, 1951); Kenneth Waltz, *Man, The State and War* (New York: Columbia University Press: 1959); and Arnold Wolfers, *Discord and Collaboration* (Baltimore: Johns Hopkins University Press, 1962). Early formulations of the problem of quasi anarchy can be found in Thucydides, as well as in the writings of Thomas Hobbes and Jean-Jacques Rousseau.

---

*Neorealism and neoliberalism are discussed in Chapter 14.

7. Thucydides, *History of the Peloponnesian War*, translated by Rex Warner (Baltimore: Penguin, 1954), p. 25.

8. This viewpoint is especially identified with the late Hans Morgenthau and his *Politics Among Nations*.

9. Note, for example, that the American Catholic bishops sought to address this dilemma in their 1983 pastoral letter on strategic nuclear deterrence. (See Chapter 6.)

10. On this theme, see especially Hedley Bull, *The Anarchical Society: A Study of Order in World Politics* (New York: Columbia University Press, 1977).

11. See Chapter 14. For a thorough discussion of the nature and development of international regimes, see especially Stephen D. Krasner, ed., special issue on international regimes, *International Organization* 36 (Spring 1982), revised in book form as *International Regimes* (Ithaca, NY: Cornell University Press, 1983).

12. See especially the analysis of Robert O. Keohane, *After Hegemony* (Princeton: Princeton University Press, 1984), Chapter 1.

13. There have been other eras in which economic interdependence has been extensive. For example, exports plus imports were 52 percent of the GNP of Great Britain in 1909–1913, compared with 41 percent in 1975. For the United States, the figure was 14 percent in the years from 1879–1898—the same as in 1975. See Kenneth Waltz, *Theory of International Politics* (Reading, MA: Addison-Wesley, 1979), p. 212.

14. Edward Morse provides a useful list of these transformations in *Modernization and the Transformation of International Relations* (New York: Free Press, 1976).

15. Criticism of this view is developed in Robert O. Keohane and Joseph S. Nye, *Power and Interdependence*, 2nd ed. (Glenview, IL: Scott, Foresman, 1989). Also see Graham T. Allison, *Essence of Decision: Explaining the Cuban Missile Crisis* (Boston: Little, Brown, 1971).

16. See Peter Gourevitch, *Politics in Hard Times: Comparative Responses to International Economic Crises* (Ithaca, NY: Cornell University Press, 1986). Also Peter B. Evans, Harold K. Jacobson and Robert D. Putnam, eds., *Double-Edged Diplomacy: International Bargaining and Domestic Politics* (Berkeley: University of California Press, 1993).

17. Also see, for example, Peter Katzenstein, *Small States in World Markets* (Ithaca, NY: Cornell University Press, 1985).

18. Figures for 1993, from *Economic Indicators*, monthly statistical publication of the Joint Economic Committee of the U.S. Congress, as reported in Paul Krugman, "Proving My Point," *Foreign Affairs*, Vol. 73, No. 4 (July/August 1994):199.

19. This concept of continuing human enlightenment and progress is perhaps best represented by the writing of the eighteenth-century French philosopher, Condorcet.

20. E. H. Carr, *The Twenty Years' Crisis, 1919–1939: An Introduction to the Study of International Relations* (New York: St. Martin's, 1939, and revised edition, 1946). The classic postwar work is Morgenthau's *Politics Among Nations*. Also see, for example, Walter Lippmann, *The Cold War: A Study in U.S. Foreign Policy* (New York: Harper & Row, 1947).

21. These concepts were specifically defined and applied by Morgenthau, in Chapter 1 of *Politics Among Nations*.

22. For a useful treatment of the realist versus idealist debate, see Robert Osgood, *Ideals and Self-Interest in America's Foreign Relations* (Chicago: University of Chicago Press, 1953), as well as the summaries in James Dougherty and Robert Pfaltzgraff, eds., *Contending Theories of International Relations: A Comprehensive Survey*, 3rd ed. (New York: Harper & Row, 1990), pp. 81–135; and in Paul R. Viotti and Mark V. Kauppi, eds., *International Relations Theory: Realism, Pluralism, Globalism*, 2nd ed. (New York: Macmillan, 1993).

23. Hedley Bull, "International Theory: The Case for a Classical Approach," *World Politics* 18 (April 1966): 366.

24. Morton Kaplan, "The New Great Debate: Traditionalism versus Science in International Relations," *World Politics* 19 (October 1966): 1–20, at p. 20. For a more extended discussion of the uses of theory and the possibilities of scientific international relations approaches, see Robert J. Lieber, *Theory and World Politics* (Boston: Winthrop Publishers and Little, Brown, 1972), pp. 4–15. See also, Yale H. Ferguson and Richard Mansbach, *The Elusive Quest: Theory and International Politics* (Columbia, SC: University of South Carolina Press, 1988); and William C. Olson and A. J. R. Groom, *International Relations Then and Now* (London: HarperCollins, 1991.)

25. Ernst Haas, "The Balance of Power: Prescription, Concept or Propaganda?" *World Politics* 5 (July 1953): 442–476.

26. Waltz, *Theory of International Politics*, pp. 194–195. Waltz's approach is also known as *structural realism.*

27. Morgenthau, 3rd ed., 1960, p. 5. For a more comprehensive treatment of power, its measurement, and definition, see Robert J. Lieber, *Theory and World Politics*, pp. 88–110.

28. K. J. Holsti, "The Concept of Power in the Study of International Relations," *Background* 7 (1964): 179–194.

29. As found by Dennis G. Sullivan, and cited by Norman Z. Alcock and Alan G. Newcombe, "The Perception of National Power," *Journal of Conflict Resolution* 14 (September 1970): 335.

30. There has been considerable controversy over the level of Soviet military spending as a percentage of GNP. The range of Western estimates has varied from as low as 11–14 percent to as high as 18–20 percent or more. For a sample of the debate among American experts, see, for example, the exchange between James E. Steiner and Franklyn D. Holtzman, "CIA Estimates of Soviet Military Spending," *International Security*, Vol. 14, No. 4 (Spring 1990): 185–198. In the late 1980s, in the midst of a series of other revelations, there were suggestions by Soviet authorities that the figure was as high as 25 percent, although the Soviets themselves appeared unsure of the exact number.

31. Henry Kissinger's book considers the way in which the Congress of Vienna restored these rules after the demise of Napoleon in 1815. See *A World Restored* (New York: Grosset and Dunlap, 1964).

32. For an assessment of neorealism, see Robert O. Keohane, ed., *Neorealism and Its Critics* (New York: Columbia University Press, 1986.) Also, Joseph S. Nye, Jr., "Neorealism and Neoliberalism," *World Politics,* Vol. 40, No. 2 (January 1988): 235–251; and Fareed Zakaria, "Realism and Domestic Politics: A Review Essay," *International Security*, Vol. 17, No. 1 (Summer 1992): 177–198.

   Note also that the term neorealism was used in the early 1980s in a different sense. This perspective understood America's world role in terms of the need for containing the USSR, but also recognized the limits of power as well as the implications of an open international economy benefitting the industrial democracies. It also took into account an increasing global diffusion of power. See Richard Feinberg, *The Intemperate Zone: The Third World Challenge to U.S. Foreign Policy* (New York: W. W. Norton, 1983), pp. 22–23. Also Richard Feinberg and Kenneth Oye, "After the Fall: U.S. Policy Toward Radical Regimes," *World Policy Journal*, Vol. 1, No. 1 (Fall 1983). The term was also used by Tom J. Farer, in "Searching for Defeat," *Foreign Policy*, No. 40 (Fall, 1980), pp. 155–174. On diffusion of power, see especially Kenneth Oye, "Constrained Confidence and the Evolution of Reagan Foreign Policy," in Kenneth Oye, Robert J. Lieber, and Donald Rothchild, eds., *Eagle Resurgent? The Reagan Era in American Foreign Policy* (Boston: Little, Brown, 1987), pp. 3–39.

chapter 2

The International System and the Modern State

For four hundred years the foreign policy of England has been to oppose the strongest, most aggressive, most dominating Power on the Continent. . . .

—WINSTON CHURCHILL[1]

The dual problem of individual and collective survival has never been lastingly solved by any civilization. It could only be definitively solved by a universal state or by the rule of law.

—RAYMOND ARON[2]

. . . while the world no longer lives under the shadow of superpower nuclear confrontation, the numbers of actual and possible conflicts, both among and within states, seem bound to grow, whether because of aggressive ambitions . . . or border disputes and rival claims over the same territory . . . or domestic crises and policies that have effects abroad.

—STANLEY HOFFMANN[3]

Nation states will remain the most powerful actors in world affairs, but the principal conflicts of global politics will occur between nations and groups of different civilizations. The clash of civilizations will dominate global politics.

—SAMUEL P. HUNTINGTON[4]

. . . civilizations do not control states, states control civilizations. States avert their gaze from blood ties when they need to; they see brotherhood and faith and kin when it is in their interest to do so.. . . .

We remain in a world of self-help. The solitude of states continues; the disorder in the contemporary world has rendered that solitude more pronounced.

—FOUAD AJAMI[5]

While there is a certain truth to the notion that we live in unique times, the record of the past is far from irrelevant in contributing to our understanding of contemporary affairs. The experience of the past is important not only for the insights it affords, but also because earlier experiences retain a lingering impact on present-day societies and their leaders.

THE MODERN NATION-STATE SYSTEM

Since the dawn of recorded time, different societies and peoples have experienced a wide range of external contacts. Some of these brought commerce, technology, religion, culture, and ideas; others led to war and conquest. As a result, the map of the world has been shaped and reshaped over thousands of years. History has seen the rise and fall of empires and the disappearances of entire civilizations and peoples.

Although much of this experience is lost in antiquity, other elements of it persist to this day—for example, in the impact of classical Greek and Roman civilization on contemporary Europe and America. It is true, of course, that many important ancient "players" were not nation-states, but either small city-states on the one hand, or empires or dynasties on the other. Even so, there are lessons to be drawn. Thus, for example, historians have cited relations among Greek city-states of the fifth century B.C. as foreshadowing the balance-of-power dynamics later to be found among Italian city-states of the Renaissance, and then among European states of recent centuries. Indeed, during the Cold War, Secretary of State Henry Kissinger could draw on the example of one of these ancient rivalries to characterize America as Athens and the Soviet Union as Sparta.[6]

Even the experiences of great empires may not be wholly irrelevant. One modern analyst identifies a pattern by which great, hegemonic power ultimately proves self-reversing. Looking not only at more recent examples (in this case, the nineteenth-century British Empire), but also at the experiences of imperial Rome, China, the Netherlands, and other states, Robert Gilpin identifies three structural causes of declining power. The first is the expense of maintaining hegemonic leadership. Typically, the strongest state pays a disproportionate cost in order to maintain existing power arrangements. These stem from the economic and military burdens of empire, or simply the costs of alliance leadership, but over time they become an increasingly heavy weight to bear. Second, there are intrinsic reasons why domestic consumption tends to rise while saving and investment fall, as both elites and publics seek to enjoy the benefits of their society's position of world preeminence. Third, there is the diffusion of technology. Though a dominant power may have achieved its rise in part through the superiority of its weaponry or technology, these often spread to other societies more easily or rapidly than they were acquired in the first place.[7]

International relations have encompassed a wide range of historical settings—by no means confined to Europe or the West. Among others, these have included the experiences of China and of South and Southeast Asia; the record of the Ottoman Empire in the Middle East, the Balkans, North Africa, and Spain; and the ebb and flow of relations among societies in sub-Saharan Africa. A number of these early non-Western experiences have been reflected in the writings of authors such as the ancient Chinese scholar, Mencius (a successor of Confucius in the late fourth century B.C.); Kautilya, a Hindu precursor of realism (c. 300 B.C.); and the leading Arab philosopher of history, Ibn Khaldun (1332–1406).[8] Nonetheless, for some three centuries until 1945, a nation-state system, anchored primarily on the European continent, gave the dominant imprint to international relations. Much of today's understanding of the attributes of statehood stems from this period. The characteristics include national sovereignty (the supremacy of a state's authority within its territorial boundaries), the concept of a national government, state boundaries, territorial integrity, diplomatic representation, multilateral treaties, and the idea—however often transgressed in practice—that states are not supposed to interfere in each other's internal affairs. Many of these elements were set forth in the writings of a Dutch jurist, Hugo Grotius,[9] and became part of a rudimentary and evolving body of international custom.

This "modern" period in international relations is often dated from the year 1648. At that time, the Peace of Westphalia brought to an end the Thirty Years' War, which had ravaged central Europe. The war that had shaken Europe through much of the first half of the seventeenth century was one in which religious and dynastic alignments cut across distinctions of territory, language, and ethnicity. Protestant and Catholic rivalries, and the designs of the Hapsburg Empire, fueled a wide-ranging struggle that involved French, English, Scottish, Dutch, Spanish, Swedish, Italian, and German rulers and forces.

In the lands of what had been called the Holy Roman Empire, religious and dynastic forces battled for control. On one side, the great Catholic family dynasties, particularly the Hapsburgs (who ruled most of what is now Austria, the Czech Republic, Slovakia, and Hungary), allied themselves with Spain and with the papacy in Rome. Meanwhile, German Protestant princes formed coalitions with the English, the Dutch, and the French Huguenots (Protestants). The conflict became more devastating than earlier wars of the feudal period, and the scale of destruction and slaughter was unmatched in Europe until the twentieth-century world wars. Over a period of time, the fighting expanded and conditions of chaos developed in central Europe as large armed bands, sometimes numbering up to 40,000 men,[10] pillaged much of what is now Germany. By the time of the 1648 peace agreement, roughly one-third of the entire population of Germany had died.

From the Peace of Westphalia onward, however, Europe began to take on many of the characteristics of international relations which would endure for centuries. These included an emergent balance-of-power system among the various states. In formal terms, a territorial *state* was a sovereign body exercising predominant authority within its geographic borders. In contrast to the earlier feudal era, these entities were no longer subject to the claims of religious, dynastic, or imperial authority at a higher level. Independent states thus became more and more the component parts of the modern international system.

Over the next two centuries, these states would come to be organized more along national lines, rather than as territorial agglomerations shaped as much by royal dynasties or religious ties as by nationality. A number of factors facilitated the increased predominance of the European territorial state, especially the eroding power of religious authorities and, from the latter part of the eighteenth century onward, the growing role of the nation-state in the process of industrialization. From these changes states derived both enhanced authority and considerably greater capability.

At times, the evolving state system was challenged by national leaders seeking to achieve dominance of the entire continent, for example, France under King Louis XIV from the late 1600s until 1713; Napoleon in the years prior to his defeat at the Battle of Waterloo in 1815; and later in the 1930s and early 1940s, Adolf Hitler. However, it was a system of independent states, organized increasingly along lines of nationality, which more or less prevailed and provided some semblance of international order.

To be sure, Europe after the Peace of Westphalia was still a long way from a comprehensive pattern of nation-states and the self-conscious nationalism of its peoples. These did not develop for another century and a half, until the time of the Napoleonic Wars. Thus, apart from the unusual ravages of the Thirty Years War, warfare tended to remain something largely apart from the practical concern of the average European. Thomas Schelling aptly describes this sense of remove:

> From about 1648 to the Napoleonic era, war in much of Western Europe was something superimposed on society. It was a contest engaged in by monarchies for stakes that were measured in territories, and, occasionally, money or dynastic claims. The troops were mostly mercenaries and the motivation for war was confined to the aristocratic elite. Monarchs fought for bits of territory, but the residents of disputed terrain were more concerned with protecting their crops and their daughters from marauding troops than with whom they owed allegiance to. . . . It is an exaggeration to refer to European war during this period as a sport of kings, but not a gross exaggeration.[11]

The French Revolution of 1789 and the subsequent period of Napoleonic rule (1802–1815) brought a growing nationalism, first in France and then throughout the European continent during the remainder of the nineteenth century. In the case of France, the rising sense of national identity enabled both the revolutionary leaders and Napoleon to mobilize a hitherto unprecedented proportion of the population in the service of the state via the mass citizen army. The concept of a *nation* here refers to a people with a shared sense of identity, usually based on characteristics such as ethnicity, language, culture, or history. Increasingly, the concept of the state would come to be linked with that of nationhood, in the *nation-state*, even though accidents of history and the mosaic of population patterns often meant that the two phenomena were by no means identical.

For three centuries after 1648, the European state pattern embodied the prevailing form of international relations. During this period, Europe enjoyed increasing global predominance.[12] The leading countries of Europe extended imperial control over much of the world, achieved economic and technological dominance, and developed the strongest military forces. In the late nineteenth and early twentieth centuries, with the increasing centralization of state power

Table 2.1 GROWTH IN POPULATION AND STEEL PRODUCTION
OF THE EUROPEAN POWERS

	Population (millions)		Steel Production (million tons)	
	1870	1914	1880	1913
Italy	27	37	—	0.93
Austria-Hungary	36	52	0.12	2.61
France	36	39	0.39	4.69
Russia	82	171	—	4.83
Great Britain	31	45	1.32	7.79
Germany	40	65	0.73	17.60

Source: Adapted from data compiled by Anton W. DePorte, in *Europe Between the Super-powers: The Enduring Balance,* 2nd ed. (New Haven: Yale University Press, 1986), pp. 12–13.

and the enormous growth in commercial and military strength fostered by the industrial revolution, Europe seemed at the height of its wealth and influence. Yet the basis for a profound change was already taking shape.

The change centered on Germany. German-speaking lands had long been separated into a large number of principalities, subject to the influence of their neighbors, and divided religiously between Protestants and Catholics. By 1871, however, Otto von Bismarck, the Chancellor of Prussia, the largest and militarily most powerful of the German states, had unified most of the German-speaking areas of Europe (with the notable exception of Austria). He achieved this through adroit political maneuver and a series of limited wars against Denmark, Austria, and France. Bismarck thus created Western and Central Europe's most populous, economically vigorous, and militarily powerful state.

From the time of German unification until the outbreak of World War I in 1914, Germany's power rapidly outdistanced that of its neighbors. For example, its population grew from forty million to sixty-five million persons, placing it far ahead of Austria-Hungary, Great Britain, and France. And its industrial might soared. Illustratively, by 1914, German steel production of 17.6 million tons dwarfed that of its individual neighbors and was not far below the *combined* production of Britain, Russia, France, Austria-Hungary, and Italy (see Table 2.1.)

The impact of this emerging German power, however, proved profoundly destabilizing to the European state system. For one thing, imperial Germany now sought a position of world prominence at least equivalent to that of its earlier rivals, Britain and France. However, much of the non-European world had already seen the culmination of the European rivalry for power and hegemony, and there was little territory left—for example, in Africa—with which to satisfy German demands. After the dismissal of the astute and diplomatically skillful Bismarck in 1890, Kaiser Wilhelm II, the German ruler from the Hohenzollern family, proved clumsy and even menacing in asserting claim to what he regarded as Germany's rightful place as a world power.

Under Wilhelm II, Germany's policies triggered a major arms race in the years after 1900. In the process, the full weight of Europe's industrialization was

increasingly thrown into the construction of ships and artillery. A sharpening polarization of power in Europe also began to take shape. For centuries, Europe had
seen a shifting balance among countries of roughly comparable strength. And
coalitions usually developed to counter the weight of any one power that threatened to achieve continental dominance. Britain in particular had often played the
role of the balancer. The British had long regarded their primary vital interest to
be the prevention of any one state achieving mastery of the European continent.
For three centuries, Britain had thrown its weight into the balance to counter the
attempted hegemony of states such as Spain and then France.

Now, with the emergence and expansion of German power and the increasing
assertiveness of that country's leaders, the British found themselves drawn increasingly into alignment with their historic foe, France. The French, in turn, who
were now overshadowed by the more populous and industrialized imperial Germany, sought alliance with Germany's eastern neighbor, imperial Russia. With
Germany now allied to the Austro-Hungarian Empire of the Hapsburgs, the European balance of power had lost its flexibility.

From 1905 to 1914, Europe experienced not only a massive arms race, but
also a series of major crises over great power rivalries in North Africa, particularly
Morocco, and in the Balkans. In the latter area, three potentially vulnerable empires maneuvered for advantage. The decaying empire of the Ottoman Turks left
a growing power vacuum in the region. As a result, rivalry between the Austro-
Hungarian Empire (allied to Germany) and the Russian Empire of the Romanov
dynasty (allied to France) came to a head. Although the details now seem esoteric,
this conflict in the Balkans triggered the cataclysm of World War I, and with it the
collapse of no fewer than four empires (German, Austrian, Russian, and Turkish)
and destruction of the European order.

The circumstances of the time made it more difficult for the major actors to
avoid war than on earlier occasions. The growth of nationalist sentiment and increased political awareness or involvement by the broader public made it harder
for governmental leaders to achieve compromises. Moreover, modern weaponry
appeared to favor the offense. Together, these factors hastened the momentum
toward war.[13]

In a sequence of events familiar to students of early twentieth-century history, the Austrian Archduke, Francis Ferdinand, was assassinated at Sarajevo on
June 28, 1914, by Serbian nationalists. In reaction, Austria (supported by Germany) issued an ultimatum to Serbia, against whom it subsequently declared war.
Russia, as Serbia's ally, mobilized its own armed forces in an effort to deter Austria from attacking Serbia. A day later, on July 31, Germany mobilized against
Russia. At the same time, after making demands on Russia's ally, France, which
included not only neutrality but the handing over of border fortifications, Germany then declared war on France as well. Under its long-practiced Schlieffen
Plan, Germany was committed to striking first against France. Imperial Germany
sought to drive France out of the war within six weeks, before turning her own full
military might against Russia without the menace of a grueling two-front war.

However, Germany's invasion of neutral Belgium, inconveniently located on
the route toward France, caused Britain—after initially vacillating—to enter the

war on the side of France. By the first week of August, Europe was plunged into full-scale war. Within weeks, the German offensive stalled at the Marne river outside Paris, and Europe now found itself doomed to four years of grinding trench warfare. In the course of the conflict, some ten million soldiers would perish and the political map would be torn apart.[14]

The war caused the political, economic, and human devastation of Europe. The flower of its youth died in the trenches: one million British, 1.3 million French, two million Germans, two million Russians, and hundreds of thousands of Italians, Turks, Romanians, Bulgarians, Americans, and others. The war also brought or accelerated the collapse of a series of old regimes. Most notably, the Russian czar was overthrown in March 1917 and replaced first by a moderate provisional government and then in October 1917 by the Bolsheviks under V. I. Lenin. In Germany, the collapse of the old order gave rise to the fragile Weimar Republic, itself left with the immense burdens of reparations for a war it had not started and the consequences of a devastating world depression it had not caused. In the end, Weimar itself collapsed with the assumption of power by Adolf Hitler and his Nazi party in January 1933.

The purpose here, however, is less to recount the catastrophic events of the interwar years than to note that the European power balance had failed disastrously. Indeed, before the end of World War I, the United States itself had been brought in to redress the balance on the Continent. By the spring of 1917 the Allied forces of Britain and France were near exhaustion and the Russians close to collapse. The American declaration of war on Germany in April 1917 came partly in response to unrestricted German submarine warfare. But it was also due to sympathy with the Allies and a commitment by President Woodrow Wilson to ideals of spreading democracy and self-government throughout the Continent. The arrival of American troops in late 1917 and early 1918 ultimately turned the tide of battle against Germany and in favor of the Allied forces.

Note, then, that the counterbalancing of German power in the center of Europe could no longer be achieved by the Europeans themselves. During the 1930s, as the menace of European fascism and especially of Nazi power grew, the European allies proved unable to contain this threat. Meanwhile, the United States had retreated into isolationism, and Russia under Stalin found itself in a relation of uneasy antagonism and suspicion with the other countries of Europe. In the end, after securing an extraordinary nonaggression pact with the USSR, Hitler unleashed war in 1939 by attacking Poland.* Europe was again plunged into world war, this time with even more horrendous consequences.

At first, in the spring of 1940, Hitler overran much of Western Europe, defeating France in his lightning "blitzkrieg" campaign. At this point, Britain stood beleaguered and alone against the Nazis. Yet within a year, in June 1941, Hitler invaded Russia, touching off four years of almost unimaginably savage warfare and laying waste vast areas of Eastern Europe. A few months later, on December 7,

---

*Following Hitler's defeat of Poland, Germany and the Soviet Union proceeded to partition the country between themselves. This action took place under terms of a secret protocol to their August 1939 treaty.

1941, Japanese forces attacked American naval installations at Pearl Harbor, Hawaii. The United States declared war on Japan. In turn, Hitler, as Japan's ally, immediately declared war against the United States. Ultimately, the Nazis were only defeated by the combined military might of the Americans and Russians, thrown onto the scales alongside the British.

World War II caused the deaths of tens of millions of soldiers and civilians while devastating much of Europe. Moreover, it witnessed the deliberate policy of genocide directed by Adolf Hitler, as Nazi Germany carried out the deportation and murder of six million Jewish men, women, and children throughout occupied Europe.[15] The deliberate savagery and unprecedented scale of the Nazi holocaust left an indelible moral scar across the face of European civilization. It also starkly illuminated the absence of effective sovereign authority above or beyond the actions of a single powerful nation-state.[16]

THE POST–WORLD WAR II PATTERN: SIMILARITIES AND DIFFERENCES

By 1945, the European nation-state system lay in ruins. The means of an intra-European balance no longer existed. The predominant European states no longer stood as leading world powers. Germany had been defeated and divided between East and West. Britain, though one of the victorious "Big Three" powers, with the United States and the Soviet Union, was drained economically and militarily and would soon divest itself of empire. France had been defeated and occupied, and its political institutions discredited; it would also abandon its imperial possessions, though only after exhausting wars in Indochina (1946–1954) and Algeria (1954–1962).

Elsewhere, Italy, after having come under the fascist rule of Benito Mussolini in 1922, and becoming Hitler's ally in the war, had also been devastated. (Italian self-respect was, however, redeemed in part by the overthrow of Mussolini in 1943.) Spain, too, was greatly weakened. Its dictator, Francisco Franco, had managed to stay out of World War II, but the country had yet to recover from the disastrous civil war of 1936–1939. Finally, the countries of Eastern Europe, many of which had endured chaotic interwar events, the collapse of their new democratic governments, and the coming to power of brutal right-wing dictatorships, were falling under Soviet hegemony in 1945–1948. Russian troops had pushed into their territory in driving back the German armies, and the principal Eastern European countries (Poland, Czechoslovakia, Hungary, Bulgaria, Romania) same under the control of Soviet-dominated communist governments.

Outside Europe, Imperial Japan, which had extended its domination over much of Southeast Asia and adjacent areas, was devastated. The atomic bombing of Hiroshima and Nagasaki in August 1945 precipitated Japan's surrender, and its military power appeared to be at an end. Elsewhere, China had been grievously weakened by a decade of war and partial occupation and would soon undergo a full-scale civil war between forces of the Nationalist government of Chiang Kai-shek and those of the Communists led by Mao Zedong.* In South Asia, meanwhile, India and Pakistan would not gain independence from Britain until 1947, and even then would undergo severe traumas of war, internal upheaval, and nation–building.

In short, three centuries of European world primacy had come to an end. Here and in Asia, previously major powers were now weakened or prostrate. Whereas international relations had mainly been centered on the European continent, power and primacy were now passing to the United States and the USSR. Both of these continental superpowers were geographically outside the area in which world politics had been focused for the previous three centuries. But they would become the principal actors in the post-1945 world.

THE INTERNATIONAL SYSTEM
DURING THE COLD WAR

The post-1945 period marked a revolution in international relations, not only because of the demise of a European-centered international system, but also because of characteristics that set it apart from anything that had previously existed.

The first of these differences involved the bipolar confrontation that developed between the United States and the USSR. By 1947, the break between the wartime allies was complete, and there now ensued a power struggle between a Soviet bloc under the control of Joseph Stalin and a group of non-Communist countries led by the United States and involving not only the European democracies but increasingly the former Axis powers of Germany, Italy, and Japan, as well as a number of non-Communist countries in Asia and Latin America. What made this struggle unusual was the element of worldwide confrontation and the competition not only in military but also economic and ideological dimensions.

A second profound difference separating the post-1945 world from previous eras in international relations was the development of nuclear weapons together with modern delivery systems. Though the true "balance of terror" envisaged by Winston Churchill did not completely take shape until the mid 1960s, the possibility now existed that an all-out war between the world's principal powers could destroy civilization. In past epochs, a decision to go to war involved calculations of potential gains and losses. In the memorable words of the nineteenth-century Prussian strategist, Karl von Clausewitz, war was the continuation of diplomacy by other means. Now, however, the means of an unlimited nuclear war—though the event remained unlikely—would imply the destruction of any conceivable purpose for which the war would have been entered in the first place.

Third, the coming to independence of much of the developing world also revolutionized world politics. Huge areas either attained formal independence in the postwar period (especially in Asia and Africa), or achieved a far greater importance in world affairs than they had previously known.

---

*This is the contemporary transliteration of Mao's name from Chinese into English. The earlier usage was *Mao Tse-tung*.

Much of what had been termed "international relations" had been an essentially European-centered matter. Now, however, while Europe remained of great importance, both intrinsically and as a focus for the confrontation of Soviet and American power, international relations had become truly global. This change encompassed the number and range of actors and areas, the expanded agenda of issues, and the totality of the stakes involved.

World politics in the decades after World War II embodied characteristics that made it distinctly different from what had gone before. The East-West conflict and the existence of nuclear weaponry represented a modern embodiment of the imperatives of power played out on an unprecedented scale and global dimension. Ironically, the magnitude of potential destruction also pushed the superpowers toward a search for order, as a means of managing the nuclear competition that threatened to destroy them both. Meanwhile, the North-South dimension involved the interplay of both power and order, especially in working out international economic relations.

THE POST–COLD WAR INTERNATIONAL SYSTEM

For more than four decades, the defining characteristic of the international system was the global confrontation between the two superpowers, the United States and the Soviet Union. During this period, as Kenneth Oye has noted, the classical state system was partially supplanted by a bloc system, each with its own zones of military protection, economic production, and political homogeneity. [17] Although the Cold War originated in Europe, largely along the demarcation line created by the deployment of American and Russian forces at the end of World War II, the confrontation subsequently extended to Asia and throughout the world.

Ironically, although the Cold War included massive military deployments in Europe, a nuclear balance of terror, the projection of superpower rivalry into remote regional conflicts, and a contest between two diametrically opposed concepts of society, the era actually provided a certain predictability and stability. Each of the superpowers tended to maintain a degree of order within its own sphere, though it is important to note that these arrangements were for the most part voluntary on the Western side (particularly in Europe), while imposed (often brutally) on the Soviet side. As a consequence of these features, as well as the restraint imposed by the specter of a nuclear armageddon, and despite the periodic eruption and intensification of regional conflicts, the Cold War never developed into a "hot" war—a direct military conflict between the forces of the United States and those of the Soviet Union. Indeed, the period produced what the historian John Lewis Gaddis has called, "the long peace."[18]

It is also important to recognize that even during this era of bipolarity, some continuities with the pre-1945 world were evident. The most important of these was the existence of an anarchic international environment and the prevalence of a nation-state model or paradigm as the predominant feature of international relations. To be sure, especially in much of the developing world, state boundaries often reflected little semblance of ethnic or national identity, nor did all states control their own economy or security. Even so, the formal manifestations of sovereignty—flags, governments, territorial borders, and even United Nations membership—remained evident in the everyday interactions of world affairs.

The sudden and unexpected end of the Cold War in 1989–1990 not only produced profound changes within Europe, but had major implications for the international system as well. With the end of the East-West conflict and the dissolution of the Soviet Union, the loose bipolar structure gave way to an increasingly multipolar and fragmented system, with one remaining superpower (the United States), a number of secondary military or economic powers (some of them still loosely linked to the United States through alliances such as NATO), and a series of regionally influential and smaller, weaker states.

The immediate aftermath of the Cold War also gave rise to a series of debates concerning international stability. Some analysts anticipated that the reduction in Soviet-American military competition would result in lower levels of violence within and among developing countries.[19] Others identified a growing capacity for international cooperation, both through organizations such as the United Nations and the European Community, and by means of regimes for informal cooperation in different issue areas. In addition, it was suggested that the unprecedented collaboration of the United States, the Soviet Union, and dozens of other countries in responding to Iraq's August 1990 invasion of Kuwait signaled the prospect of a new world order. Moreover, the enormously increased importance of international economic activity, including trade, investment, financial flows, and the spread of technology, along with a dense network of international communication and interchange, and growing international concern with global issues (the environment, population, human rights, public health) were cited as signaling the evolution of a post–Cold War world in which traditional forms of sovereignty and attention to military security would prove to be outmoded or superseded.

In practice, with the passage of time, many of these propositions concerning the future of the post–Cold War system began to appear less persuasive. Illustratively, military conflict showed little sign of waning. Indeed, the end of the Cold War saw a surge in fierce ethnic and nationalistic rivalries and the outbreak of a series of brutal wars, both domestic and interstate. Among the more conspicuous of these were savage communal violence in the former Yugoslavia, particularly as a result of efforts to create a Greater Serbia; starvation and civil war in Somalia; the renewal of civil wars in Angola and Afghanistan (which had appeared to end with the withdrawal of superpower involvement); a deadly onslaught by Saddam Hussein against Shiite Arabs living in the marshes of Southern Iraq; and the eruption of violent struggles involving many of the former Soviet Republics in the Caucasus and Central Asia (Georgia, Armenia, Azerbaijan, Tajikistan).

These and other cases illustrated not only the multiple sources of conflict and war in the post–Cold War international system, but also the disappointingly limited means of conflict resolution and international peacemaking. Despite a number of apparent successes, for example by the United Nations in Cambodia, no such effective result was achieved in Bosnia, where nearly 200,000 people (mostly Bosnian Moslems) perished within two years. The machinery of the United Nations was often cumbersome and ineffective, and was further limited by difficulty in gaining consensus (as well as financial and military resources) from the key member states of the Security Council.

Moreover, despite the presence of the most destructive conflict in Europe since World War II, the European Community was effectively paralyzed from acting in the former Yugoslavia by disagreements among France, Germany and Britain. At the same time, the Community's own pace of integration slowed, with the at least temporary collapse of efforts to achieve monetary union, as well as difficulties in implementing the December 1991 Maastricht Treaty, which had aimed to accelerate European unity.

In sum, despite enormous changes during the half-century after 1945—including development of regional and global institutions; extraordinary growth in trade, economic interdependence and communications; the spread of market-oriented economies; the emergence of new global issues; and even the diffusion of democracy—which made the boundaries of states much more porous, there remains ample evidence of continuing conflict and war, as well as conspicuous limitation on the ability of existing international organizations to foster cooperation and enforce order. These experiences mean that the post–Cold War international system continues to exhibit important characteristics of the traditional state-centric international system which predated the Cold War.

NOTES

1. *The Second World War: The Gathering Storm* (Boston: Houghton Mifflin, 1948), p. 207.
2. *Peace and War: A Theory of International Relations* (Garden City, NY: Anchor/Doubleday, 1973), p. 15.
3. "Delusions of World Order," *New York Review of Books*, 9 April 1992, p. 37.
4. "The Clash of Civilizations?" *Foreign Affairs*, Vol. 72, No. 3 (Summer 1993): 22–49, at 22.
5. "The Summoning," *Foreign Affairs*, Vol. 72, No. 4 (September/October 1993): 2–9, at 9.
6. According to Admiral Elmo Zumwalt, then Chief of Naval Operations, in 1974 Kissinger depicted the American people as lacking the stamina to stay the course against the Russians, who are "Sparta to our Athens." Elmo R. Zumwalt, Jr., *On Watch: A Memoir* (New York: Quadrangle/New York Times Book Co., 1976), p. 319.
7. Robert Gilpin, *War and Change in World Politics* (New York: Cambridge University Press, 1981).
8. Mencius, *The Works of Mencius*, translated and with notes by James Legge (New York: Dover Publications, 1970). Kautalya, *The Kautilya Arthasastra*, translated by R. Shamasastry (Mysore, India: Mysore Printers and Publishing House, 1967); Ibn Khaldun, *An Arab Philosophy of History*, translated by Charles Issawi (Princeton: Darwin Press, 1987).
9. Grotius's principal work, written in 1625, was *On the Law of War and Peace (De Jure Bellis ac Pacis)*. For the relationship of this to international law, see Chapter 12.
10. For a concise account of this period, see John A. Garraty and Peter Gay, eds., *The Columbia History of the World* (New York: Harper & Row, 1972, and Dorset Press, 1981), pp. 584–591.

11. Thomas C. Schelling, *Arms and Influence* (New Haven: Yale University Press, 1966), pp. 27–28.
12. For the process by which Europe became increasingly connected to the wider world, see, for example, Hedley Bull and Adam Watson, eds., *The Expansion of International Society* (New York: Oxford University Press, 1984).
13. The causes of World War I are considered at length in Chapter 7.
14. For a lucid treatment of the outbreak of World War I, see Barbara Tuchman's work, *The Guns of August* (New York: Macmillan, 1962). Also see Laurence Lafore, *The Long Fuse: An Interpretation of the Origins of World War I*, 2nd ed. (New York: Lippincott and Harper & Row, 1971).
15. Although large-scale massacres had begun earlier, the decision to destroy Europe's Jewish population was made by Hitler and a group of Nazi leaders at a conference on January 2, 1942, in the Berlin suburb of Wannsee. Three of the most comprehensive and authoritative accounts of the holocaust are Raul Hilberg, *The Destruction of the European Jews* (New York: Holmes and Meier, rev. ed., 1985); Lucy S. Dawidowicz, *The War Against the Jews, 1933–1945* (New York: Free Press, 1986); and Leni Kahl, *The Holocaust: The Fate of European Jewry* (New York: Oxford University Press, 1990). For an eyewitness account by a member of the Polish underground who brought word of the death camps to the West, see Jan Karski, *Story of a Secret State* (Boston: Houghton Mifflin, 1944). A moving personal memoir of a teenage boy's deportation to the concentration camps at Auschwitz and Buchenwald is Elie Wiesel's *Night* (London: Hill and Wang, 1960, and New York: Bantam, 1982).
16. On the failure of the allied countries to intervene against the Nazi slaughter of the Jews, see Martin Gilbert, *Auschwitz and the Allies* (New York: Holt, Rinehart & Winston, 1981); and Walter Laqueur, *The Terrible Secret: Suppression of the Truth about Hitler's "Final Solution"* (Boston: Little, Brown, 1981, and New York: Penguin, 1982).
17. Kenneth A. Oye, "Beyond Postwar Order and New World Order: American Foreign Policy in Transition," in K. Oye, R. Lieber, and D. Rothchild, eds., *Eagle in a New World: American Grand Strategy in the Post–Cold War Era* (New York: Harper-Collins, 1992), p. 5.
18. John Lewis Gaddis, *The Long Peace: Inquiries into the History of the Cold War* (New York: Oxford University Press, 1987.)
19. Oye et al., p. 19.

PART 2

Conflict in the
Postwar and
Post–Cold War
Systems

chapter 3

The East-West Conflict: Origins

There are at the present time two great nations in the world, which started from different points, but seem to tend towards the same end. . . .

All other nations seem to have nearly reached their natural limits. . . . these alone are proceeding with ease and celerity along a path to which no limit can be perceived. The American struggles against the obstacles that nature poses to him; the adversaries of the Russians are men. The former combats the wilderness and savage life; the latter, civilization with all its arms. The conquests of the American are therefore gained by the plowshare; those of the Russian by the sword. The Anglo-American relies upon personal interest to accomplish his ends and gives free scope to the unguided strength and common sense of the people; the Russian centers all the authority of society in a single arm. The principal instrument of the former is freedom; of the latter, servitude. Their starting point is different and their courses are not the same; yet each of them seems marked out by the will of Heaven to sway the destinies of half the globe.

—ALEXIS DE TOCQUEVILLE, 1835[1]

The Soviet Union, unlike previous aspirants to hegemony, is animated by a new fanatic faith, antithetical to our own, and seeks to impose its absolute authority over the rest of the world.

—NSC 68 (NATIONAL SECURITY COUNCIL DIRECTIVE), SPRING 1950

The Communists are not to the left, but to the East.

—ATTRIBUTED TO FRENCH SOCIALIST LEADER GUY MOLLET

F or almost half a century, from the end of World War II in 1945 until the dissolution of the USSR in December 1991, relations between the United States and the Soviet Union were at the center of world politics. At times these relations were marked by intense hostility, bitter competition, and even regional wars (for example, in Korea, Vietnam, Afghanistan) involving one or the other of the superpowers. At other times, as in the early 1970s and more so after Mikhail Gorbachev's rise to power in 1985, there was considerable relaxation of tension and even cooperation. Although the division of Europe and the global bipolar confrontation of the superpowers ultimately came to an end, it is impossible to understand the post–Cold War world without an effective knowledge of the Cold War and its profound impact on the international system.

The origins of this Cold War have long been the subject of attention and debate. At the outset, ideology received a great deal of attention as the chief causal factor. For example, in the words of one contemporary American observer:

> the crux of the Soviet battle is not primarily for physical things. . . . It is for dominion over the soul. For the first time a powerful adversary not only rejects our civilization but fights to destroy everything we value.[2]

Subsequently, additional explanations for the bipolar confrontation have been suggested: the brutal character of Stalin as Soviet leader, perception and misperception among the key actors, the interaction of domestic politics and foreign policy, and the imperatives of international power politics which brought the United States and the USSR—the world's preeminent states after 1945—into a struggle for regional and global influence in the postwar era.

In reality, the origins of the Cold War are multicausal. Major historical epochs are rarely shaped by a single, unique cause. However, considerations of power in the Soviet-American confrontation, initially in Europe and then more widespread, proved fundamental. Thus, to a considerable extent, the East-West division of Europe was foreshadowed by the location of American and Western forces on the one side, and Soviet troops on the other, as the Allies completed the defeat of Nazi Germany in June 1945. Subsequent events were of enormous importance, yet much of the evolving Cold War was shaped by immediate power realities at the end of World War II.

BACKGROUND: AMERICA AND RUSSIA
BEFORE THE COLD WAR

Until the outbreak of World War II, the United States and the USSR by no means possessed the superpower roles with which they were to emerge at the end of the conflict. From the conclusion of World War I in 1918 to the onset of World War II in 1939, Britain, France, and Germany (the major states of Western and Central Europe), together with Japan, held the central position in world affairs.

The United States had made a major impact in 1917 by intervening in the war. In the aftermath of the conflict, America's physical size, population, resources, and economic and potential military power made it a force to be reckoned with. But there was disillusion with the results of this "war to end all wars." After 1919, America withdrew into isolationism, rejecting a more active role in European or Pacific affairs. Congress even passed a series of neutrality acts aimed at preventing the United States from being drawn into any future world conflict, and the country remained aloof from much of the turmoil which swept Europe and the Far East during the 1920s and 1930s.

For its part, Russia had suffered greatly as a result of World War I. As Europe's largest but most backward country, its already fragile social fabric and institutions had been severely shaken by the conflict. In March 1917, the czarist regime collapsed, giving way to a weak parliamentary regime. This provisional government, under Alexander Kerensky, was unable to achieve Russian withdrawal from the war, and in October 1917 it was overthrown by a small but tightly organized Communist party under the leadership of V. I. Lenin. The Bolshevik seizure of power was followed by Russia's withdrawal from the war in February 1918, under the Treaty of Brest-Litovsk. However, the Soviet Union soon found itself in the midst of a savage civil war. The civil war ended in 1920, but the USSR was slow to recover from the ravages of war, revolution, and famine. This, together with Soviet distrust of the outside world—contingents of British, French, Japanese, and American troops had taken part in a haphazard intervention against the Communists—and Western suspicion of the new regime and its proclaimed commitment to world revolution left the USSR substantially isolated.

Following the Nazi seizure of power in January 1933, the risks of a new European war began to grow. The regimes of Adolf Hitler in Germany and of Joseph Stalin in the Soviet Union denounced each other in increasingly strident terms. Hitler also sought to overturn the existing European order and establish the ultimate world dominance of Nazi Germany. The Western European powers, particularly Britain and France, vacillated between strategies of appeasement and resistance to Nazi expansion and aggression. Despite efforts by President Franklin Roosevelt, the United States avoided involvement in attempts to contain the increasingly belligerent actions of Nazi Germany, Fascist Italy, and Imperial Japan. Mutual suspicion made cooperation even more difficult between the Western Europeans and the Soviet Union.

Ironically, both the United States and the USSR had sought to avoid involvement in World War II. Although the Soviets initially appeared ready to defend Czechoslovakia against Germany in 1938, their position changed after the French and British appeasement of Hitler at Munich in September 1938. Indeed, the USSR actually signed a treaty of nonaggression with Nazi Germany in August 1939. A secret provision of the pact allowed the Soviets to occupy the Eastern half of Poland after the Nazis invaded that country in September. Less than two years later, however, Russia found itself at war with Germany. In June 1941, having already conquered most of Europe except Britain, Hitler launched a ferocious assault against the Soviet Union. In turn, the United States entered the war in December 1941, following the Japanese attack at Pearl Harbor.

Whatever their reluctance or limited involvement during the interwar years of the 1920s and 1930s, the Americans and Soviets emerged from the devastation of World War II as the world's two most powerful countries. Their temporary wartime alliance against Germany quickly disintegrated, and within two years a bitter animosity had risen between them.

IDEOLOGY AND POWER IN SOVIET BEHAVIOR

What drove Soviet behavior during the Cold War? Scholars and policymakers have long debated this question. Can Soviet conduct best be understood by reference to the importance of Marxist-Leninist ideology? Or, was it the case that Russian power, history, and national interest were more fundamental factors in shaping the behavior of the USSR? After all, Russia under the czars was an expansionist and imperial power in Siberia, Central Asia, and Eastern Europe well before the Bolsheviks seized power. It was also a country that displayed suspicion and paranoia toward the outside world and maintained a rudimentary apparatus for domestic political repression.

In reality, diverse elements influenced Soviet actions. While ideology became greatly corrupted and diluted in practice, it played a certain part. At minimum, its existence served as a device to legitimate the monopoly of power by the leaders of the Soviet Union in their own eyes and to some extent among the Soviet population. It also facilitated Soviet influence and domination over foreign Communist parties for more than half a century.

Nonetheless, in many respects, the ideology of the Soviet Union was greatly blunted in its practical application. More often than not, it served as little more than a cover for the pursuit of Soviet national interests defined in terms of power. Thus Stalin, who ruled the Soviet Union until his death in 1953, pursued policies that—while extraordinarily ruthless in their application of power—minimized the practical importance of ideology. For example, the antagonism with Leon Trotsky and the preference for "socialism in one country"[3] were dictated less by Marxism-Leninism than by a drive to consolidate control within the USSR. Whenever the priorities of the Soviet Communist leadership conflicted with those of foreign Communist parties, the latter were inevitably sacrificed in the interests of the former.

Soviet policy toward Germany provided a clear illustration of this. In dealing with the German Weimar Republic (1919–1933) and with the Nazi Third Reich (1933–1945), Soviet leaders pursued policies that provided narrow benefits to their own country (for example, in trade and technology), but sacrificed the chances of the German Communist party and even—by their opposition to cooperation with other anti-Nazi forces in German politics—enhanced the opportunities for Hitler to take power in 1933. The most flagrant example of this Soviet behavior came in August 1939, with the Nazi-Soviet Pact. This allowed Hitler to launch his *blitzkrieg* against the countries of Central and Western Europe without fear of a hostile Soviet Union at his back. Ultimately, it is not surprising that many of those Western intellectuals who were sympathetic to the Soviet Union in its early years developed a sense of bitter disillusionment as a result of the disastrous events of the 1930s.[4]

The inclination of Soviet leaders to give priority to their national interest over considerations of ideology long outlived Stalin. But other factors added to the blunting of whatever remaining edge Soviet Communism may have had. Among these factors was the consolidation of the Soviet regime, which gave its leaders a vested interest in the protection of their own positions of power and privilege within Soviet society. Even more important, however, and well before Mikhail Gorbachev and Boris Yeltsin, the advent of nuclear weapons and of a Soviet-American balance of strategic nuclear power made it difficult for Soviet leaders to pursue revolutionary objectives that would run the risk of a nuclear confrontation with the United States.[5]

EARLY YEARS OF THE COLD WAR, 1945–1948

World War II and the struggle against Nazi Germany had made allies of the United States and the Soviet Union. However, the prior relationship between the two powers was one of suspicion and animosity, and the end of the war gave rise to growing tension between them. By 1947, the dimensions of a major confrontation had begun to take shape, and the outlines of a bipolar division of Europe and of much of the rest of the world became increasingly clear.

As the conclusion of the war against Hitler approached, the Allied powers held a series of important meetings to plan for the immediate postwar situation in Europe. These meetings already contained the seeds of discord. For their part, the Russians insisted on security as their overwhelming priority. The United States and Britain, although accepting the Soviets' demand for nonhostile countries along their borders, emphasized the need for self-determination and free elections for the peoples of Europe. This concerned not only those countries that had been exposed to the ravages of Nazi occupation, but also Germany itself.

Although much of the explanation for the Cold War lies in the actions and personality of Stalin and the Soviet drive for control over Eastern Europe, the basis for a confrontation was already latent in differing Soviet and Western priorities: throughout Eastern Europe, the combination of security *and* self-determination was unlikely. With one or two exceptions, for example, Czechoslovakia, freely elected governments in Eastern Europe were unlikely to look with friendship on the Russians. Poland, after experiencing the horrors of Nazi occupation, including the slaughter of six million people (half of whom were Jews*),[6] had been betrayed and occupied by the Soviets, and had been the victim of Russian power and influence for centuries. Elsewhere throughout Eastern Europe, and in different forms, historical animosity toward the Soviets was also widespread.

On the part of the British, Prime Minister Winston Churchill acquiesced in the shaping of spheres of influence in the Balkans. In his memoirs, Churchill recounted his October 1944 meeting with Stalin in Moscow. Noting that Soviet

---

*These account for approximately half the six million European Jews murdered by the Nazis in the Holocaust.

armies had already moved into Rumania and Bulgaria, as they drove back the German armies, Churchill suggested to Stalin that Britain and Russia avoid getting at "cross-purposes." He therefore put the following proposition to Stalin:

> "So far as Britain and Russia are concerned, how would it do for you to have ninety per cent predominance in Rumania, for us to have ninety per cent of the say in Greece, and go fifty-fifty about Yugoslavia?" While this was being translated I wrote out on a half-sheet of paper:
>
> Rumania
>
> | | |
> |---|---|
> | Russia | 90% |
> | The others | 10% |
>
> Greece
>
> | | |
> |---|---|
> | Great Britain (in accord with USA) | 90% |
> | Russia | 10% |
> | Yugoslavia | 50–50% |
> | Hungaria | 50–50% |
>
> Bulgaria
>
> | | |
> |---|---|
> | Russia | 75% |
> | The others | 25% |
>
> I pushed this across to Stalin, who had by then heard the translation. There was a slight pause. Then he took his blue pencil and made a large tick upon it, and passed it back to me. It was all settled in no more time than it takes to set down.[7]

In the most important and subsequently controversial of the wartime agreements, Churchill, Stalin, and Roosevelt met at the Black Sea resort of Yalta in February 1945. There, the leaders of the Big Three powers signed a "Declaration on Liberated Europe." Although Yalta was later depicted by some critics as deliberately dividing Europe between a Soviet-dominated East and an American-dominated west, the Declaration actually pledged Allied assistance in the formation of interim governments. These were to be "broadly representative of all the democratic elements in the population and pledged to the earliest possible establishment through free elections of governments responsive to the will of the people."[8]

Following the Yalta summit, and even before Roosevelt's death in April, Soviet policy toward the Allies became tougher and less cooperative. The issues concerned not only the treatment of Germany, but especially the postwar arrangements for Poland. The subject was not only important to the Polish people, but had a far greater symbolic significance. After all, the immediate cause over which Britain and France had gone to war with Hitler was the German invasion of Poland in 1939. Now, Stalin was insisting on the imposition of a Soviet-sponsored Polish government, based in the liberated Polish city of Lublin, while opposing the return to power of the Polish government in exile, which had been located in London during the war.

From 1944 to 1947, the Soviets gradually tightened their control over the countries of Eastern Europe which the Red Army had occupied in driving Hitler's armies from the region. It was this presence of military forces, far more than wartime Allied agreements such as Yalta, that made the Soviet actions possible. In Poland, Hungary, East Germany, Bulgaria, and Romania, interim elected governments based on coalitions of anti-Nazi parties and groups were gradually replaced or destroyed. With Soviet backing, local Communist parties exploited ethnic and regional rivalries as well as the divisions among parties representing democratic socialists, peasants, nationalists, and others. In the end, non-Communist political leaders were forced into exile, imprisoned, or murdered. Only in Albania and Yugoslavia did Communist regimes take power based on their own successful resistance movements, rather than under the aegis of the Soviets, though these governments too—even in Yugoslavia at first—were no less brutal.

Stalin also imposed a series of territorial changes all along Russia's Western borders. Each of his Eastern European neighbors was forced to cede territory to the USSR. The Soviets thus incorporated land from Finland, 70,000 square miles of Eastern Poland, the Czechoslovak province of Ruthenia, the Romanian provinces of Bukovina and Bessarabia, and East Prussia from Germany. Stalin also forcibly reannexed the Baltic states of Estonia, Latvia and Lithuania, which had existed as independent republics during the interwar years.[9]

As a result of these events, Churchill could, by March 1946, deliver an address in which he spoke of an "iron curtain" having descended across Europe, from Stettin on the Baltic Sea, southward to Trieste on the Adriatic.

The American Response

The immediate postwar relations between the United States and the USSR had quickly begun to cool. Although the Big Three had reached agreement on establishment of the United Nations and on occupation arrangements for Germany, there were disputes on many issues. At the war's end, the United States had immediately terminated the huge program of lend-lease aid which had been vital to Russia's war effort. President Truman had gotten along badly with Soviet Foreign Minister Molotov in their initial meeting shortly after the new President had assumed office. And a Soviet request for a major postwar loan had been ignored. In Germany, the Soviets had begun keeping the railroad boxcars in which food and raw materials were being sent to their occupation sector, and the Western allies retaliated by curtailing these shipments.

The escalation of tension between the United States and the Soviet Union encompassed disputes over lesser issues as well as basic conflicts over matters of profound importance. Together, these events contradicted initial expectations of American policymakers about the postwar world. President Roosevelt had originally entertained the hope that it would be possible for the Big Three powers to maintain a cooperative working relationship. His objective had been for the major powers, working with the United Nations organization, to preserve order in the postwar world, and hence avert the slide into conflict and renewed war that had occurred after World War I. Thus, for example, he had expected that the occupation of Germany would be managed by a Joint Allied Control Council that would operate successfully on the basis of unanimity.

President Roosevelt's views were also shaped by a second major assumption: that postwar America would revert to an isolationist posture. This assumption was based on America's experience in the aftermath of World War I. And, if anything, it was significantly more important than the belief about the need for and possibility of postwar collaboration with the Soviets. Roosevelt possessed an astute sense of domestic American politics. He had observed the way in which a massive political reaction against foreign involvement occurred in the United States after the 1918 armistice. This had frustrated President Wilson's efforts to obtain support for the Versailles Peace Agreement and for the United States' entry into the League of Nations. It had also ushered in a period of deep-seated isolationism, which kept the United States from playing a more constructive role in preventing international economic chaos and in arresting the spread of fascism prior to World War II. Indeed, President Roosevelt's own efforts to resist aggression by the Axis powers had been frustrated by continuing congressional and public opposition until a little more than a year before Pearl Harbor. Consider, for example, that the August 1941 renewal of legislation maintaining a military draft passed the House of Representatives by only one vote—at a time when World War II in Europe had already been underway for two years.

The point about this domestic political environment is fundamental. For while Roosevelt has sometimes been criticized for entertaining exaggerated hopes about postwar relations with the Soviets, far less attention has been focused on the domestic political context on which his assumption rested. To be sure, the United States possessed unparalleled military power at the end of World War II, with more than twelve million men and women under arms, and a monopoly on the atomic bomb. Yet, no foreign policy is viable without a solid basis of public and congressional support. Before his death in April 1945, Roosevelt assumed that isolationist sentiment would again prove to be an overwhelming public and congressional force as soon as the war ended. He thus took it for granted that there would be no domestic support for maintaining American troops in Europe for more than a year or two after the end of the war.

As a result, Roosevelt assumed that the exercise of Western power in Europe would have to be carried out by the British. These assumptions about postwar political constraints within the United States shaped American strategy in dealing with Stalin. For if an American administration faced these stiff domestic limits on its exercise of power in the postwar world, then more emphasis would have to be placed on shaping Soviet behavior through accommodation than on acting from a position of enduring practical power.

Following the surrender of Japan on September 2, 1945, America began a very rapid demobilization. Nevertheless, there were public protests at the end of 1945 that the pace of demobilization was not fast enough. These included massive letter- and postcard-writing campaigns to members of Congress, and isolated sit-down strikes by draftees still in uniform. Within one year, army strength alone fell from 8.3 million persons to 1.9 million.[10] Meanwhile, the Republicans captured control of Congress in the 1946 elections, and sentiment in Congress seemed to be moving in an isolationist direction.

Profound changes were occurring, however, that would reshape the entire international disposition of the United States. To begin with, the growing animosity between Russia and the Western allies ran counter to initial Allied expectations and Roosevelt's original assumption. In addition to their consolidation of power in Eastern Europe, the Soviets also began to put pressure on Iran and Turkey. As early as April 1945, Stalin ordered a tougher anti-Western line for foreign Communist parties,[11] and at the start of 1946 the Soviet leader resumed the hostile ideological language toward the West that the Soviets had abandoned at the outset of the war. Elsewhere in Europe, the hoped-for postwar recovery had not begun to materialize. By the winter of 1946–1947, Western Europe appeared to be on the edge of economic and political collapse. Powerful and pro-Soviet Communist parties were active contenders for power in Italy, France, Belgium, and Greece. Even Britain was forced to resort to bread rationing, something which had not been necessary in the most desperate days of the war.

A Revolution in American Policy

The deteriorating situation in Europe and the evolution of events there were very different from what United States policymakers had initially expected. The result would be to draw America back into Europe and bring about a revolution in peacetime foreign policy. During an extraordinary fifteen-week period, beginning on February 21, 1947, and extending to June 5,[12] the basic elements of America's postwar policy took shape. The consequences of these policy changes profoundly affected United States foreign policy and international relations.

The Truman Doctrine. On February 21, 1947, the British government notified the U.S. State Department that it would be ending the economic and military assistance which it had been providing to Greece and Turkey. This decision reflected the waning wealth and power of Great Britain and the course of its own retreat from empire. It also stemmed from the fact that among the Big Three allied countries, Britain no longer had the resources of a true world power. American assumptions that Britain could play the predominant role in maintaining stability and Western interests on the European continent now called for reexamination.

The Truman administration opted to seek authorization from Congress to take the place of Britain in providing aid to Greece and Turkey. Secretary of State George C. Marshall presented the request to leaders of Congress, but they were not receptive. Dean Acheson, then Undersecretary of State and later to replace Marshall, subsequently restated the case. Acheson, however, put the matter in more stark geopolitical and moral terms. At one level, he expressed the fear that without American support, the governments of both countries might succumb to the combined weight of internal opposition and external pressure from the USSR, and give way to pro-Soviet regimes. At another level, Acheson posed the problem as part of a Soviet challenge to Western civilization for which the United States was compelled to provide world leadership.

Given the Democrats' massive election losses in 1946 and Republican control of the Congress, bipartisan support for the administration's request was critical. The key figure was the Republican chairman of the Senate Foreign Relations Committee, Arthur H. Vandenberg of Michigan. At Vandenberg's request, Acheson and the administration agreed that the request would be presented in a presidential speech to Congress and the country. This would state the grave realities of the developing confrontation with the Soviets, and the global danger which the United States and the West faced.

On March 12, President Truman addressed a joint session of Congress. While requesting 400 million dollars in economic and military assistance for Greece and Turkey, the president framed the issue in dramatic terms, implying that the peace of the world and the security of the United States were at stake. He posed the issue as a choice between two ways of life:

> One way of life is based upon the will of the majority, and is distinguished by free institutions, representative government, free elections, guarantees of individual liberty, freedom of speech and religion, and freedom from political oppression.
>
> The second way of life is based upon the will of a minority forcibly imposed upon the majority. It relies upon terror and oppression, a controlled press and radio; fixed elections, and the suppression of personal freedoms.

Truman then went on to enunciate what has come to be called the Truman Doctrine:

> I believe that it must be the policy of the United States to support free peoples who are resisting attempted subjugation by armed minorities or by outside pressures.
>
> I believe that we must assist free peoples to work out their own destinies in their own way.
>
> I believe that our help should be primarily through economic and financial aid which is essential to economic stability and orderly political processes.[13]

In effect, President Truman had framed the matter of aid for Greece and Turkey in terms of a global doctrine which was to gain broad support from congress and the public. In the future, its application would commit the United States to intervention in areas far distant from Europe and the Eastern Mediterranean. Ironically, the Truman Doctrine began to appear so far-reaching that a number of prominent Americans influential in its conception began to warn of overextension. George Kennan, director of policy planning at the State Department, and Walter Lippmann, the influential columnist, both argued that the president's formulation had become excessive and too apocalyptic in tone.

In any case, the request for aid was approved by Congress. This ushered in an era in which the United States would play an increasingly active world role, not only in counterbalancing Soviet power, but in resisting the establishment of pro-Soviet regimes. At first, this intervention took place mainly in Europe, where it proved highly successful. In later years, however, the application of these policies to the developing world would prove far more difficult and controversial. Eventually it would even influence the American decision to intervene in Vietnam.

The Marshall Plan. A second critical component of the new American response concerned the increasingly desperate economic situation of the Western Europeans. The massive wartime destruction of railways, bridges, ports, power plants, and factories—the infrastructure of modern industrial life—blocked a rapid recovery. The European states lacked the immediate resources to repair or replace these facilities, and the absence of progress had damaged public confidence and seemed to threaten a decline toward economic collapse and political anarchy. On March 5, Dean Acheson took the initiative in establishing an interagency working group to determine what countries might need American aid. The committee found that the populations of France and Italy were suffering from growing hunger, cold, and social discontent. Both countries were likely to run out of gold and foreign currency reserves before the year's end. Britain was expected to exhaust its reserves in the following year.[14]

On May 8, 1947, and with the approval of President Truman, Acheson proposed a massive aid plan in a speech delivered in Cleveland, Mississippi. Although initial press accounts of the speech were fragmentary, subsequent reaction to the plan was favorable. Ultimately, what came to be known as the Marshall Plan was proposed by Secretary of State George C. Marshall in a historic address to the Harvard University commencement on June 5, 1947.

The program, which became law within less than a year, emphasized active European cooperation in making use of a massive transfusion of American economic aid. Initially, in order to minimize the conflictive aspects of the growing Soviet-American confrontation and appeal to European public opinion, the proposal by General Marshall was framed so that it was open to all European states, including the Soviet Union. While there would have been serious domestic political problems—and possibly unmanageable economic costs—had the Soviets and the Eastern European countries accepted the offer, the Russians reacted with suspicion and hostility instead. Although Foreign Minister Molotov did attend an initial European planning session in Paris in June 1947, the Soviets took the position that the requirement of making public their budget information would constitute an unacceptable intrusion in their internal affairs. The Soviets even managed to force Czechoslovakia, which then had Communists in government but had not yet experienced the February 1948 coup d'état, to reject the offer of Marshall Plan aid.

A generation later, the scale and success of Marshall Plan aid still seem remarkable. Conceived at a time of deepening concern over the Soviet threat, the program approved by Congress in the spring of 1948 and extending over four years provided an extraordinary transfusion for the prostrate economies and societies of Western Europe. In its first year alone, the cost of the program amounted to approximately *fourteen times* the percentage of gross national product (GNP) that the United States would spend on foreign aid some four decades later. Specifically, the cost was 2.8 percent of annual GNP, as contrasted with 0.2 percent in the early 1990s. As for the results, consider that in 1947 European economies were producing at only one-fourth to two-thirds of their prewar industrial capacity. Within four years, they were outproducing the 1939 levels by some 43 percent.[15]

Not only did the Marshall Plan avert economic collapse in Western Europe, but it also underwrote a growing political stability while reducing the opportunities for domestic Communist parties in France and Italy. The improved economic climate helped to usher in a quarter-century of unprecedented economic growth and expansion of trade among the industrial democracies.

Containment. The third critical component of America's policy response was the doctrine of containment. In what may be the most widely quoted *Foreign Affairs* article ever written, George Kennan, under the pseudonym of "X," outlined the intellectual and strategic rationale for what would become the policy of the United States in coping with the challenge of the Soviets throughout the more than four decades of Cold War. The argument, which Kennan had previously set out in a December 1946 dispatch (the "long telegram") to Washington from the American Embassy in Moscow, and which had been widely circulated within the government, was summed up in the following passage:

> Soviet pressure against the free institutions of the western world is something that can be contained by the adroit and vigilant application of counterforce at a series of constantly shifting geographical and political points, corresponding to the shifts and manoeuvres of Soviet policy, but which cannot be charmed or talked out of existence.[16]

Kennan assumed that containment could serve to prevent Soviet expansion and—over a period of time—to create the conditions for the "break-up" or "gradual mellowing" of Soviet power. Although he subsequently observed that containment was meant to be primarily political rather than military in nature,[17] the argument came to be interpreted as the basis for a worldwide application of American power.

Whatever the later evolution of doctrine, the spring of 1947 had ushered in nothing less than a revolutionary transformation of American foreign policy. The country was now committed to an immense international involvement, including the defense of Europe, unprecedented in its *peacetime* history. And this revolution was accomplished with a wide measure of bipartisan support. As we shall see, bipartisanship was not to last indefinitely, but its presence in 1947–1949 was fundamental in shaping the Truman administration's actions.

FROM THE CZECH COUP TO THE DEATH OF STALIN

Even before the end of World War II, the United States and Britain had found themselves in growing disagreement with the Soviet Union. Over time, the Soviet stance became increasingly hardline and the disputes more and more acrimonious. Consider some of the more important events in this escalation of tension:

May 6, 1945: Victory in Europe; Germany surrenders.

July 15 to August 2, 1945: Potsdam Conference; Allies unable to agree on elections in Eastern Europe.

August 6–9, 1945: United States drops atomic bombs on Hiroshima and Nagasaki; Japan surrenders and World War II ends.

August 16, 1945: Winston Churchill criticizes "police governments" being established in Eastern Europe; uses term *iron curtain* to describe division of Europe and the tragic events unfolding there.[18]

August 20, 1945: United States cancels lend-lease aid over Soviet objections.

January 19, 1946: Iran complains to United Nations about Soviet unwillingness to evacuate Northern Iran; Soviets ultimately withdraw in May.

September 1946: Fighting between Greek government and Communist guerrillas; Greece complains about support for guerrillas by Albania, Bulgaria, and Yugoslavia.

October and November 1946: United States and Britain criticize Bulgarian and Rumanian elections in which Communists and their allies obtain majorities as unfair.

January 1947: United States and Britain denounce Polish elections organized by Communists as violation of Yalta; moderate Peasant party is defeated and its leader leaves for exile in West.

February 1947: Fighting renewed in Chinese civil war between Communists of Mao Zedong and Nationalists (Kuomintang) of Chiang Kai-shek.

March 1947: Announcement of Truman Doctrine.

May 1947: France and Italy oust Communists from their coalition governments.

June 1947: Marshall Plan proposed.

July 1947: Publication of Kennan's "X" article on containment.

August 1947: Communists-dominate coalition in Hungary.

September 1947: Soviets establish Cominform (Communist Information Bureau); this replaces Comintern (Communist International), which was abolished in 1943, and provides device for closer supervision of foreign Communist parties.

February 1948: Communists seize power in Czechoslovakia.

March–June 1948: Increasing Soviet and Western disputes over Germany; Soviets quit Allied control council; United States, Britain, and France agree to consolidate their own zones of occupation, carry out currency reform, and establish a federal constitution for West Germany plus West Berlin.

June–July 1948: Soviets begin blockade of West Berlin; Allies respond with airlift.

July 1948: Soviets oust Yugoslavia from Cominform.

April 1949: Signing of North Atlantic Treaty provides basis for NATO and the United States' commitment to defense of Western Europe.

May 1949: Berlin blockade ends.

July 1949: USSR tests its first atomic bomb.

October 1949: Communists win Chinese civil war.

June 24, 1950: North Korea attacks South Korea; United States provides troops to support South Korea; United Nations Security Council supports allied effort under "Uniting for Peace" resolution, in absence of Soviet delegation.

October 1950: Chinese troops enter Korean War as forces of General MacArthur approach Yalu River border.

May 1951: United States tests hydrogen bomb.

March 5, 1953: Stalin dies.

This unfolding of events brought into being a Cold War between the United States and the Soviet Union, each buttressed by its own group of allies or—in the case of the USSR—satellites. While no one event by itself had the unique importance of, for example, a Pearl Harbor, the Communist coup d'état in Czechoslovakia provided a watershed in the early years of the Cold War. Coming as it did in February 1948, the Czech coup also helped to solidify a domestic American political consensus behind the new direction in foreign policy that the Truman administration had set out in the spring of 1947. The event also had the effect of dampening opposition to the new policy, both from those who would have preferred a more traditional, isolationist policy for the United States and from those who had entertained a more sympathetic view toward the USSR.

Ironically, Czechoslovakia had been the one country in Eastern Europe in which the tension between self-determination for its own people and security for the USSR might have been least acute. Unlike Poland, Czechoslovakia had not historically come under Russian threat or domination. Nor had there been conflict with the USSR during the years after World War I. Instead, Czechoslovakia had gained its independence in 1918, after centuries of rule by the Hapsburg Empire based in Vienna. The bulk of Czechoslovakia had been liberated from Nazi occupation by the Soviets (although American troops had freed the western area of the country). As a result, a genuinely free election in Czechoslovakia seemed not incompatible with the creation of a government friendly to the Soviet Union. Nor did Czechoslovakia suffer from grave internal instability. It was an economically developed country that had had one of the highest standards of living in Europe prior to World War II. It had been the most stable and democratic country in Eastern Europe during the interwar years. The experience of the late 1930s had also left a painful legacy concerning the need to adapt to the wishes of larger and more powerful neighbors. For, in October 1938, Czechoslovakia had been abandoned by the British and French as a result of the Munich agreement. The Western allies had acquiesced in Hitler's demand that the Czech region of the Sudentenland land be ceded to him. Terrified of the risk of war, and without consulting the Czechs, the British and French had ultimately complied.

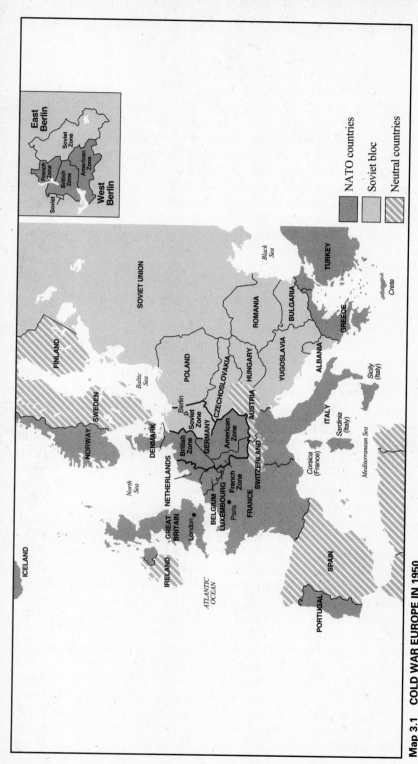

Map 3.1 COLD WAR EUROPE IN 1950

Source: Gary B. Nash and Julie R. Jeffrey, et al (eds.), *The American People,* 3rd ed. (New York: HarperCollins, 1994), p. 902.

Though the agreement may have postponed war, it lasted only briefly. In March 1939, Nazi Germany seized most of the rest of the now-indefensible country, while Poland and Hungary also helped themselves to small pieces of territory. Thus, after 1945, the Czech president, Edvard Beneš, perceived that dependence on the Western allies could offer little protection. Rather than put up futile resistance, and reflecting perhaps the accommodating tradition immortalized in the novel *The Good Soldier Svejk*,[19] Beneš and his colleagues in the Czechoslovak political leadership sought to find a *modus vivendi* with the Soviet Union.

At first, the Soviets did not seem threatening. Beneš organized a provisional government in Moscow in March 1945, in which some seven of twenty-five cabinet positions were allocated to the Communist party. These included the positions of prime minister and minister of the interior—the latter being the member of the government responsible for the security forces. In the spring of 1945, the provisional government returned to Prague, where it took office and accepted a foreign policy based on alliance with the USSR. Free elections then followed in May 1946. In these, the Communists gained approximately 35 percent of the popular vote.

With the worsening in East-West relations, however, the situation inside Czechoslovakia became more tense. During the latter part of 1947, the Soviets forced the Czechs to reject the American offer of Marshall Plan aid. As the year drew to a close, Communist strength in the country began to weaken in reaction to the repressive actions of Communist parties and the Soviet Union throughout Eastern Europe.

Matters finally came to a head in February 1948. The non-Communist cabinet majority sought to regain control from the Communist prime minister and interior minister. A few days later a Soviet deputy foreign minister flew to Prague to orchestrate the Communist response. Following disturbances, action by the police and Communist worker militias took place. There was bloodshed. Jan Masaryk, then foreign minister and a pivotol figure for non-Communist Czechs, plunged from a window to a suspicious death. Parliamentary democracy was abolished, and the Communist takeover throughout Eastern Europe was now complete.

Ironically, a series of purges would soon take place, in Czechoslovakia as well as elsewhere in the region, aimed at many of those local Communist leaders who had participated in the seizure of power. From 1950 to 1952, at the behest of Stalin and the Soviet leadership, individuals suspected of a "leftist" or "cosmopolitan" bent were imprisoned, tried, and in some cases executed. Their fate was soon shared by those Communist leaders with too "rightist" or nationalist an orientation, as the Stalinists sought to prevent any other Eastern European regime from repeating the independent course chosen by Marshall Tito of Yugoslavia.

By the time of Stalin's death in March 1953, the Soviets had not only presided over the seizure of power by Communist parties throughout Eastern Europe, but they had also seen to it that the surviving leaders were beholden to Soviet sponsorship and unlikely to assert any independent policies of their own. However, whether or not the Soviets had any immediate aggressive intention toward Western Europe, their consolidation of power in Eastern Europe led to a stiffening in Western policy and attitudes.

Beyond Eastern Europe, the outbreak of the Korean War, whether caused by direct Soviet involvement or chiefly due to the initiative of the North Koreans, prompted a significant military buildup among Western countries.[20] Coming as it did after Soviet detonation of the atomic bomb and the Communist victory in China, Korea caused the Western allies increasingly to view the USSR as presenting a major European and even global military threat. In reaction to these circumstances, the Truman administration sent four American army divisions to Europe, took steps that approximately tripled the defense budget, and determined to rearm West Germany, even though the appalling experience of World War II was only five years past.

THE INTERACTION OF DOMESTIC AND FOREIGN POLICY

Observers of foreign policy often treat it in isolation from domestic politics. Countries are frequently personified, that is, regarded as individuals writ large, reacting as rational actors in direct response to the actions of other countries. Thus commentators tell us that country A has reacted in a given way to the action of country B, without taking into account the multiple influences on foreign policymaking. While later chapters of this book treat the problem in more detail, it should be noted here that the early Cold War period was marked by especially important reciprocal effects of domestic politics on foreign policy, and vice versa. Specifically, the Roosevelt administration approached its summit meetings with the Soviet Union on the assumption that domestic political constraints, in particular a postwar reversion to isolationism similar to that occurring after World War I, would restrict the ability to deploy American power abroad in the aftermath of World War II.

Conversely, the intensification of the Cold War began to feed back into American domestic politics. Just as foreign policy was shaped profoundly by domestic affairs, so too domestic politics did not unfold in isolation from the broader external world. Initially, massive Republican gains in the 1946 congressional elections had been followed by a practical bipartisan approach toward foreign policy during the critical spring events of 1947. By and large, this disposition persisted well into 1948, helped along by a pervasive sense that Harry S. Truman, who had succeeded to the office on Roosevelt's sudden death in April 1945, was a lame duck president. This perception was strengthened by Democratic party splits, with the departure of part of the party's left for the cause of the Progressive party and the candidacy of Henry Wallace, and of segregationist Southerners for the splinter "Dixiecrat" candidacy of Strom Thurmond.

To the surprise of almost everyone except Harry Truman, however, the incumbent president scored a stunning upset victory over the Republican nominee, Thomas E. Dewey, in the 1948 election. Yet Republican frustration, the shock of postwar events, and disappointed aspirations for the postwar world began to shape increasingly acrimonious domestic politics. The mood of resentment and accusation began to build slowly in 1949, then intensified. It fed on anger and frustration over the fate of Eastern Europe, especially toward the tragedies experienced by the peoples of Poland and Czechoslovakia. At almost the same time, Americans experienced yet another shock with the "loss of China." Then, too, the July 1949 explosion of the Soviet atomic bomb stimulated a current of anxiety. The American atomic monopoly was no more, and it was now foreseeable—though not immediately so—that the United States would face vulnerability to attack that two vast oceans had previously prevented. Finally, the outbreak of the Korean War propelled American combat troops onto an Asian battlefield less than five years after they had defeated Japan.

Other factors impinged as well, including a series of spy cases in the United States and Britain. An often excessive and uncritical enthusiasm for Russia as America's world war ally was now replaced by widespread anxiety over a global struggle with a monolithic Communist menace directed from the Kremlin.

Of these various factors, the loss of China may well have been the most profound. An almost romantic sense of attachment and uplift toward China had once been pervasive. This missionary and condescending view had been typified by the words of Senator Kenneth Wherry (Republican) of Nebraska, who told a cheering crowd in 1940, "With God's help, we will lift Shanghai up and up, ever up, until it is just like Kansas City."[21] The victory of Mao's Communists in the civil war, however, conjured up a sense of peril, and attention began to shift to finding traitors within the United States on whom the blame for this enormous loss could be placed.

The moment came with a speech by the then little-known junior senator from Wisconsin, Joseph McCarthy. On February 9, 1950, at Wheeling, West Virginia, he charged: "Men in high places are concerting to deliver us to disaster." The senator went on to speak of a "great conspiracy dwarfing any previous venture," and he claimed to have a list (never actually produced) of 205 Communists in the State Department. A few weeks later, on March 30, McCarthy expanded his charge, claiming that "Soviet Russia conquered China, and an important ally of this conqueror was the small left-wing element in our Department of State."

The United States had in fact intervened in China, with weapons, equipment, and money, to support the Nationalist forces of Chiang Kai-shek. However, it is doubtful that the Maoist victory could have been prevented short of American intervention with combat troops on a scale comparable to that of World War II.

The Communist victory in China had a significant impact on American politics. It fed the search for scapegoats or traitors at home, thereby ushering in a period of McCarthyism that lasted several years and had corrosive effects on the domestic political climate in which foreign policy was debated. Indeed, the climate of opinion had a major impact even on the administration of President Truman which McCarthy was in the process of vilifying. In early 1950, Secretary of State Dean Acheson directed the preparation of a key document by the National Security Council. Known as NSC 68, this report emphasized the serious nature of the Soviet threat and called for massive expansion of America's military establishment. The document, largely written by Paul Nitze, a senior government official, also contained passages conveying an intolerance of dissent. NSC 68 spoke of the present crisis as demanding that the individual "exercise discrimination: while pursuing through free inquiry the search for truth he knows when he should commit an act of faith; that he distinguish between the necessity for tolerance and the necessity for just suppression." In going on to warn that a free society is vulnerable, the document cautioned against "the excess of tolerance degenerating into indulgence of conspiracy."[22]

The prose of NSC 68 was relatively elevated in tone as it grappled with philosophical issues and the competitive claims of freedom versus security. Ironically, the cut and thrust of domestic politics soon turned discussion of these foreign and security issues into crude *ad hominem* attacks—even directed at Acheson himself. Acheson, along with General George C. Marshall, the commander in chief of American forces in World War II and Acheson's predecessor as secretary of state, was vilified by McCarthy. Indeed, Richard Nixon added his own denunciation of the Secretary of State, with a memorable condemnation of "Dean Acheson's College of Cowardly Communist Containment."[23]

After the loss of China, the government of Mao Zedong was perceived as little more than a puppet of the Soviets. Thus, even a figure such as Dean Rusk, then Assistant Secretary of State for Far Eastern affairs, and later to become Secretary of State under Presidents Kennedy and Johnson, could describe China in the following terms:

> The Peiping regime may be a colonial Russian government—a slavic Manchuko on a larger scale. It is not the Government of China. It does not pass the first test. *It is not Chinese.*[24]

The United States adopted a policy of nonrecognition of the People's Republic of China (PRC), choosing to treat the Nationalists (the Republic of China), whose officials had fled to the island of Taiwan in 1949, as the official government. During these years, a number of State Department officials who had been China experts were driven out of government, despite the absence of evidence that they had been disloyal. The resultant loss of expertise, coupled with the climate of intimidation about the loss of China, made successive administrations slow to recognize the reality of the growing Sino-Soviet split.

Ironically, beginning with the Nixon presidency, the belated awareness of this bitter rivalry between Russia and China would later make possible not only diplomatic recognition but a de facto alliance between the United States and the PRC, in which the United States would even manage to establish electronic ground stations within China in order to monitor Soviet missile tests after the loss of facilities in Iran.

WHAT CAUSED THE COLD WAR?

Major historical events can rarely be explained by a single factor. More often they are multicausal in nature. In the case of the Cold War, a number of competing explanations or causes have been set forth to account for the origins of the East-West struggle. Indeed, a number of revisionist interpretations have suggested either that the United States and USSR shared comparable responsibility[25] or even that the Cold War was actually caused by the United States.[26]

Nonetheless, the most important factor remains that of concrete Soviet actions in Eastern Europe at the time. Although other significant causes existed, these actions galvanized Western and American reactions and policies.[27] This does not exclude other contributory causes, yet the regime of Joseph Stalin, which had already been responsible for the deaths of more than twenty million of its own subjects through purges, executions, collectivization of agriculture, and the vast system of forced labor camps in Siberia (the "Gulag"),[28] can hardly be credited with a postwar policy that was merely the result of misunderstandings, differences of interest, or misperceptions.

A second cause of the Cold War was great power conflict. That is to say, major powers tend to compete for power and influence, regardless of their ideological coloration. From this perspective, it is important to bear in mind that Russia under the czars had been a contender for European power as well. It had sought to expand its influence in the Balkans, against Turkey and the Austro-Hungarian Empire, as well as elsewhere in Eastern Europe and along its Asian periphery. Indeed, it was under nineteenth-century czarist regimes that Russia vastly extended its territorial domain across Siberia to the Far East.* From this perspective, we can appreciate how the demise of Nazi Germany left a power vacuum in Central Europe which was ultimately filled by the United States and the USSR.

This is not to ignore the specifically ideological component of Soviet policy under Lenin, Stalin, and their successors. Nonetheless, it is well to remember that power rivalries between Marxist-Leninist states became very bitter, as the struggle between Vietnam and Cambodia, and the competition between the Soviet Union and China later attested. (Nor were Communist countries the only ones susceptible to such fratricidal struggles. Consider too the bitter 1980–1988 war between two Islamic countries, Iran and Iraq, as well as the outbreak of World War I in 1914 among countries with identities that were mainly capitalist and Christian.)

Third, there exists the realm of ideology as an explanation for the Cold War. While the Soviet domination of Eastern Europe involved a deliberate exercise of Soviet power, it is also true that the Soviet Union on the one hand, and the United States and the industrial democracies on the other, represented significantly different beliefs about political, social, and economic ways of life and, indeed, human values. While these differences were sometimes depicted in oversimplified, manichean terms, the contrasts of belief and ideology, and of national historical experience, were real.

Soviet ideology, however, was doubly removed from the nineteenth-century philosophy of Karl Marx and the working class movements that resulted from it. Under Lenin and Stalin, the belief system itself became transformed into the rationalization for a totalitarian police state and the interests of a narrow, bureau-

---

*During the nineteenth century, the United States was expanding its own domain across the North American continent, ultimately reaching the Pacific.

cratic, collectivist dictatorship. Ideological commitment to the liberation of "workers of the world" was replaced by the interests of this narrow party elite. Moreover, Soviet priorities became those of "socialism in one country," with the ideology increasingly a vehicle for the advancement of Russian national interests.

Finally, there remain matters of misperception. That is, the components of emotional hostility and an escalating cycle of rivalries and disputes did exist. No doubt they worsened relations among the superpowers, not least in exacerbating the conflict between the Soviets' perceived (and often exaggerated) claim to security and competing desires of the Eastern European countries for self-determination. In this respect, however, the assertions of revisionist historians that place great emphasis on Soviet responses to initial Western actions seem excessive. To be sure, the Soviets may have been offended by a number of U.S. actions. These included the Truman administration's canceling of lend-lease, the United States' mishandling of the Soviet postwar loan request, and President Truman's abrasive first meeting with Foreign Minister Molotov.[29] The Soviet historic memory of Western (including American) intervention in the Russian civil war also existed. Yet all these factors taken together still carry far less weight in explaining the outbreak of the Cold War than the facts of Stalin's concrete actions, the realities of great power conflict, and the clash of ideology.[30]

ASSESSING THE SOVIET THREAT

Was it the case, then, that the Soviets presented an immediate threat of a planned military invasion of Western Europe in the years after 1945? In all probability, the answer is that they did not. To begin with, the USSR had suffered grievously from the ravages of the war. More than twenty million Russians had died, vast stretches of western Russia lay in ruins, and the Soviets faced a daunting task of reconstruction. Thus the ability of the country to sustain a drive into the West was probably minimal if directed against a viable Western Europe. Stalin almost certainly appreciated the consequences of any attempt to attack Western Europe in the face of U.S. nuclear superiority. On the other hand, had there been no Western resistance to Soviet expansion nor major risk to the USSR, Soviet behavior might have been more adventurous. In this sense, the American commitment was crucial in restoring stability to Western Europe.

Was NATO actually necessary to deter the Soviets from a military onslaught on Western Europe? One of Europe's foremost strategic analysts observes that we cannot know for certain, but that "it is . . . improbable, given both their historical record and their political philosophy, that they would have seriously contemplated such an action unless and until a recognizable 'revolutionary situation' had developed in the West in which they could plausibly intervene to give fraternal support to the toiling masses and to a powerful indigenous communist party that would act as their agent in controlling the region after its conquest."[31] Thus, the American contribution to economic recovery and the restoration of political self-confidence and stability were critical, while the commitment to NATO provided a vital accompanying element of reassurance.

Here it is also useful to consider a sober assessment by the late Edward Crankshaw. He described the Bolshevik regime as "even more vile than it was possible for anyone who had not experienced it to imagine." Yet he observed that although the Soviets found it "hard to resist every opportunity for easy expansionism and subversion, there was next to no danger of the Kremlin launching a formal war and it could always be stopped by a firm and clear declaration of the line it must not cross—backed by sufficient force to make that declaration credible." At the same time, Crankshaw insisted on a realistic view of the Soviets. He was critical of a return in the early 1980s to a "panic fear of the Communist menace," an "ideological crusade," and of a "general loss of a sense of proportion."[32]

These realist assessments depict the Soviet Union as a powerful and antagonistic power, but with practical limits on the threat it posed to Western Europe at the onset of the Cold War. However, it is also worth asking whether there might have been anything the United States could have done at the time to prevent the Russians from imposing their control over Eastern Europe. This domination, after all, exacted a severe human cost from the inhabitants of the region. Indeed, a series of popular rebellions against rule by the Soviets or by Communist parties closely allied to the USSR did take place. These included East Berlin in 1953, Hungary and Poland in 1956, Czechoslovakia in 1968, and Poland in 1980–1981.

In retrospect, it is difficult to identify what might have been done by the West to arrive at a better outcome. On the one hand, a tougher strategy, possibly coupled with economic incentives, might have served to force the Soviets to follow a less hegemonic policy toward Eastern Europe. And it is impossible to say that this would not have worked. Stalin's hard line masked enormous Soviet weakness at the time, and the Soviets might have been content to drive a bargain in which Eastern Europe was part of the stakes. Yet the problem of this argument is not only that it is based on a series of "what ifs." More important, domestic American political support for a tougher policy did not coalesce until the spring of 1947, by which time the Soviets had consolidated their position everywhere but in Czechoslovakia. And, for a Soviet dictator who had asked the question, "How many divisions has the Pope?" the massive American military demobilization could hardly have gone unnoticed. By the middle of 1946, the presence of U.S. forces in Europe had been greatly reduced, along with the practical possibility of using force as a lever against the Soviet presence in Eastern Europe.

Conversely, the United States might have sought to pursue a much more accommodating position toward the Soviet role in Eastern Europe. Yet this effort to maintain a postwar *modus vivendi* with Stalin in order to avert the division of Europe into two hostile blocs would have required turning a blind eye toward a blatant pattern of abuses of democratic freedoms and human rights in the Soviet sphere. Not only is it doubtful that benign neglect by the United States would have measurably alleviated the situation within Eastern Europe, but it is nearly inconceivable that public and congressional opinion would have allowed an American administration to remain mute about the unfolding events in Poland and the other states under Soviet occupation.

In sum, the United States was neither in a position to intervene forcefully in, say, 1946, to compel Stalin to withdraw from Eastern Europe, nor would it have been able to pursue a path of passive acquiescence toward Soviet actions. In the end, the postwar division of Germany and Europe, and with it the onset of the Cold War, seem to have been virtually unavoidable. In fact, the location of what Churchill termed the iron curtain roughly paralleled the demarcation line between American and other Western troops[33] on the one side, and of Soviet forces on the other, as they completed their defeat of Nazi Germany in 1945. While there were exceptions to this grim power reality, in particular for Finland, Austria, and Northern Iran, the outcome largely reflected the facts of armed strength on the ground as it existed in 1945. The long experience of the East-West conflict and Cold War reflected this fact.

NOTES

1. *Democracy in America* (New York: Knopf, 1945), p. 452.
2. Anne O'Hare McCormick, "Faith for a Troubled Christmas Time," *New York Times Magazine,* 2 December 1950, quoted in Arnold S. Kaufman, "The Cold War in Retrospect," in Irving Howe, ed., *A Dissenter's Guide to Foreign Policy* (Garden City, NY: Anchor, 1968), p. 65.
3. Adam B. Ulam puts greater emphasis on personal rivalries for power among Soviet leaders than on ideological differences among them. See *Expansion and Coexistence: Soviet Foreign Policy, 1917–1973* (New York: Holt, Rinehart & Winston, 1973), p. 136.
4. For a compelling collection of these reactions, see the accounts of six intellectuals (André Gide, Richard Wright, Ignazio Silone, Stephen Spender, Arthur Koestler, and Louis Fischer), in Richard Crossman, ed., *The God That Failed* (New York: Harper, 1950).
5. See Chapter 6.
6. See, for example, Raul Hilberg, *The Destruction of the European Jews* (Chicago: Quadrangle Books, 1961, and New York: New Viewpoints/Franklin Watts, 1973).
7. Winston S. Churchill, *Triumph and Tragedy* (Boston: Houghton Mifflin, 1953), pp. 227–228.
8. See Louis Halle, *The Cold War As History* (New York: Harper & Row, 1967), p. 69. Halle provides a detailed elaboration of the clash between security and self-determination.
9. The Soviets were unsuccessful in seeking to extract territorial concessions from Turkey. The USSR gained legalization of many of these changes in a series of treaties during 1947. Incorporation of East Prussia was recognized in the Helsinki accords of 1975, but the United States never formally accepted Soviet annexation of the Baltic states, and they regained their independence in September 1991. See Alvin Z. Rubinstein, *Soviet Foreign Policy Since World War II: Imperial and Global,* 2nd ed. (Boston: Little, Brown, 1985), pp. 46-47, 52–53.
10. On June 30, 1945, army military personnel on active duty totaled 8,266,373. One year later, the number had fallen to 1,889,690. Note that the data include the Army Air Forces (the predecessor of the U.S. Air Force). Source: Newspaper Enterprise Association, *The World Almanac* (New York: 1981), p. 329. For stories on troop protests and demands for faster demobilization, see *New York Times,* January 7, 8, 10, 1946.
11. Stalin ordered a purge of Communist party members who favored "peaceful coexistence" and were unwilling to support Moscow's new line of political war against Western government policies. This was done by means of an article signed by the leader of

the French Communist Party, Jacques Duclos, which appeared in that party's theoretical journal, *Cahiers du Communisme*. See Rubenstein, p. 48.

12. For a detailed treatment of this period, see Joseph Marion Jones, *The Fifteen Weeks* (New York: Harcourt, Brace & World, 1955).

13. The text of Truman's address can be found in Jones, *The Fifteen Weeks,* pp. 269–274.

14. Jones, *The Fifteen Weeks,* pp. 207 ff.

15. Data from David Schoenbaum, *New York Times,* 5 June 1982, and World Bank, *World Development Report,* 1993 (New York: Oxford University Press, 1993), p. 274.

16. George F. Kennan, "The Sources of Soviet Conduct," *Foreign Affairs* 25 (July 1947): 566–582, at p. 576.

17. See George F. Kennan, *Memoirs: 1925–1950* (Boston: Little, Brown, 1967). Also see Charles Gati, ed., *Caging the Bear: Containment and the Cold War* (Indianapolis: Bobbs-Merrill, 1974).

18. Evan Luard, ed., *The Cold War: A Re-appraisal* (New York: Praeger, 1964), p. 20. Luard's excellent volume provides a useful account of the events in this period, and the chronology here draws in part on his treatment. Another useful source is John W. Young, *The Longman Companion to Cold War and Detente 1941–91* (New York: Longman, 1993.)

19. Jaroslav Hasek, *The Good Soldier Svejk and His Fortunes in the World War* (Harmondsworth, Middlesex, England: Penguin, 1973). The book was written in 1921–1922.

20. For analysis of the war's effects on policy, see also Robert Jervis, "The Impact of the Korean War on the Cold War," *Journal of Conflict Resolution* 24 (December 1980): 563–592.

21. Quoted, *New Republic,* 26 October 1974.

22. See Gaddis Smith, *New York Times,* 12 September 1976, and David S. McLellan, *Dean Acheson: The State Department Years* (New York: Dodd, Mead, 1976). The text of NSC 68 was declassified in 1975.

23. The Nixon statement has been widely cited. See, for example, David Halberstam, *The Best and the Brightest* (Greenwich, CT: Fawcett Crest, 1972), p. 395.

24. Address before the China Institute, New York, May 18, 1951, in U.S. *Department of State Bulletin,* Vol. XXIV, No. 621, 28 May 1951, pp. 846–848, at p. 847; italics added. See also *New York Times,* 19 May 1951, italics added.

25. For example, William Appleman Williams, *The Tragedy of American Diplomacy,* rev. ed. (New York: Delta Books, 1962).

26. Especially Joyce and Gabriel Kolko, *The Limits of Power: The World and United States Foreign Policy, 1945–54* (New York: Harper & Row, 1972).

27. John Gaddis notes that American diplomats did not initially view the Soviets as an adversary. Instead, even if later U.S. policies may have involved overreactions, Soviet unilateralism caused the changes in America's outlook during the initial postwar years. See John Lewis Gaddis, *The Long Peace: Inquiries into the History of the Cold War* (New York: Oxford University Press, 1987).

28. Use of the term *Gulag* to describe the Soviet system of repression and especially its vast network of forced labor camps gained prominence with the publication of Aleksander I. Solzhenitsyn's major work, *The Gulag Archipelago 1918–1956: An Experiment in Literary Investigation* (New York: Harper & Row, 1973, 1974). A considerable body of information had long been available, however, and even included a widely circulated secret speech by Nikita Khrushchev to the Soviet Communist Party Congress in February 1956, denouncing the crimes of Stalin.

A number of Western historians have estimated deaths from the executions, agricultural collectivization, punitive famine, and labor camps at up to 20 million. See

Robert Conquest, *The Great Terror: Stalin's Purge of the Thirties* (New York: Macmillan, 1973); and *The Harvest of Sorrow: Soviet Collectivization and the Terror-famine* (New York: Oxford University Press, 1986), also Stephen F. Cohen, *Rethinking the Soviet Experience: Politics and History Since 1917* (New York: Oxford University Press, 1985). A dissident Russian Marxist historian, Roy Medvedev, has put forward a similar estimate, as published in the Soviet weekly tabloid, *Argumenti i Fakti* and cited in *New York Times*, 4 February 1989, p. 1. Another report puts Medvedev's estimate at 12 million. See *The Economist* (London), 10 December, 1988, p. 98. For a substantially lower estimate, of 4.5 to 5 million, see Jerry F. Hough, *How the Soviet Union Is Governed* (Cambridge, MA: Harvard University Press, 1979). Note that Hough's figure covers the years from 1926 through 1939. While some of the higher estimates, such as Medvedev's, encompass the years until Stalin's death in 1953, others are limited to the prewar period. Yet another estimate, by a Soviet demographer named Maksudov, is of 17.5 million deaths, of which 7.5 million are attributed to the period up to 1939 and 9 to 11 million for the years from 1939 to 1953. See *Cahier du monde russe et sovietique* (Paris: Mouton editeur, Vol. XVII, No. 3, July–September 1977: 223–267), summarized in *Le Monde* (Paris), 2 May 1979.

29. For views of the Cold War by other revisionist historians, see, for example, D. F. Fleming, *The Cold War and Its Origins* (New York: Doubleday, 1961) and Gar Alperowitz, *Atomic Diplomacy: Hiroshima and Potsdam* (New York: Simon & Schuster, 1965).

30. For views of the Cold War that stress Soviet responsibility and power rivalries, see, for example, Hans J. Morgenthau, *In Defense of the National Interest* (New York: Knopf, 1951); Louis Halle, *The Cold War As History* (New York: Harper & Row, 1967); Dean Acheson, *Present at the Creation* (New York: Norton, 1969).

31. Michael Howard, "Reassurance and Deterrence," *Foreign Affairs* 61 (Winter 1982–83): 311.

32. Edward Crankshaw, *Putting Up With the Russians* (New York: Viking-Penguin, 1985).

33. One exception occurred on July 1, 1945, when British and American forces withdrew from parts of Germany (Mecklenberg, Thuringia, and Saxony) they had occupied but which wartime Allied agreements had allotted to Soviet occupation.

chapter 4

East-West Relations and the End of the Cold War

[The Soviet Union is] . . . the focus of evil in the modern world . . . an evil empire. . . .

—PRESIDENT RONALD REAGAN,
SPEECH TO THE NATIONAL ASSOCIATION OF EVANGELICALS, MARCH 8, 1983[1]

The longest peace yet known rested on two pillars: bipolarity and nuclear weapons.

—KENNETH N. WALTZ[2]

It was a unique event in human history. . . . Never before has there been a case of an empire that caved in without a war, revolution or an invasion.

—SIR ISAIAH BERLIN[3]

The bipolar era severely limited the sovereignty and the freedom of states (particularly within the Soviet sphere).. . . Thus it was natural that communism's decline would encourage the rebirth of nations and increase their openness to external influences. What was unclear was whether the future would feature a new bipolar cleavage (this time based on a North-South confrontation), a new multipolar equilibrium or global cooperation. . . . The surprise is that, although indications in the direction of each model have emerged, their course has been troubled, distorted and, in some respects, dominated by another more powerful development—political decomposition and anarchy.

—PIERRE HASSNER[4]

The postwar order that emerged from the ruins of World War II came to an abrupt end some forty-five years later. A series of popular and largely peaceful revolutions in Eastern Europe, the opening of the Berlin Wall on November 9, 1989, and a profound change in Soviet policy toward the region marked a surprisingly rapid transformation.

The causes of change lay both in the origins of the Cold War and in the contradictions of the Soviet political and economic system itself. The imposition of both Soviet domination and Moscow–oriented Communist regimes throughout Eastern Europe never achieved acceptance by the peoples of Eastern Europe. This left the region in unstable equilibrium. It meant that while a surface stability could be maintained, though broken by periodic bursts of resistance (as in East Berlin in 1953, Hungary in 1956, Czechoslovakia in 1968, and Poland in 1980–1981), it rested on the expectation that the Soviet Union would maintain the Eastern European status quo, and would do so by force if necessary. For the USSR, however, preservation of control in Eastern Europe was becoming increasingly costly and problematic.

With Mikhail Gorbachev's coming to power in March 1985, a gradual transformation began. This was driven by the Soviet system's increasing inability to provide for the needs of its people, by the USSR's failure to compete with other advanced industrial societies amid a modern technological revolution, and by a change in Soviet society itself, whose population was increasingly urban, professional, and well educated, but who found their system unable to meet the needs of an increasingly modernized society.[5] The failure of the Soviet system was aptly summarized by Boris Yeltsin, who in 1991 became the first elected President of Russia. Shortly before the dissolution of the USSR itself, Yeltsin observed:

> I think this experiment which was conducted on our soil was a tragedy for our people and it was too bad that it happened on our territory. . . . I think gradually this will come to be understood by other countries where supporters of the idea of communism still exist.[6]

In addition to Soviet domestic failure, major foreign policy initiatives had proven counterproductive, leading both to a reintensified arms race with the West, which the Soviet Union was hard pressed to afford, and to growing resistance to heavy-handed Soviet interventions—as in the bitter guerilla war in Afghanistan.

The end of the postwar era did not, however, come smoothly, nor was the Gorbachev period the first time that Soviet and American leaders had moved toward a relaxation of East-West tensions. A series of earlier efforts had also taken place. The first of these had occurred after the death of Stalin in 1953. Subsequent periods of détente took place following the Cuban missile crisis of October 1962, and later in 1969–1972 with the actions of the Nixon administration and its de-escalation of the Vietnam War. In each case, it appeared that the Cold War was coming to an end and that East-West relations were in the process of transformation. However, these assessments proved premature. Each of these periods of détente deteriorated and even gave way to a serious confrontation—the Cuban missile crisis, Vietnam, the October 1973 Middle East War, Afghanistan, and a crisis over the deployment of Euromissiles at the beginning of the 1980s.

To appreciate the nature of East-West relations at the end of the twentieth century, as well as to comprehend why the transformation that occurred at the end of the 1980s constituted a break with the postwar order, it is necessary to assess the long period from the early 1950s onward, in which each of these early détente efforts was undertaken and then collapsed. While these steps in the 1950s, 1960s, and 1970s entailed significant relaxation of tensions and the undertaking of important agreements in trade, human contacts, and arms control, none of them eliminated the basic cause of the Cold War: the imposition of Soviet control over Eastern Europe. Once Gorbachev finally moved to accept the need for change, however, there followed both extraordinary, even dizzying, transformation of the region in 1989–1991 and ultimately the end of the Cold War itself.

FROM COLD WAR TO DÉTENTE

With the death of Stalin and the end of the Korean War in 1953, the initial phase of the Cold War began to give way to a less intense form of East-West conflict. This by no means brought the Soviet-American confrontation to an end, but marked the beginning of a transition to a more stable, long-term competition. The deep-seated sources of antagonism remained, but it became increasingly apparent that the superpowers would grope toward means of managing their conflict in ways short of war.

East-West relations did not, however, follow a steady path of relaxation. While a gradual thaw did take place as the legacy of Stalin faded, there were major oscillations between relaxation and crisis. Consider some of the most prominent of these events. In May 1955, the Big Four powers (United States, USSR, Britain, and France) reached agreement on the Austrian State Treaty. This provided for the departure of occupation troops from Austria and establishment of its neutrality. In July 1955, American, Soviet, and British leaders held a summit meeting at Geneva. Here they discussed a number of proposals to reduce tensions and improve their mutual security. These efforts were followed in February 1956 by Soviet leader Nikita Khrushchev's secret speech to the Twentieth Congress of the Soviet Communist party in which he delivered a long, dramatic denunciation of the crimes of Stalin. Later, in the spring of 1956, Khrushchev announced plans for a reduction of more than one million men in the Soviet armed forces.

However, these events were soon followed in October and November by simultaneous crises in Hungary and the Middle East. In Budapest, massive public resistance to the Stalinist regime led to its replacement by an independent-minded government under Imre Nagy. Nagy had once headed a Communist regime but had been imprisoned as a result of purges during the Stalin period. At the beginning of November 1956, this new government announced Hungarian withdrawal from the Soviet-led Warsaw Pact and declared Hungary's neutrality. At the same time, Soviet troops, which had briefly withdrawn, launched a massive invasion of Hungary. This culminated in bloody fighting, the suppression of the

Hungarian government, and its replacement by a pro-Soviet regime under János Kádár.

Meanwhile, in the Middle East, escalating conflict and threats to Israel by President Nasser of Egypt led to war. As a result, Israel occupied the Sinai Peninsula. A coordinated British and French operation almost simultaneously took over the Suez Canal. The Soviets responded by threatening to use missiles against France and Britain. More important, strong economic and political pressure from the United States forced the occupying powers to withdraw from Egypt.

Eventually this crisis atmosphere gave way to another relaxation in Soviet-American relations. Despite continuing competition outside of Europe, the superpowers conducted a series of efforts aimed at easing their relations. These included further negotiations in Geneva and a September 1959 visit to the United States by Nikita Khrushchev.

Once again, however, there occurred a sharp turn toward crisis. In May 1960, Khrushchev disrupted a summit meeting in Paris after the Soviets shot down an American U-2 spy plane overflying their territory. In rapid succession, East-West tensions escalated over the status of Berlin, events in Indochina, and growing animosity between the United States and the Cuban government of Fidel Castro. In a period of little more than two years, there occurred the April 1961 Bay of Pigs episode, in which a CIA-coordinated invasion by Cuban exiles was defeated by the Castro regime; the August 1961 construction of the Berlin wall by the Communist government of East Germany; and the October 1962 Cuban missile crisis. The latter event brought the United States and Russia closer to the brink of nuclear war than at any time in their postwar history. Ironically, its resolution helped to usher in yet another period of relaxation. In 1963, the superpowers negotiated a hotline agreement, linking Washington and Moscow for the purposes of crisis communication. They also agreed to a treaty that suspended the testing of nuclear weapons in the atmosphere.

Yet again, the growing improvement in East-West relations was reversed. One of the major issues was the escalation of fighting in Vietnam. In 1965, this brought the American commitment of combat troops on a major scale and the expanded Soviet provision of aid to North Vietnam. In addition, August 1968 saw the ruthless Soviet suppression of the moderate Dubček government in Czechoslovakia and its effort at constructing "communism with a human face." The Soviets also proclaimed what came to be called the Brezhnev Doctrine—in effect committing the USSR to intervention wherever the existence of a pro-Moscow government was in danger.

EVOLUTION OF THE SOVIET-AMERICAN RELATIONSHIP

One of the great paradoxes of the Cold War was that it marked a long period of stability between the two greatest powers of the time, the United States and the Soviet Union. While their interactions were characterized by periods of both great tension and accommodation, a series of changes in their relationship during the 1950s and 1960s created conditions for a greater regularization of their conflict and thus made possible a form of competitive coexistence. It is well worth considering each of these changes in turn, not only because each was intrinsically important, but also because they helped to shape the East-West conflict.

Stability of the European Balance

In the initial years of the Cold War, the United States' concern was to stabilize the economies and political systems of those European countries that had not been occupied by the Soviets at the end of the war and thus had avoided early Stalinist domination. Development of the Truman Doctrine and Marshall Plan make this quite clear. At the same time, Soviet leaders may have entertained hopes that a repetition of instability characteristic of the 1930s would ultimately create upheaval and revolution in the West.

Meanwhile, there remained Western hopes that Soviet subjugation of Eastern Europe might somehow be reversed. Prior to the 1952 American presidential election, Republican leaders were critical of the Truman administration for its policy of seeking to "contain" Soviet Communism without making a concerted effort to push it back from the lands of Eastern Europe. Indeed, President Eisenhower's key advisor and secretary of state, John Foster Dulles, spoke of the need to "roll back" the Soviets from that region.

An uprising of East Berlin workers on June 17, 1953, demonstrated the continued instability of the Soviet hold on Eastern Europe, though allied countries were unable to act as the revolt was put down by Soviet tanks.[7] The subsequent experience of the Hungarian uprising proved sobering. It demonstrated anew the deep-seated hostility of their own people toward pro-Soviet regimes. During the revolt, external radio broadcasts suggested that American forces might intervene in support of the Hungarians. In the end, however, the Eisenhower administration was unable to act with force to aid the revolution. In effect, it stood by helplessly as the Soviets crushed the Hungarian army and civilian resistance.

It is striking to note that this American caution in the use of force occurred at a time when the United States still maintained strategic nuclear superiority over the USSR. That is, in the event of a major nuclear war between the superpowers, the United States possessed at least the hypothetical ability to prevail, although not without the risk of suffering a small number of nuclear attacks against the North American continent.

The Eisenhower administration refrained from intervening during the Hungarian revolution for two major reasons. Both of them rested on fundamental considerations of power. First, and most immediately, the Soviets possessed superiority of conventional forces within Hungary and the immediate region, and geography made American intervention impractical. Hungary was bordered on the east by the USSR, which could thus send troops directly into that country. To the north was Czechoslovakia, to the south, Yugoslavia, and to the west, neutral Austria. Hungary was not contiguous with any NATO country, and for American troops to intervene would have required a massive violation of Austrian neutrality, as well as exposure of the intervening force to being outflanked and cut off by Soviet troops operating through the territory of their Czech ally.

Second, even had the conditions on the ground been less daunting, Hungary lay within the Soviet sphere of influence. As a consequence of World War II, the Soviets had achieved hegemony in Eastern Europe, while the United States had become the most influential power in Western Europe. Although the conditions of these spheres of influence differed profoundly—in that the Americans were present with the consent of local populations—it had become increasingly clear that an overt effort by either superpower to intervene in the other's realm would be likely to precipitate war. Both sides appeared wary of touching off World War III, regardless of whether such a conflict would escalate to the nuclear level or remain entirely conventional.

Meanwhile, other developments seemed to make the European balance durable. By the mid 1950s, the countries of Western Europe were in the midst of a period of sustained prosperity and economic growth. They had recovered from the material ravages of war, and their political systems had successfully resisted the challenges initially presented by large Communist movements, especially in Italy and France. In addition, the consolidation of the American, British, and French occupation zones of Germany and the establishment of the Federal Republic of Germany had proved a resounding success. West Germany proved to be economically dynamic. And authoritarian challenges to its domestic political system from both the far right (neo-Nazis) and far left (pro-Moscow Communists) appeared to be minimal.

Western Europe remained firmly linked to the United States in security terms, through the establishment of NATO and the rebuilding of armed forces by the member countries. In addition, economic links among the Western Europeans were burgeoning, especially with the creation of the six-member European Coal and Steel Community in 1952, and its metamorphosis into the European Common Market in 1957.

For their part, the Soviets appeared to consolidate control in Eastern Europe. They achieved this through a combination of pro-Soviet indigenous regimes, political repression, military occupation forces in a number of countries, establishment of the Warsaw Pact as a military alliance, and construction of the Council for Mutual Economic Assistance (Comecon) as a means of economic integration. They also created an East German state, the German Democratic Republic (GDR), from their own occupation sector of Germany. And although the August 1961 construction of the Berlin wall to prevent East Germans from fleeing to the West testified to the political bankruptcy of the regime, the GDR seemed to become the most economically successful of the Soviet bloc countries.

Thus, viewed as a whole, Europe had attained a degree of stability by the late 1950s. The division of the Continent along the military demarcation lines established in 1945 appeared increasingly durable. Prospects for revolutionary upheaval or instability in the West were minimal. Meanwhile, the Soviets controlled Eastern Europe. Europe remained divided into two rival blocs, the one allied militarily and economically to the United States, the other tied to the Soviet Union.

This division gave the United States and the USSR spheres of influence in their respective regions of Europe. However, this apparent symmetry masked basic differences. The Western Europeans had built—or rebuilt—stable democratic systems. Their membership in regional groupings and in NATO itself remained voluntary—as the French departure from NATO's integrated military command structure demonstrated in 1966.* By contrast, Hungary's effort to withdraw from the Warsaw Pact in 1956 had been crushed by Soviet tanks, and Hungarian Prime Minister Nagy had been executed for his efforts. In any event, the increasingly stable configuration in Europe suggested that major change was remote. Despite periodic suggestions for reexamining the division of Germany or for doing away with the division of Europe, it appeared that the postwar status quo was unlikely to be overturned.

Strategic Stability

A second change, in this case in the military realm, gradually took shape during the late 1950s and early 1960s. Here too, an initially fluid situation had become more stable. Initially, in the aftermath of World War II and in the early years of the Cold War, the Soviet-American military balance in Europe had rested on an asymmetrical standoff.

While the Russians maintained a numerical advantage in conventional military forces, including troops, tanks, and artillery, the United States offset this with its preponderance of strategic nuclear power. The United States could deter any possibility of a Soviet military threat to Western Europe through the prospect that, although the Russians might be able to occupy a significant portion of the region, the Americans had the ability to retaliate by inflicting nuclear devastation on the USSR. This situation was put graphically in a March 1954 memorandum of the U.S. Strategic Air Command. Under its "Optimum Plan," Russia would be hit with between 600 and 700 bombs. As the memorandum put it, "The final impression was that virtually all of Russia would be nothing but a smoking, radiating ruin at the end of two hours."[8]

With the Soviets' autumn 1957 launching of Sputnik, the world's first orbiting man-made satellite, the prospect of a major change in the strategic balance began to emerge. At the time, it appeared that the Soviets were about to acquire a major missile capability for use against the United States, and that they might well be forging ahead of the United States in strategic weapons. This gave rise to a "missile gap" controversy in 1959–1960, during which Democratic opponents of the Eisenhower administration and of the Republican 1960 presidential nominee, Richard Nixon, accused the administration of allowing a potentially dangerous margin of Soviet military advantage to emerge.

In fact, by the middle of 1961, new American satellite surveillance indicated that no such missile gap was occurring, and indeed the United States had maintained a considerable lead in intercontinental strategic weaponry. Nonetheless, it was only a matter of time before the Soviets would acquire a reliable second-strike capability[9] for use against the United States. The sense of mutual vulnerability of the two superpowers, spoken of for many years, was first vividly dramatized by the

---

*France did not, however, renounce its obligations under the North Atlantic Treaty.

events of the October 1962 Cuban missile crisis. Though the United States ultimately prevailed, particularly because of the superiority of its conventional forces in the region, the crisis created a perception that the two superpowers had come to the very brink of a nuclear war.

Later in the 1960s, the United States and the Soviet Union moved to a situation of strategic parity. In this nuclear balance, each now appeared capable of responding to a nuclear first strike against itself by inflicting similarly unacceptable damage on the attacker. This condition of nuclear deterrence, together with the mutual vulnerability on which it rested, seemed to lend a certain stability to the strategic arms race. It did not halt the development and deployment of new weapons, but it contributed to an increasing perception among policymakers on both sides that whatever the hostility and profound differences between the superpowers, neither could prevail in the event of a major nuclear war.

While the emerging vulnerability of the United States gave way to growing misgivings in Europe about the credibility of the American commitment, stability continued to characterize the European theater. The presence of more than 300,000 American troops, along with the existence of battlefield and theater nuclear weapons and British and French nuclear forces, served credibly enough as a potential detonator for the American strategic arsenal in the unlikely event that the Soviets were to consider a military threat to Western Europe.

In sum, although the strategic arms race continued, there was a more pervasive sense of the unacceptable consequences of a nuclear war and of the increasingly robust nature of the strategic balance. These circumstances made it more feasible—though by no means easy—for the superpowers to contemplate negotiations aimed at stabilizing or even limiting their nuclear competition.

Challenges to Bipolarity

During the height of the Cold War, the world appeared at times to be divided into two unified, hierarchic, and opposing blocs: one led by the United States, the other by the Soviet Union. From Washington, it was sometimes assumed that events were orchestrated in the Kremlin. Hence, it was often asserted that the People's Republic of China (PRC) was no more than a Soviet satellite, that communism was monolithic, and that international upheaval or instability of any kind was likely to have its roots in Moscow.

Even from the outset, however, this perception of a rigidly bipolar world had its limitations. As early as 1948, for example, the Communist—and thoroughly nationalist—Yugoslav regime of Marshal Tito broke with Stalin. The Yugoslavs soon received economic and military aid from the United States, even while Tito preserved a Communist political system internally. During the 1950s and 1960s, additional challenges to the unity of the Soviet bloc arose. These included the hardline but independent course taken by Communist Albania—which benefited from the fact that it did not share a common border with the USSR. Romania also managed to adopt a prickly autonomy in foreign policy, refusing the stationing of Soviet troops on its soil, while remaining a member of the Warsaw Pact and Comecon and maintaining one of the most internally repressive political systems of any country in the Communist world.

The most important of the challenges to Soviet leadership, however, came from China. There, Mao Zedong had long followed a course of action and an ideology distinctly different from that of the Soviets. This contributed to increasing tension between the two giant Communist powers. In 1958, their growing animosity led to a split between them. The Khrushchev regime immediately ordered a halt to numerous construction and aid projects. Soviet personnel withdrew at once, often taking the blueprints with them. Increasingly, the Soviets and Chinese found themselves at odds: they supported rival contenders for power in third-world conflicts, increased their military deployments along the 4,000-mile Sino-Soviet border, and in 1969 fought a series of small but deadly skirmishes.

Meanwhile, the West also experienced a loosening of allied cohesion. The approach of nuclear parity between the superpowers accentuated the sense among Western European governments that strategic interests among the NATO allies were not always identical. Specifically, given the small geographic area of the Continent and their catastrophic experience of war, the Europeans preferred that maximum priority be given to preventing the outbreak of war on their territory, even if the tradeoff made strategic nuclear war between the superpowers more likely—though still remote.

The most assertive challenge to American leadership was mounted by France, under the leadership of Charles de Gaulle. The French president sought not only to restore French power and autonomy, but to enhance France's world role by gaining the leadership of an increasingly independent Europe. Although there remained limits to the degree of autonomy that de Gaulle could exercise, he nonetheless posed serious challenges to the United States in key areas. In monetary policy he attacked the primacy of the dollar, not least by converting large amounts of dollars for gold at a time when American currency flowing abroad had begun to outrun United States gold reserves (then available for exchange at the official price of $35 per ounce). In European affairs, de Gaulle vetoed Britain's bid for membership in the Common Market. He took this action in January 1963 on the grounds that the UK was not yet European enough in its outlook, and especially because he regarded Britain as compromised by its close relationship to the United States.

In the realm of security, de Gaulle first proposed in 1958 the creation of a three-power (American-British-French) directorate to run NATO affairs. Later, in 1966, he withdrew France from the integrated military command of NATO on the grounds that this military cooperation contradicted France's independence. De Gaulle also sought to act as an intermediary between East and West. He pursued improved ties with the Soviet Union and China, opposed American intervention in Vietnam, and tried to weaken the cohesion of both blocs in order to achieve greater latitude for secondary powers such as France in the West and China in the East. Ultimately, de Gaulle's efforts proved to be overextended, first by the May 1968 events in France involving massive disturbances by students and workers, and then by the Soviet invasion of Czechoslovakia in August 1968, which demonstrated the brutal limitations to independence faced by countries within the Warsaw Pact.

French actions were by no means the only factors shaping a less tightly organized Western bloc. With economic recovery, allied countries were in a better position to pursue their own interests and policies while being less deferential to American wishes. Differences began to widen over such matters as monetary policy, agricultural trade, détente with the Soviet Union, and the growing American involvement in Vietnam.

The cumulative effect of these and other developments in both East and West was to make both blocs significantly less cohesive. While the United States and the Soviet Union each remained the paramount power in its sphere of influence, there were increasing elements of multipolarity, not only within the blocs, but on the part of countries elsewhere in the world that did not adhere to either grouping.

Increased Importance of the Developing World

At the onset of the Cold War, the United Nations included some fifty countries. Its members came primarily from Europe and the Americas. Not surprisingly, many of them were parties to the East-West conflict. During the mid 1950s, the number and importance of nonaligned countries began to grow as a result of the process of decolonization. Although President Eisenhower's secretary of state, John Foster Dulles, could make a statement describing neutrality as immoral, the fact remained that more and more states emerged for whom the East-West conflict was not a central preoccupation. Indeed, within two decades, UN membership had tripled, to more than 150 states. With the exception of a few countries (such as the two Germanies, admitted in 1973), most of the new states belonged to the developing world.

This change in the composition of the United Nations symbolized a broader underlying shift. While the East-West conflict remained intrinsically important, and in no other realm did states possess military strength comparable to that of the superpowers, the new states brought with them an agenda often different from that which had absorbed the Soviets and Americans. This did not preclude the expansion of the Soviet-American contest into the developing world. However, for many of the newer actors, regional rivalries, bitter ethnic disputes, territorial questions, and a host of local factors dominated their attention. Illustratively, conflicts between India and Pakistan, Egypt and Israel, Ethiopia and Somalia, and even Vietnam and Cambodia often cut across matters of ideology or of loyalties to one or the other of the superpowers.

By the early 1970s, it had become possible to speak of a multipower world. President Nixon, for example, in a widely cited 1972 "Man of the Year"[10] interview, described an emergent balance among five major centers of power: the United States, the Soviet Union, China, Western Europe, and Japan. In important respects this formulation was exaggerated, not least because only the United States and the USSR were true military superpowers, and only the United States among the five mentioned centers was both a military *and* an economic superpower. Nonetheless, by the early 1970s, the international arena encompassed a group of actors and agendas vastly expanded from those that had monopolized the stage in the late 1940s and early 1950s.

Lessening Ideological Militancy

The death of Stalin in 1953, as well as that of one of his top lieutenants, Andrei Zhdanov, in 1948, helped to ease some of the intensity of the Cold War. Added to this, the end of the Korean War, the Austrian State (peace) Treaty, Khrushchev's revelations about the crimes of Stalin, the growing number of contacts and summits between representatives of East and West, and widening recognition that the East-West competition, especially in Europe, would not soon be resolved, led to a gradual reduction in the explicitly ideological composition of the East-West conflict.

The waning of this strident language did not signal the disappearance of deep underlying differences of interest, nor of strikingly different sets of political and economic systems and human values. Nonetheless, the East-West conflict began to settle into a pattern based more on power—especially the maintenance of the Soviet sphere of influence in Eastern Europe and periodic Soviet challenges to American and Western interests as targets of opportunity arose. With the declining international credibility of Soviet claims to speak for or represent anything except Russian self-interest, as opposed to some higher notion of international communist solidarity, yet another component of the Cold War eroded. To be sure (and as noted in Chapter 3), Soviet claims to ideals that transcended mere national interest had long been subordinate to Russian power and purposes. But even the ritualistic proclamations of ideology and belief now declined.

At the same time, American policymakers followed an increasingly pragmatic disposition in international affairs. The language of free-world solidarity had always been tempered in practice. This was evident early on, not only in support for the Communist but anti-Soviet government of Yugoslavia, but also in a periodic willingness to support right-wing authoritarian regimes as long as they were anti-Communist or anti-Soviet in their foreign policy. The inclination to make foreign policy judgments based on power politics rather than belief reached its culmination in the Nixon opening to the People's Republic of China. It was ironic that one of the most vociferous advocates of anti-Communism within American politics and an early and relentless opponent of the PRC should be the architect of a major realignment in international affairs. President Nixon's dramatic 1972 visit to Peking signaled a recognition that despite vast differences in beliefs and in political systems, China and the United States could find common interest in counterbalancing the weight of Soviet power. To say that this meant minimizing the importance of ideology in world affairs is an understatement.

NIXON, KISSINGER, AND DÉTENTE

Together, the above factors produced significant change in the climate of Soviet-American relations. Moreover, domestic priorities within the two countries pointed in the same direction. Given the subsequent disintegration of détente in the latter part of the 1970s, as well as the tendency for Soviet-American relations to fluctuate between cycles of tension and relaxation, it is important to understand the initial motivations for détente.[11]

First, for the Nixon-Kissinger administration, engaged in the tortuous process of extricating the United States from Vietnam, a relaxation of tensions with the Soviet Union appeared to offer a means for putting pressure on North Vietnam and thus facilitating an orderly American withdrawal without conveying the impression of disarray or humiliation. The administration regarded this as important for maintaining the international credibility of the United States. Second, at a time when the Soviets had attained rough overall nuclear parity with the United States, détente could provide a means to regulate the military competition with the USSR and to lessen the risk of the two superpowers being pulled into a major conflict as a result of escalation over some secondary issue or involvement with a dependent ally. Third, détente appeared to offer a means of entwining the Soviets in a web of interdependence. By elaborating a wide array of diplomatic, economic, technical, scientific, agricultural, and even cultural relationships, the administration hoped that it could shape an environment in which the Soviets would be reluctant to disturb the international status quo for fear of damaging their own national interests. In short, if détente succeeded, it could conceivably constrain Soviet behavior.

The Soviets had their own reasons for pursuing a course of improved relations with the United States. Their massive military buildup, launched after the Cuban missile crisis, had brought them to a position of rough equivalence with the United States. They would now negotiate on strategic issues with the Americans from a position not of inferiority but of equality. Like the Americans, the Soviets had a basic national interest in lessening the risk of war by escalation, accident, or miscalculation. They found it especially important to avoid being drawn into a nuclear confrontation by the actions of a client state. The growing antagonism with China also gave Moscow an incentive for seeking improved relations with the United States, in order to lessen the likelihood that the United States and the PRC would increasingly make common cause against the Soviet Union.

Finally, there existed a major economic motivation. Despite the hopes Khrushchev had so colorfully expressed ("we will bury you") about the Soviet Union outdistancing the United States in a peaceful competition, actual Soviet performance had lagged very badly. The system remained plagued with outmoded technology, inefficiency, stagnation, and corruption. Expanded trade with the West—and particularly with the Americans, who the Soviets tended to assume were the leading force in any given field—seemed to offer a means of modernizing Soviet industry and technology.

The same could be said of agriculture, where Soviet performance had continued to be grossly inadequate. Fewer than 3 percent of Americans were employed in agriculture, where they nonetheless managed to produce enough food to feed the entire American population and a good deal of the rest of the world as well, yet the one-quarter of the Soviet work force still employed on the land had proved incapable of providing an improved diet for the Soviet population. Indeed, as late as the 1975 harvest, Soviet grain production of 137 million tons provided a per capita yield no better than that of 1913, the last prewar year of the czarist regime.[12] Not surprisingly, the Soviets were interested in purchasing American grain, as well as in obtaining American technology in order to improve their agricultural productivity.

Détente itself comprised three sometimes related sets of negotiations and agreements. These included arrangements to regularize the European status quo, a series of political and economic understandings with the United States, and measures to regulate the strategic military competition between the superpowers.

Détente in Europe and the CSCE

The overriding Soviet objective in Europe was to secure acceptance of the status quo. That is, the Russians sought to gain legitimization for the postwar division of Germany, equality of status for the German Democratic Republic, and acceptance of the territorial changes and boundaries they had imposed in Eastern Europe. The Soviet interest in détente also coincided with a change of political power within the Federal Republic of Germany. In 1969, Willy Brandt became the West German chancellor, heading a coalition government led by the Social Democrats. The Brandt government accepted the need for recognizing the postwar status quo, both as an unavoidable legacy of Hitler's war and as something that Germany appeared powerless to change.

The early 1970s ushered in a series of major agreements. Initially, in August 1970, West Germany and the USSR signed a treaty renouncing the use of force and accepting all European frontiers as inviolable. The Soviets thereby secured West German recognition of the division of Germany as well as acceptance of the Oder-Neisse line (the border between East Germany and Poland) and hence of the loss of prewar German lands to Poland and the USSR.[13]

In rapid succession, there followed agreements between West Germany and Poland (December 1970), a four-power agreement regularizing the status of Berlin (June 1972), and a treaty between the two Germanies (December 1972). The culmination of the détente process in Europe, however, was the thirty-five nation negotiation known as the CSCE (Conference on Security and Cooperation in Europe). This brought together all the countries of Europe (except Albania), plus the United States and Canada. On August 1, 1975, the participants signed the Final Act of the CSCE. Though not technically a treaty, the "Helsinki Declaration" recognized the inviolability of European borders and thus legitimized the postwar status quo—which had been an overriding Soviet objective. However, Helsinki also provided for a series of major human rights measures. These included respect for basic human freedoms (including freedom of religion), rights of travel and emigration, reunification of divided families, wider circulation of information and newspapers, and a host of related measures. The incorporation of these measures had been strongly advocated by the Western Europeans and the neutral countries. Their inclusion evoked widespread popular interest and helped to stir opinion in Eastern Europe. However, the nature of the Soviet system would make Russian compliance with these commitments problematic.

Soviet-American Détente

Two key themes of this book concern the importance of national power consider-ations and of domestic factors in shaping the international behavior of states. These elements are clearly evident in the American and Soviet approaches to dé-tente during the 1970s. For the Nixon administration, détente with the Russians offered a means of countering the electoral challenge presented by the anti-Viet-nam War position of the Democrats and then of their 1972 presidential nominee, Senator George McGovern. It also provided a way to pressure the North Viet-namese toward an acceptable formula for negotiations.

On the Soviet side, once the decision to pursue détente had been made, the interests of other parties were relegated to the background. Specifically, the spring of 1972 had seen a major increase in fighting in Vietnam. The Nixon ad-ministration responded to a North Vietnamese offensive by expanding the bomb-ing around the North Vietnamese capital of Hanoi and by mining the port of Haiphong. These actions came only fifteen days before a scheduled Moscow sum-mit meeting between President Nixon and the Soviet leader, Leonid Brezhnev. Nonetheless, the summit took place as planned.

During the last week of May 1972, Nixon and Brezhnev agreed on a series of steps to improve relations between the two countries. These went beyond agree-ments reached during the previous eight months, which had included improving the hotline between Moscow and Washington, measures against accidental use of nuclear weapons, a consular agreement, and the outlawing of biological warfare. In Moscow, there were additional agreements on the environment, science and technology, public health, incidents on the high seas, and commercial arrange-ments. More important, however, were conclusion of an arms control package (SALT I, discussed below) and the adoption of a statement of basic principles of relations between the United States and the USSR. Among its key points, this "Moscow Declaration" pledged the two parties to avoid military confrontation, pursue restraint in their mutual relations, recognize the sovereign rights of all states, and promote conditions in which no countries would be subject to outside influence in their internal affairs.

The Moscow meeting was followed a year later by a June 1973 summit in Washington. This came after a massive Soviet purchase of American grain in the fall of 1972 and the January 1973 conclusion of a peace agreement between the United States and North Vietnam.[14] At their Washington summit meeting, the two leaders signed an "Agreement on the Prevention of Nuclear War." This com-mitted the two sides to refrain from the threat or use of force against other coun-tries, in circumstances that might endanger peace and security. The eruption of the Yom Kippur War less than four months later would put Soviet compliance with this agreement to a severe test. Nonetheless, the momentum generated by these two summits led to an array of lesser agreements, major expansion of trade, and even a joint Soyuz-Apollo space flight in 1975.

Arms Control Negotiations

From the time of the Cuban missile crisis in October 1962, efforts had been underway to limit the nuclear arms race between the United States and the USSR. As far back as 1963, these had resulted in the hotline agreement and the limited atmospheric test ban. Subsequent agreements included 1967 treaties against introducing nuclear weapons in Latin America (the Treaty of Tlatelolco) and in outer space, the July 1968 Nuclear Non-proliferation Treaty, and three 1971 arrangements (the Seabed Arms Control Treaty, the Hotline Modernization Treaty, and the Soviet-American Agreement on Prevention of Accidental Nuclear War).

The principal achievement, however, came with the Moscow Meeting of May 1972. This brought to a culmination the Strategic Arms Limitation Talks (SALT). The SALT I Agreements, signed on May 26, 1972, included a formal treaty to limit each side's deployment of antiballistic missiles (ABM) to no more than two sites. They also contained a five-year Interim Agreement in which each side agreed to abide by limitations on the number of its offensive strategic missiles. In effect, this agreement held the number of missiles at their existing levels pending a set of new negotiations (SALT II) aimed at achieving permanent and more far-reaching measures.[15] In the meantime, neither side was to exceed its total of missiles deployed or under construction. These totaled 1,054 ICBMs and 710 SLBMs for the United States, and 1,618 ICBMs and 950 SLBMs for the USSR.[16]

President Nixon resigned in August 1974 as a result of the Watergate scandal. However, guidelines for Salt II were set out in a meeting between Brezhnev and President Gerald Ford in the far eastern Soviet city of Vladivostok in November 1974. The guidelines provided that each side would have a total of 2,400 delivery vehicles (that is, submarine launched ballistic missiles, ICBMs, and intercontinental bombers). Within the 2,400 figure, 1,320 of each side's missiles could be MIRVed, that is, equipped with multiple, independently targetable reentry vehicles.

The administration of Jimmy Carter and the Brezhnev leadership found great difficulty in negotiating a mutually satisfactory SALT II agreement. Delays first occurred as a result of April 1977 proposals by the Carter administration for more sweeping reductions than the Soviets were willing to consider. By the time a draft SALT II treaty was arrived at in 1979, the worsening international climate and the increasingly shaky domestic political situation of the Carter administration created new problems. These, followed by the Soviet invasion of Afghanistan in December 1979, ultimately brought the demise of détente and the SALT II treaty was left unsigned.

THE DEMISE OF DÉTENTE

Almost from its inception, détente encountered challenges. While specific issues and incidents were often important in themselves, the broader problem stemmed from the fact that the United States and the Soviet Union did not share sufficiently common assumptions about the international status quo. By contrast, in 1815 the great powers represented at the Congress of Vienna had restored the European order, based on a more-or-less shared conservative view and a rejection of the revolutionary nationalism that the French Revolution and Napoleon had introduced. While Russia of the 1970s was a very different country from that in which the Bolsheviks had come to power, and Brezhnev and his elderly colleagues in the Soviet politburo had a significantly greater interest in the European status quo than their predecessors a half-century before, the basis for overall agreement with the United States remained tenuous.

This problem was particularly acute in three areas. First, although the situation in Europe, where the Cold War had originated, seemed to be in a kind of equilibrium, no such basis existed in the developing world. The American conception of détente implied that the Soviet-American understandings were to be global in scope. But the Soviet approach provided for continued and strenuous competition in the third world. As a result, developments in the Middle East and in Africa (especially Angola and Ethiopia) would subject détente to enormous strains.

Second, Soviet undertakings at Helsinki and elsewhere required commitments to human rights practices and policies that were antithetical to the nature of Soviet communism. When contradictions arose, as was bound to occur, Moscow would place greater priority on its habitual practices than on compliance with international standards. These practices would be maintained behind the pretense that external discussion of human rights violations in the Soviet Union constituted an unacceptable intervention in its internal affairs, and that raising such matters constituted "provocation" by the enemies of détente. Nonetheless, the human rights policies at issue were ones the Soviets had agreed to at Helsinki (as earlier in the Universal Declaration of Human Rights and the United Nations Charter), and the Soviet response could not dispel wider international concern.

Third, domestic American politics were also bound to impinge. The reciprocal influences of international and domestic affairs on each other insured that the pursuit of détente could not and would not be carried out as though on an abstract and insulated diplomatic chessboard. Soviet actions in the developing world, Soviet abuses of human rights, particularly in regard to Jewish emigration, Soviet actions to maintain control over Eastern Europe, and continuing Soviet military programs all combined to galvanize American domestic opponents of détente—on both the right and left of the political spectrum—and to influence the course of Soviet-American relations.

These patterns became evident in a series of specific arenas. First, and as one of the earliest signs of deep trouble, there was the matter of Soviet behavior during the October 1973 Middle East War. Despite the 1972 and 1973 summit agreements, with their provisions for preventing conflict and providing mutual warnings about threats to the maintenance of peace, Moscow's actions in advance of and during the Yom Kippur War seemed to contravene the spirit of these East-West accords. The Soviets took an active role in building up Egyptian and Syrian supplies prior to the Arab attack on October 6. Soviet civilian dependents were evacuated three days prior to the war, without prior warning to the United States that hostilities were imminent. Soviet military advisors were present with the Syrians on the Golan Heights against the Israelis, and Moscow encouraged Algeria and other countries to enter the war. The Soviets mounted a huge airborne resupply effort to Egypt and Syria within days of the outbreak of the war—despite Secretary of State Kissinger's delay in resupplying Israel until a week had passed, in hopes of moving the belligerents toward a negotiated settlement. And finally, after the tide of battle had turned, the Soviets threatened to deploy up to seven airborne divisions of their own troops to prevent the total collapse of the Egyptian Third Army Corps, which the Israelis had surrounded on the west bank of the Suez Canal.[17]

In the realm of human rights, the signing of the 1975 Helsinki Declaration galvanized widespread hopes throughout Eastern Europe. While some relaxation did appear to occur, groups sprang up to monitor compliance with the provisions of the CSCE. The Soviets responded with harsh repression against their own citizens who took part in this effort. These actions contradicted both the letter and spirit of the August 1975 agreement.

Meanwhile, the Soviet interest in expanded trade required that the Nixon administration obtain congressional authorization on most-favored-nation (MFN) status for them. This would have enabled Russian exports to the United States to face tariffs no greater than those levied on America's other trading partners. However, Congress attached a series of conditions (the Jackson-Vanik and Stevenson amendments) to the legislation. These specified that as a condition for granting MFN status and favorable credit terms, the USSR was required to ease domestic obstacles to emigration from the Soviet Union of Jews and other minorities. The Soviets regarded this as an unacceptable intervention in their internal affairs (although the provisions simply made explicit the obligations to which the Soviet Union had previously agreed in the Universal Declaration on Human Rights), and in early 1975 the Russians renounced the trade agreement.

Events in Africa delivered another major blow to détente. In November 1975, the former Portuguese colony of Angola gained its independence. The country was torn by a three-sided civil war, which pitted two tribal-based groups (UNITA and the FNLA) against a Soviet-supported group, the MPLA, centered in the capital, Luanda. During fighting in late 1975 and early 1976, a diverse coalition of countries supported UNITA and the FNLA. These included Zaire, the United States, China, and South Africa. The South Africans intervened with several thousand troops, reaching the suburbs of Luanda. However, they withdrew when the United States Congress passed the Clark amendment, cutting off funds for the war in Angola, at almost the same time that more than 11,000 Cuban troops, supported and transported by the Soviets, intervened in force.[18] Ultimately, the weight of Soviet weapons and Cuban troops allowed the MPLA to consolidate its hold (though a long guerrilla war continued in which UNITA managed to maintain control of a large portion of the hinterland populated by the Ovimbundu—Angola's largest tribal group).

Meanwhile, on the northeast coast of Africa along the Red Sea, a different—but no less complex—struggle was erupting in Ethiopia. There, a spring 1977 coup brought Marxist-Leninist military officers to power. Within a year, a fierce, multisided civil war and a border conflict with Somalia were transformed by Soviet weapons, advisors, and the intervention of Cuban troops in numbers comparable to those deployed in Angola. Here, too, Soviet and Cuban support proved pivotal, and the regime of President Menghistu Haile Mariam was further aided in its consolidation of power by the introduction of police security advisors from East Germany.

The death knell of détente was finally rung at the end of 1979. This occurred when a Soviet-led coup deposed Afghanistan's Marxist President Amin and replaced him with a more compliant figure, Babrak Karmal. Soviet involvement in this bloody series of events was blatant. Although the Soviets claimed to have been invited in, their actions put Karmal in power. For example, Soviet military advisors had acted to disable Afghan army tanks on the day before the coup by removing their batteries for "maintenance," Soviet airborne troops were landed at the airport, and Karmal's seizure of power was announced by an Afghan radio station actually located on the Soviet side of the border. The Soviet action caused the escalation of a civil war already being fought in the countryside by Islamic rebels against the Amin government. However, with the near-collapse of the Afghan army, the brunt of the fighting was borne by the more than 100,000 Soviet troops introduced into Afghanistan. More to the point, this marked the first occasion in which Soviet combat troops had been committed outside the sphere of influence established in Eastern Europe at the end of World War II. It stimulated growing concern in the United States about the expansion of Soviet power and the overall objectives of the Soviets. It also brought to an end the process of détente as the 1970s came to a close.

While this series of Soviet actions provided ample cause for the collapse of détente, Moscow compiled its own list of complaints about American policies during the 1970s. These included the administration's inability to provide anticipated MFN trade status and credits, CIA support for the anti-Communist FNLA movement in Angola, the Carter administration's initial rejection of the Vladivostok arms control understandings that President Ford and Leonid Brezhnev had tentatively agreed on, and even Western attention and encouragement to Soviet dissidents. As a result of these and other factors, the USSR found fewer advantages than originally anticipated in its own pursuit of détente.

MANAGING THE SOVIET-AMERICAN CONFLICT

Changes in the Soviet-American relationship that had made détente possible in the 1960s and 1970s proved to be more ambiguous than they first seemed. This became clear for each of the basic elements. First, the European balance involved an unstable Soviet equilibrium in Eastern Europe. There, periodic Soviet-sponsored repression, as in Poland during the rise of the Solidarity movement (1979–1981), was bound to provoke friction with the West.

Second, strategic stability provided rough equivalence at the nuclear level, but it by no means eliminated controversies about long-term maintenance of the strategic balance nor disputes over specific weapons programs and deployments.

Such issues as American debate over the "window of vulnerability" (an issue in 1979–1980 in reaction to vulnerability of U.S. land-based ICBMs), deployment of Soviet SS-20s and then American Intermediate-range Nuclear Forces (INF) in Europe, compliance with the unratified SALT II agreement, and the Reagan administration's 1983 Strategic Defense Initiative ("Star Wars") were prominent examples of Soviet-American tension. While mutual recognition of the necessity to avoid nuclear war remained high, there was also a Western concern to insure a sufficient balance of conventional (i.e., nonnuclear) forces in order to deter conflict in Europe and elsewhere.

Third, while the global configuration of international relations had certainly become less rigidly bipolar this shift did not eliminate the primacy of the Soviet-American competition nor did it displace the superpowers from their standing as the world's predominant military powers. Nor did growing multipolarity lessen the amount of international conflict. If anything, the incidence increased, and with it the proliferation of opportunities for the Americans and Soviets to find themselves in acrimonious confrontations.

Fourth, the developing world had in fact become more important in international politics. Yet the change in focus away from Europe and Japan did not bring a relaxation in superpower relations. Détente was primarily applicable to Europe, but the shift to a North-South arena had not eliminated the East-West rivalry. Instead, the Soviet-American competition continued in new arenas and issues. Indeed, endemic instability throughout the developing world insured that there would be no shortage of such issues. In the end, fundamental disagreement about the applicability of détente to the third world may have been the single most important factor in bringing about the demise of détente.

Fifth, ideological militancy had lessened, especially in terms of the declining appeal of Soviet communism in Europe—East or West—and the developing world. Yet in power terms, the challenge presented by the Soviets remained considerable based on their efforts to make use of targets of opportunity as these arose during the 1970s.

THE GORBACHEV ERA

The postwar order became transformed at the end of the 1980s. A prevailing pattern (or *paradigm*) of East-West relations that had changed and evolved during the prior forty-five years, but had nonetheless endured in its essentials, came to an end. Important developments had occurred during the previous decades, some giving rise to premature assessments that the postwar era was over. However, the scope and importance of the events ending the Cold War deserve to be enumerated here, in order to convey just how fundamental and rapid were the departures from the past that they represented. Among the most central of these were the following:

> December 1987: INF Treaty signed by Reagan and Gorbachev, eliminating U.S. and Soviet arsenals of intermediate-range nuclear missiles.

February 1988: Moscow announces plans to withdraw troops from Afghanistan and to seek accommodation in Cambodia and Namibia conflicts.

June 1988: Gorbachev calls for major changes in Soviet government, including stronger Soviet presidency, limit of two five-year terms, and multicandidate elections.

December 1988: Gorbachev UN speech announces plan to cut 500,000 Soviet troops over two years; withdraw 5,000 tanks and amphibious assault equipment from East Germany, Czechoslovakia, and Hungary, and remove and dismantle six tank divisions.

January 1989: Hungary legalizes freedom of assembly and association; in February, approves creation of independent political parties; in October, ruling party abandons Communist ideology; in March 1990, non-Communist parties win free elections.

February 1989: Soviets complete withdrawal of combat troops from Afghanistan.

March 1989: Gorbachev announces failure of collectivized agriculture and proposes land be returned to families.

March 1989: Free elections held in USSR for first time since 1918.

June 1989: Solidarity candidates sweep Polish elections; in August, a non-Communist, Tadeusz Mazowiecki, becomes Prime Minister, marking first loss of power through democratic process by any Communist regime.

July 6, 1989: Gorbachev renounces interference or use of force in affairs of Eastern Europe; October 25, declares Brezhnev doctrine dead; December 4, Warsaw Pact condemns its August 1968 Czech invasion.

August 11, 1989: United States opens seismic listening posts in USSR, providing means to monitor nuclear tests.

September 1989: East Germans by the tens of thousands flee to West Germany via Hungary and Austria.

October 7, 1989: Gorbachev visits East Berlin and is cheered by crowds; privately urges East German Communist leaders to adopt reforms.

October 23, 1989: Foreign Minister Shevardnadze tells Soviet legislature that actions in Afghanistan violated Soviet law and international norms of behavior; admits Krasnoyarsk radar station violated ABM Treaty.

October–November 1989: mass prodemocracy demonstrations in East Germany and Czechoslovakia.

November 9, 1989: East German government opens Berlin Wall; jubilant East Germans throng West Berlin.

November 10, 1989: Bulgarian Communist leader, Todor Zhivkov, removed after thirty-five years in power.

November 18, 1989: East Germany hard-line Communist leader Erik Honecker is ousted.

November 24, 1989: Hardline Czechoslovak leaders resign; on December 10, new government with non-Communist majority of ministers takes power; Vaclav Havel becomes President on December 29.

December 15–22, 1989: Hundreds killed by security forces after demonstrations in Timisoara and Bucharest, Romania; army supports protesters; Ceausescu and wife executed on December 25.

December 25, 1989: Soviet Congress of People's Deputies condemns August 1939 Nazi-Soviet Pact.

February 2–10, 1990: Gorbachev and Shevardnadze acknowledge the right of East and West Germans to decide on unity.

February 26, 1990: Soviets agree to remove troops from Czechoslovakia by July 1, 1991.

March 11, 1990: Soviets agree to remove troops from Hungary by July 1, 1991.

March 1990: Amendments to Article 6 of Soviet Constitution end Communist Party's guaranteed monopoly of power; Gorbachev assumes new position as executive President of USSR, inaugural speech pledges rapid moves to market economy, says "Cold War has been done away with, but military confrontation has not been overcome."

March 18, 1990: East Germany holds free elections; non-Communist parties, led by Christian Democrats, begin steps to form a government.

March 22, 1990: Soviets reported removing last of some 1,000 military advisors from Ethiopia.

September 12, 1990: Treaty on the Final Settlement with Regard to Germany signed by the United States, the USSR, Britain, France, East and West Germany. Allies relinquish occupation rights and leave Germany free to unify.

October 3, 1990: German unification.

November 19, 1990: NATO and Warsaw Pact leaders sign Conventional Forces in Europe Treaty (CFE), for major armed forces reductions in Europe.

June 12, 1991: Boris Yeltsin elected Russian President with 57 percent of popular vote.

July 1, 1991: Warsaw Pact dissolved.

July 31, 1991: Bush and Yeltsin sign START I Treaty, reducing strategic weapons.

August 19–22, 1991: Coup attempt in Moscow. Yeltsin rallies public and hard-line leaders are arrested. On August 24, Gorbachev resigns as Communist Party head.

September 6, 1991: Soviet Union recognizes independence of Latvia, Lithuania, and Estonia.

December 8, 1991: Yeltsin and leaders of Ukraine and Belarus agree to establish a Commonwealth of Independent States. Eleven of the fifteen former Republics of USSR later agree to join.

December 25, 1991: Gorbachev resigns as Soviet President.

December 31, 1991: Soviet Union ceases to exist.

February 1, 1992: Bush and Yeltsin declare formal end to Cold War.

January 4, 1993: Bush and Yeltsin sign START II Treaty, for 75 percent reduction of nuclear warheads over 10 years.

October 2–4, 1993: Yeltsin and his government defeat takeover attempt by Communists and nationalists. Hundreds killed in Moscow fighting.

That these events were revolutionary in their impact, there can be no doubt. However, two questions require attention here. First, what brought about the changes, and, second, what implications do they have for international relations?

The Sources of Change

The road to these changes was by no means smooth or steady. Gorbachev, himself a protégé of former KGB leader Yuri Andropov (who briefly led the USSR from the death of Leonid Brezhnev in November 1982 until his own death in February 1984), at first undertook to run the Soviet Union with greater efficiency and rationality, rather than to transform the existing system. But efforts to eliminate corruption, drunkenness, and bureaucratic paralysis did not address the causes of Soviet stagnation. With the Soviet system unable to meet the needs of its own people, and more and more uncompetitive with the industrial democracies of Western Europe, North America, and Japan, Gorbachev turned to a more radical series of measures, labeled *glasnost* (openness) and *perestroika* (economic restructuring).[19] These measures would take him and his country on a course it had never known before, the eventual outcome of which could not be foreseen.

The changes themselves were, however, due to far more than the whim of a single leader. In part they were a reaction to the accumulated deficiencies of seventy years of the Soviet system of rigid dictatorship and a centrally planned economy. At the same time, however, the dramatic changes Gorbachev undertook stemmed from the deep-seated modernization process taking place within Soviet society.

Russia, under the czars and then under Communist rule by Lenin, Stalin, and their successors, was a backward land. Its population was heavily rural, lived in primitive circumstances, had experienced generations of subservience in the conditions of daily life, and had low levels of education and of exposure to the outside world. As such, the population was prepared to endure harsh conditions and severely repressive rule. These included civil war, forced draft industrialization, and a desperate and bloody war effort after Hitler invaded Russia in 1941.

At the end of World War II, in 1945, half the Russian population were still peasants. As late as the early 1960s, no more than 25 million people had finished secondary school. However, eventual recovery from the war and the widening impact of industrialization, urbanization, and mass education were propelling the modernization of Soviet society. By the end of the 1980s, only one-eighth of the population remained as peasants,[20] and some 125 million Soviets had completed either secondary school or some kind of higher education.[21]

The demands of a new era in world technology and economics, sometimes described as the third industrial revolution, also had a profound impact. The first industrial revolution had taken place in the late eighteenth century and involved the application of steam power and machinery to production, while the second occurred in the late nineteenth century, incorporating electricity, chemistry, and the internal combustion engine. Indeed, it was sometimes joked that Russian Communism equaled Soviets (worker collectives) plus electricity. However, the massive, heavy industrial development that had spread throughout the USSR since the 1930s was becoming increasingly irrelevant to the needs of modern economic life. Sheer tonnages of coal, steel, cement, chemicals, and other industrial products were no longer sufficient in themselves.

The demands of a new era in world technology and economics were different. These incorporated knowledge-based industries and services, telecommunications, computers, and rapid innovation, all bringing with them the need for a highly educated work force, the free flow of information, and a relaxation of central control. The Soviet Union was already lagging in its performance and, in failing to adapt, the country was being left far behind the pace of global economic and technological development.

Consequently, a far more urban and educated population, attuned to and aware of world events, and increasingly knowledgeable about standards of living and lifestyles in Western Europe and the United States, made up a different social foundation on which the Soviet political and economic system would be based. Once a Soviet leader appeared who possessed both the will and the political power to embark on rapid change, he could proceed with substantial elite support and at least a popular readiness for change, even if skepticism or frustration were widespread.

In sum, change was a product both of deep-seated economic and social evolution within the USSR and the appearance of Gorbachev and then Yeltsin. And despite the great uncertainties that remained concerning the path of political and economic development in the USSR, the clock could not be turned back to reimpose the policies of an earlier era.

Gorbachev's domestic and foreign policies developed slowly and unevenly. Initially, the Soviet leader reaffirmed many of the existing slogans and policies, apparently seeking only to run the existing system with greater skill and efficiency. However, over time, as he consolidated his political power, driven by necessity as well as by the development of his own ideas, he departed further and further from both the political legacy of Soviet communism and from the foreign policy legacy of the USSR's world role since 1945.

"New Thinking" in Soviet Foreign Policy

In the waning years of the Soviet era, Gorbachev and his colleagues articulated the concept of "new thinking" in Soviet foreign policy. Its essentials, as described by Soviet leaders in sometimes grandiose language, included the ideas that war was no longer a rational policy; new approaches to resolving international problems were required, based on peaceful coexistence and cooperation; mankind shared a common destiny in the face of global threats; interdependence required a new level of political cooperation; interstate relations should be freed from ideological constraint; organizations such as the United Nations deserved a greater importance in efforts to preserve peace; and there should be more reliance on international law in interstate relations.[22]

The history of Soviet foreign policy was replete with universalistic statements about the ideals of humanity and peaceful coexistence—which were then cynically contradicted by Soviet actions and policies. However, Gorbachev's foreign policy actions represented a significant break with past practices. The need for change in foreign policy was driven by the enormous economic and political costs of maintaining control over Eastern Europe as well as sustaining with expensive economic and military aid a series of far-flung pro-Moscow regimes. The latter included Cuba (costing some $5 to $6 billion per year), Ethiopia (supplied with $10 billion worth of weaponry), Vietnam ($2.5 billion per year), Nicaragua (with a bankrupt economy then under Sandinista control), Afghanistan, and the desperately poor African states of Angola and Mozambique, among others. Moreover, the Soviet defense budget itself amounted to as much as 20 to 25 percent of GNP, a burden three to four times that of the United States.

Changes in foreign policy, including reductions in military and economic assistance and cuts in Soviet troops and weapons, provided a means for freeing resources badly needed for the domestic economy. Moreover, Gorbachev had hoped that a significant reduction in international tension would facilitate economic cooperation with the West, including trade, investment, technology transfer, and other means for improving Soviet economic performance.

Change in Soviet foreign policy also was driven by the recognition that hardline foreign policies of the 1970s and early 1980s had failed, and that the Soviet Union could not attain strategic superiority.[23] Rather than achieving the political gains Moscow had sought, Soviet policies had instead galvanized stiffer American and allied reactions—as in the 1979 NATO decision to proceed with deployment of Euromissiles and subsequent action in 1983.

In practice, the implementation of Gorbachev's new policy in Eastern Europe was revolutionary. The Soviet leader not only tolerated regime changes throughout Eastern Europe, he appeared to have welcomed and encouraged them. Leaders in Poland and Hungary were themselves disposed to proceed with reform and chiefly needed reassurance that the Soviets would not intervene to thwart change—as had happened in the past. Elsewhere, however, as in Czechoslovakia and East Germany, whose leaders had been unsupportive of the changes taking place within the Soviet Union, Gorbachev prodded hard-line regimes on the need for change in their own countries. Indeed, one of the steps that proved critical was his signal that Soviet troops would not leave their barracks to save these old-line Communist leaders from the demands of their own people. With this prop removed, a key symbolic underpinning of these regimes was eliminated, both in the eyes of their own leaders and in terms of popular appreciation of the possibilities for a democratic revolution.

Internal Soviet problems also had a foreign policy dimension. Though Moscow had proved surprisingly willing to relinquish its "outer empire" (its control over neighboring countries in Eastern Europe and perhaps Afghanistan), a still more difficult problem existed concerning its "inner empire" (made up of lands and peoples incorporated into Russia by both Czarist and Communist leaders.)[24] The Baltic republics of Latvia, Lithuania, and Estonia, seized by the Soviet Union in 1940, sought complete independence, but their actions were at first opposed by Gorbachev. While Moscow had signaled greater flexibility than in the past, the issue posed the risk of internal conflict within the USSR (40 percent of whose total population were ethnically non-Russians), where it was being watched as a precedent by many of the peoples who had been incorporated into the Central Asian republics of the USSR, as well as by the large and strategically vital population of the Ukraine.

Ultimately, in September 1991, faced with the stubborn determination of the Baltic states, pressure from the United States, and the aftermath of the August coup attempt, the Soviet Union formally recognized the independence of Lithuania, Latvia, and Estonia. The departure of these three former republics was only a prelude, however, to the breakup of the USSR itself. On December 1, Ukrainians voted for independence, and on December 8, President Boris Yeltsin met with the leaders of Ukraine and Belarus to declare the formation of a loose Commonwealth of Independent States (CIS), open to all 15 of the former Soviet republics. Two weeks later, on December 21, the leaders of 11 former republics met in the capital of Kazakhstan to establish the CIS. Their agreement provided for cooperation in economic matters and in other realms, but the CIS was not to have the attributes of a state and there were to be no central government ministries. Moreover, the republics made clear that each would insist on its own right as an independent state, including application for membership in the United Nations. In the Alma-Ata Declaration which ended their meeting they announced, "With the formation of the Commonwealth of Independent States, the Union of Soviet Socialist Republics ceases to exist."[25]

INTERNATIONAL RELATIONS AFTER THE EAST-WEST CONFLICT

The dissolution of the Soviet Union and the end of the Cold War have brought profound change to the international system. As discussed in Chapters 2 and 3, the superpower confrontation and the East-West conflict were the dominant characteristics of world politics for nearly half a century. The end of the Cold War, and of the bipolar system that accompanied it, has brought an end to the division of Europe and an almost complete cessation of superpower competition in regional conflicts.

At least in its initial phase, the post–Cold War world has seen unprecedented cooperation between Russia and the West. During a relatively brief period of time following the end of the Cold War, Moscow joined with the United States in permitting UN action against Iraq for its invasion of Kuwait, acted as a formal cosponsor of the Middle East peace process, signed major arms control treaties to reduce conventional and nuclear weapons, removed its troops from Eastern Europe, and collaborated in efforts to resolve bitter conflicts in Ethiopia, Cambodia, and Namibia.

Reciprocally, the United States and the industrial democracies offered outside support for the efforts of Gorbachev, and then Yeltsin, to undertake democratization and the transition to a market economy. For example, in April 1992, Western leaders announced a package of measures representing as much as $24 billion in aid. Moreover, the United States also offered important political support to Yeltsin and the reformers at the time of hard-line coup attempts in August 1991 and again in October 1993.

Despite this cooperation, it would be wise to avoid the simple assumption that the end of the Cold War necessarily implies a more stable, orderly, and peaceful world. Even before its end, assessments of the Cold War era had already noted its paradoxical effect in producing what John Gaddis has called the "long peace."[26] As authors such as Raymond Aron, Kenneth Waltz, and others have noted, general nuclear deterrence prevented war between East and West. The perception of a balance of terror worked to stabilize the relationship and to produce peace through fear.[27] As Erich Weede observes, extended deterrence, in its linkages between the superpowers and their allies or regional client states, also reduced the inclination of each superpower to interfere vigorously in the other's sphere of interest. Of equal importance, as noted elsewhere in this book, each of the superpowers provided a form of order within its own sphere. In essence, this had the effect of resolving the problem of formal anarchy within each of the blocs. Weede states this another way: "Unipolarity within the Soviet and American blocs made the superpowers into potential substitutes for an order-creating central authority at the subsystemic level."[28]

The end of the Cold War and the dissolution of the Soviet Union has removed a major source of tension, but it has also meant the waning or even disappearance of factors that were conducive to stability. These include extended deterrence and the central authority each superpower represented in its own arena. On the Western side, this is not likely to upset peace and stability because of the presence of stable democratic regimes and the experience of almost a half-century of mutually beneficial economic interdependence and even integration. In Eastern Europe and the former Soviet Union, however, the change has unleashed a torrent of pent-up ethnic, regional, and nationalistic forces. In the case of Eastern Europe, tensions are evident, for example, in each of the Baltic countries over the status of Russians living in these states; in Hungary, which has expressed concern over the treatment of Hungarians living in Romania and Slovakia; in the Czech Republic and Slovakia; and in savage conflict among the peoples and states of the former Yugoslavia. Altogether, in the new states formed after the breakup of the Soviet Union, there are some 200 border disputes, at least four civil wars, and numerous power struggles involving competing groups of democrats, communists, religious fundamentalists, and nationalists.[29]

Despite the dissolution of the USSR, Russia remains a formidable military power. Though the country is in the midst of a severe decline, with its economy and society in chaos, Russia retains a population of 150 million, and a vast land area amounting to 75 percent of the former Soviet Union. Though considerably reduced, its strategic nuclear forces will (for the foreseeable future) continue to give it a durable deterrent vis-à-vis the United States, and its conventional forces remain by far the most powerful on the European continent.

Within the Russian Federation itself, the pattern of cooperative relations with the West faces significant opposition from a variety of forces. These include traditional communists, extreme nationalists, and important parts of the military. While a return to the Cold War pattern no longer appears possible, the reassertion of Russian power and a less cooperative position toward the outside world are far more plausible. If coup attempts in 1991 or 1993 had succeeded, Russian foreign policy would have become more antagonistic on such issues as regional arms sales; alliances with radical anti-Western regimes in Iraq, Cuba, and Libya; UN sanctions toward Libya and Iraq; compliance with arms control agreements; and efforts to control former Soviet republics.[30] Confrontation on these issues is also possible in the future if those favoring more hardline or ultranationalistic policies come to power in Moscow.

Indeed, even under Yeltsin, the Russian military has carried out an increasingly assertive policy toward what they term the "near abroad" (i.e., the former Soviet republics.) Russian forces have intervened covertly in bitter conflicts between Azerbaijan and Armenia, in Georgia, Moldova, Tajikistan and elsewhere. In some cases they have done so to protect the interests of 25 million Russians living in the republics. Moreover, as Table 4.1 illustrates, the presence of these ethnic Russians outside Russia creates a potentially explosive situation. In other cases, intervention has been used to influence the struggle for power within these republics or to encourage them to draw closer to Russia. Thus, for example, in the autumn of 1993, the leader of Georgia, Eduard Shevardnadze, was forced to seek Russian help against Abkhazian separatists who threatened to overwhelm his beleaguered forces. In return, he agreed to accept the stationing of Russian troops in Georgia and to join the CIS.

In essence, though the old Marxist-Leninist Soviet Union has disappeared, Russia remains a major military power and its policy toward countries along its periphery, particularly in the Caucasus and Central Asia, may well exhibit the kind of influence characteristic of the czars who extended Russian power throughout the region in the centuries before the Bolshevik takeover in 1917. More broadly, the end of the Cold War and the withdrawal of the Soviet Union from Eastern Europe have left greater scope for bitter regional, national, and ethnic rivalries. In this sense, there is a risk of the "anarchy" problem reemerging if new mechanisms do not arise to aid in the resolution of disputes and maintenance of order in the region.[31] Thus, ironically, while there is no reason to entertain "nostalgia" for the Cold War, its passing has allowed other regional conflicts to take its place.

Table 4.1 RUSSIANS IN THE NON-RUSSIAN REPUBLICS
OF THE FORMER SOVIET UNION

Republic	% Russian	Republic pop.	Russian pop.
Ukraine	22%	51.7 million	11.4 million
Kazakhstan	38	16.5	6.3
Uzbekistan	8	19.9	1.6
Belarus	13	10.2	1.3
Latvia	34	2.7	0.9
Kirgizstan	22	4.3	0.9
Moldova	13	4.3	0.6
Estonia	30	1.6	0.5
Turkmenistan	10	3.5	0.4
Tajikistan	8	5.1	0.4
Azerbaijan	6	7.0	0.4
Georgia	6	5.4	0.3
Lithuania	9	3.7	0.3
Armenia	2	3.3	0.06

Sources: Calculations from data in *The Economist,* 10 July 1993, p. 39, and *One Nation Becomes Many: The Access Guide to the Former Soviet Union* (Washington, DC: Access, 1992).

NOTES

1. The text of the Reagan address, delivered at Orlando, Florida, is reprinted in Strobe Talbott, *The Russians and Reagan* (New York: Vintage, 1984), pp. 105–118. The above quotation can be found in Talbott, pp. 116 and 117.
2. "The Emerging Structure of International Politics," *International Security,* Vol. 18, No. 2 (Fall 1993): 44–79, at 44.
3. Quoted in *The Economist* (London), December 26, 1992–January 8, 1993, p. 67.
4. "Beyond Nationalism and Internationalism: Ethnicity and World Order," *Survival,* Vol. 35, No. 2 (Summer 1993): 49–65, at 50.
5. Lucian W. Pye, "Political Science and the Crisis of Authoritarianism," *American Political Science Review,* Vol. 84, No. 1 (March 1990): 3–19.
6. Quoted from remarks on ABC television, September 6, 1991, in *Washington Post,* September 7, 1991.
7. There were also demonstrations in more than 250 East German towns. Western estimates put the death toll at more than 200 demonstrators and 100 police, with thousands injured. The uprising began on April 16 with worker strikes against increased work norms imposed by the state. As the demonstrations expanded, there were attacks on offices of the ruling Party and demands for the government's resignation and the holding of free elections. Armed police and Russian troops crushed the revolt. For a brief account, see the *German Tribune* (Hamburg), No. 1185, 30 June 1985.
8. See David Alan Rosenberg, "'A Smoking, Radiating Ruin at the End of Two Hours.' Documents on American Plans for Nuclear War with the Soviet Union, 1954–1955," *International Security* 6 (Winter 1981/82): 3–38, at p. 25. The memorandum (Op–36C/jm) quoted above is dated 18 March 1954, and is an account of a briefing given to representatives of all services at SAC Headquarters, Omaha, Nebraska, on 15 March 1954.

9. That is the ability to withstand a nuclear first strike and then retaliate by inflicting unacceptable damage on the attacker (see Chapter 6).

10. *Time,* 3 January 1972.

11. For a detailed analysis of détente, see Raynmond L. Garthoff, *Détente and Confrontation: American-Soviet Relations from Nixon to Reagan* (Washington, DC: The Brookings Institution, 1985). For a different interpretation, see Adam B. Ulam, *Dangerous Relations: The Soviet Union in World Politics, 1920–1982* (New York: Oxford University Press, 1983).

12. *New York Times,* 10 December 1975.

13. For a detailed account of the development of détente in Europe, see Garthoff, *Détente and Confrontation,* pp. 105–125. A brief but useful description of these and related European agreements can be found in Joseph Nogee and Robert H. Donaldson, *Soviet Foreign Policy Since World War II,* 4th ed. (New York: Macmillan, 1992). Also see Ulam, *Dangerous Relations.*

14. The agreement between the United States and North Vietnam had followed protracted negotiations in Paris and the Christmas bombing of Hanoi by American B-52s.

15. For a widely cited account of the SALT negotiations, see John Newhouse, *Cold Dawn: The Story of SALT* (New York: Holt, Rinehart & Winston, 1973).

16. Actual deployments at this time, May 1972, were less for SLBMs: the United States had 656, the Soviets 740. Within the overall missile limits, each side could substitute new weapons for old or ICBMs for SLBMs and vice versa. See Newhouse; see also Richard Smoke, *National Security and the Nuclear Dilemma* (Reading, MA: Addison-Wesley, 1984), p. 155.

17. Garthoff provides a detailed account of this period. However, his interpretation emphasizes Brezhnev's efforts during the previous year to discourage the Arabs from going to war (on the grounds that they were likely to lose). See *Détente and Confrontation,* pp. 361–382.

18. Donald Rothchild, "U.S. Policy Styles in Africa; From Minimal Engagement to Liberal Internationalism," in Kenneth Oye, D. Rothchild, and Robert J. Lieber, eds., *Eagle Entangled: U.S. Foreign Policy in a Complex World* (New York: Longman, 1979), pp. 310–311.

19. See Mikhail Gorbachev, *Perestroika: New Thinking for Our Country and the World* (London: Fontana/Collins, 1988). His book, originally published in November 1987, contains more use of references to Lenin and other ideological terminology than a number of his major speeches in 1989 and 1990.

20. Pye, "Political Science and the Crisis of Authoritarianism," 10.

21. Jerry F. Hough, "Gorbachev's Politics," *Foreign Affairs,* Vol. 68, No. 5 (Winter 1989/90): 26–41, at p. 30.

22. See especially the description of "new thinking" in foreign policy by Vladimir Petrovsky, Soviet Deputy Foreign Minister, published by the USSR Academy of Sciences in its journal, *Social Sciences,* No. 2, 1990, and in *PS: Political Science and Politics* (Washington, DC: American Political Science Association, March 1990): 30–32. Also see Gorbachev's speech to the UN General Assembly on 7 December, 1988, *New York Times,* 8 December, 1988. And see "Gorbachev's Era of New Thinking," special issue of *Journal of International Affairs,* Vol. 42, No. 2 (Spring 1989).

23. Seweryn Bialer, "'New Thinking' and Soviet Foreign Policy," *Survival,* Vol. XXX, No. 4 (July/August 1988): 291–309, at p. 293.

24. The terms "outer" and "inner" empires are used by Zbigniew Brzezinski, in "Post-Communist Nationalism," *Foreign Affairs,* Vol. 68, No. 5 (Winter 1989/90): 1–25.

25. *Washington Post,* 22 December 1991.

26. John Lewis Gaddis, *The Long Peace: Inquiries into the History of the Cold War* (New York: Oxford University Press, 1987).

27. See, for example, Raymond Aron, "The Anarchical Order of Power," *Daedalus,* Vol. 95 (1966): 479–502; Waltz, *Theory of International Politics* (New York: McGraw-Hill, 1979); "The Emerging Structure of International Politics," *International Security* (Fall 1993); and Erich Weede, "Extended Deterrence, Superpower Control, and Militarized Interstate Disputes, 1962–1976," *Journal of Peace Research* 26 (1989): 7–17.

28. Erich Weede, "Conflict Patterns During the Cold War Period and Thereafter," paper presented at Conference on The Impact of Global Political Change on the Middle East, Haifa University, May 4-6, 1993, p. 6.

29. *The Economist,* 28 August 1993, p. 13.

30. See, for example, Alexei G. Arbatov, "Russia's Foreign Policy Alternatives," *International Security,* Vol. 18, No. 2 (Fall 1993): 5–43, at p. 15.

31. See the more detailed discussion of anarchy and order in Chapter 11. For an exploration of the anarchy problem in Europe after the transformation of the Soviet bloc, see Jack Snyder, "Averting Anarchy in the New Europe," *International Security,* Vol. 14, No. 4 (Spring 1990): 5–41.

chapter 5

The North-South Conflict

With the end of the Cold War, international politics moves out of its Western phase, and its centerpiece becomes the interaction between the Western and non-Western civilizations and among non-Western civilizations.
—SAMUEL P. HUNTINGTON[1]

. . . ethnic conflict poses as great a danger to common world security as did the Cold War.
—UNITED NATIONS SECRETARY GENERAL BOUTROS BOUTROS-GHALI[2]

On the whole (there are exceptions) the failure of the polities has matched the failure of the economies; and the twin failures merge. Ghana, the most advanced of all the territories of colonial Africa, and the first to gain its independence, is today in economic ruin, apprehensively and incompetently guarded by a puritanical military dictatorship. And Ghana has been lucky, compared with some.
—CONOR CRUISE O'BRIEN[3]

Students of world politics make frequent reference to the "South" and to the "North-South conflict." Indeed, these terms have become commonplace. Yet this attention is a relatively recent phenomenon. For many years—at least from the vantage point of the United States and Western Europe—international relations was primarily concerned with events on the European continent, with periodic involvement of the great powers in Asia (especially China and Japan), and then with the Soviet-American conflict.

However, a great wave of decolonization occurred in the aftermath of World War II. This first involved the Asian subcontinent (India, Pakistan, Ceylon) and then in the 1950s and early 1960s spread much more widely throughout Africa, Asia, and the Caribbean. Together with countries (especially in Latin America) that had achieved independence much earlier, large numbers of new states now appeared on the world scene as at least nominally independent actors. Collectively, these countries and virtually all those other than the advanced industrial democracies and the Soviet bloc in Europe came to be labeled as the "South." The shift was symbolized by a tripling of United Nations membership. As a result, "international relations" have become more truly international. The interplay of world politics, economics, and even cultural relations is more literally global in scope than at any previous time in human history.

The countries of the developing world had become increasingly visible after 1955. In April of that year, a widely publicized international conference at Bandung in Indonesia, led by Indonesia's President Sukarno, Prime Minister Nehru of India, and President Tito of Yugoslavia, had taken place.[4] This meeting of 29 nonaligned countries was followed over the years by a burgeoning in the ranks of third-world countries, especially as decolonization gained momentum in Africa during the late 1950s and early 1960s. A decade later, the importance of the South seemed to take on still greater weight. In the aftermath of the 1973–1974 oil shock, it was widely believed that a fundamental shift of wealth and global power toward the oil-exporting countries of the world was in progress.[5]

In the later 1970s, however, emphasis on the North-South distinction as the overriding characteristic of international relations proved to be premature. The détente of the early 1970s was reversible, and important elements of the East-West conflict were played out within the developing world (as in the Soviet invasion of Afghanistan, conflicts in Ethiopia and Angola, and guerrilla wars in Central America). Moreover, divisions among countries of the South themselves were profound. Major conflicts or even full-scale wars erupted, for example, between India and Pakistan, China and Vietnam, Ethiopia and Somalia, and Iran and Iraq. In addition, bitter internal civil conflicts and political upheaval took place within many states of the developing world.

Nonetheless, North-South divisions remained very real. From a Southern perspective, problems of poverty, population, development, trade, national identity, and ethnic strife often made issues on Soviet-American or East-West agendas seem distant or artificial. Other important issues—for example, debt, protectionism, environment, proliferation of missiles and chemical or nuclear weapons— sometimes pitted countries of the South against important states of the North. Indeed, with the momentous changes in Eastern Europe and the Soviet Union at the end of the 1980s and the beginning of the 1990s, superpower confrontation in the developing world came to an end. As a consequence, fundamental North-South distinctions, and issues intrinsic to the South, increasingly stood as international problems in their own right, rather than as matters often bound up with the older East-West cleavages. Ironically, the end of East-West competition sometimes coincided with a decline in attention and involvement by outside powers—particularly for countries which were of less interest for trade and investment.

What, then, accounts for role of the developing countries in the South and of their appearance on the stage of world politics? Why have these changes occurred relatively recently? For answers that go beyond the ephemeral level of day-to-day events or the actions of individual national leaders, we must look to the deep-rooted phenomena of nationalism, modernization, and development.

THE REVOLUTIONS OF MODERNIZATION AND NATIONALISM

Over the course of some four centuries, the countries of Europe achieved and maintained domination over much of the non-Western world. Vast areas of North and South America, Asia, and Africa were controlled directly or indirectly by major colonizing powers such as Spain, England, and France. Indeed, most European states at one time or another participated in the process of exploration and conquest. These included the Dutch, Portuguese, Belgians, Russians, Germans, and others (see Table 5.1). It is worth noting that this was a fluid process. Some regions—for example, Latin America during the nineteenth century—underwent nearly complete decolonization while others—sub-Saharan Africa in the last quarter of the same century—came under imperial control relatively late.

Further, the phenomenon of imperialism[6] was by no means a unique activity of developed Northern countries against less developed—and often nonwhite—Southern peoples. The course of civilization over thousands of years is full of the activities of premodern societies asserting their dominance over neighboring peoples. The actors in these conquests, some of them benign, others devastatingly brutal, include Babylonians, Assyrians, Persians, Egyptians, Greeks, Romans, Aztecs, Arabs, Mongols, Turks, Chinese, Africans, and countless others. The forms of imperialism too have varied immensely, from the assertion of political, economic, or cultural influence, through the spread of religion, the imposition of political rule, enslavement, and the settling of empty—or depopulated—lands.

Those societies that came under Western influence were extremely diverse. Some were relatively primitive, others possessed quite advanced levels of literacy and bureaucratic complexity, at least among their local elites—as in the case of China and India, for example. However, they tended to share a lag in both technology and economic development vis-à-vis the dominating external powers.

They were also highly traditional, or premodern in their forms of social organization. This observation involves much more than an ethnocentric assertion that the societies of the outside powers were more "advanced" or "enlightened." In

Table 5.1 MAJOR COLONIZING COUNTRIES AS OF 1900

	Number of Colonies	Area (square miles)		Population	
		Mother Country	Colonies, etc.	Mother Country	Colonies, etc.
United Kingdom	50	120,979	11,605,238	40,559,954	345,222,239
France	33	204,092	3,740,756	38,517,975	56,401,860
Germany	13	208,830	1,027,120	52,279,901	14,687,000
Netherlands	3	12,648	782,862	5,074,632	35,115,711
Portugal	9	36,038	801,100	5,049,729	9,148,707
Spain	3	197,670	243,877	17,565,632	136,000
Italy	2	110,646	188,500	31,856,675	850,000
Austria-Hungary	2	241,032	23,570	41,244,811	1,568,092
Denmark	3	15,289	86,634	2,185,335	114,229
Russia	3	8,660,395	255,550	128,932,173	15,684,000
Turkey	4	1,111,741	465,000	23,834,500	14,956,236
China	5	1,336,841	2,881,560	386,000,000	16,680,000
United States	6	3,557,000	172,091	77,000,000	10,544,617
Total	136	15,813,201	22,273,858	850,103,317	521,108,791

Source: Data compiled by H. C. Morris, *The Statesman's Yearbook* (London, 1900), as presented in J. A. Hobson, *Imperialism: A Study* (London: Allen & Unwin, 1902).

some cases the colonizing power brought literacy, expanded educational opportunities, improved health and living standards, roads and railroads, and even the nucleus of legal and democratic institutions. In other cases, for example, in the Belgian Congo, the imposition of outside control was brutal and crudely exploitative.

The differences between traditional and modern society can be summarized in the types of authority relations that are prevalent. The German sociologist Max Weber (1864–1920) set out categories, or sets of "ideal types," that summarize these differences. In premodern society, the *basis of legitimacy* rests on belief in tradition. By contrast, modern or bureaucratic society requires belief in rationally established rules. Next, the *type of organization* of authority in premodern society is often patriarchal as opposed to bureaucratic. The *characteristic basis of action* is one of habit in traditional society, in contrast to rational calculation in modern society. *Recruitment of staff* is on the basis of status or favoritism in traditional society (for example, a person enters a particular career because of family or clan membership). In modern bureaucratic society, recruitment is—at least in principle—on the basis of training or examination. Finally, *relations between staff members* are personal and according to status in traditional society, whereas modernity dictates "impersonal" relations.[7]

These categories are not rigid, and there are important exceptions and qualifications to these concepts. The point is that the types of authority reflect profound contrasts in social organization. These tend to apply independent of differences in geography and politics. Traditional societies have generally been more inert and more likely to come under the influence of modern societies.

In a more specific sense, modernization affects politics. Samuel Huntington provides a useful analysis of *political* modernization. Its three characteristics are worth quoting at length:

> First . . . the *rationalization of authority:* the replacement of a large number of traditional, religious, familial, and ethnic political authorities by a single, secular, national political authority. . . . Secondly . . . the *differentiation of new political functions and the development of specialized structures* to perform those functions. Areas of peculiar competence—legal, military, administrative—become separated from the political realm, and autonomous, specialized but subordinate, organs arise to discharge those tasks. . . . Thirdly . . . *increased participation in politics* by social groups throughout society and the development of new political institutions—such as political parties and interest associations—to organize this participation.[8]

An important and sometimes destabilizing aspect of modernization concerns the rate at which this process occurs. Huntington argues that political stability depends on the relationship between political mobilization (popular participation in politics) and political institutionalization (the development of state authority and institutions). In his view, instability is likely to increase to the extent that mobilization outpaces institutionalization.[9]

Along with modernization, nationalism developed. Invariably, however, it brought upheaval to traditional societies. First, what does the term mean? *Nationalism* can usefully be defined as a people's common awareness of belonging together. It is intensified by common ties of ethnicity, language, history, religion, and culture. In addition, it is often associated with a particular geographic location.[10]

Nationalism is a typically modern concept whose origins lie in Western Europe. Significantly, broad groups of people within a society come for the first time to identify with their nation. One of the most commonly cited cases in point is that of the French Revolution. By contrast, traditional societies have usually been more or less inert. This was especially the case among the vast bulk of the population living on the land. For many centuries, the populations of countries such as India or China were almost indifferent to those who ruled them—one group of rulers replaced another, for better or worse, but little sense of national identity existed among the common people. Of course, there have been exceptions. Even passive peasants sometimes rose up in revolt against their rulers. But these occasions were sporadic and not sustained. Thus it was possible, for example, for the British to rule India with only a few thousand civil servants. But when Ghandi succeeded in galvanizing massive public involvement during the 1920s and 1930s through civil disobedience, the British faced growing resistance and ultimately chose to withdraw.

Nationalism has taken on very different forms. In nineteenth-century Europe, it was often identified with political liberalism. That is, it was frequently associated with middle-class and popular aspiration for self-determination or democratic forms of government, whether against a national aristocratic elite—as in France—or against foreign or imperial rule—as in the case of the Dutch against Spain, or Italy against a combination of influences which kept that land fragmented until 1861.

Twentieth-century nationalism has had a more varied record. In Italy and Germany, for example, it degenerated into fascism and nazism—with a virulent and deadly form of hatred directed at people identified as outsiders or scapegoats. Parts of Eastern Europe also experienced extreme forms of nationalism and protofascism in the same period. Subsequently, however, nationalism proved a rallying point for resistance to occupation in World War II and to Soviet domination during the Cold War. In the developing world, nationalism frequently provided the impetus for resistance to imperial or colonial rule—whether through political means or armed movements. However, in both post–Cold War Eastern Europe and in large parts of the developing world, nationalism and ethnicity have often been the source of bitter antagonism.

Ironically, imperialism tended to stimulate both modernization and nationalism in traditional societies. These, in turn, undercut the authority and rule of the outside powers. Yet nationalism in the third world has proved to be very much double-edged. On the one hand, it provided a stimulus to self-determination and to the notion that foreign control was unacceptable. Cases in point include Algerian opposition to the French during 1954–1962, and Afghan resistance to the Soviets after 1979. On the other hand, the phenomenon of nationalism, especially as linked to ethnicity, has also proved devastatingly divisive to many developing countries whose national identity is by no means homogeneous.

In nineteenth-century Europe, a people or nation (that is, a group sharing a common identity, typically based on language, culture, or ethnicity) was often strongly associated with a particular territory (France, Britain, Ireland, Italy, Poland). In these circumstances, it is possible to speak of a nation-state: a place where a people with a common identity and a territorially based form of government more or less coincide.

But throughout vast areas of the developing world, as well as much of Eastern Europe and the former Soviet Union, the boundaries of states, that is, of legal and political entities, more often than not cut across those of ethnic groups. As a result, borders inherited from colonial times, or from earlier patterns of conquest by indigenous peoples, are subject to bitter challenge. Ethnic and communal rivalry thus pose profound problems for countries throughout the developing world. Illustratively, Nigeria, the largest and most populous country of black Africa, was torn by a civil war from 1967 to 1970. This pitted the Ibo group of tribes, a largely Christian ethnic group in eastern Nigeria, against the dominant and more numerous Moslem Hausas of northern Nigeria. The resultant conflict (which also included other important regions and ethnic groups such as the Yorubas) caused more than one million deaths before the effort of the Ibos to secede and to form their own country (Biafra) was defeated.

Other cases abound. In one major instance, such conflict led to the formation of a new country when the people of East Bengal rebelled against Pakistan and—as a result of a subsequent war between India and Pakistan—managed to establish the country of Bangladesh. In most circumstances, however (Kurds in Iraq, Tamils in Sri Lanka, Sikhs in India—to cite only a few among numerous cases), the result has been an ongoing process of political unrest interspersed with sporadic outbursts of violence or even guerrilla war.

Some of the groups in question are quite sizeable in numbers and cohesive in ethnic identity. There are, for example, approximately twenty million Kurdish people living in the mountainous regions extending across the borders of Iraq, Iran, and Turkey, with smaller numbers in Syria and the USSR. Yet despite possessing a language and culture of their own, and having waged intermittent warfare since the 1920s to gain self-determination from Iraq, Turkey, and Iran, the Kurds have been unable to acquire an independent state.

Growing modernization and nationalism were not the only factors that caused the decline of colonialism. Education, both in the subject country and in the metropolitan capitals of the colonizing powers, often proved important. The ideas inculcated at secondary schools and universities in Paris, London, and Oxford were ultimately subversive to colonial rule. Western values of liberty and equality could not easily be reconciled with the practices of empire, and the experience of education spawned a generation of opponents to continued foreign rule.

In some instances, though typically much later (not until the late 1950s and the 1960s), education took place in such Communist bloc locations as the Patrice Lumumba University in Moscow, established specifically for students from the developing world. Here the values inculcated were decidedly different, emphasizing Marxism-Leninism, a Soviet-centric perspective on world affairs, and the dynamics of underdevelopment and imperialism. The effect was to influence an educated elite in ways of thinking hostile not only to the already fading rule of the old colonial powers of the West, but also to successor regimes. In cases where pro-Soviet governments had managed to attain power, this educational process was aimed at providing cadres of political, technical, and bureaucratic personnel to maintain and staff the governmental apparatus. For the Soviets, the overall results remained mixed, however, inasmuch as students were often exposed to crude racism in their limited contact with Russians, and—more important—their own local priorities, problems, and ethnic conflicts often proved more crucial than the ideological viewpoints imparted by the Soviets.

The expansion of commerce also proved important, as did the creation of an infrastructure of transportation, communications, and national institutions. By widening the horizons and contacts of people previously confined to limited geographical areas, these developments did as much to shape a growing sense of nationhood as the impact of education itself.

World War II provided a strong impetus for decolonization. In the years from 1940 to 1942, countries that—from the view of the colonized—had appeared impregnable suffered a series of stunning defeats. In 1940, Germany defeated and occupied France, Belgium, and the Netherlands. In Asia, Japan inflicted defeats on the British and French. Yet, before long, the Germans and Japanese were themselves overcome and occupied. The lesson of this experience was that dominating external powers, whose role had often been reinforced by concepts of racial or cultural superiority, were not invulnerable after all.

In the next few years, the process of decolonization developed with extraordinary rapidity. Britain relinquished its Indian empire (the "jewel in the crown") in 1947. The Dutch gave up in Indonesia—after sometimes heavy fighting—in 1949. In the ensuing years, vast areas of the Middle East, Asia, Africa, and the

Caribbean gained independence as well. In a quarter-century, the map of world politics was redrawn.

HOW IMPORTANT IS THE SOUTH?

As we shall see below, some of the countries of the South remain afflicted with immense poverty and human want, problems of development and debt, and grave political and social instability. Apart from some altruistic sense of involvement or attention to the exotic, why should students of international relations bother to study the South? The answer, in part, is that countries of the Southern world have assumed an intrinsic importance that those interested in world affairs overlook at their own peril.

First, a number of developing countries have become regional powers of considerable importance in their own right. As a result, the interplay of international relations in a given geographic region is increasingly subject to the political, economic, and military influence of these regional "hegemons." Consider a number of cases in point:

In Central America, Venezuela and Mexico have exercised a considerable role by virtue of their oil resources, population, and political contacts. For example, in circumstances in which the United States had surprisingly limited scope for maneuver, Venezuela intervened with arms shipments and political influence to hasten the fall of the authoritarian leader of Nicaragua, Anastasio Somoza, in 1979. The fact that events in Nicaragua then unfolded in ways which the Venezuelan government of the day, and its successors, opposed—especially in the development of the Sandinista regime supported by Cuba and the Soviet Union and hostile to the United States—does not lessen the influence it exercised.

In East Asia, China has become one of the fastest growing economies on earth. Based on traditional calculations of gross national product (GNP), it possesses the world's tenth largest economy. However, in terms of IMF and World Bank calculations based on purchasing power parity (the value of a country's goods and services in purchasing power at home rather than on the basis of its currency on international exchanges), China actually ranks third overall—just behind Japan and ahead of Germany. Indeed, as Table 5.2 indicates, these calculations place four developing countries (China, India, Brazil, and Mexico) among the world's ten largest economies, even though their per capita income levels remain far lower.[11] Moreover, China's population, land area, and military strength, including nuclear weapons and missiles, make it the leading power in all of Asia. Elsewhere in the region—as in the case of Taiwan, Singapore, South Korea, and Hong Kong—the resources of local actors rest on their role as vigorous exporters and competitors in the area and throughout the world economy.

In South America, Brazil, with its 151 million people and giant economic base is the most important country on the continent. Despite severe problems of inflation and poverty, its economy ranks ninth in the world. In turn, its smaller neighbor, Argentina, with 33 million people, stretched Britain's capabilities in military power projection to their limit before being defeated in the battle for the Falkland Islands.

In South Asia, India has become a player of immense importance. Its population of 867 million makes it second only to China, and despite the poverty of many of its people, India has the world's sixth largest economy. It exercises a regional role of considerable military and economic influence, and its growing industrial base and military power make it a force to be reckoned with.

In sub-Saharan Africa, Nigeria remains a power without equal. Despite daunting economic problems—made still worse by massive corruption, political instability, and a decline in oil revenues—its large armed forces, oil, economic weight, and population give it a major presence in the region.

In the Middle East, a series of major players contend: Egypt, Israel, Iran, Iraq, Syria, and Saudi Arabia, each with its own strengths and vulnerabilities. These encompass, variously, oil wealth; population; religious influence; tank forces (in the case of Syria and Iraq) greater than those of Britain, France, or Germany; a skilled and powerful air force (in the case of Israel); and (in the case of Saudi Arabia) the largest concentration of proven oil reserves on earth.

Second, not only have regional powers or hegemons become important, so has the incidence of local conflicts in which outside powers play only modest roles in shaping outcomes. Consider, for example, the rivalries and wars between India and Pakistan, or the complex conflict that previously involved China, Vietnam, and Cambodia. As another illustration, the rivalry between Iraq and Iran rests on antagonisms reaching as far back as the year A.D. 637 and the historic Battle of Qadisiya. This strife pits Arabs against Persians for dominance of the Tigris and Euphrates river basins—an arena of local power rivalry since antiquity.

These regional rivalries and conflicts involve a blend of old and new: Iranian Shi'ite fundamentalists invoked the names of seventh-century religious leaders in firing surface-to-surface missiles at Baghdad, for example. Consider, too, the fact that China has existed as a vast nation-state for several millennia, but has now emerged as more relevant to international affairs than at any time since the European nation-state system's ascendance to world leadership after 1648. In essence, after having been more or less acted on for several centuries, countries of the developing world have been emerging, or reemerging, as more independent actors in their own right. In the process, their internal upheavals and conflicts with neighbors have taken on an importance well beyond the merely regional.

WHAT CHARACTERIZES THE SOUTH?

Poverty is often said to be a characteristic of the developing world, and the North-South dividing line does, to some extent, reflect a rich versus poor distinction. This is, however, a matter that must be approached with care. The World Bank

Table 5.2 LARGEST ECONOMIES RANKED BY PURCHASING POWER PARITY

Rank by Overall Size of Economy	Purchasing Power Parity per Capita	GNP per Capita
1. United States	$22,204	$22,204
2. Japan	19,107	27,132
3. China	1,450	370
4. Germany	19,500	24,585
5. France	18,227	21,022
6. India	1,150	330
7. Italy	16,896	19,911
8. Britain	15,720	17,596
9. Brazil	5,240	2,940
10. Mexico	7,170	3,030

Source: Data from International Monetary Fund. Table based on data in *New York Times,* 20 May 1993, p. A1. NB: GNP per capita figures vary slightly from those used by World Bank and reported in Table 5.3.

categorizes the world's countries in three broad groups: low-income economies (less than $635 GNP per capita), middle-income (above $635 but less than $7,911, with a subcategory of upper-middle income at $2,555 and above), and high-income ($7,911 and above).[12] The World Bank classifies 40 countries as low income, 65 as middle income (of which 43 are lower-middle), and an additional 22 as high income (see Table 5.3).

All 40 of the world's low-income countries are from the developing world. Among the five poorest countries in the group, Mozambique has the lowest average annual per capita income, with only $80 per person and a population of 16 million people. The next poorest countries include states with quite small populations—Bhutan ($180 per capita and 1.5 million people)—as well as large ones—Ethiopia ($120 and 52.8 million).[13] Yet there are other developing countries that are rich. This is especially true of certain oil-exporting countries. For example, the United Arab Emirates has a per capita GNP of $15,830, which is one of the highest in the entire world.

The income data are complicated. Indonesia is oil rich, yet it has a population of 181 million, and its per capita income of $610 places it in the low-income group. Other developing countries, largely from East Asia and Latin America, can be found in the middle-income category. These include such states as Brazil ($2,940), Malaysia ($2,520), Trinidad and Tobago ($3,670), and others. Indeed, even a poor country such as India, with average GNP per capita of just $330, presents a much more complex picture than the figures suggest. Among India's 866 million people, the most well-off one-tenth of the population comprises a group of some 86 million persons, with educational and income levels characteristic of much wealthier and more developed societies. Bear in mind, as well, that India has a considerable industrial export sector in its economy which is especially adept at competing in other countries of the developing world. India also possesses considerable armed forces and was the sixth country in the world (after the United States, the USSR, Britain, France, and China) to explode an atomic device.

Table 5.3 BASIC INDICATORS

Population, Area, Income, Inflation, Life Expectancy

	Population (millions) mid 1991	Area (thousands of square kilometers)	GNP per capita		Average annual rate of inflation (percent)		Life expectancy at birth (years) 1991	Adult illiteracy (percent)	
			Dollars 1991	Average annual growth rate (percent) 1980–1991	1970–1980	1980–1991		Female 1990	Total 1990
Low-income economies	3,127.3 t	38,828 t	350 w	3.9 w	8.2 w	12.6 w	62 w	52 w	40 w
China and India	2,016.0 t	12,849 t	350 w	5.6 w	4.3 w	6.9 w	66 w	50 w	37 w
Other low-income	1,111.2 t	25,980 t	350 w	1.0 w	15.7 w	23.4 w	55 w	56 w	45 w
1 Mozambique	16.1	802	80	-1.1	..	37.6	47	79	67
2 Tanzania	25.2	945	100	-0.8	14.1	25.7	51	..	..
3 Ethiopia	52.8	1,222	120	-1.6	4.3	2.4	48	..	..
4 Uganda	16.9	236	170	..	..	..	46	65	52
5 Bhutan	1.5	47	180	..	..	8.4	48	75	62
6 Guinea-Bissau	1.0	36	180	1.1	5.7	56.2	39	76	64
7 Nepal	19.4	141	180	2.1	8.5	9.1	53	87	74
8 Burundi	5.7	28	210	1.3	10.7	4.3	48	60	50
9 Chad	5.8	1,284	210	3.8	7.7	1.1	47	82	70
10 Madagascar	12.0	587	210	-2.5	9.9	16.8	51	27	20
11 Sierra Leone	4.2	72	210	-1.6	12.5	59.3	42	89	79
12 Bangladesh	110.6	144	220	1.9	20.8	9.3	51	78	65
13 Lao PDR	4.3	237	220	..	..	..	50	..	..
14 Malawi	8.8	118	230	0.1	8.8	14.9	45	..	..
15 Rwanda	7.1	26	270	-2.4	15.1	4.1	46	63	50
16 Mali	8.7	1,240	280	-0.1	9.7	4.4	48	76	68
17 Burkina Faso	9.3	274	290	1.2	8.6	3.8	48	91	82

(continued on next page)

Table 5.3 (continued)

	Population (millions) mid 1991	Area (thousands of square kilometers)	GNP per capita Dollars 1991	GNP per capita Average annual growth rate (percent) 1980–1991	Average annual rate of inflation (percent) 1970–1980	Average annual rate of inflation (percent) 1980–1991	Life expectancy at birth (years) 1991	Adult illiteracy (percent) Female 1990	Adult illiteracy (percent) Total 1990
18 Niger	7.9	1,267	300	-4.1	9.7	2.3	46	83	72
19 India	866.5	3,288	330	3.2	8.4	8.2	60	66	52
20 Kenya	25.0	580	340	0.3	10.1	9.2	59	42	31
21 Nigeria	99.0	924	340	-2.3	15.2	18.1	52	61	49
22 China	1,149.5	9,561	370	7.8	0.9	5.8	69	38	27
23 Haiti	6.6	28	370	-2.4	9.3	7.1	55	53	47
24 Benin	4.9	113	380	-0.9	10.3	1.6	51	84	77
25 Central African Rep.	3.1	623	390	-1.4	12.1	5.1	47	75	62
26 Ghana	15.3	239	400	-0.3	35.2	40.0	55	49	40
27 Pakistan	115.8	796	400	3.2	13.4	7.0	59	79	65
28 Togo	3.8	57	410	-1.3	8.9	4.4	54	69	57
29 Guinea	5.9	246	460	..	..	..	44	87	76
30 Nicaragua	3.8	130	460	-4.4	12.8	583.7	66	..	..
31 Sri Lanka	17.2	66	500	2.5	12.3	11.2	71	17	12
32 Mauritania	2.0	1,026	510	-1.8	9.9	8.7	47	79	66
33 Yemen, Rep.	12.5	528	520	..	..	..	52	74	62
34 Honduras	5.3	112	580	-0.5	8.1	6.8	65	29	27
35 Lesotho	1.8	30	580	-0.5	9.7	13.6	56	..	..
36 Indonesia	181.3	1,905	610	3.9	21.5	8.5	60	32	23
37 Egypt, Arab Rep.	53.6	1,001	610	1.9	9.6	12.5	61	66	52
38 Zimbabwe	10.1	391	650	-0.2	9.4	12.5	60	40	33
39 Sudan	25.8	2,506	..	..	14.5	..	51	88	73
40 Zambia	8.3	753	..	..	7.6	..	49	35	27
Middle-income economies	**1,401.0 t**	**40,796 t**	**2,480 w**	**0.3 w**	**28.4 w**	**67.1 w**	**68 w**	**26 w**	**21 w**
Lower-middle-income	**773.8 t**	**19,309 t**	**1,590 w**	**-0.1 w**	**22.8 w**	**23.1 w**	**67 w**	**32 w**	**26 w**

41	Bolivia	7.3	1,099	650	-2.0	21.0	263.4	59	29	23
42	Côte d'Ivoire	12.4	322	690	-4.6	13.0	3.8	52	60	46
43	Senegal	7.6	197	720	0.1	8.5	6.0	48	75	62
44	Philippines	62.9	300	730	-1.2	13.3	14.6	65	11	10
45	Papua New Guinea	4.0	463	830	-0.6	9.1	5.2	56	62	48
46	Cameroon	11.9	475	850	-1.0	9.8	4.5	55	57	46
47	Guatemala	9.5	109	930	-1.8	10.5	15.9	64	53	45
48	Dominican Rep.	7.2	49	940	-0.2	9.1	24.5	67	18	17
49	Ecuador	10.8	284	1,000	-0.6	13.8	38.0	66	16	14
50	Morocco	25.7	447	1,030	*1.6*	8.3	7.1	63	62	51
51	Jordan	3.7	89	1,050	-1.7	..	*1.6*	69	30	20
52	Tajikistan	5.5	143	1,050	..	..	..	69	..	..
53	Peru	21.9	1,285	1,070	2.4	30.1	287.3	64	21	15
54	El Salvador	5.3	21	1,080	-0.3	10.7	17.4	66	30	27
55	Congo	2.4	342	1,120	-0.2	8.4	0.4	52	56	43
56	Syrian Arab Rep.	12.5	185	1,160	-1.4	11.8	14.3	67	49	36
57	Colombia	32.8	1,139	1,260	1.2	22.3	25.0	69	14	13
58	Paraguay	4.4	407	1,270	-0.8	12.7	25.1	67	12	10
59	Uzbekistan	20.9	447	1,350	..	..	..	69	..	..
60	Jamaica	2.4	11	1,380	0.0	17.3	19.6	73	1	2
61	Romania	23.0	238	1,390	0.0	..	6.2	70	..	..
62	Namibia	1.5	824	1,460	-1.2	..	12.6	58	..	..
63	Tunisia	8.2	164	1,500	1.1	8.7	7.3	67	44	35
64	Kyrgyzstan	4.5	199	1,550	..	..	..	66	..	..
65	Thailand	57.2	513	1,570	5.9	9.2	3.7	69	10	7
66	Georgia	5.5	70	1,640	..	..	..	73	..	..
67	Azerbaijan	7.1	87	1,670	..	..	..	71	..	..
68	Turkmenistan	3.8	488	1,700	..	..	..	66	..	..
69	Turkey	57.3	779	1,780	2.9	29.4	44.7	67	29	19
70	Poland	38.2	313	1,790	0.6	..	63.1	71	..	..
71	Bulgaria	9.0	111	1,840	1.7	..	7.8	72	..	..
72	Costa Rica	3.1	51	1,850	0.7	15.3	22.9	76	7	7

(continued on next page)

Table 5.3 (continued)

	Population (millions) mid 1991	Area (thousands of square kilometers)	GNP per capita		Average annual rate of inflation (percent)		Life expectancy at birth (years) 1991	Adult illiteracy (percent)	
			Dollars 1991	Average annual growth rate (percent) 1980–1991	1970–1980	1980–1991		Female 1990	Total 1990
73 Algeria	25.7	2,382	1,980	–0.7	14.5	10.1	66	55	43
74 Panama	2.5	77	2,130	–1.8	7.5	2.4	73	12	12
75 Armenia	3.4	30	2,150	..	..	..	72	..	..
76 Chile	13.4	757	2,160	1.6	..	20.5	72	7	7
77 Iran, Islamic Rep.	57.7	1,648	2,170	–1.3	188.1	13.8	65	57	46
78 Moldova	4.4	34	2,170	..	22.4	..	69	..	..
79 Ukraine	52.0	604	2,340	..	..	..	70	..	..
80 Mauritius	1.1	2	2,410	6.1	15.3	8.1	70	..	..
81 Czechoslovakia	15.7	128	2,470	0.5	..	3.5	72	..	..
82 Kazakhstan	16.8	2,717	2,470	..	..	..	69	..	..
83 Malaysia	18.2	330	2,520	2.9	7.3	1.7	71	30	22
Upper-middle-income	**627.0 t**	**21,486 t**	**3,530 w**	**0.6 w**	**31.7 w**	**95.4 w**	**69 w**	**17 w**	**14 w**
84 Botswana	1.3	582	2,530	5.6	11.6	13.2	68	35	26
85 South Africa	38.9	1,221	2,560	0.7	13.0	14.4	63	..	..
86 Lithuania	3.7	65	2,710	..	..	..	71	..	..
87 Hungary	10.3	93	2,720	0.7	2.8	10.3	70	..	..
88 Venezuela	19.8	912	2,730	–1.3	14.0	21.2	70	10	12
89 Argentina	32.7	2,767	2,790	–1.5	133.9	416.9	71	5	5
90 Uruguay	3.1	177	2,840	–0.4	65.1	64.4	73	4	4
91 Brazil	151.4	8,512	2,940	0.5	38.6	327.6	66	20	19
92 Mexico	83.3	1,958	3,030	–0.5	18.1	66.5	70	15	13
93 Belarus	10.3	208	3,110	..	..	..	71	..	..
94 Russian Federation	148.7	17,075	3,220	..	..	..	69	..	..

95 Latvia	2.6	65	3,410	..	..	..	69	..	..
96 Trinidad and Tobago	1.3	5	3,670	-5.2	18.5	6.5	71	52	39
97 Gabon	1.2	268	3,780	-4.2	17.5	1.5	54	52	..
98 Estonia	1.6	45	3,830	.		.	70	19	15
99 Portugal	9.9	92	5,930	3.1	16.7	17.4	74	..	..
100 Oman	1.6	212	6,120	4.4	28.0	-3.1	69	..	..
101 Puerto Rico	3.6	9	6,320	0.9	6.5	3.4	76	..	..
102 Korea, Rep.	43.3	99	6,330	8.7	20.1	5.6	70	7	4
103 Greece	10.3	132	6,340	1.1	14.5	17.7	77	11	7
104 Saudi Arabia	15.4	2,150	7,820	-3.4	24.9	-2.4	69	52	38
105 *Yugoslavia*	23.9	256		..	18.4	123.0	73	12	7
Low- and middle-income	**4,528.0 t**	**79,624 t**	**1,010 w**	**1.0 w**	**21.8 w**	**53.9 w**	**64 w**	**46 w**	**35 w**
Sub-Saharan Africa	488.9 t	23,066 t	350 w	-1.2 w	13.9 w	18.4 w	51 w	62 w	50 w
East Asia & Pacific	1,666.5 t	16,369 t	650 w	6.1 w	9.1 w	6.3 w	68 w	34 w	24 w
South Asia	1,152.2 t	5,133 t	320 w	3.1 w	9.7 w	8.3 w	59 w	69 w	54 w
Europe and Central Asia	492.0 t	2,314 t	2,670 w	0.9 w	18.7 w	18.2 w	70 w	22 w	16 w
Middle East & N. Africa	244.1 t	11,015 t	1,940 w	-2.4 w	18.8 w	8.6 w	64 w	57 w	45 w
Latin American & Caribbean	445.3 t	20,507 t	2,390 w	-0.3 w	43.1 w	208.2 w	68 w	17 w	16 w
Severely indebted	**486.2 t**	**23,574 t**	**2,350 w**	**-1.0 w**	**39.1 w**	**189.6 w**	**67 w**	**27 w**	**22 w**
High-income economies	**822.3 t**	**31,682 t**	**21,050 w**	**2.3 w**	**9.1 w**	**4.5 w**	**77 w**	**5 w**	**4 w**
OECD members	783.1 t	31,135 t	21,530 w	2.3 w	9.0 w	4.3 w	77 w	5 w	4 w
106 Ireland	3.5	70	11,120	3.3	14.2	5.8	75	..	..
107 †Israel	4.9	21	11,950	1.7	39.5	89.0	76	..	5
108 New Zealand	3.4	271	12,350	0.7	12.5	10.3	76	f	f
109 Spain	39.0	505	12,450	2.8	16.1	8.9	77	f	f
110 †Hong Kong	5.8	1	13,430	5.6	9.2	7.5	78	7	5
111 †Singapore	2.8	1	14,210	5.3	5.9	1.9	74	..	..
112 United Kingdom	57.6	245	16,550	2.6	14.5	5.8	75	f	f
113 Australia	17.3	7,687	17,050	1.6	11.8	7.0	77	f	f
114 Italy	57.8	301	18,520	2.2	15.6	9.5	77	f	f
115 Netherlands	15.1	37	18,780	1.6	7.9	1.8	77	f	f

(continued on next page)

Table 5.3 (continued)

	Population (millions) mid 1991	Area (thousands of square kilometers)	GNP per capita		Average annual rate of inflation (percent)		Life expectancy at birth (years) 1991	Adult illiteracy (percent)	
			Dollars 1991	Average annual growth rate (percent) 1980–1991	1970–1980	1980–1991		Female 1990	Total 1990
116 Belgium	10.0	31	18,950	2.0	7.8	4.2	76	f	f
117 Austria	7.8	84	20,140	2.1	6.5	3.6	76	f	f
118 France	57.0	552	20,380	1.8	10.2	5.7	77	f	f
119 Canada	27.3	9,976	20,440	2.0	8.7	4.3	77	f	f
120 United States	252.7	9,373	22,240	1.7	7.5	4.2	76	f	f
121 Germanyᵉ	80.1	357	23,650	2.2	5.1	2.8	76	f	f
122 Denmark	5.2	43	23,700	2.2	10.1	5.2	75	f	f
123 Finland	5.0	338	23,980	2.5	12.3	6.6	76	f	f
124 Norway	4.3	324	24,220	2.3	8.4	5.2	77	f	f
125 Sweden	8.6	450	25,110	1.7	10.0	7.4	78	f	f
126 Japan	123.9	378	26,930	3.6	8.5	1.5	79	f	f
127 Switzerland	6.8	41	33,610	1.6	5.0	3.8	78	f	f
World	**5,351.0 t**	**111,306 t**	**4,010 w**	**1.2 w**	**11.2 w**	**15.4 w**	**66 w**	**45 w**	**35 w**
Fuel exporters	**262.8 t**	**12,387 t**	**1,990 w**	**-3.1 w**	**19.6 w**	**9.6 w**	**60 w**	**54 w**	**44 w**

Figures in italics are for years other than those specified.

Note: *w* = weighted average

   t = total

   ᵗ = economies classified as developing

   ᵉ = data for Federal Republic of Germany before unification

   f = illiteracy less than 5%

Source: World Bank, *World Development Report 1993* (New York: Oxford University Press, 1993), pp. 238–239. Reprinted by permission of Oxford University Press.

In sum, while poverty is common in much of the developing world, it is by no means uniform. Also note that developing countries are very unequal in population. Some are ministates with tiny populations. Others, notably China, with more than one billion people, and India, are massive. Similar differences can be found for population density, life expectancy, literacy, and other demographic indicators.

Here too, numbers alone do not always convey a sufficiently clear picture of realities in the developing world. One important effort to obtain a more useful composite indicator has led to the calculation of a Human Development Index by the United Nations Human Development Program. This assigns each country a score ranging from zero to a maximum of 1.000, based on levels of health, education, and individual purchasing power. The data show that, especially in the developing world, income per capita is not always the most accurate indicator of the average level of well-being and living standards among a population. For example, although Brazil ranks fifty-third among all countries in GNP per capita, and would thus appear to be well ahead of seventy-sixth ranked Costa Rica, the latter's accomplishments in education and health actually mean that its population has a higher quality of life. On the UN's Human Development scale, Costa Rica (with a "score" of .852) ranks forty-second, while Brazil (at .730) is in seventieth place.[14] A precursor of the UN Index can be found in the Physical Quality of Life Index (PQLI) calculated in the mid 1980s. That index incorporated life expectancy as of age one, literacy, and infant mortality. While the PQLI broadly corresponded to income level, it too identified cases where income per capita was not an accurate predictor of quality of life.[15]

THIRD AND FOURTH WORLDS

In making sense of the South, it is helpful to distinguish between *third* and *fourth* worlds. These terms rest on a division between those developing countries that have achieved some degree of progress in economic growth and quality of life for their people, and others whose performance has proven far weaker during the past decade, and whose future prospects appear much more grim.

A word about the origin of the term *third world* is in order here. The concept was originally meant to distinguish the developing countries from those states that were either part of the existing Western countries (chiefly the established industrial democracies) or part of the Soviet bloc. The implication was that the Western states made up a first world and the Soviet bloc countries a second world, though the terms were not generally used. However, the idea of the third world requires further clarification.

Based on the World Bank data, there exist major differences among developing countries based on income levels as well as geography (see Table 5.4). For example, during the years from 1980 to 1991, the 40 countries in the low-income group had real GNP per capita growth rates of 3.9 percent. Excluding China and India, which grew at an impressive rate of 5.6 percent, the other countries in this group averaged a meager 1.0 percent during the same period. Indeed, for some of them, owing to problems of debt, political instability, high birth rates, and disastrous economic policy choices, the record was far worse. For example, Latin

Table 5.4 CATEGORIES OF DEVELOPMENT

Income Category	No. of Countries 1991	Population (billions) 1991	Per capita GNP$ 1991	Per capita % GNP Growth 1980–1991	Annual Population Growth 1980–1991
Low (below $635)	40	3.127	350	3.9	2.0
Low (China & India)	2	2.016	350	5.6	1.7
Low (excluding China & India)	38	1.111	350	1.0	2.6
Lower–Middle ($635–2,555)	43	.774	1,590	-0.1	2.0
Upper–Middle ($2,555–$7,911)	22	.627	3,530	0.6	1.5
High (above $7,911)	22	.822	21,050	2.3	0.6
World	167	5.351	4,010	1.2	1.7

Source: Based on data from World Bank, World Development Report, 1993, pp. 238–39, 288–89. Also see Table 5.3.

American economies saw their GNP per capita decline by 0.3 percent per year, sub-Saharan African countries averaged negative economic growth of 1.2 percent, and the countries of the Middle East and North Africa experienced an average annual decline of 2.4 percent. In short, many of the poorest countries as a group have actually been losing the battle to develop and to improve the living conditions of their people.

What accounts for these major differences among the developing countries? In some cases, progress in development has been aided by the presence of raw materials for export. Countries such as Indonesia and Malaysia, for example, have benefited. Next there are countries that have succeeded in achieving rapid economic development (the newly industrializing countries known as the "NICs"), or at least have been able to achieve results in processing raw materials or intermediate industrial goods. Not only does this category include the dynamic East Asian economies such as Singapore, Taiwan, South Korea, Hong Kong and others, it also encompasses large countries such as Brazil and India that have been able to achieve considerable development of their domestic industries and technology.

By contrast, the poorest countries, for our purposes the "fourth world," have much more dire prospects. Portions of sub-Saharan Africa (e.g., Chad, Ethiopia, Mali, Burkina Faso), parts of Central and South Asia (Bangladesh, Nepal, Afghanistan), and sections of the Caribbean (particularly Haiti) are included here. Excluding China and India, they account for more than a billion people. Countries in the low-income group are by no means identical in their degree of poverty—just as a number of countries in the lower-middle-income category actually find themselves in desperate circumstances. Nonetheless, fourth-world countries typically suffer from severe lack of energy and other natural resources, population pressure,[16] and the absence of revenues to pay for the food, machinery, and oil they need for their economies to function at more than the barest level of subsistence. For many of these states, particularly in the drought-stricken Sahel area just below the Sahara desert, bankruptcy and famine are constant perils.

Indeed there are even growing risks of "de-development." Living standards have actually fallen in some countries. In Ghana, for example, there has been a deterioration of physical facilities as well as the disruption of a skilled professional administrative class the country once had. In some instances the failures are due to outrageously bad political leaders. Ghana is a case in point, but there are others far worse—as the cases of Uganda, Zaire, and Somalia tragically illustrate. Thus, to such physical difficulties as climate, lack of resources, and natural disaster, there have been added a series of human failures:[17] corruption, repression, civil war, and regional conflict. Together these factors have contributed to a grim prospect in significant areas of the developing world.

In sum, generalizations about the South should be made with care. Poor but vast and populous countries such as India and China nonetheless possess important economic or military strengths and have become major powers in their regions. In other cases, developing countries such as South Korea, Taiwan, and Brazil have become significant economic competitors—as aggressive and successful exporters of steel and electronics, for example, or even as arms suppliers in the developing world.

DILEMMAS OF DEVELOPMENT

Throughout vast areas of the South, the problem of development is far more than a narrow, technical matter. Instead, it concerns the basic economic, political, and social conditions of human life. Progress in dealing with poverty, disease, illiteracy, unemployment, infant mortality, and other ills requires both economic improvement *and* development of stable social and political institutions.

Despite grave problems, important changes have occurred in the developing world during recent decades. For both third- and fourth-world countries, there have been substantial advances in adult literacy, urbanization, increased life expectancy, reduced infant mortality, and other indicators. Indeed, even an otherwise gloomy assessment of world development notes that average life expectancy has risen by 16 years and adult literacy by 40 percent, while child mortality has declined by 50 percent.[18] However, in the process, new perils have emerged. For example, movement from the countryside to the cities has brought about the creation of vast slums and shantytowns, with inadequate provision for safe drinking water, sewage disposal, transportation, and jobs.

Capital formation has been stimulated with grants from abroad, in the form of foreign aid, as well as by loans and foreign investment. However, for some developing countries, foreign investment failed to generate domestic capital formation, and for many states the problem of paying the interest—let alone the principal—on their accumulated foreign debt poses extraordinary problems.

The Debt Crisis

During the 1970s, especially in the aftermath of the oil shocks of 1973–1974 and 1979–1980, many countries of the developing world borrowed heavily from banks and multilateral agencies in the Northern world. The banks themselves held large amounts of "petrodollars"—earnings that oil-producing states had deposited as oil prices soared—and they were eager to lend money. For their part, developing countries borrowed to finance large infrastructure projects (highways, harbors, airports, hospitals, power plants, government buildings) and industrial development efforts. However, a substantial amount of the borrowed money was used inefficiently or simply wasted. Vast sums went to finance imports of consumer goods, grandiose projects that became "white elephants," unrealistic exchange rates, capital flight, and outright corruption.

During the early 1980s, however, as debt mounted, the price of oil stagnated and then began to decline and Western banks became increasingly reluctant to lend new money. At the same time, a severe economic recession in 1981–1982 and high interest rates combined to make a massive debt problem apparent. Moreover, indebtedness made the developing countries highly sensitive and vulnerable to economic changes taking place in the West. Thus, for example, each 1 percent increase in interest rates added $2.7 billion to Latin America's external interest payments and reduced annual GNP for a country such as Mexico by half of 1 percent.[19]

The developing countries had built a mountain of debt that they faced great difficulty in repaying. This posed serious problems for the banks, and indeed a massive financial crisis was narrowly averted in 1982. For many low-income countries, however, the economic and social consequences of the debt crisis were disastrous. The soaring burdens of interest payments alone ate up large portions of earnings from exports. Indeed, beginning in 1984, overall debt repayments actually amounted to a significant annual net transfer of resources from the poor to the rich countries. By 1988, the net annual outflow from Latin America amounted to $24 billion, and as a group the developing countries transferred $50.1 billion more in debt repayment than they received in loans and foreign assistance.[20] Indeed, from 1982 to 1989, a single country, Mexico, actually transferred a staggering total of $56 billion more in debt payments than it received.[21]

The effect of the debt crisis and the burden of interest payments was worsened by population growth as well as by external factors such as recession, high interest rates, and sagging commodity prices. Economic growth became severely retarded, and unemployment soared. In some countries, governments found themselves without the resources to provide sufficiently for such basic services as health care, sanitation, education, and public transportation. Average per capita economic growth stagnated or even declined.

The debt burden has been particularly serious in Africa. For sub-Saharan Africa, external debt is actually equivalent to 108.8 percent of GNP—a level triple that of Latin America, South Asia, or East Asia (see Table 5.5). Servicing this debt, which for the African continent as a whole amounted to $290 billion in 1992, cost more than $26 billion in 1991 alone. As a consequence, countries in the region found themselves spending four times more on debt service than for all health-care services to 600 million people. This burden has led to urgent calls for debt relief.

Foreign Aid

The urgency of these problems has caused many observers to emphasize the importance of foreign aid. This assistance includes humanitarian help to relieve temporary conditions of famine, drought, and natural disaster. It encompasses education, medical assistance in relieving and preventing disease, technical assistance in improving agricultural productivity, and the provision of a wide range of aid to build and maintain the physical infrastructure needed by a developing society. Importantly, it also includes money, both to improve infrastructure and sometimes to meet current needs and even interest payments. These funds include loans, capital transfers from governmental and international agencies, and other actions.

While educational and health measures have had a major impact on literacy, infant mortality, and life expectancy, the long-term effects of financial aid remain subject to fierce debate. Some observers have emphasized additional aid as the key to improved development, along with other measures to better the terms and conditions of trade and to open markets for the products of developing countries. Among the most widely known of these recommendations were those of the

Table 5.5 DEBT BURDEN BY REGION:
External Debt as % of GNP, 1992

Sub-Saharan Africa	108.8%
Latin American and Caribbean	37.6
South Asia	36.3
East Asia and Pacific	27.9

Source: World Bank data, in *African Debt Crisis: A Continuing Impediment to Development* (New York: Africa Recovery Unit, United Nations, 1993.)

Brandt Commission, an independent group of international figures, headed by the former German chancellor, Willy Brandt. In the early 1980s it called for a series of sweeping measures to ward off starvation, lessen the burden of armaments, encourage trade, and reshape the conditions of the world economy, which were seen as operating to the detriment of the South. Indeed, the authors of two Brandt Commission reports argued that cooperation in these measures was essential for economic recovery and growth in the North as well as in the South.[22]

Other observers, by contrast, tended to place more emphasis on indigenous problems and argued that no amount of foreign aid could eliminate the need for greater efforts on the part of those living in the region, together with necessary steps in economic and political reform.[23] It is, however, useful to consider that among LDCs that have achieved more rapid economic growth, some of the most successful (particularly South Korea and Taiwan) have benefited *both* from generous American aid and from major internal reforms, particularly in land distribution. On the other hand, China has attained one of the world's highest growth rates, without foreign aid but with substantial foreign investment.

The Dependency Debate

From the perspective of the South, a series of very different ideas have been brought to bear concerning the problems of economic growth and the blame for poverty. The concept of *dependency theory* or *dependencia* has been put forward by both political leaders and writers in Latin America, Africa, and Asia, as well as by a number of theorists of development in the North. In essence, dependency theory holds that the established liberal economic order has been at fault for exploiting the less developed countries. It considers that third-world poverty is the result of the Northern world's wealth. Variations of this approach include both Marxist and non-Marxist interpretations, more or less emphasis on the role of colonialism and imperialism, divergent views on the role of the state and of economic and social classes within both the Northern and Southern worlds, and different degrees of reliance on moral, philosophical, economic, or historical precepts.[24]

From the dependency perspective, and beginning in the mid 1970s, important spokesmen and groups representing developing countries argued for creation of a "New International Economic Order" (NIEO). As initially proposed in 1974 by a group of 77 developing countries (the "Group of 77"), and adopted by the

Sixth Special Session of the United Nations General Assembly, this called for a major restructuring of international economic and financial relationships, with large increases in foreign aid, credit, and debt relief; higher prices for LDC commodity exports; greatly expanded access to Northern markets; and a significantly enhanced voice for the countries of the South in international economic decision making. However, many of these original proposals were vague, contradictory, or even utopian, while others reflected a more practical sense of the need for expanded trade, capital flows, investment, and technology transfers.[25]

Regardless of the merits of the various aid and dependency arguments, it is useful to note that many of the difficulties in which developing countries are mired have fundamental internal causes. For example, corruption has become a way of life in many of the poorest developing countries. The issue goes far beyond that of offending the moral or legal sensitivities of outside observers. Instead, corruption imposes a crushing tax on economic activity and an obstacle to development.[26] As one otherwise sympathetic but uncompromising observer comments about Ghana, "The main damage was the destruction of the most valuable part of Ghana's inheritance from the colonial days: its honest and competent civil service, the best in tropical Africa. But the honest and competent administrators had to be shoved aside, because they stood between Nkrumah's socialist cronies and the loot."[27] As a result, a country that at the time of independence in 1957 had a gross domestic product (GDP) per capita comparable to that of South Korea plunged into a quarter-century of steadily falling real income at the average rate of 1 percent per year.[28]

More broadly, in African countries with low incomes, weak economic development, and relatively new state structures, an additional problem arises. Whether these states appear to be socialist or capitalist, the key means of acquiring wealth is often less by productive or entrepreneurial economic activity than through access to the power of the state. And, a leading Nigerian observer adds, political repression "may well be the greatest single obstacle to development." This is especially evident in food shortages, which are not merely a result of natural disasters, but "essentially the failure of policies," specifically the abuse and coercion of peasant producers.[29] Both external and internal causes thus shape the problems of development.

Given the discrepancies within the developing world, it is not surprising that economic growth has varied sharply. This is not only the case between countries of the third and fourth worlds, but (as evident in Table 5.6) significant regional differences can also be identified. While the causes of these differences are complex, domestic policies of the countries involved appear to play a crucial role, particularly in the need for economic and market reforms. These typically include increases in the prices farmers receive for their produce, realistic exchange rates, low state budget deficits, interest rates above the rate of inflation, and greater latitude for the market mechanism to operate.[30] Indeed, a World Bank study indicates that during a three-year period in the late 1980s, African countries that adopted economic reforms managed growth rates more than double those of countries that did not.[31]

Table 5.6 REGIONAL DIFFERENCES IN ECONOMIC GROWTH AND INCOME AMONG LOW- AND MIDDLE-INCOME COUNTRIES

Region	Population (billions) 1991	Per capita GNP $ 1991	Per capita % GNP growth 1980–1991	Annual % Population Growth 1980–1991
Sub-Saharan Africa	.489	350	-1.2	3.1
East Asia & Pacific	1.667	650	6.1	1.6
South Asia	1.152	320	3.1	2.2
Europe & Central Asia	.420	2,670	0.9	0.9
Mid East & N. Africa	.244	1,940	-2.4	3.2
L. America & Caribbean	.445	2,390	-0.3	2.0
ALL LOW- & MID-INCOME	4.538	1,010	1.0	2.0

Source: Adapted from data in World Bank, *World Development Report, 1993*, p. 239. Also see Table 5.3.

ETHNICITY AS A MAJOR SOURCE OF CONFLICT

If problems of development, misrule, and nation building continue as major difficulties for the countries of the South, so too do deep-rooted ethnic conflicts. As noted above in the analysis of nationalism, very few developing countries possess the relative ethnic homogeneity of a nation-state such as France or Norway. Instead, loyalties to one's ethnic, linguistic, or religious group frequently cut across national loyalties. Consider several cases in point.

In India, the world's most populous democracy, the community of 14 million Sikhs has been involved in bitter controversy with the national government. The Sikhs themselves have been a relatively successful and visible minority, both in their commercial activity and in service to India's armed forces. But beginning in the early 1980s, an action-reaction cycle led to a crisis. After pressures for increased autonomy within India by a more extreme element among the Sikhs were rejected, there followed the occupation and fortification of the Sikh national shrine, the Golden Temple, by a diehard group. In response, the Indian Army intervened, taking over the facility and killing hundreds of Sikhs in the process. Ultimately, Sikh terrorists retaliated by carrying out the assassination of Prime Minister Indira Gandhi. This in turn was followed by fierce rioting and reprisals, in which—sometimes with the complicity of police—as many as a thousand innocent Sikhs were murdered.

In Angola, where ideological and political considerations were once a driving force, ethnicity has fueled a continuing civil war. In this case, the UNITA movement, though no longer backed by the United States, retains the support of half the country's population, stemming from its base in the Ovimbundu tribe—the largest single ethnic group in Angola. U.S.-mediated agreements in 1988 and 1991 helped end the role of outside powers (including Cuban troops and Soviet support for the MPLA government in the capital, Luanda), brought a temporary halt to the fighting, and led to internationally sponsored elections in 1992, under a UN operation known as UNAVEM II. However, the weakness of the UN presence, with fewer than 500 military and police observers and a few hundred others to observe the elections in a vast country, and the absence of UN troops to enforce the settlement, led to renewed civil war between the UNITA and MPLA forces.[32] In the subsequent fighting, tens of thousands of Angolans died from warfare and starvation.

In Sri Lanka, once a country with a widely recognized level of achievement in meeting the needs of its population, years of bloody conflict between the country's Tamil minority and the majority Sinhalese community have killed thousands of people since 1987, caused thousands to flee to India, and at one point prompted a temporary intervention by the armed forces of India.

Other examples of ethnic conflict abound: between Arabs and black Africans along the border between Mauritania and Senegal, Hutu and Tutsi peoples in Rwanda, Kikuyu and Kalenjin in Kenya, Turks and Kurds in Turkey, Moslems and Hindus in India, Christians and Moslems in Lebanon, Cambodians and Vietnamese in Southeast Asia, and in countless other countries and regions.

Nor is conflict over ethnicity, language, and religion confined to the developing world. The savage ethnic conflict within the former Yugoslavia is a case in point, and significant problems exist elsewhere—within Northern Ireland (Catholics versus Protestants), Belgium (French versus Flemish speakers), Spain (Basque and Catalan separatism), and Bulgaria (brutality against a minority population of one million ethnic Turks.) Moreover, following the end of the Cold War and the dissolution of the Soviet Union, previously suppressed hatreds within the former Soviet sphere have burst into the open. This has been exemplified in brutalities and bloody fighting between Azerbaijani and Armenian peoples, in the transcaucasus region, and elsewhere in portions of what was once Soviet Central Asia. For the most part, however, the intensity of ethnic cleavages within the developing world tends to be more severe, as a result of the tumultuous process of modernization and development, often exacerbated by problems of weak or bad government.

THE SOUTH AND WORLD POLITICS

This book is organized around the dual themes of anarchy and order as systemic concepts. Certainly, the bulk of the South in the late twentieth-century world has become an arena in which problems of instability are endemic. As Stanley Hoffmann has summarized the problem, "The shakiness of the political structures of so many states; the communal conflicts, ideological antagonisms, religious hatreds, and social cleavages. . . ; the lack of fit between political regimes imposed by past masters (foreign or domestic); and societies undergoing an almost unmanageable process of transformation guarantee endless cycles of revolution, external interventions, and counter-revolutions."[33]

In essence, problems of development and modernization, weak states, and ethnic conflicts virtually assure an unstable and at times anarchic environment in many areas of the South. Indeed, since the end of World War II, the great majority of international conflicts—whether in the form of wars between states, civil wars, or even terrorism—have occurred there. Although the South has become the scene of great instability as its relevance to international relations has increased, the principal fracture line of contemporary international relations is unlikely to become simply a North-South affair. Instead, intraregional problems (i.e., "South-South" conflict) and endemic instability can often inflict appalling human costs—as exemplified in settings as diverse as Somalia, Cambodia, the Sudan, Rwanda, the Persian Gulf, Lebanon, Afghanistan, and a number of the former Soviet republics. Conflicts such as these are driven by deep-seated ethnic, political, economic, and regional animosities. Developments within the South have generally become more difficult for external actors to influence effectively, whether those actors are Americans, Russians, French, British, Chinese, Germans, Japanese or even bodies such as the Organization of African Unity, the Organization of American States, and the United Nations itself.

The implications are thus mixed. Some areas have achieved progress in grappling with problems of poverty, economic development, and the establishment or consolidation of pluralistic governmental institutions. Moreover, a number of important regional and civil conflicts have been mitigated or even brought to a halt with the involvement of outside powers cooperating through the United Nations. (Though the UN is not always in a position to intervene, and when it does the outcome—as evident in Somalia or Angola—is not always success.) Meanwhile, the consequences for some of the occupants of these lands remain painful, with worsening problems of poverty, population, political upheaval, environmental degradation, ethnic conflict, and regional rivalry. To observe these troubles is not to condone them, but their recognition remains a precondition for comprehending world politics in the remaining years of the twentieth century.

NOTES

1. "The Clash of Civilizations?" *Foreign Affairs*, Vol. 72, No. 3 (Summer 1993): 22–49, at 27.
2. Speech to the National Defense University, quoted in *Washington Post*, 9 November 1993, p. A13.
3. *New Republic*, 18 March 1985, p. 32.
4. The "spirit of Bandung" is discussed by Robert A. Mortimer, *The Third World Coalition in International Politics*, 2nd ed. (Boulder: Westview Press, 1984), pp. 5ff.
5. The implications of the oil decade are assessed in Chapter 10.
6. Definitions of imperialism abound. For the purposes of this volume, the one offered by John Strachey seems useful: "By imperialism I mean the process by which peoples or nations conquer, subdue and then permanently dominate (either *de jure* or *de facto*) other peoples or nations. By empire I mean the state of things in this way established." *The End of Empire* (New York: Frederick A. Praeger, 1964), p. 7.

   A different definition is provided by the late Hans J. Morgenthau: "A nation whose foreign policy aims at acquiring more power than it actually has, through a reversal of existing power relations—whose foreign policy, in other words, seeks a favorable change in power status—pursues a policy of imperialism." *Politics Among Nations* (New York: Knopf, 5th ed., 1978), p. 43. While this definition is original in focusing on change in the status quo as its indicator, it is less satisfactory here because it does not identify countries and regions where power is already being imposed.

7. See, for example, the discussion of Weber's approach in David Willer, *Scientific Sociology: Theory and Method* (Englewood Cliffs, NJ: Prentice-Hall, 1967), p. 45.

8. Samuel Huntington, "Political Modernization: America versus Europe," *World Politics* 18 (April 1966): 378. Italics added.

9. *Political Order in Changing Societies* (New Haven: Yale University Press, 1968). Karl Deutsch made an analogous point concerning political mobilization and social integration. See *Nationalism and Social Communication: An Inquiry into the Foundations of Nationality*, 2nd ed. (Cambridge: MIT Press, 1966).

10. See Jack C. Plano and Ray Olton, *The International Relations Dictionary*, 3rd ed. (Santa Barbara: ABC-Clio, 1982), p. 33. For a much more sophisticated analysis of nationalism, see Deutsch, *Nationalism and Social Communication*. Also see Chalmers A. Johnson, *Peasant Nationalism and Social Communication: The Emergence of Revolutionary China, 1937–1945* (Stanford: Stanford University Press, 1962), especially pp. 19–30.

11. *New York Times*, 20 May 1993, pp. A1 and A8.

12. Unless otherwise indicated, data are from World Bank, *World Development Report, 1993* (New York: Oxford University Press, 1993). The World Bank's basic income indicators are from pp. x–xi and 238–239 and are drawn from 1991 data.

13. Data from World Bank, *World Development Report, 1993*, pp. 238–239. Data for UAE from 1989 edition, pp. 164–165.

14. See *Human Development Report* (New York: Oxford University Press, 1993), pp. 128, 135–137.

15. The data on PQLI are drawn from John W. Sewell et al., *U.S. Policy and the Developing Countries: Agenda 1988* (Washington, DC: Overseas Development Council, and New Brunswick, NJ: Transaction Books, 1988), pp. 199 and 246 ff. The PQLI calculations were prepared for the Overseas Development Council by Morris D. Morris and Chenkuo Pang of the Brown University Center for Comparative Study of Development. The PQLI data are for 1985.

16. A study places particular emphasis on the relationship between rapid population growth and deteriorating living conditions—especially in Africa, the Middle East, South Asia, and Latin America. Lester Brown and Jodi Jacobson argue that the more successful developing countries (e.g., in East Asia) have slowed their population growth rates. See *Our Demographically Divided World* (Washington, DC: Worldwatch Institute, 1986).

17. A number of works provide vivid portraits of deception and misrule in the developing world. On problems in the Islamic world, see the acerbic critique by V. S. Naipaul, *Among the Believers: An Islamic Journey* (New York: Vintage/Random House, 1982). For accounts of corruption, misrule, and repression in Communist countries, see two impressive and deeply felt accounts by disillusioned revolutionaries: Truong Nhu Tang, *Vietcong Memoir* (New York: Harcourt Brace Jovanovich, 1985), and Carlos Franqui, *Family Portrait with Fidel* (New York: Random House, 1984). And, for striking fictional portrayals of misrule in West Africa, see V. S. Naipaul, *A Bend in the River* (New York: Knopf, 1979), and Chinua Achebe, *Anthills of the Savannah* (New York: Anchor/Doubleday, 1988).

18. Council of the Club of Rome, *The First Global Revolution* (New York: Simon & Schuster, 1991), and *The Economist*, 19 October 1991, p. 104.

19. Data from Pedro-Pablo Kuczynski, managing director of the First Boston Corporation. See "Periling Debtor Countries," *New York Times,* 24 May 1984.

20. *The Economist* (London), 24 June 1989; *New York Times* and *Washington Post,* 18 September 1989.

21. *New York Times,* 25 July 1989. On debt, more broadly, see Miles Kahler, *The Politics of International Debt* (Ithaca, NY: Cornell University Press, 1986), and Robert A. Pastor, ed., *Latin America's Debt Crisis: Adjusting to the Past or Planning for the Future?* (Boulder: Lynne Reinner, 1987).

22. See *North-South: A Programme for Survival. Report of the Independent Commission on International Development Issues* (Cambridge: MIT Press, 1980). See also the Brandt Commission, *Common Crisis: North-South Cooperation for World Recovery* (Cambridge: MIT Press, 1983).

23. See, for example, P. T. Bauer, *Equality, the Third World, and Economic Delusion* (Cambridge: Harvard University Press, 1981). Bauer stridently criticizes the dominant weight of opinion among developmental specialists for placing what he considers to be excess emphasis on equality and on the evils inherited from colonialism.

24. There is a huge, diverse literature on dependency. One of the best selections of this work—and of alternative approaches and criticisms—is Edward Weisband, ed., *Poverty Amidst Plenty: World Politics and Distributive Justice* (Boulder: Westview, 1989). For a critical assessment of the dependency approach and the agenda of its advocates in the third world, see Stephen D. Krasner, *Structural Conflict: The Third World Against Global Liberalism* (Berkeley: University of California Press, 1985), especially pp. 1–4 and 174 ff.

25. See Richard Feinberg, *The Intemperate Zone: The Third World Challenge to U.S. Foreign Policy* (New York: Norton, 1983), pp. 118–122.

26. In some instances, corruption and the looting of national wealth by rulers has become a problem of grave proportions. According to one account, a former Mexican president was reported to have left the country with more than one billion dollars at the end of his term in office. See James S. Henry, "Where the Money Went," *New Republic,* 14 April 1986, p. 20. By another estimate, the deposed Philippine president, Ferdinand Marcos, had amassed a personal fortune of more than $6.5 *billion* before his ouster. See *New York Times,* 9 February 1987, p. 1.

27. Conor Cruise O'Brien, *New Republic,* 18 March 1985, p. 34. Crawford Young argues that as state power becomes the prize, this also serves to exacerbate indigenous ethnic conflict. See *The Politics of Cultural Pluralism* (Madison: University of Wisconsin Press, 1976).

28. Data from *The Economist,* 12 July 1986, p. 40.

29. Claude Ake, "Does Western Aid Develop Africa?" *The Wilson Center Reports* (Washington, DC: Woodrow Wilson International Center for Scholars, May 1985).

30. *The Economist,* 4 March 1989, p. 13.

31. *Ibid.,* pp. 13 and 63.

32. See Chester Crocker, "Angola: Can This Outrageous Spectacle Be Stopped?" *New York Times,* 13 October 1993.

33. Stanley Hoffmann, "The Future of the International Political System: A Sketch," in Samuel P. Huntington and Joseph S. Nye, Jr., eds., *Global Dilemmas* (Lanham, MD: University Press of America, 1985), p. 291.

chapter 6

Nuclear Weapons and World Politics

The most important points often are simplest ones. No one can win an all out nuclear war.

—ROBERT JERVIS[1]

With nuclear weapons, however, short of a breakthrough that would give the United States either a first-strike capability or an effective defense, Russia need not keep pace militarily with American technology.

—KENNETH WALTZ[2]

... more than a dozen countries have operational ballistic missiles, ... more than 25 countries, many of them hostile to the United States and our allies, may have or may be developing nuclear, biological and chemical weapons.

—CIA DIRECTOR JAMES WOOLSEY[3]

The end of the Cold War and a series of major agreements to reduce American and Russian nuclear forces have had a significant impact on the nuclear arms race that took place during the East-West conflict. Many of the concerns that preoccupied strategists, government leaders, and scholars have been overtaken by events. Nonetheless, basic realities concerning nuclear weapons continue to be durable features of the international landscape, and it is vital to understand their implications. The subject remains relevant, not only because of its importance for understanding the recent past, but also because it is part of the continuing reality of international relations. It also has implications for the future, both in terms of superpower relations and in understanding the problem of nuclear proliferation.

Nuclear weapons continue to exist in significant numbers, not only in the possession of the United States and Russia, but also in the hands of Britain, France, and China. Moreover, in small numbers and less openly, they appear to be in the possession of several other countries in Asia, the Middle East, and Africa. Given the existence of independent states, the absence of overarching authority, and the unlikelihood that such a proven and devastatingly powerful technology can ever be abandoned, these weapons of potential mass destruction are here to stay.

Since their introduction in 1945, nuclear weapons have wrought a revolution in international relations. The invention of atomic and thermonuclear bombs, coupled with advanced delivery systems (aircraft, land-based missiles, submarines), represents more than a technological evolution. Major advances in weaponry have occurred before: the longbow, gunpowder, armor, artillery, the machine gun, tanks, and airplanes are among numerous past innovations in weapons technology. Yet the nuclear revolution brings with it unique features. The speed and distance of weapons delivery, and especially the destructive force unleashed, create the possibility of destroying the very things for which war might have been fought in the first place.

In a sense, innovations in weaponry have outrun human social and political institutions. Mankind is organized in separate states; the international environment in which these states interact remains structurally anarchic, and conflicts—sometimes leading to wars—are a fact of international life. Yet the means of conflict have become progressively more deadly. One early observer of nuclear weapons and world politics thus questioned whether these weapons were compatible with the continued existence of people organized in nation-states.[4]

THE IMPACT OF THE NUCLEAR ERA

While nuclear weapons do not by any means preclude the occurrence of war, they do make *total* war no longer a rational instrument of national strategy. In the past, a world power could contemplate the possibility of war in the event that its security or objectives could not be attained by peaceful means. Hence the maxim of the Prussian strategist Karl von Clausewitz that war is a continuation of diplomacy by other means. Indeed, a great number of past wars have shaped the course of human civilization—for good or ill. In these circumstances, war could be a rational (though nonetheless brutal) course of action if its probable gains were thought to exceed significantly the likely costs. For major powers today, however, such calculations about a war in which nuclear weapons would be used have become very different.

In a sense, the impact of the nuclear era represents the culmination of industrialization and science as applied to warfare. According to one study, each half-century since the 1820s has seen roughly comparable numbers of wars (about 100 measurable interstate conflicts in each period), yet the graph of destruction and death has risen exponentially over each successive period. Thus, there were approximately 2 million battle deaths in the years from 1820 to 1863, 4.5 million from 1864 to 1907, and more than 40 million from 1907 to 1950.[5] By implication, humanity has not become any more prone to wage war, but the advance of technology has simply made these conflicts more and more deadly.

THE NUCLEAR BALANCE

Although the end of the Cold War and the breakup of the Soviet Union have greatly changed the international system, the United States and Russia remain the two paramount nuclear powers. The two countries have greatly reduced their level of conventional (nonnuclear) military confrontation. Indeed, with the withdrawal of Russian forces from Eastern Europe, an enormous decline in the size and capability of the Russian armed forces, and withdrawal of almost two-thirds of the American forces previously stationed in Western Europe, the situation in the European continent has been transformed. Nonetheless, America and Russia continue to possess significant numbers of long-range, strategic nuclear weapons and likely will for the foreseeable future. As a consequence, and indeed as has been the case since the mid 1960s, a strategic nuclear balance between the two countries rests on a virtually ineluctable basis: nuclear superiority is unattainable in any meaningful sense. Neither side is likely—under any plausible set of conditions—to acquire a usable strategic nuclear advantage. The balance of deterrent power endures because each side has the ability, in the event of an all-out war, to destroy the other.

In the familiar jargon of the strategic community, the Americans and Russians possess *second-strike capability:* each has the capability, in the event it suffers even a devastating nuclear first strike, of nonetheless retaliating with its remaining nuclear weapons and inflicting unacceptable damage upon the attacker.[6] Such a capacity is achieved by building a nuclear force able to survive an attack and then be utilized in retaliation. This is not merely a question of numbers; second-strike capability is achieved through a combination of methods. These include *hardening* (i.e., protecting the weapons so that they cannot easily be destroyed), *dispersal* (so that all the weapons are not concentrated as large targets in one or a few places), and *mobility* (so that their location may not always be known in advance by a potential attacker).

What constitutes *unacceptable damage* remains imprecise. It is partly a psychological and political question, but it implies a level of harm to a society that its leaders find intolerable. As a very rough approximation, perhaps two hundred nuclear weapons exploded on the industrial centers of either the United States or the USSR would kill one-third of the country's population and destroy two-thirds of its industrial capacity. These consequences would be a result merely of the immediate effects (blast, heat, and radiation) of the attack, and do not measure the longer-term human and material toll (disease, radiation sickness, famine, environmental damage) that would ensue.

The situation in which the United States and Russia find themselves has been termed "mutual assured destruction" (MAD), and has been criticized repeatedly, both as a description of the existing balance and as a depiction of current policy. Yet the concept reflects a basic reality: the existence of mutual assured destruction is a fact, regardless of policy. As Robert Jervis puts it, *"nuclear weapons enable the state that is losing a war to destroy the other side."*[7]

This reality imposes its logic on the superpowers. It represents a revolution in the meaning of warfare.[8] As a result, many concepts and understandings derived from conventional warfare have become inappropriate. Efforts to utilize them result in the fallacy of conventionalization.[9] This implies an effort to treat nuclear weapons in business-as-usual terms, as though these weapons merely represented another addition to the arsenals of mankind, or "more bang for the buck," as a phrase of the early 1950s once avowed.

These realities also suggest a lesson for those most committed to nuclear disarmament; it is that effective abandonment of nuclear weapons is a practical impossibility. Despite widespread appeals for the ultimate elimination of nuclear weapons, the nuclear genie will not be shoved back into the bottle. In a partially anarchic international environment, rivalries involving major powers are unlikely to disappear. Moreover, neither of the superpowers will abandon its arsenal and knowledge nor surrender these to some broader international authority. Indeed, even if the United States and Russia were somehow willing to disarm, they would not do so unless certain that all other nuclear weapons states would take the same action. However, the number of countries with nuclear weapons has grown to include not only Britain, France and China, but—at least temporarily—includes three Republics of the former Soviet Union (Ukraine, Belarus, and Kazakhstan), and is believed to include Pakistan, India, and Israel as well. In addition, countries such as North Korea, Iran, Iraq and Libya are said to have ambitious programs aimed at acquiring nuclear weapons capability. The willingness of nuclear states even to contemplate total nuclear disarmament is further reduced by the knowledge that in a hypothetical nuclear-disarmed world, the covert retention of even a handful of warheads could radically alter the balance of military power.

Major increments to strategic nuclear weaponry have limited utility except insofar as they are essential to maintain assured destruction capability and—though this is a difficult matter to specify with precision—to maintain credibility with allies, adversaries, and one's own population. In this sense, possession of more than a minimal deterrent may be important. These same considerations also call for attention to command, control, and communications facilities in an effort to preserve control if deterrence ever breaks down, and thereby maintain the possibility of keeping the war limited.[10]

TABLE 6.1 THE COLD WAR NUCLEAR BALANCE:
United States and Soviet Strategic Nuclear Forces in 1989

	USA		USSR	
	Launchers	Warheads & Bombs	Launchers	Warheads & Bombs
ICBMs	1000	2450	1451	6657
SLBMs	608	6208	942	3806
Long-Range Bombers	360	5872	195	1940
Totals	1968	14,530	2588	12,403

Source: Based on data from International Institute for Strategic Studies, *The Military Balance 1989–1990* (London: Autumn 1989), p. 212. (Warhead figures are based on SALT counting rules.)

Apart from the focus on weapons and hardware, however, it is essential to note severe practical and human limitations on the employment of nuclear forces. Problems of command and control are likely to be acute, and even a limited nuclear war may very quickly escalate out of control. Moreover, the superiority that the United States possessed in strategic nuclear weaponry during the 1950s and early 1960s was not easily converted into political influence. The United States could not, for example, prevent the Soviet Union from crushing the Hungarian revolution with tanks, or deter Castro from adopting a pro-Soviet position in Cuba. Indeed, the surviving members of the Kennedy administration who took part in the deliberations of the "ExCom" of the National Security Council during the October 1962 Cuban missile crisis have maintained that United States' strategic nuclear capability offered little usable leverage on the crisis. Instead, proximity and a preponderance of American conventional forces in the region were thought to have been decisive.[11]

CAN THERE BE MEANINGFUL NUCLEAR SUPERIORITY?

During the Cold War the United States and the Soviet Union confronted one another with large and diverse arsenals of nuclear weapons. Each side possessed advantages in specific categories (see Table 6.1). The Soviets had a larger number of launchers or delivery vehicles (i.e., their combined total of missiles and long-range bombers). They possessed a heavier missile throw-weight and megatonnage, meaning that their strategic missiles were mostly larger and could carry a heavier payload of explosive warheads and penetration aids. The Soviets also had a greater number of land-based intercontinental ballistic missiles (ICBMs) capable of striking the United States, as well as more submarine-launched missiles. Moreover, a number of their ICBMs were mobile rather than based in fixed sites.

The United States had the advantage in several other areas. As a rule, American technology was more advanced and sophisticated than that of the Soviets. This permitted American weapons to attain greater degrees of accuracy. In addition, the United States led in miniaturization, or the ability to achieve greater power and distance in a warhead payload. These attributes of accuracy and miniaturization helped to offset Soviet advantages in throw-weight and megatonnage. In addition, the United States continued to hold a small lead in the number of strategic (i.e., intercontinental) warheads. Moreover, the U.S. held an advantage in the proportion of strategic nuclear warheads that were submarine launched. By the time the Cold War ended in 1989–1990, more than half of Soviet warheads were on land-based ICBMs, with just over 30 percent accounted for by submarines, whereas the United States had less than 17 percent of its force on ICBMs and almost 43 percent at sea. The significance of these numbers lies in their relationship to second-strike capability. Land-based missiles are—at least theoretically—vulnerable to an adversary's first strike. However, American missile submarines at sea could escape instant detection and thus could not be destroyed by surprise attack. As a result, they would be available for retaliatory use in the event of a Soviet first strike against the United States. This was more than sufficient to give the American side a credible deterrent, that is, one that deterred a Soviet attack.

Thus, during the Cold War, although United States and the USSR each held advantages in certain areas, the overall strategic nuclear picture remained one in which neither side had any margin of usable nuclear superiority. Since no more than several hundred strategic warheads, from among the more than 14,500 American and more than 12,400 Soviet warheads, would have sufficed to devastate either side, meaningful superiority was unattainable. These imperatives of the nuclear environment left both sides without a practical alternative to coexistence.

In the aftermath of the Cold War and in view of the momentous changes in Europe and the former Soviet Union, the issue of nuclear superiority is raised in a manner different from that of the last three decades of the Cold War. What do the breakup of the USSR, the large-scale reductions in Russia's armed forces, the economic and social chaos evident during the effort at transition to a market economy, and the planned reductions in nuclear forces under the START II agreement (discussed below) imply for the nuclear balance? Despite the technological gap that Russia faces, it does not need to keep pace with American military technology in order to maintain effective deterrence. As Waltz has noted, "So long as a country can retaliate after being struck, or appears to be able to do so, its nuclear forces cannot be made obsolete by an adversary's technological advances."[12] Given the dynamics of strategic nuclear deterrence, it is thus possible to anticipate a durable nuclear balance so long as the United States develops neither a first-strike capability nor an effective defense against strategic missiles.[13] For the foreseeable future, neither event seems likely.

ARMS CONTROL AND THE SUPERPOWERS

During the latter years of the Cold War, nuclear disarmament—the abandonment of nuclear weapons—became the proclaimed objective of both the United States and the Soviet Union. For example, former President Ronald Reagan stated flatly that, "Our ultimate goal is the complete elimination of nuclear weapons."[14] And a series of Soviet leaders made comparable statements.[15] Yet there is little in the record of human history to suggest that technologies once developed and deployed are ever voluntarily relinquished.[16] Thus, efforts to mitigate the Soviet-American nuclear confrontation focused on the limitation and control of nuclear arms.

The United States and the Control of Nuclear Arms

Consider first the situation of the United States. It originally held nuclear superiority over the Soviet Union. This began with the dawn of the nuclear age and the explosion of the first atomic bombs in 1945. Although the Soviets detonated their first atomic weapon in 1949, the United States maintained a significant lead based on its larger nuclear arsenal, superior delivery systems, and more advanced technology. This American edge permitted Secretary of State John Foster Dulles to announce, in 1954, a policy of "massive retaliation." Rather than attempt to match the Soviets in costly deployment of troops and conventional forces, the United States would reserve the right to retaliate against any Soviet aggression—especially in Western Europe, but globally as well—with its nuclear forces and at times and places of its own choosing.

The dramatic Soviet launching of the first Sputnik earth satellite in October 1957,[17] however, appeared to signal a major strategic transformation. Though American territory had lost its invulnerability by the early to mid 1950s, owing to the assumption that at least some Soviet long-range bombers would be able to reach it in the event of war, the United States had maintained a strategic nuclear superiority in long-range forces able to strike the adversary's homeland. However, as a result of Sputnik, it was widely believed that the Soviets had managed to leap ahead of the United States in the deployment of ICBMs. In fact, as in the case of earlier fears about a "bomber gap," this "missile gap" did not materialize. By 1961 it was clear that the United States continued to possess strategic advantage—in this case both in ICBMs and sea-based SLBMs. The American superiority did not really end until the mid to late 1960s, when the USSR finally attained second-strike capability.

From that time on, the United States and the Soviet Union maintained a rough balance of strategic nuclear power. This was described under a variety of names: parity, balance of terror, essential equivalence, robust deterrence, nuclear balance, mutual assured destruction. The tenacity of this strategic balance tended to impose itself despite the preferences of policymakers. For example, when the Reagan administration took office in January 1981, some of its strategic thinkers questioned the durability of the status quo. A number of them had previously expressed alarm that the Soviet Union might be acquiring a strategic nuclear advantage over the United States. They advocated that urgent steps be taken to redress this shift. Some proponents of the Reagan position argued that—if worse came to worst—America must be able to fight and win a nuclear war. Indeed, the 1980 Republican platform called for the attainment of nuclear superiority by the United States.

Reagan administration strategists initially expressed alarm at the "window of vulnerability" which they—and strategic experts in the latter years of the Carter administration—feared would occur in the early 1980s. It was postulated that, in a worst-case situation, the Soviets would be able to use their landbased ICBMs to mount a successful first strike against America's land-based Minuteman missile force and much of the strategic bomber force as well. This, it was feared, would leave the United States at a serious disadvantage. After such an attack, and with only a fraction of America's lethal and highly accurate ("hard-target kill capability") land-based missiles remaining, possessing less accurate submarine-launched ballistic missiles (SLBMs) and facing an extensive Soviet antiaircraft defense, an American president would be reluctant to order a reprisal attack against Soviet population centers, since the Soviets would then be able to retaliate against U.S. cities with the large number of their own land-based missiles.

There were, however, a series of important counterarguments to these points: major components of America's strategic nuclear force would survive a Soviet nuclear first strike; these forces would include most of the SLBMs, some strategic bombers, and shorter-range weapons deployed on United States aircraft carriers and at bases in England and elsewhere within striking distance of the USSR; and it was by no means certain that the entire American ICBM force could be destroyed in a surprise attack. Even in a worst-case situation the United States would have been able to retaliate and to inflict unacceptable damage on the Soviet Union. More important still, it was exceptionally difficult to imagine circumstances in which the Soviets would have the motivation or would be so reckless as to unleash a nuclear first strike when the accompanying risk of their own destruction remained so compelling.

Ultimately, the Reagan administration revised its original views of the strategic nuclear arms race.[18] For example, the presidentially appointed Scowcroft Commission de-emphasized the "window of vulnerability," and discussion of nuclear superiority and of fighting a nuclear war also diminished, though it was soon replaced by sweeping talk about defensive systems to protect America against strategic nuclear attack.

During its initial four-year term, the Reagan administration was the first since Eisenhower's not to have reached a significant arms control agreement with the Soviet Union. Yet overall constraints shaping the superpower nuclear arms race, coupled with practical experience and political pressures from the domestic political realm as well as from allies, made an American effort at arms control a more prominent part of the United States agenda during the second Reagan administration, as well as in the Bush administration which followed. Thus, in December 1987, the Soviet Union and the United States agreed to eliminate their intermediate-range nuclear missiles,* via the INF Treaty. This was followed by major agreements in November 1990 (the Conventional Forces in Europe Treaty), July 1991 (The Strategic Arms Reduction Treaty, or START I), and January 1993 (START II).

---

*These missiles had ranges of 300–600 and 600–3500 miles, respectively.

The Soviet Union and the Control of Nuclear Arms

Strategic nuclear deterrence has had the effect of constraining the Soviet Union as well as the United States. Following the October 1962 Cuban missile crisis, the Soviet Union launched a major buildup of both its nuclear and conventional forces. This expansion made the USSR a global superpower, with some ability to project forces around the world. Yet the United States continued to maintain a rough overall balance vis-à-vis the USSR. More important, no decisive strategic advantage followed from this increase of Soviet forces. Regardless of aspirations on the part of Marxist-Leninist ideologues for a change in the "correlation of forces," the continuing strategic nuclear deterrence between the superpowers precluded any meaningful shift in the power relationship between the United States and the Soviet Union.

Nor did Soviet weapons buildups bring major advantages in Europe. For example, deployment of Soviet SS-20 intermediate-range missiles targeted against Western Europe did not stimulate "finlandization" nor increased fragmentation within NATO. In fact, the allocation of scarce resources to a costly and long-term program of arms spending imposed enormous burdens on the Soviets themselves. Not only were commitments to military spending made at the expense of investment in agriculture, consumer goods, housing, energy, and other sectors, but there was an unmistakable human cost that Soviet leaders inflicted on their own society.[19]

As a result, the USSR was more willing to contemplate negotiation with the United States on a variety of arms control measures. Under Mikhail Gorbachev, who assumed control in March 1985 after the deaths of three elderly predecessors (Brezhnev, Andropov, and Chernenko) in three years, the Soviets sought to reduce the risks posed by the strategic arms competition and lessen the costs of it.

ARMS CONTROL AGREEMENTS

Numerical reductions in weapons do not by themselves bring about greater stability. The number of strategic nuclear warheads has been so large and the number needed to inflict unacceptable damage so small that reductions per se do not alter the strategic relationship between the superpowers nor greatly lessen the perils to which their populations are exposed. This is not to say that reductions are undesirable: they can be important as symbols, in creating momentum toward further negotiations, and in slowing the pace of strategic arms competition.

The crux of any effort to restrain or mitigate the arms race, however, lies in efforts to provide greater durability to the superpowers' strategic relationship. That is, the test of any efforts and agreements must be whether they enhance the stability of deterrence.

Against the postwar background of Soviet-American relations, the dilemmas of deterrence, and the realities of international relations as a "self-help" system, the superpowers have been involved in a long series of negotiations and agreements aimed at controlling their competition. Two early agreements came in the aftermath of the October 1962 Cuban missile crisis. In 1963, the United States and USSR signed a *Hot Line Agreement,* creating a direct link for communications between their leaders in times of emergency. In the same year, this was followed by the *Limited Test Ban Treaty,* banning atmospheric and outer space testing of nuclear weapons. Britain was also a negotiator of the agreement, and the Treaty was subsequently signed by 116 countries. France and China refused to sign, and at first tested their own weapons in the atmosphere. Eventually, however, they agreed to comply with its provisions without actually becoming signatories.[20]

The later 1960s also saw agreement on an *Outer Space Treaty* (1967), banning placement of nuclear weapons in space or on the moon or other celestrial bodies, and signed by the United States, USSR, United Kingdom and 86 other states; the *Tlatelolco Treaty,* creating a *Latin American Nuclear Free Zone* (1967), and signed by 24 countries of the region plus the five big nuclear powers; and the 1968 *Nuclear Non-Proliferation Treaty,* in which the United States, USSR, United Kingdom, and 133 nonnuclear weapons countries sought to discourage the spread of nuclear weapons, facilitate peaceful uses of nuclear energy, and encourage measures to halt the nuclear arms race.

During the 1970s, the more significant agreements included two major 1972 arrangements. The *SALT I ABM Treaty* (as amended in 1974) limited the United States and USSR to no more than one site for antiballistic missile systems, with a maximum of 100 launchers and missiles. Moreover, it prohibited development, testing, and deployment of systems and components. A companion measure, *The SALT I Interim Agreement,* froze the number of American and Soviet ballistic missiles at 1972 levels for a period of five years. At the end of the decade, in 1979, the governments of the United States and USSR signed the *SALT II Treaty.* The unratified agreement established overall ceilings and sublimits on strategic weapons, including a limit of 1400 strategic delivery vehicles. In 1986, the United States announced that it would no longer be bound by the SALT II limits.

The 1980s saw no major agreements during the first half of the decade, which coincided with a period of sometimes intense confrontation in East-West relations. However, a series of agreements were successfully negotiated during the latter part of the decade. These included a 1987 *Nuclear Risk Reduction Centers Agreement,* in which Washington and Moscow agreed on measures to reduce the risk of accidental war. Much more important, however, was the December 1987 signing of the *INF Treaty.* This agreement required the United States and USSR to destroy all their intermediate range missiles. It was the first agreement that actually eliminated an entire class of nuclear weapons. Moreover, the Treaty included intrusive on-site inspection procedures so that each country could verify compliance on the territory of the other.

Subsequently, in the waning years of the Cold War and in its immediate aftermath, American and Russian leaders reached agreement on two successive START (Strategic Arms Reduction Talks) Treaties, based on a framework established during the latter part of the Reagan administration and embraced on the American side by the Bush and then the Clinton administrations, and in Moscow by Presidents Gorbachev and then Yeltsin. Whereas the SALT agreements had

TABLE 6.2 UNITED STATES AND RUSSIAN STRATEGIC
NUCLEAR WARHEADS BEFORE AND AFTER START II TREATY

	Air-launched	Sea-Launched(SLBM)	ICBM	TOTAL
1990				
U.S.	4,436	5,760	2,450	12,646
USSR	1,596	2,804	6,612	11,012
START I (July 1991 Treaty)				
U.S.	3,700	3,456	1,400	8,556
RUSSIA	1,266	1,744	3,153	6,163
START II (January 1993 Treaty—Reductions for year 2003)				
U.S.	1,272	1,728	500	3,500
RUSSIA	752	1,744	504	3,000

Source: Arms Control Association, Washington, DC, 3 September 1992; see also *New York Times,* 30 December 1992.

the effect of slowing the nuclear arms race, the START agreements called for large decreases in existing levels of strategic nuclear warheads. Thus, the START I Treaty, signed in July 1991, provided for reductions of one-third in the number of American warheads and more than 40 percent on the Soviet side. The Start II Treaty, signed by Presidents Bush and Yeltsin in January 1993, committed the two sides to even more drastic cuts (see Table 6.2), so that over a ten year period, the total of American strategic nuclear warheads would be reduced to 3,500 and Soviet warheads to 3,000.[21]

PROBLEMS OF DETERRENCE

Does the long period of stability in Russian-American nuclear deterrence as well as the pattern of arms control negotiations mean that nuclear deterrence is entirely stable and untroubled? Hardly. There remain moral, military, technical, and political challenges. A review of these is useful because they are likely to remain relevant over the longer term, regardless of the course of events in Moscow and Washington, and because of their relationship to other nuclear weapons states.

The Moral Challenge

First, there exists a cruel logic to a strategic balance that has maintained peace for some four decades but does so by, in effect, holding mass publics as hostages. Not surprisingly, the prospect of slaughtering vast numbers of innocent civilians has given rise to considerable moral objection. This has led to proposals for some kind of alternative to the nuclear deterrent. The moral and theological implications have been wrestled with, for example, in a pastoral letter issued by the American

Catholic bishops. They have adopted the position that nuclear weapons may be retained for deterrence, but their argument implies that the actual use of these weapons would be immoral.[22] Even though MAD may well be inescapable, as long as it exists it is likely to engender deep concern.

Countervailing Strategies and Nuclear War Fighting

Policies for how nuclear weapons would actually be employed have also come into question. At one level, and as an alternative to MAD, it has been argued that the strategy should be to target strictly military sites (missile bases, troop concentrations, weapons plants, communications and transportation facilities, refineries, and command centers) rather than to employ terror attacks on civilian populations.

Prior to the Gorbachev-Yeltsin era, advocates of such a countervailing strategy posed a considerable challenge to deterrence. In their judgment, the United States had to be prepared in the event that deterrence ever broke down. They added that wars have occurred in the past, and that if a nuclear war were to erupt in the future, the United States must be prepared to control the process of nuclear escalation, to achieve "escalation dominance," or even to aim at traditional objectives, that is, "winning."[23]

The response to the countervailing strategy, as well as the controlled nuclear escalation argument, however, is that even a targeting strategy aimed at strictly military sites would kill vast numbers of civilians. In 1980, for example, the U.S. Office of Technology Assessment estimated that a Soviet attack aimed only at Minuteman missile silos would nonetheless kill between 2 and 20 million Americans.[24] A subsequent study concluded that more than 10 million deaths could result from "limited" attacks aimed at industrial or material targets and not at the American population per se.[25] By implication, such a conflict would become very difficult to control. In any case, the debate over attacking military or civilian targets (sometimes described as "counterforce" versus "countervalue") can be overdrawn. In fact, American nuclear targeting had not originally concentrated specifically on Soviet civilian targets. More important, modern societies are not neatly divided into separable civilian and military components. If a major war occurred, the distinction would blur, largely because many military and military-related facilities are so close to cities and concentrations of the civilian population. Because of the high degree of "co-location" of military-industrial sites with United States urban areas, one estimate puts deaths from an attack at only 20 to 30 percent lower than those estimated for a deliberate attack on city centers.[26]

Another critical problem for any doctrine of controlling nuclear war is that loss of control would occur if either side successfully targeted the other's political-military leadership. During the Cold War, some advocates of fighting such a nuclear war suggested that if war occurred the United States should aim to decapitate the Soviet leadership, and with it their ability to rule. Yet it is at least imaginable that if the centralized leadership were destroyed, and no one had the authority to "turn off" the war, a decapitated military would continue the struggle in a desperate and spasmodic form.[27]

Deterrence versus Defense

There are paradoxes of deterrence versus defense.[28] To deter means to dissuade an adversary from taking a particular action, especially the use of force. Ironically, the most deadly weapons ever invented have a principal task that is one of deterrence rather than of use. Deterrence is made more credible by making war more terrible as well as by having second-strike capability. This is meant to leave no doubt in the mind of the adversary about the retaliatory consequences if it ever unleashes a first strike. Yet for deterrence to be *credible,* elaborate steps must be taken to design weapons, delivery systems, military deployments, and command systems so that nuclear forces actually could be used if necessary. Paradoxically, preparations demanded by the logic of deterrence could enhance the possibility of one side or the other ultimately resorting to the use of nuclear weapons, thereby negating the purpose of deterrence itself.

One of the most important challenges to the maintenance of deterrence involves the risk of conflict through escalation. For credibility, deterrence requires the appearance of resolve. The adversary must be convinced that there are matters of national or allied interest so compelling that a country is willing to contemplate nuclear war rather than to see the loss of a value or interest it cherishes. Indeed, throughout the Cold War, NATO strategy for the defense of Western Europe against Soviet conventional forces called for the use of nuclear weapons in the event a Warsaw Pact attack could not be repelled without them. Under those circumstances, a conventional war in Europe, or for that matter in the Middle East, Asia, or elsewhere, had the potential to escalate into a nuclear conflict. In the post–Cold War world, nuclear weapons continue to provide deterrence (though in Europe, the potential threats appear to be remote), and they may do so in Asia as well (for example in discouraging a North Korean attack against South Korea).

Decision Making under Crisis Conditions

Under certain circumstances, crisis behavior by decision-makers can enhance the risks of conflict. A powerful example is the outbreak of war in 1914. World War I had devastating consequences for many of the belligerents, but national leaders were unable to avert the conflict.

In conventional wars, policymakers who initiate conflict have frequently devoted more attention to their own domestic and strategic political situation than to the capabilities and interests of their opponents.[29] An important study suggests that domestic political needs shaped the decisions of the United States in Korea in 1950, of Egypt in initiating the October 1973 Middle East War, and of the Argentine junta and Britain in the Falkland Islands in 1982. While nuclear confrontations pose very different issues from conventional ones, the same studies suggest that irrational confidence can stem from situations in which "signals" are numerous and ambiguous.[30]

Any national leadership faced with the almost unimaginable task of fighting a nuclear war would experience extraordinary problems of judgment, stress, and rationality. Under extreme circumstances, the stakes could become ones not only of national but even of human survival. Yet loss of control—whether through human or technical causes—becomes a critical danger.

Even in small-scale conventional conflicts, there can be loss of control. Military strategists have called attention to the "fog of war,"[31] and chaotic circumstances or loss of communication have often produced unintended and sometimes lethal results. Examples of such cases include the Gulf of Tonkin incident of August 4, 1964; the attack on the USS *Liberty* in June 1967; the *Mayaguez* incident in April 1975; and the shooting down of an Iran Air passenger plane over the Persian Gulf in July 1988. In the first instance, there was uncertainty over whether the second of two North Vietnamese torpedo boat attacks on American destroyers actually occurred. In another case, in June 1967, Israel inadvertently attacked an American surveillance ship off the coast of the Suez peninsula after important communications were delayed or misdirected in both American and Israeli military command systems.[32] In the third instance, United States marines landed on a Cambodian island to rescue American sailors. It was later learned that the sailors had been released a half-hour before the assault, but some three dozen marines lost their lives in the operation. Finally, in the Persian Gulf tragedy, a U.S. naval cruiser, the *Vincennes,* mistakenly shot down Iran Air flight 655 in the belief it was an Iranian F-14 fighter plane. This took place in the aftermath of a clash between the USS *Vincennes* and three Iranian gunboats. All 290 civilians aboard the passenger plane were killed.

Technical Problems of Command and Control

Technical difficulties with command, control, communication, and intelligence (the C^3I problem) have also received considerable attention. One respected study in the early 1980s indicated that if one to five nuclear weapons were exploded high in the atmosphere over the continental United States, the entire country would be subject to intense electromagnetic pulses, possibly disabling all unprotected solid-state military communications. The same author suggested that some 50 nuclear weapons would probably be sufficient "to eliminate the ability to direct U.S. strategic forces to coherent purposes."[33]

The relevance of these problems is twofold. On the one hand, they imply that the ability to manage a nuclear war in a controlled and rational manner is a daunting task. On the other, they represent a potential threat to deterrence, for if it were the case that a preemptive or first-strike nuclear attack carried with it the possibility of preventing the adversary from retaliating (through devastation of command and control systems), the stability of deterrence could be lessened. In reaction to this problem, the United States undertook substantial and costly improvements and hardening of its communication and command systems during the 1980s.

Nuclear Disarmament

There are two major challenges to deterrence, which aim at escaping from it. One of these is nuclear disarmament, the other is strategic defense. As for the first, there is little prospect that the two superpowers, let alone France, Britain, China, and a half-dozen other countries on the threshold of nuclear status, will abandon or forgo a known weapons technology.

Despite the dangers inherent in the nuclear status quo, the nuclear genie is out of the bottle, and the prospect of real nuclear disarmament seems impossibly remote. Nuclear weapons remain a fact of international life—and a peril. The problem thus is how to lessen the chances of their being used, to limit or control the nuclear arms race, and to provide greater stability for deterrence and thereby lessen the likelihood of war.

Strategic Defense

During the early and mid 1980s, the Reagan administration put forward the concept of strategic missile defense. Its 1983 Strategic Defense Initiative (SDI or "Star Wars") sought escape from deterrence by proposing a defensive shield to protect the continental United States against Soviet missiles.[34] In Reagan's words, SDI offered "a way out of the nuclear dilemma that has confounded mankind for four decades."[35] The subject became one of extensive political and strategic debate. Yet, no matter how desirable it might seem to provide a shield for the population of the United States, and thereby to eliminate a catastrophic peril,[36] the capability has not been realistically available. While SDI might ultimately have offered enhanced protection for selected areas (e.g., "point defense" of missile sites), no reliable protection for the bulk of the American people was attainable.

Among the most telling points made by the critics of strategic defense (or ballistic missile defense) were the following: the program did not provide defense against nuclear attack by means other than long-range missiles (bombers, cruise missiles); a deployed system would have to be virtually 100 percent effective to be of any value because even a small number of warheads would still inflict unacceptable damage on the United States; new warheads to overwhelm any defensive system, and other countermeasures, would probably be cheaper and easier to build than the SDI itself, whose cost was likely to be prohibitive.[37]

Although strategic defense continued to receive rhetorical support from governmental officials, Congressional and scientific experts remained skeptical. Indeed, a series of high-ranking former defense officials, including past Chairmen of the Joint Chiefs of Staff and two former Secretaries of Defense, criticized or disparaged the SDI program. While tending to find useful some degree of continued research effort, they—and the mainstream of the scientific community—found little basis on which to anticipate the feasibility of the program and thus to provide a plausible case for actual deployment. Moreover, even some former officials were critical of what a one-time national security advisor to President Reagan described as "romantic and manipulative hyperbole" that had characterized administration efforts to promote SDI.[38]

Some kind of strategic defense ultimately could prove valuable against a missile launched by accident or a very small-scale attack by a country that had recently acquired nuclear weapons. Yet, at the broader strategic level, elements of the SDI could actually be destablizing to the nuclear balance. The risk could occur if one side felt pressured to unleash a first strike in fear that it would lack sufficient force to retaliate effectively against a defensive shield after it had suffered a first strike. By contrast, while disagreeing with unilateral efforts to build strategic defenses, Thomas Schelling has noted:

> I like the notion that East and West have exchanged hostages on a massive scale and that as long as they are unprotected, civilization depends on the avoidance of military aggression that could escalate to nuclear war.[39]

Indeed, even if a workable and affordable population defense somehow could be deployed, it would not offer protection against other kinds of nuclear perils. These could include air- or sea-launched cruise missiles as well as more exotic threats such as the bomb in the suitcase, or the weapon in a ship sailing into an American port. In short, no matter how desirable and how ardently sought after, there is no foreseeable escape from what remains a grim set of risks.

In recognition of the above considerations, the Clinton administration ended the SDI program shortly after coming to office. The previous effort, which had cost $32 billion over a decade, had not produced any antimissile weapons. The administration instead directed that the program and its technologies be refocused on creating an antimissile system with more limited missions. In light of the end of the Cold War, as well as the experience of the Gulf War against Iraq, the program was given the purpose of seeking to defend American forces in the field as well as defending the United States from attack, particularly from a nuclear armed "terrorist state."[40]

PROLIFERATION

Assessments of deterrence have customarily centered on the United States and the Soviet Union. Limited attention was devoted to the other existing nuclear states: Britain, France, and China. For the most part, this was due to the assumption that they were allied to one of the superpowers, that their nuclear arsenals were modest and not likely to affect the overall balance, or (after some initial trepidation concerning China) that none of them were likely to precipitate a nuclear war.

In the aftermath of the Cold War, the essential conceptions of nuclear deterrence continue to remain valid, but the evolving threat of proliferation becomes much more dangerous (see Table 6.3). Although they have not publicly acknowledged it, several additional countries have nuclear weapons capabilities—or the ability to assemble the weapons—in some form. They include India, which exploded a "peaceful" nuclear device in 1974, Pakistan, and Israel. South Africa actually constructed six nuclear weapons in the 1980s, but destroyed them in 1989 before the country moved to end apartheid and establish majority rule.[41]

In addition, the breakup of the Soviet Union has left nuclear weapons in the hands of three republics outside Russia: Ukraine, Kazakhstan, and Belarus. These are nominally under the command of the Commonwealth of Independent States

TABLE 6.3 COUNTRIES WITH NUCLEAR WEAPONS

Declared	Undeclared	Actively Seeking to Develop
United States	India	North Korea
Russia	Pakistan	Iran
Britain	Israel	Iraq
France	....	Libya
China	South Africa**	....
Ukraine*		Argentina***
Belarus*		Brazil***
Kazakhstan*		

*Under unified command of CIS
**Weapons destroyed
***Programs apparently discontinued

(CIS), but Ukraine in particular has sought to use its possession of 176 missiles, 37 long-range bombers and some 1,500 warheads in order to bargain for Western security guarantees, economic aid, and Russian energy supplies. Even if the weapons are not seen as posing a likely danger to neighboring countries, they are cause for concern because they complicate efforts to implement existing arms control agreements such as START I and II, and because of uncertainties over their control.

In addition, at least four other countries have undertaken major efforts to acquire nuclear weapons. These include Iraq, whose program was temporarily destroyed by a preemptive Israeli attack in 1981, then relaunched so that it was within 18 months of success at the time of the 1991 Gulf War. Bombing damage and subsequent UN inspections led to the apparent dismantlement of what had been a vast program, but despite acceptance of UN monitoring, the regime of Saddam Hussein has not relinquished its long-term nuclear ambitions. Iran and Libya have active programs of their own, and their ability to acquire Western technology and equipment in this effort has been a source of friction among the advanced industrial countries. The North Korean nuclear program has been conducted with great secrecy in one of the world's most isolated and reclusive countries, and concerns over the advanced status of its program have led to growing tension in the Korean peninsula and East Asia. Finally, although Brazil and Argentina had begun programs in the 1970s, both are believed to have halted these efforts after democratic governments came to office.

The risks posed by proliferation are serious. They include the possible acquisition of weapons by regimes that are dangerous, aggressive, or unstable; dangers concerning command and control, accidents, or terrorism; the introduction of nuclear weapons in areas of intense conflict where the risk of war is great; the potential instability of deterrence in regional nuclear rivalries where states are unlikely to possess second-strike capability; and the growing availability of missiles and high-performance aircraft, which make these weapons a potential threat to countries thousands of miles away. Indeed, at least 10 developing countries have or are seeking to acquire nuclear weapons, 22 have been at work on chemical or biological weapons, and 25 have acquired ballistic missiles.[42]

Efforts to control proliferation have been under way since at least 1968 and the signing of the NPT. The International Atomic Energy Agency in Vienna (IAEA) conducts inspections of peaceful nuclear programs under the terms of the Treaty, but there are limits to the effectiveness of these efforts when member states are determined to evade detection. This problem is exemplified by the history of the Iraqi program. The regime of Saddam Hussein posed an evident risk of deception and proliferation, yet the IAEA, as a consequence of its institutional weakness, did not give priority to monitoring the Iraqi program to insure that its purposes were peaceful. Indeed, approximately 70 percent of the Agency's budget was used for inspections in Canada, Japan, and Germany, countries that did not pose a proliferation danger.

Remarkably, IAEA inspections prior to the 1990 Gulf crisis failed to detect evidence of Iraq's massive covert effort to acquire nuclear weapons. Not only did this failure provide a veil of legitimacy for Iraq, but it gave IAEA officials a vested institutional interest in defending their assessment of the Iraqi program. For example, not long before Iraq's invasion of Kuwait, the IAEA's safeguards director described Iraq's behavior as "exemplary," adding that fears of Iraq making a bomb from its nuclear fuel did not "make sense."[43] Indeed, even after the Gulf War, the UN-mandated inspection which followed, and the discovery of the vast Iraqi program, a leading IAEA official at one point rushed to Baghdad seeking to convince an inspection team that what they had discovered was not actually what they knew it to be.[44] Yet Iraq itself later admitted that it had secretly produced plutonium while under IAEA safeguards,[45] and the scale of the Iraqi program was then found to have exceeded even the suspicions of many of its most active critics.

By contrast, inspection and monitoring of Iraq's nuclear program after the Gulf War were conducted by a UN Special Commission for the Disarmament of Iraq (UNSCOM), established in April 1991 and operating under the terms of UN Security Resolutions 687 and 715, which required the dismantling of Iraq's weapons of mass destruction. These UN measures were backed by strong international economic sanctions, and in October 1993 the Baghdad government finally announced that it would comply with these requirements. While these efforts seemed to prove effective, they were unique in comparison with previous international nonproliferation efforts.

An example of an important, but less authoritative, effort to control proliferation can be found in the April 1992 agreement by 27 countries to halt the spread of equipment used in making atomic weapons. Prompted in part by experience with Iraq, this agreement received the support of many of the world's leading countries, including the United States, Russia, France, Germany, Britain, Italy, Switzerland, and others—many of whom had been lax in preventing sensitive exports of such equipment in the past.[46] The agreement covered 65 classes of equipment and material with "dual-use" (in the sense of both peaceful and military) applications. The effort was organized by the Nuclear Suppliers Group, a body linking the leading high-technology countries, originally established after the 1974 explosion of a nuclear device by India. Although measures such as these can have some effect in coordinating efforts to restrict the spread of nuclear weapons, they embody many of the characteristic limitations of cooperation among independent states. In this case, the accord is strictly voluntary and contains no provisions for enforcement. Moreover, a number of states that have been important sources of nuclear exports have not signed the agreement. These include China, Argentina, Brazil, Pakistan, and India.[47]

THE FUTURE OF NUCLEAR DETERRENCE

Given the experience of more than four decades of Soviet-American nuclear rivalry, followed by the end of the Cold War, the risk of major powers waging nuclear war against one another appears remote. Indeed, in retrospect, the nuclear stalemate provided an important component of stability during the Cold War era. It is evident, however, that nuclear proliferation poses new risks, and the greater danger may well be of a localized regional conflict involving lesser powers that acquire or use nuclear weapons in the future. In the absence of more effective and binding international measures, such as those adopted after the Gulf War to monitor Iraq's compliance with UN Security Council disarmament resolutions, the long-term prospects of preventing additional proliferation of nuclear weapons are not encouraging.

Deterrence among the acknowledged nuclear powers, however, is likely to continue more or less intact. While there have been significant achievements in the reduction of nuclear arms, the disappearance of these weapons is extremely unlikely.

NOTES

1. Robert Jervis, *The Meaning of the Nuclear Revolution: Statecraft and the Prospect of Armageddon* (Ithaca, NY: Cornell University Press, 1989), p. 1.
2. Kenneth N. Waltz, "The Emerging Structure of International Politics," *International Security*, Vol. 18, No. 2 (Fall 1993): 51.
3. Testimony by James Woolsey, quoted, *Washington Post*, 21 May 1993, p. A25.
4. See John H. Herz, *International Politics in the Atomic Age* (New York: Columbia University Press, 1959), especially his section on "The Security Dilemma in the Atomic Age," pp. 231ff.
5. Bruce Russett, *Trends in World Politics* (New York: Macmillan, 1965), pp. 12–13.
6. For an alternative view, which asserted that the Soviets' historical view gave them a much higher threshold of "acceptable damage," see Richard Pipes, "Why the Soviet Union Thinks It Could Fight and Win a Nuclear War," *Commentary* 64 (July 1977).
7. Robert Jervis, *The Illogic of American Nuclear Strategy* (Ithaca, NY: Cornell University Press, 1984), p. 12. Italics added. Jervis provides an incisive elaboration and updating of concepts originally developed by strategists such as Thomas Schelling, Glenn Snyder,

Bernard Brodie, and James King. Also see Jervis, *The Meaning of the Nuclear Revolution: Statecraft and the Prospect of Armageddon* (Ithaca, NY: Cornell University Press, 1989); and *International Security*, Vol. 13, No. 3 (Winter 1988–1989): 142n, 143n.

8. This concept is developed not only in Jervis, but also in Michael Mandelbaum, *The Nuclear Revolution* (New York: Cambridge University Press, 1983), and especially in Hans J. Morgenthau, "The Four Paradoxes of Nuclear Strategy," *American Political Science Review* 58 (March 1964). It was also set out in the writing of early postwar thinkers such as John Herz and Bernard Brodie.

9. The term "conventionalization" was that of Hans Morgenthau; see "The Four Paradoxes of Nuclear Strategy." See also "The Fallacy of Thinking Conventionally about Nuclear Weapons," in David Carlton and Carlo Schaerf, eds., *Arms Control and Technological Innovation* (New York: Wiley, 1976), pp. 256ff. A lucid application of the concept to subsequent analyses of nuclear strategy can be found in Robert Jervis, *The Illogic of American Nuclear Strategy*, pp. 56–64.

10. The term and the point that follows are cogently set out by Robert Art, in "Between Assured Destruction and Nuclear Victory: The Case for the 'MAD-Plus' Posture," *Ethics* 95 (April 1985): 497–516, at p. 500.

11. See the statements by Robert MacNamara, Dean Rusk, and others, interviewed on the twentieth anniversary of the crisis, *Time,* 27 September 1982, pp. 85–86. Also see the thoughtful analysis by Richard Ned Lebow, "The Cuban Missile Crisis: Reading the Lessons Correctly," *Political Science Quarterly* (Fall 1983): 431–458.

12. Waltz, "The Emerging Structure of International Politics," p. 51.

13. *Ibid*.

14. Press conference, 9 January 1985.

15. For example, Mikhail Gorbachev: "The Soviet Union is preparing a step by step . . . process of ridding the earth of nuclear weapons . . . within the next fifteen years. . . ." Official statement on arms control, provided by Tass, the Soviet news agency, and reprinted in the *New York Times,* 17 January 1986.

16. Poison gas was widely used in World War I, then outlawed by international treaties after the end of the war. For the most part it was not used in World War II against combatants (though Nazi slaughter of noncombatant civilians included methods that were worse, and Japan used poison gas against the Chinese). Poison gas has proved difficult to employ in combat without risking harm to the side using it. However, the weapon has been used on occasion—for example, by the Egyptian army in the Yemen war during the mid 1960s and by Iraq against Iran in the early 1980s. Iraq also used poison gas in 1988, when it killed thousands of Iraqi Kurds at the town of Halabja. See *Amnesty International Report 1989* (New York and London, 1989), pp. 257–260. The United States and the Soviet Union both developed stocks of nerve gas for use in the contingency that the other side resorted to it and more than 20 other countries are believed to possess chemical weapons, including China, India, Pakistan, Iran, Iraq, Libya, and Israel. However, the United States, Russia, and more than 145 countries have signed a January 1993 treaty to ban the production, stockpiling, and use of chemical weapons. This Chemical Weapons Convention (CWC) provides for the destruction of all chemical weapons within ten years of the treaty's entry into force, and it also establishes a system of on-site inspections to verify compliance. See Alan Riding, "Signing of a Chemical Arms Pact Begins," *New York Times,* 14 January 1993, p. A16, and Amy E. Smithson, ed., *The Chemical Weapons Convention Handbook,* (Washington, DC: Henry L. Stimson Center, 1993).

17. See, for example, Raymond Aron's important book, which considered the consequences for European security stemming from the prospect that American territory would be

vulnerable to Soviet nuclear weapons, *The Great Debate* (Garden City, NY: Doubleday, 1961). For a useful overview of the development of American nuclear strategy, see Richard Smoke, *National Security and the Nuclear Dilemma*, 2nd ed., (New York: Random, 1987).

18. For statements of concern about the window of vulnerability, see Paul Nitze and others in Charles Tyroler, ed., *Alerting America: The Papers of the Committee on the Present Danger* (New York: Pergamon-Brassey's International Defense Publishers, 1984), especially pp. 105–107.

19. As one indication, by 1984 the life expectancy of the adult male population of the USSR actually had declined by some four years as compared with figures approximately a decade earlier. On Soviet views of arms control, see Michael Mandelbaum, ed., *The Other Side of the Table: The Soviet Approach to Arms Control* (New York: Council on Foreign Relations, 1990).

20. Details of the major arms control agreements discussed here are based on information provided in the valuable compendium published by the Arms Control Association. See *Arms Control and National Security* (Washington, DC: 1989), pp. 166–168. Two other useful studies of arms control are Albert Carnesale and Richard N. Haass, eds., *Superpower Arms Control: Setting the Record Straight* (Cambridge, MA: Ballinger, 1987); and Morris McCain, *Understanding Arms Control* (New York: Norton, 1989).

21. *New York Times*, 30 December 1992, pp. A1 and A6.

22. National Conference of Catholic Bishops, *The Challenge of Peace: God's Promise and Our Response* (Washington, DC: United States Catholic Conference, 1983). And see the valuable discussion of the issues posed by the bishops' pastoral letter in Judith A. Dwyer, S.S.J., ed., *The Catholic Bishops and Nuclear War: A Critique and Analysis of the Pastoral, the Challenge of Peace* (Washington, DC: Georgetown University Press, 1984). Also see William V. O'Brien and John Langan, eds., *The Nuclear Dilemma and the Just War Tradition* (Lexington, MA: Lexington Books, 1986); and Joseph S. Nye, *Nuclear Ethics* (New York: Free Press, 1988).

23. Colin Gray, "Nuclear Strategy: A Case for a Theory of Victory," *International Security* 4 (Summer 1979). Gray's article, and a number of others providing a range of views on problems of nuclear deterrence, are reprinted in Steven E. Miller, ed., *Strategy and Nuclear Deterrence* (Princeton: Princeton University Press, 1984). See also Spurgeon M. Keeny, Jr., and Wolfgang Panofsky, "MAD versus NUTS: Can Doctrine or Weaponry Remedy the Mutual Hostage Relationship of the Superpowers?" *Foreign Affairs* 60 (Winter 1981/82).

24. Congress of the United States, Office of Technology Assessment, *The Effects of Nuclear War* (Totowa, NJ: Allanheld, Osmun and Croom Helm Publishers, 1980).

25. William Daugherty, Barbara Levi, and Frank von Hippel, "The Consequences of 'Limited' Nuclear Attacks on the United States," *International Security* 10 (Spring 1986): 4. Note, however, a 1987 study by the Federal Emergency Management Agency estimating that more than 111 million Americans live in areas that in a nuclear war would probably be hit by direct atomic blasts; they would be likely to die immediately. See *New York Times*, 4 June 1987.

26. Daugherty et al., p. 25.

27. For a fictional treatment of this problem, see William Prochnau, *Trinity's Child* (New York: G. P. Putnam's Sons, 1983).

28. Glenn H. Snyder, *Deterrence and Defense: Toward a Theory of National Security* (Princeton: Princeton University Press, 1961).

29. Richard Ned Lebow, "Deterrence Reconsidered: The Challenge of Recent Research," *Survival* 27 (January/February 1985): 20–29, at p. 26.

30. Lebow, p. 27. For a view contending that military forces are not designed for signaling, see Samuel P. Huntington, "Playing to Win," *The National Interest,* no. 3 (Spring 1986): 8–16.

31. See B. H. Liddell Hart, *Through the Fog of War* (New York: Random, 1938).

32. There are studies of these cases. One of the most compelling is on the *Liberty* incident. See Hirsh Goodman and Zeev Schiff, "The Attack on the *Liberty,*" *Atlantic Monthly,* (September 1984): 78–84.

33. See John D. Steinbruner, "The Great Strategic Debate: Nuclear Decapitation," *Foreign Policy* 45 (Winter 1981–1982): 16–28, at pp. 18 and 26. Also Desmond Ball, *Can Nuclear War Be Controlled?* Adelphi Paper No. 169 (London: International Institute for Strategic Studies, Autumn 1981); Kurt Gottfried and Bruce Blair, *Crisis Stability and Nuclear War* (New York: Oxford University Press, 1988); and Paul Bracken, *The Command and Control of Nuclear Forces* (New Haven: Yale University Press, 1983).

34. In addition to the presidential statement of 23 March 1983, see the statement by the director of the SDI organization, Lt. Gen. James Abrahamson, to the Sub-committee on Defense of the Appropriations Committee, U.S. House of Representatives, 9 May 1984. Also see the statement on "The President's Strategic Defense Initiative" (Washington, DC: U.S. Government Printing Office, 3 January 1985). Both documents are excerpted in *Survival* 27 (March/April 1985): 75–83. In addition, a brief descriptive overview can be found in U.S. Department of State, Bureau of Public Affairs, Special Report No. 129, "The Strategic Defense Initiative" (Washington, DC: June 1985).

35. Speech to the Republican party of California, 22 August 1985, quoted in the *New York Times,* 23 August 1985, p. 1.

36. For strong advocacies of the program, see Colin S. Gray, "A Case for Strategic Defense," *Survival* (March/April 1985): 34–50; Keith Payne and Colin S. Gray, "Nuclear Policy and the Defense Transition," *Foreign Affairs* 62 (Spring 1984): 820–842; Fred S. Hoffmann, Study Director, *Ballistic Missile Defense and U.S. National Security: Summary Report* (Washington, DC: Future Security Strategy Study, October 1983); and Fred S. Hoffmann, "The SDI in U.S. Nuclear Strategy," *International Security* 10 (Summer 1985): 13–24.

37. Among the more important critiques, see Hans A. Bethe *et al.,* letter to the *Wall Street Journal,* 2 January 1985; Harold Brown, "The Strategic Defense Initiative: Defensive Systems and the Strategic Debate," *Survival* (March/April 1985): 55–64; Lawrence Freedman, "The 'Star Wars' Debate: The Western Alliance and Strategic Defense: Part II," Adelphi Papers No. 199 (London: International Institute for Strategic Studies, Summer 1985), pp. 34–50; Sidney Drell, Philip J. Farley, and David Holloway, "Preserving the ABM Treaty: A Critique of the Reagan Strategic Defense Initiative," *International Security* 9 (Fall 1984): 51–91; Sidney Drell and Wolfgang Panofsky, "The Case Against Strategic Defense: Technical and Strategic Realities," *Issues in Science and Technology* (Fall 1984): 45–65; Charles L. Glaser, "Do We Want the Missile Defenses We Can Build?" *International Security* 10 (Summer 1985): 25–57; and Samuel F. Wells, Jr., and Robert S. Litwak, eds., *Strategic Defenses and Soviet-American Relations* (Cambridge, MA: Ballinger, 1987).

38. Robert C. McFarlane, quoted in the *Washington Post,* 18 February, 1990, p. A18. Criticism also came from former Secretaries of Defense, Harold Brown and James Schlesinger, and from former Chairmen of the Joint Chiefs of Staff, including General David C. Jones and Admiral William J. Crowe (chairman from 1985 to 1989).

39. Thomas C. Schelling, "What Went Wrong with Arms Control," *Foreign Affairs* 64 (Winter 1985/86): 219–233, at p. 233.

40. Announcement by Defense Secretary Les Aspin, in *Washington Post,* 14 May 1993, pp. A1 and A18.

41. *New York Times,* 23 March 1993, pp. A1 and A12.
42. Estimate by U.S. intelligence sources, cited in *Washington Post,* 21 June 1992, p. A20. Also see CIA Director James Woolsey's assessment, *Washington Post,* 21 May 1993, counting a dozen countries with missiles and 25 with chemical, biological, or nuclear programs.
43. Jennifer Scarlott, "Nuclear Proliferation After the Cold War," *World Policy Journal* (Fall 1991): 691.
44. Author's interview on 20 April 1992, with a scientist from the Lawrence Livermore National Laboratory, who served as a leader of one of the UN nuclear inspection teams. Also see Lieber, "Existential Realism After the Cold War," *The Washington Quarterly,* (Winter 1993): 166.
45. *New York Times,* 6 August 1991, p. A1.
46. A detailed list of countries whose private companies or even governments provided technology and equipment to Iraq's nuclear and missile programs before the 1991 Gulf War has been compiled by Gary Milholin and Diana L. Edensword of the Wisconsin Project on Nuclear Arms Control. The countries are listed in Douglas Jehl, "Who Armed Iraq," *New York Times,* 18 July 1993, p. E5.
47. *New York Times,* 18 July 1992.

PART 3

Watersheds in Twentieth-Century International Relations

chapter 7

Interpretations of the Past: 1914 Versus 1938

You will be home before the leaves have fallen from the trees.
—KAISER WILHELM II, TO DEPARTING GERMAN TROOPS
IN THE FIRST WEEK OF AUGUST, 1914[1]

World War I "lies like a band of scorched earth" across modern history, dividing what came before from what came after.
—BARBARA TUCHMAN[2]

My good friends . . . there has come back from Germany to Downing Street peace with honor. I believe it is peace for our time.
—BRITISH PRIME MINISTER NEVILLE CHAMBERLAIN,
AFTER THE MUNICH AGREEMENT WITH HITLER, ADDRESSING A CROWD
OUTSIDE HIS LONDON RESIDENCE, OCTOBER 1, 1938[3]

You tell us that the situation today is like 1914, when the world was falling into a war it did not want but could not stop. . . .

That is not true. Your Majesty, we are today in a period like the 1930s, when a madman decided to annex his neighbors and the world did nothing. That led to World War II.
—SAUDI AMBASSADOR BANDAR BIN SULTAN AL-SAUD,
TO KING HUSSEIN OF JORDAN, ASSESSING IRAQ'S INVASION OF KUWAIT[4]

In an era of intercontinental ballistic missiles and nuclear weaponry, of global interdependence and North-South conflict, why recall the origins of two wars fought with conventional arms and touched off by events largely confined to the heart of Europe?

The answer is that both the outbreak of World War I in August 1914 and the appeasement of Hitler by Britain and France in the Munich agreement of October 1938 (which destroyed Czechoslovakia and paved the way for World War II) stand as watersheds in twentieth-century world politics.

Succeeding generations of foreign policy decision-makers find their understanding of international relations shaped by both their own experiences and those of their predecessors. Landmark events etch themselves into the consciousness of those who make and interpret foreign policy, and of the societies from which they come. Among other experiences widely cited as watersheds in this century are the Russian Revolution of 1917; the Great Depression of the 1930s; the rise of nazism, culminating in World War II, with its appalling carnage and genocide; Stalinism and the Soviet "Gulag"; the onset of the Cold War; decolonization of the developing world; the Cuban missile crisis of October 1962; the Vietnam War; the energy crisis of the 1970s; and the end of the Cold War in 1989–1990.

Each of these occurrences possesses an importance far beyond its dramatic details. Events such as those of 1914 and 1938 can also influence how countries respond to new experiences. Statesmen regard the present from the perspective of the past. To understand the flow of contemporary events, observers and policy-makers inevitably rely on screening devices to help them make sense of a complex reality. Previous experiences, and the understandings these seem to convey, help us to filter a torrent of information, thus deciding which facts and events to emphasize and which to minimize or ignore. In this regard, Ernest R. May makes three related points about the uses of history: first, that "framers of foreign policy are often influenced by beliefs about what history teaches or portends"; second, that "policy-makers ordinarily use history badly"; and third, that "policy-makers can, if they will, use history more discriminately."[5]

Consider, for example, President Harry S Truman's June 1950 decision to commit American troops to the defense of South Korea. From accounts by key participants, including Truman himself, it appears that memories of the Western democracies' failure to resist Nazi and Japanese aggression during the 1930s played an important role in shaping Truman's response. In Truman's own words, as he weighed the American response to North Korea's attack:

> In my generation, this was not the first occasion when the strong had attacked the weak. I recalled some earlier instances: Manchuria, Ethiopia, Austria. I remembered how each time that the democracies failed to act it had encouraged the aggressors to keep going ahead. Communism was acting in Korea just as Hitler, Mussolini, and the Japanese had acted ten, fifteen and twenty years earlier. . . . If this was allowed to go unchallenged it would mean a third world war, just as similar incidents had brought on a second world war.[6]

A decade later, President John F. Kennedy's actions in the Cuban missile crisis were conditioned in part by his explicit concern to avoid a 1914-style escalation of events beyond the control of himself and Soviet leader Nikita Khrushchev. By contrast, President Lyndon Johnson's initial response to the Vietnam conflict, like Truman's to Korea, was shaped by memories of the 1930s and appeasement.

In the late 1970s and early 1980s, the responses of some American observers were again shaped by reference to the years prior to World War II. In this case, a series of reversals for the United States (the collapse in Vietnam, the energy shocks of 1973–1974 and 1979–1980, the fall of the Shah of Iran), and assertive Soviet actions (expansion of military power, intervention in Ethiopia, Angola, and Afghanistan) stimulated warnings of a dangerous shift in world power (the "correlation of forces")[7] suggestive of Germany's rise during the 1930s. These observers also pointed to what they regarded as an insufficiently resolute Western (especially European) response to international crises as reminiscent of appeasement nearly a half-century earlier.[8]

More recently, after Saddam Hussein's August 1990 invasion and occupation of Kuwait, American President George Bush reacted by invoking comparisons with the aggressive actions of Adolph Hitler:

> Czechoslovakia, they know first-hand about the folly of appeasement. They know about the tyranny of dictatorial conquests. And in the World War that followed, the world paid dearly for appeasing an aggressor who should and could have been stopped. We're not going to make that mistake again. We will not appease this aggressor.[9]

In order to judge the applicability of the World War I and II analogies, it is thus essential to consider each of these experiences in more detail.

1914 AND THE OUTBREAK OF WORLD WAR I

The world of 1914 had experienced rising tension between the major powers of the day. Three of them, France, Russia, and England, became allied through the Triple Entente. The others—Germany, Austria-Hungary, and, more loosely, Italy—were joined in the Triple Alliance.

Although European countries had been embroiled in lesser wars, for example between Austria and Prussia (1866), Prussia and France (1870), Russia and Turkey (1877), Britain and South Africa (1899–1902), Russia and Japan (1904–1905), and in the Balkans (1912–1913), there had been no massive general conflict on the continent since the end of the Napoleonic Wars in 1815. There was, however, no shortage of rivalries and of maneuvering for power and position among the powers. The race to control sub-Saharan Africa had absorbed considerable European energies during the last two decades of the nineteenth century. The closing of this colonial frontier after 1900 (by which time virtually the entire African continent had fallen under European control) was followed by growing tensions and arms races within Europe itself. One of the most dangerous areas lay in southeastern Europe, where the decline of the Turkish Ottoman Empire left a potentially explosive power vacuum in the Balkans.

The Rigidifying Balance of Power

Some historians and analysts of this period focus on the unique personalities—and extraordinary weaknesses and idiosyncrasies—of the statesmen involved. One account, for example, depicts Germany's Kaiser Wilhelm as a "moody man with a mercurial temper"; Emperor Franz Joseph of Austria-Hungary as an "exhausted old man"; and Czar Nicholas II of Russia as the "epitome of apathy and indifference in matters of public policy."[10] Yet it was the international environment in which these men and their governments acted that created the explosive conditions for war to occur. During the decade before 1914, the balance of power in Europe had rigidified. The key players found themselves locked into increasingly static alignments. Moreover, the problems of coping with growing German economic and military power caused Britain to commit herself to the side of France after 1909. This meant that the British could no longer play the role of balancer.

In the past, whenever a European power had seemed to threaten domination of the continent, Britain had thrown her weight behind those opposing this threat. In previous centuries, this challenge had been posed by Spain and then France. Now, however, the weight of an ascendant Germany could barely be offset, even with Britain's commitment to the role of counterbalance.

Illustratively, from 1890 to 1914, Germany's population had risen from 49 million to 65 million, an increase of 32.7 percent. This was almost double the rate of growth experienced by Britain, and it contrasted even more sharply with France, whose population had remained nearly static (see Table 7.1).

More important, in the generation from 1880 to 1913, Germany underwent spectacular industrial growth. In 1880, its share of world manufacturing production had stood at just 8.5 percent—a level only slightly above that of France and little more than one-third that of Britain. By 1913, however, Germany had far outdistanced France, and its figure of 14.8 percent even exceeded that of England, at 13.6 percent (see Table 7.2).

An even more portentous set of changes was occurring outside Western and Central Europe. From 1890 to 1914, the populations of both the United States and Russia had risen by some 55 percent—a rate well above that of the leading European countries. From 1890 to 1913, America's share of world manufacturing grew from barely half that of Britain to a position of world ascendancy. With 32 percent of the entire world's production, the United States now accounted for more than double the *combined* output of Europe's two leading powers, Germany and Britain. The implications of this shift would only become fully apparent after the Europeans had bled themselves on the field of battle.

The Schlieffen Plan

As the rivalries for power and primacy among Europe's leading countries became more intense, national military leaders began to prepare contingency plans for use in the event that war were to break out. The most elaborate of these was developed by Germany's General Staff. Ultimately, it was to become another factor creating conditions for a European explosion in 1914. Completed in 1906, the design had been prepared by Count Alfred von Schlieffen. The Schlieffen Plan

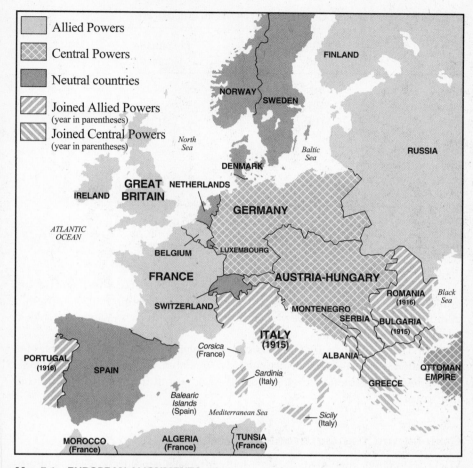

Map 7.1 EUROPEAN ALIGNMENTS, 1914
Source: Gary B. Nash and Julie R. Jeffrey, et al. (eds.) *The American People,* 3rd ed. (New York: Harper-Collins, 1994), p. 749.

sought to overcome the menace of a grinding two-front war. It was designed to forestall a long, deadly conflict, in which Germany would face protracted struggle against her two principal adversaries, France and Russia.

The Schlieffen Plan called for a temporary holding action in the East, using no more than one-eighth of German forces against the huge but ponderous and more slowly mobilized forces of czarist Russia. In the meantime, the full weight of German offensive power would be rapidly mobilized, then thrown against France in a swift advance. The right wing of the German armies would sweep through (neutral) Belgium, brush the Channel coast, envelop and crush the flanks of the French army, and—having lured the French into a lunge toward their lost border territory of Alsace-Lorraine—wheel around to take Paris from the north. In six weeks the war would be over, with France decisively beaten, as at the Battle of Sedan in 1870.

Table 7.1 POPULATION OF THE GREAT POWERS (MILLIONS)

	1890	1914	Percentage Increase
Britain	38	45	18.4
France	38	39	2.6
Russia	110	171	55.4
Germany	49	65	32.7
Italy	30	37	23.3
Austria-Hungary	41	52	26.8
United States	63	98	55.6
Japan	40	55	37.5

Source: Author's percentage calculations, from data in Quincy Wright, *A Study of War*, 2nd ed. (Chicago & London: University of Chicago Press, 1965), pp. 670–671, as cited in Paul M. Kennedy, "The First World War and the International Power System," *International Security* 9 (Summer 1984): 10.

Having defeated France, Germany could then turn the full might of her armies against Russia. The czar's forces would be beaten within four months, thus ending the war well before the weight of British seapower and a maritime blockade could take full effect.[11]

For years, German forces practiced and planned based on the Schlieffen Plan. Railroad timetables were meticulously calculated, and everything was staked on the fastest possible mobilization for full-scale war at the very instant the conflict began.

Beliefs and the Outbreak of War

While systemic factors created increasingly explosive conditions, a series of attitudes and beliefs accelerated the slide toward war as well. Perhaps the most insidious of these was a misplaced application of the ideas of Charles Darwin. In the late nineteenth century, Darwin's hypotheses about nature, including natural selection and the survival of the fittest, were transposed from the realm of evolution and the plant and animal kingdoms to the affairs of states. "Social Darwinism," together with the grandiose philosophical conceptions of theorists such as Hegel, were used by some to suggest that war was a biological necessity and that there were epochs in human history in which the dominance of a particular civilization—namely Germany—was destined to occur.

For example, the German general von Bernhardi published a book in 1911, *Germany and the Next War*, which stridently propounded these ideas. In this influential volume, he maintained that war was the "natural law upon which all the laws of nature rest, the law of the struggle for existence." Germany, he argued, needed to choose "world power or downfall"; and "conquest thus becomes a law of necessity."[12]

Other beliefs, too, shaped popular and governmental outlooks toward war. German leaders and strategists widely—and probably erroneously—believed that

Table 7.2 PERCENTAGE SHARE
OF WORLD MANUFACTURING PRODUCTION

	1880	1913	Change in Percentage Share 1880–1913
Britain	22.9	13.6	−9.3
France	7.8	6.1	−1.7
Russia	7.6	8.2	+0.6
Germany	8.5	14.8	+6.3
Austria-Hungary	4.4	4.4	—
Italy	2.5	2.4	−0.1
Japan	2.4	2.7	+0.3
United States	14.7	32.0	+17.3

Source: Author's percentage calculations from data in Paul Bairoch, "International IIndustrialization Levels from 1750 to 1980," *Journal of European Economic History* 11 (Spring 1982): 297, as cited in Paul M. Kennedy, "The First World War and the International Power System," *International Security* 9 (Summer 1984): 12

time was working against their country and feared that the passage of years would allow the Slavic Russia of the czars to complete a massive military buildup that would present a mortal peril. Meanwhile, the rulers of Austria-Hungary feared that rising nationalism could tear their multinational empire apart. In the summer of 1914 they would conclude that war against Serbia was required to counteract these forces.

Europe had not experienced a general conflagration for almost a hundred years. Throughout the continent, particularly in popular and often crudely written newspapers and cheap novels aimed at newly literate mass publics, combat and warfare were romanticized with an aura of drama and excitement that gave meaning and purpose to otherwise mundane lives.

More specific notions about war also contributed to the general climate of opinion. In defiance of the lessons of the American Civil War and of subsequent conflicts, such as the Russo-Japanese War of 1904–1905, strategists and military leaders throughout Europe for the most part minimized the impact of industrialization and technology on modern warfare. The chief exception, however, was the railway, which offered a means of rapid and intensive mobilization. Overlooking the devastating effects of the machine gun, heavy artillery, and barbed wire, France's chief of staff, General Joffre, could declare that the French army "no longer knows any other law than the offensive. . . . Any other conception ought to be rejected as contrary to the very nature of war."[13]

To this "cult of the offensive," which suggested that any conflict would be sharp but short, were added the ideas of economists. In a widely cited work, *The Grand Illusion*, written in 1910, Norman Angell asserted that the costs of a protracted modern war would be far too great for countries to bear. As a result, the British author concluded that any such conflict would necessarily be brief.

Offensive military doctrines were, however, not only a product of beliefs and expansionist war aims. As Scott Sagan has noted, they also resulted from the need of each of the major states to protect an exposed ally:

> Thus, the Russians needed an offensive capability against Austria-Hungary, in order to be able to prevent the Austrians from attacking Serbia with overwhelming offensive superiority. The French required offensive capabilities against Germany in order to support Russia. Germany needed an offense to protect Austria-Hungary if Russia launched an attack against Germany's ally.[14]

The Onset of War

By 1914 Europe had already experienced a number of war scares. The major powers were heavily armed, arrayed against each other in competing alliances, and fortified with beliefs about the inevitability of war. Their strategic conceptions assumed the supremacy of the offense and the need for rapid mobilization in the event that war was about to begin, lest their opponents gain dangerous, even fatal, advantage. This perilous environment was further exacerbated by the existence of decrepit multinational empires, undergoing challenges from growing nationalism among their subject peoples. Among these were not only the decaying Ottoman Empire and the Russia of the czars, but above all the faltering Austro-Hungarian monarchy whose hold on large areas of Eastern Europe and the Balkans had become increasingly fragile.

In this geopolitical tinderbox, on June 28, 1914, the dramatic assassination of the heir to the Austrian throne, the Archduke Francis Ferdinand, provided the spark. The murder took place at Sarajevo in Bosnia (then part of the Austrian Empire) and was carried out by a secret society of Serbian nationalists. Feeding on ferocious regional and ethnic rivalries (which even then seemed obsure to most Europeans), it triggered a deadly escalation.

Austria-Hungary, having been given political support and encouragement by her much more powerful ally, Germany, sought revenge against Serbia. On July 23, she delivered an ultimatum demanding political subjugation on the part of the Serbs. Three days later, despite Serbia's nearly complete capitulation, Austria rejected the response. On July 28, Austria declared war against Serbia and the next day shelled its capitol, Belgrade. Alliances now sucked the great powers into what had been a regional conflict. Russia, as Serbia's ally, declared partial mobilization on July 29 in an effort to force the Austrians to back down. The following day, both Russia and Austria-Hungary moved to full-scale mobilization of their armies. The Germans, in turn, began mobilization on July 31 and issued ultimatums to both Russia and France.

The German ultimatum to Russia called for the latter's demobilization. From France, the Kaiser demanded neutrality and the handing over of French border fortifications. With the expiration of the ultimatum to Russia, the Kaiser decreed general mobilization and war against Russia on August 1. And when France refused to agree to Germany's demands, particularly for neutrality, Germany declared war against France on August 3. In conformity with the discipline of the Schlieffen Plan, some 10,000 trains began moving two million German soldiers into position. German forces plunged into Belgium. In so doing, they rejected a British demand that the neutrality of Belgium be respected. In consequence, and as a result of their commitments to France, the British entered the war on August 4.

The final days of July had seen a frantic scramble within and among the European capitals, as national leaders sought ways to avoid general war. But the last-minute doubts of the Kaiser, the Czar, and their counterparts in Paris, London, and Vienna were overtaken by the onrush of events. Amid the chaos, both a sense of foreboding and an epitaph for the old European order were expressed by the British foreign secretary, Sir Edward Grey: "The lamps are going out all over Europe; we shall not see them lit again in our lifetime."

The Lessons of 1914

World War I left an indelible imprint on the twentieth-century world. Some of its lessons were immediate and clear-cut, others contradictory. Perhaps the most enduring lessons concern the risks of escalation and the consequences of unexpected events. Despite their antagonisms, alliances, and some bellicose policies, and as incredible as it may seem, it is doubtful that any of the European rivals had consciously planned to initiate a world war in August 1914—and certainly not a conflict that would last more than four bloody years, inflicting unimaginable casualties and social and political upheaval. Yet the pattern of their relations, the character of their armed forces and mobilization plans, and the onrush of events ignited a short and rapidly burning fuse that none could extinguish in time.[15]

The role of the unexpected proved equally dramatic. Among the most central elements was the unraveling of the Schlieffen Plan.[16] To begin with, though hopelessly overpowered, the Belgians fought rather than surrendering. In doing so, they briefly delayed the schedule of the German offensive and—given the German violation of their neutrality and its impact on British domestic politics—thus insured Britain's immediate entry into the war.

The Schlieffen Plan was ultimately undone, in substantial part, by events in Berlin. The original design had called for a holding action in the East while German forces delivered a knockout blow against France in the West. However, the menace of Russian forces to East Prussia caused widespread anxiety among the Junkers (the aristocratic political and military elite of Germany). Many of their ancestral estates lay in the path of the likely Russian advance. Their outcry over this looming threat finally succeeded in pressuring the Kaiser to override his military command and order the transfer of two German army corps from the Western front to the East. By doing so, he fatally weakened the crucial right flank of the German forces as they swept into northeastern France. Though they achieved huge advances, the overextended and fatigued armies of the Kaiser were ultimately stopped by the French at the Battle of the Marne on September 7–11. In turn the Germans, who had plunged to within 35 miles of Paris, were thrown back. As a final irony, this most critical battle of the war took place while German troops being transferred to the East were still in transit. In the meantime, before reinforcements arrived, existing German forces succeeded in defeating the Russians at the Battle of Tannenberg.

Within weeks, fighting on the Western front had stabilized in trench warfare stretching through northern and eastern France, from the English Channel to the Swiss border. Germany thus found itself facing exactly the two-front war its strategists had struggled to avoid and for which they had insisted on early mobilization and attack. This bloody and largely inconclusive fighting would drag on for more than four years, as strategies of attrition replaced the cult of the offensive. Battles would be fought at places such as Ypres, Passchendaele, and the Somme, with tens of thousands of men killed in a single day, often for gains measured in a few hundred yards or less. The most memorable of these clashes took place at Verdun, where in four months during 1916 the French repelled a furious German onslaught against a key fortress—at a cost of more than 800,000 dead on the two sides.

Nor were escalation, the role of the unexpected, and the overwhelming onrush of events the only major lessons. The risks posed by a decaying empire, as it lashed out to preserve itself from disintegration, also remain noteworthy. So, too, do the dangers of a regional war acting to trigger a major conflict among the great powers of the day. The explosive consequences of Balkan rivalries in a European backwater—and not directly involving Germany, France, or Britain—ultimately led to the slaughter of a generation of Germans, Frenchmen, and Britons on battlefields a thousand miles distant.

Ambiguous Lessons

Other lessons of 1914 remain less clear. One of these concerns the problem of status quo powers accommodating the growing power of another state. Some have suggested that the war might have been averted if ways had been found to grant enhanced power and recognition to imperial Germany as it gained strength in the decades after German unification in 1870. Others draw a contrasting lesson and find the origins of the war less in escalation and miscalculation than in an aggressive German drive for world power. This is the argument, for example, of the distinguished German historian, Fritz Fischer, who identifies expansionist German war aims as fundamental to our comprehension of this period.[17] Fischer notes the impact of domestic problems in motivating German leaders to follow aggressive policies. He emphasizes the plans of the German chancellor, Bethmann-Hollweg, to gain territory in Europe and to seize colonies elsewhere, as well as the desire of political leaders to seek a confrontation with Germany's adversaries. Other authors have emphasized a willingness for war on the part of the German General Staff.[18]

Indeed, not only is there compelling evidence that the leaders of Germany and Austria-Hungary possessed a "strike now better than later" outlook in the summer of 1914, accepting the risk of a wider European conflict to enhance German hegemony, but also that the German governmental bureaucracy subsequently mounted a largely successful campaign of disinformation to manipulate opinion concerning the origins of the war. This effort—pursued into the mid

1920s—even included measures affecting the treatment of the subject by German and American historians.[19]

Another widely debated question concerns the role of Britain and the importance of signaling clearly to ally and adversary alike. Some have argued that a less ambiguous commitment by the British government to intervene in the event of war might have caused Germany to adopt a more cautious position and Germany would likely have been deterred in 1914 had London issued a "clear and credible threat" to intervene early in the crisis.[20] Others, however, note that the Schlieffen Plan expressly aimed at France's defeat before the full weight of British seapower could be brought to bear. They also point to a July 1911 meeting between General Joseph Joffre, France's chief of staff, and General Sir Henry Wilson, director of military operations in Britain's War Office, at which contingency planning for the commitment of British forces had been agreed on. A year earlier, in a previous meeting between the two men, when asked what kind of tangible sign of Britain's engagement France would require, Joffre had replied: "A single British soldier, and we will see to it that he is killed." The remark also illustrates the effect that the scale of twentieth-century warfare has had since then on matters of credibility and alliance commitment. Half a century later, a comparable guarantee of American participation in the NATO defense of Western Europe would come to require not one, but 300,000 men.

Finally, questions remain about the relationship between offensive and defensive forces in wartime. A number of authors have dissected the widespread—and erroneous—belief of the time in the supremacy of the offensive. This not only shaped each side's requirement for urgent mobilization and the desire to take the offensive at the earliest available point; it also led to almost unimaginable carnage on the battlefield. Moreover, British and French attachment to this lesson, not only on the part of generals prone to refighting the "last" war, was to have disastrous consequences in the years preceding World War II.

APPEASEMENT AND THE ORIGINS OF WORLD WAR II

During the mid to late 1930s, Nazi Germany, Italy (under the Fascist dictatorship of Mussolini), and Japan sharply increased their military power and carried out policies of expansion at the expense of their neighbors. Meanwhile, the other major powers of the time failed to act decisively and in common against this growing threat. The United States maintained a largely isolationist policy, while France and Britain vacillated between accommodation and resistance. Russia, meanwhile, remained largely aloof, in a climate of mutual suspicion.

With some exceptions, the record of this period is one of indecision and appeasement of the accelerating demands of the Axis powers. The process culminated with the disastrous Munich agreement of September 30, 1938, whereby Britain and France agreed to the demands of Hitler. In an effort to keep the peace, they abandoned Czechoslovakia. However, Munich did not provide "peace for our time." Instead it signaled a demoralizing reversal for the Allies and a major conquest for Nazi Germany on the path toward World War II. Indeed, when war did come, on September 1, 1939, it did so amid conditions more perilous for the Western democracies than had existed a year earlier.

The Legacy of World War I

The trauma of the 1914–1918 war profoundly affected the climate of the 1920s and 1930s. It was widely assumed, particularly in Britain, that "the Great War" could have been averted had the parties been less ready to mobilize and do battle and more prepared for careful diplomacy. This made them reluctant to issue firm warnings or threats. In addition, British military leaders examining the recent war drew the lesson that the defense had predominated over the offense. They assumed that any future conflict would present a similar pattern, and thus they and political leaders saw less need for a more assertive military posture.[21]

The fearsome human cost of World War I was demoralizing. Throughout much of Europe, there was a sense that the war had been fought for nothing. There was also widespread popular belief that the slide toward war had been accelerated by the arms merchants, who profited from defense buildups and arms races. These feelings contributed to strong antiwar and pacifist sentiment, especially in Britain.

Beyond the level of the individual states, diplomatic and geopolitical factors shaped the post–World War I climate. The aftermath of the war and the Versailles treaty brought about the creation of a bloc of new states in Eastern Europe. Caught between their far stronger neighbors, Germany and Russia, most of them were weak, politically unstable, and frequently torn by deep ethnic rifts. For a time, there was hope that the security of these countries, and indeed the peace in Europe, could be kept by means of the new League of Nations. Collective security, in which the League's members would cooperate against any threat to the peace, was also meant to take the place of the alliances whose existence had helped to trigger the guns of August in 1914.

The postwar status quo soon faced major challenges. Germany, under the weak Weimar Republic and then, after 1933, as the Third Reich of Adolf Hitler, remained discontented with the punitive terms of the Versailles settlement. In addition to costly war reparations and limitations on its military forces, Versailles had cost Germany more than 10 percent of its prewar population and territory. Italy, Russia, and Japan also bore grievances against the terms of the postwar international order. Thus, even in the 1920s, more than half the population of Europe lived in countries opposed to the continental status quo.

Decisive cooperation among the victorious Allied powers was essential to preserve the peace in Europe. However, the United States Senate had rejected American membership in the League of Nations and refused to ratify the Versailles treaty. After having intervened decisively in 1917, the United States now abandoned an assertive role in Europe. Instead, it turned inward, in a mood of sometimes virulent reaction against the outside world. Amid a climate of disillusion with the results of a war fought "to end all wars," America adopted policies of disarmanent and neutrality. Even after President Franklin Roosevelt took office in

1933, and despite increasingly threatening events in Europe during the next several years, the country remained deeply divided. Roosevelt was unable to effectively rally the country to active opposition against the threat from the Axis powers. Indeed, as late as August 1941, with Europe already at war, the House of Representatives only passed legislation to renew the draft by a margin of one vote.

France, as the principal Allied power on the Continent, favored a more vigorous effort to restrain the growth of German might and to keep the provisions of the postwar peace. However, the French found their position gravely weakened. Wartime losses of 1.3 million men made France reluctant to risk future casualties. Its planners thus adopted a defensive strategy, erecting vast fortifications, the Maginot Line, along their border with Germany. This made them unwilling to act offensively if war threatened. (Ironically, in 1940 the Nazi blitzkrieg simply outflanked the Maginot Line from the north, by breaking through the Ardennes forest and invading across France's more lightly defended border with Belgium.) More important, the French feared facing the more numerous Germans without full support from Britain. Thus, no firm policy by France was possible unless Britain concurred.

Domestic politics also impinged on France's foreign policy. Increasingly in the 1930s, France was riven by political polarization. Forces of the extreme right made an abortive attempt to seize power in February 1934. And after a center-left coalition, the Popular Front, won the elections in 1936, some rightist politicians muttered their resentment against the new prime minister with the words, "Better Hitler than Blum."*

Britain, finally, failed to provide the forceful support for France and opposition to aggression in Europe that might have preserved the peace. If anything, the trauma of World War I proved even stronger in Britain than in France. Although Britain did enter into a cautious policy of alliance with France, successive governments were mostly unwilling to take a firm stand in maintaining the provisions of Versailles and in restraining German rearmament. Indeed, after Hitler's accession to power in 1933, the British position tended to weaken as that of Germany became more aggressive. This was increasingly the case after Neville Chamberlain became prime minister in May 1937.

The Road to Munich

The fragile Weimar Republic had succeeded imperial Germany at the end of the war. At the request of German military leaders, it had had to sue for peace to avoid the collapse of Germany's armies and the invasion of the country by foreign troops. Yet Weimar was forced to accept the costly terms imposed at Versailles. The infant republic soon bore the brunt not only of opposition from the remnants of the old imperial order, including much of the military, the civil service, and the

---

*Leon Blum was a distinguished democratic socialist and French Jew who served as prime minister from June 1936 until June 1937.

landed aristocracy, but as Germany plunged into depression after 1929 the regime also experienced attacks from the large and anti-democratic Nazi and Communist parties.

In January 1933, Hitler came to office as chancellor. He and his followers quickly destroyed the democratic parties and imposed a Nazi dictatorship. Within a short period of time, Hitler began to challenge the provisions of Versailles. In March 1935, he repudiated the disarmament clauses of the treaty. A year later, he sent German troops to occupy the demilitarized zone of the Rhineland (the portion of Germany on the western side of the Rhine river). By doing so, he broke the treaties of Versailles and Locarno, but France—in the absence of support from Britain—failed to act to stop him.

Later in the year, the German air force intervened in the Spanish civil war, taking the side of General Francisco Franco, whose troops had launched a war against a shaky republican government. In November, Hitler agreed to establish an alliance with Mussolini, whose own troops had invaded Ethiopia in December 1935. Several months later, this Fascist grouping was expanded to include Japan.

Hitler, while intensifying a savage persecution against democrats, moderates, liberals, socialists, Communists, trade unionists, and—above all—Jews, continued to seek expansion of German power within Europe and enlarge the borders of the Third Reich. In doing so, he adopted a policy of bellicose threats and ultimatums. Repeatedly, in view of the indecisive Western response, he met with success. While many observers were increasingly horrified at Hitler's rise, this reaction was not universal. At the time, some claimed to see the German dictator as no more than a misunderstood nationalist, seeking recompense for a harsh peace. Others regarded him with indifference or viewed him as a crude but useful force against communism and the Soviets. Still others shared a degree of sympathy with the tenets of nazism. For example, this was the case among a small but influential segment of the British upper class.

The climate in Europe became especially menacing in March 1938, after Hitler succeeded in annexing the German-speaking but previously independent country of Austria. This action, known as the Anschluss, was soon followed by aggressive demands against Czechoslovakia.

As the threat from Germany intensified, France, Britain, and the smaller countries of Europe faced a limited number of choices. The initial hope of using the League of Nations for a policy of collective security against aggression had proved fruitless. The League had failed to act effectively after Italy invaded Ethiopia, and it had been equally inadequate as a means of countering Japanese aggression in China. An alternative course of action would have required a firm policy of alliance against the Axis countries. However, the United States refused active involvement, both because of continuing opposition in the Senate and deeply divided public opinion. The Soviet Union, meanwhile, was undergoing the ravages of Stalin's purges. Though its foreign minister, Maxim Litvinov, offered cooperation in resistance to Nazi Germany, deep mistrust and suspicion remained between the USSR and the Allies, particularly Great Britain.

The British government of Neville Chamberlain devoted its principal efforts to a policy of appeasement. The country had been slow to rearm in response to rising German military power, and the British prime minister viewed appeasement as a method of compromise. He resorted to it in the hope of avoiding war at any cost. The policy had a domestic side as well. The government sought to manipulate the press and discredit journalists and politicians who opposed appeasement. Indeed, journalists who questioned the good intentions of Hitler and Mussolini were described as susceptible to "Jewish-Communist propaganda."[22]

The Tragedy of Czechoslovakia

Hitler sought to expand the Third Reich in order to incorporate all the German-speaking people of Europe, regardless of where they lived, and to find "lebensraum" (living space) for a greater Germany. Moreover, he sought political and military domination of the entire European continent and the subjugation or destruction of other ethnic groups. In April 1938, he demanded that Czechoslovakia hand over a portion of its territory, the Sudetenland, in which some three million ethnic Germans lived.

Czechoslovakia at this time was a prosperous, stable, and democratic country of some 13 million people. Among all the countries of Eastern Europe, it had achieved the greatest economic and political success of the interwar period. Despite its modest size, Czechoslovakia held a strategic position that was by no means hopeless. It possessed defensible territory and strong border fortifications. Its well-equipped army of some 36 divisions was prepared to fight. Above all, the country had treaties of alliance with two major European powers, France and Russia.[23]

In the face of Nazi demands, the Czechs were fully prepared to resist and the French were willing to support them in this. However, France sought assurances from Britain that if war did occur France would not be left alone to face Germany. Here, Chamberlain moved to undercut the Czechs in a frantic effort to avoid war at whatever cost. Even so, when the crisis escalated in May, with partial Czech mobilization and declarations by France and Russia that they would act to support their small ally, the British reluctantly warned Germany that they too might intervene if war occurred. Hitler then backed down, but not before announcing an October 1 deadline for settling the Sudeten German question.[24]

In effect, Chamberlain sought to resolve the crisis not by standing firm and causing Hitler to abandon his demands, but instead by maneuvering to weaken the position of France and force President Beneš of Czechoslovakia to give in. The importance of the British role might have seemed secondary, in contrast to that of the French and Russians, who were closer geographically and allied to the Czechs. However, British influence stemmed from the experiences of World War I and France anxieties about facing Germany on the field of battle without Britain. Meanwhile, the Soviets, while continuing to express their support, were also fearful of facing Germany alone.[25] Russia would not fight without France. In turn, the Czechs, though prepared for war, would find themselves in a gallant but hopeless struggle if not supported by their allies.

With the approach of Hitler's deadline, the crisis intensified. However, on September 4 the Czech president, Edvard Beneš, sought to resolve the crisis by

granting the principal demand of the Sudeten Germans, local autonomy, while re-
jecting their and Hitler's insistence on change in the country's foreign policy.
Hitler rejected this major concession as inadequate, and war appeared imminent.
On September 13, at the request of French Prime Minister Edouard Daladier,
Chamberlain sought a meeting with Hitler. Two days later, the British leader (ig-
noring the Russians) flew to meet the Nazi leader at Berchtesgaden, in Bavaria.
This dramatic rendezvous, as a leading historian of this period acidly observes,
persuaded Chamberlain that Hitler would fight to get his way, and convinced
Hitler that Chamberlain would not fight.[26]

In the next few days, Britain and then France accepted Germany's demand
for the transfer to the Third Reich of Czech districts with 50 percent or more German population—without the formality of any kind of referendum or consultation
with the local population to see if this accorded with their wishes. President Beneš
at first refused. But in the early morning hours of September 21, he was presented
with an Anglo-French ultimatum: Prague must accept Hitler's demands or they
would abandon Czechoslovakia. Indeed, if war occurred, they would hold
Czechoslovakia responsible. Thus abandoned by its Western allies, the Beneš government reluctantly gave in.[27]

Remarkably, Hitler now escalated his demands. The next day, in a meeting
with Chamberlain at Bad Godesberg, he demanded *immediate* occupation by
German troops, to occur on September 26–28. Ironically, the British prime minister refused to concede. Hitler's demand conflicted with Chamberlain's insistence
on the *appearance* of negotiation, rather than settling matters through force. War
now appeared certain, and on September 23 the Czechs mobilized their 800,000
man army. During the following two days, September 24 and 25, the British and
French cabinets rejected the Bad Godesberg demands, and France herself began
partial mobilization.

In Britain, public and press sentiment rallied against giving in to Hitler, and
the country prepared for war. The fleet was mobilized and preparations for defense against air raids were begun. On the evening of Sunday, September 27,
Prime Minister Chamberlain delivered a dramatic—and demoralizing—radio address to the British people. It contained words that would later be widely quoted
as a caution to the wishful thinking that a greater power could escape the effect of
foreign events:

> How horrible, fantastic, incredible, it is that we should be digging trenches and trying
> on gas masks here because of a quarrel in *a faraway country between people of whom
> we know nothing.*[28]

Once more, however, Chamberlain moved to fatally undercut his allies. On
September 26 he had notified Hitler that Britain would see that the German demands on Czechoslovakia were accepted, only provided that this was implemented through discussion rather than force. Incredibly, only hours after his radio
address, he responded to a message from Hitler by offering to meet again with the
German chancellor, adding, "I feel certain that you can get all the essentials without war and without delay."[29] The next day, he warned Benes that the Nazis would
invade on the September 28 and that the only alternative was for the Czechs to ac-

cept German military occupation of the territories, under a slightly modified schedule that Britain would supervise!

The Munich Conference

On September 29–30, Chamberlain and Daladier met with Hitler and Mussolini in Munich, where they capitulated completely to Hitler's Bad Godesberg demands. At 2:30 in the morning, Czech representatives, who had not been allowed to participate or even comment at this meeting that sealed their fate, were abruptly summoned to the conference room by the British and French. They were summarily ordered to accept the decision of the four-power meeting.

On October 1–7, Nazi troops occupied the Sudetenland without firing a shot. The "peace for our time" that Chamberlain bore to a relieved British public proved illusory. Although the agreement was supported by a majority in Parliament and by much of the press and public opinion, it was denounced by the opposition Labour and Liberal parties, and by a group of some forty Conservative members of Parliament led by Winston Churchill.

The disastrous consequences of Munich soon became apparent: Czechoslovakia was ruined, and despite Hitler's assurances to the British leader that Germany had no further demands to make, he seized the remainder of Czechoslovakia less than six months later. France was left isolated and humiliated, having failed to honor its 1924 treaty obligation. Russia was alienated and less than a year later, on August 23, 1939, signed a nonaggression pact with Germany. Hitler further solidified his position within Germany, having achieved a major conquest without war. Ironically, the Allied capitulation even prevented a military plot to overthrow the Nazi leader. General Halder and his associates had warned that German forces were unprepared for war, and there is evidence that they had planned to oust Hitler in a military coup.

In the end, the Munich capitulation did not forestall the general European war Chamberlain had frantically sought to prevent—an irony that Churchill bitterly noted. Less than a year later, on September 1, 1939, Nazi Germany invaded Poland, and World War II had begun. Only now, Britain and France fought without Czechoslovakia and, even more important, without the Soviet Union on their side.

As the war began, Chamberlain's words to the House of Commons provided a fitting epitaph for his disastrous prewar policy of appeasement:

> Everything that I have believed in during my public life has crashed in ruins.[30]

IMPLICATIONS

What, then, is the enduring meaning of these watershed events? Munich and appeasement remain a traumatic memory of the consequences of failure to resist aggression. In this classic case, Britain's desperate search for peace at any price only emboldened Hitler. In the end, appeasement not only failed to prevent war; it insured that when war did occur, it would do so in circumstances nearly catastrophic for the Allies. A decade after Munich, recognition of these lessons conditioned the

American and Western response to the Soviet Union, the start of the Cold War, and the Korean conflict.

The record of 1938–1939 also suggests that the consequences of human actions are often ambiguous and can even prove to be the reverse of what was intended. Chamberlain was a peaceful man, bent on applying what he thought were the lessons of 1914 to avoid war. Churchill was combative, willing to exercise power and to contemplate war. In the end, Chamberlain's actions brought the precise opposite of what he intended. By contrast, had Churchill and those advocating resistance to Nazi threats prevailed, it is conceivable that Hitler might have backed down and even been overthrown in a military coup. While historical might-have-beens are inherently dubious, it is at least arguable that the more resolute course of action might even have prevented the outbreak of World War II in Europe.

Yet, before jumping to the conclusion that the lessons of appeasement can be universalized, it would be wise to reflect more broadly. Few evils are so unambiguous as the menace Hitler presented in 1938. The implications of 1914 are also relevant, and the stakes of warfare in a nuclear world remain unique.

The events of July–August 1914 should serve to remind us of the perils of escalation.[31] and the outbreak of World War I should serve as a reminder that smaller states can trigger a conflict among larger ones, that decision-makers can lose control of events, and that the participants can find themselves drawn into a war whose consequences are far more devastating than expected. Here too, however, we must be wary of simple repetition of lessons. There is nothing inevitable about escalation of a crisis. Nor do states, even expansionist ones, automatically avail themselves of the opportunity to launch a war at the first moment that a favorable opening presents itself.[32]

Finally, during the Cold War, the existence of robust nuclear deterrence not only made the United States more cautious about the risks of a direct superpower confrontation. It also imposed a "reality constraint"[33] on Soviet aspirations. There can be little serious doubt that Soviet leaders appreciated the consequences of assured destruction. Whereas in 1914 there were reasons for genuine uncertainty about the consequences of war, modern great powers are now acutely aware of the incomparable devastation that a major conflict would unleash. As analyzed in Chapter 8, this knowledge did constitute an ultimate restraint on American and Soviet behavior on the one occasion when the two superpowers moved closest to the brink of nuclear war: the Cuban missile crisis.

NOTES

1. Quoted in Barbara Tuchman, *The Guns of August* (New York: Dell, 1963), p. 142.
2. Quoted in *International Security* 9 (Summer 1984): 5.
3. The quotation can be found in the *Times* (London), 1 October 1938, p. 14; and in Charles Loch Mowat, *Britain Between the Wars, 1918–1940* (Chicago: University of Chicago Press, 1955), p. 619.
4. "Facts Are Stubborn, Your Majesty," *New York Times,* 26 September 1990.
5. *"Lessons" of the Past: The Use and Misuse of History in American Foreign Policy* (New York: Oxford University Press, 1973), pp. x–xii. Also see Richard E. Neustadt and

Ernest R. May, *Thinking in Time: The Uses of History for Decision-Makers* (New York: Free Press, 1986).

6. Harry S Truman, *Memoirs,* Vol. 2 (Garden City, NY: Doubleday, 1956), pp. 332–333; quoted in May, *"Lessons" of the Past,* pp. 81–82.

7. The risks of a shift, or of Soviet belief in a shift, in the correlation of forces were cited, for example, by Paul Nitze, in "Strategy in the Decade of the 1980s," *Foreign Affairs* 59 (Fall 1980): 82–101.

8. See, for example Walter Laqueur, "The Psychology of Appeasement," *Commentary* (October 1978): 44–50.

9. Excerpts from President Bush's remarks at a Marine outpost in northeastern Saudi Arabia, 22 November 1990, as published in the *New York Times,* 23 November 1990, p. A16.

10. John G. Stoessinger, *Why Nations Go to War,* 4th ed. (New York: St. Martin's, 1985), pp. 3–9.

11. Tuchman provides a lucid account of the Schlieffen Plan—and of its undoing. Also see James Joll, *The Origins of the First World War* (London & New York: Longman, 1984); Laurence Lafore, *The Long Fuse: An Interpretation of the Origins of World War I,* 2nd ed. (New York: Lippincott, 1971); and Arden Bucholz, *Moltke, Schlieffen and Prussian War Planning* (New York: Berg, 1991).

12. Quoted in Tuchman, *The Guns of August,* pp. 25–26.

13. Statement in 1912, quoted in John Ellis, *The Social History of the Machine Gun* (New York: Pantheon, 1975), pp. 53–54, cited in Stephen Van Evera, "The Cult of the Offensive and the Origins of the First World War," *International Security* 9 (Summer 1984): 60. Also see Van Evera, "Why Cooperation Failed in 1914," in Kenneth Oye, ed., *Cooperation Under Anarchy* (Princeton: Princeton University Press, 1986), pp. 80–117.

14. Scott D. Sagan, "1914 Revisited: Allies, Offense and Instability," *International Security,* Vol. 11, No. 2: (Fall 1986) 151–175, at p. 163.

15. For an analysis of the role of the Schlieffen Plan in this pattern, see Glenn H. Snyder and Paul Diesing, *Conflict Among Nations: Bargaining, Decision Making and System Structure in International Crises* (Princeton: Princeton University Press, 1977), especially pp. 500–503.

16. For a more general criticism, see, for example, Gerhard Ritter, *The Schlieffen Plan: Critique of a Myth* (New York: Praeger, 1958, and Westport, C: Greenwood, 1979).

17. See *Germany's Aims in the First World War* (New York: Norton, 1967); and *War of Illusions: German Policies from 1911 to 1914* (New York: Norton, 1975). Also see Fischer's *World Power or Decline? The Controversy Over Germany's Aims in the First World War* (New York: Norton, 1974); John A. Moses, *The Politics of Illusion: The Fischer Controversy in German Historiography* (London: George Prior, 1975); and Michael R. Gordon, "Domestic Conflict and the Origins of the First World War: The British and German Cases," *Journal of Modern History* 46 (June 1974): 191–226. (Gordon also stresses the impact of domestic considerations in shaping Germany's external policies.)

18. See, for example, Martin Kitchen, *The German Officer Corps: 1890–1914* (Oxford: Oxford University Press, 1968); Gerhard Ritter, *The Sword and the Scepter: The Problem of Militarism in Germany* (Coral Gables: University of Miami Press, 2 vols., 1969 and 1973); and Richard Ned Lebow, "Windows of Opportunity: Do States Jump Through Them?" *International Security* 9 (Summer 1984): 147–186.

19. Holger H. Herwig describes this campaign of censorship, distortion, and influence. See "Clio Deceived: Patriotic Self-Censorship in Germany after the Great War," *International Security,* Vol. 12, No. 2 (Fall 1987): 5–44, especially pp. 5–7 and 26.

20. Sagan, p. 154.

21. For a thoughtful discussion of assumptions about offense and defense, see Robert Jervis, "Cooperation Under the Security Dilemma," *World Politics* 30 (January 1978): 186–214. On the impact of the decline in Britain's relative economic power in affecting the country's position, see J. L. Richardson, "New Perspectives on Appeasement: Some Implications for International Relations," *World Politics*, Vol. XL, No. 3 (April 1988); 289–316.

22. Quoted by Michael Barber, *The Sunday Times* (London), 2 April 1989, reviewing Richard Crockett, *Twilight of Truth: Chamberlain, Appeasement and the Manipulation of the Press* (London: Weidenfeld, 1989). Even after Hitler's forces broke the Munich agreement by marching into Prague in March 1939, much of the British press continued to praise Chamberlain's conduct of foreign policy.

23. The treaty with France dated from 1924; that with Russia was signed in 1935. Soviet commitment was contingent on France fulfilling its obligations to Czechoslovakia. See Josef Korbel, *Twentieth Century Czechoslovakia: The Meaning of Its History* (New York: Columbia University Press, 1977), p. 122.

    A lucid and detailed account of the Czech crisis can be found in Mowat, *Britain Between the Wars, 1918–1940*, pp. 604–620. The definitive work is by Telford Taylor, *Munich: The Price of Peace* (Garden City, NY: Doubleday, 1979).

24. Mowat, pp. 605–606.

25. For a discussion of British leverage over the Allies in the Czech crisis, see Arnold Wolfers, *Britain and France Between two Wars* (New York: Norton, 1966), p. 280.

26. Mowat, p. 610.

27. For a moving account of these events seen from the perspective of Czechoslovakia, see Korbel, *Twentieth Century Czechoslovakia,* pp. 124ff.

28. *Times* (London), 28 September 1938. Italics added.

29. Quoted in Mowat, p. 615.

30. Statement of 3 October 1939, quoted in Mowat, p. 650.

31. The importance of the 1914 analogy is emphasized by Miles Kahler. He suggests that it points to weaknesses in deterrence theory and notes that in Europe the event has had a more powerful hold than 1938–1939. See "Rumors of War: The 1914 Analogy," *Foreign Affairs* 58 (Winter 1979/80): 374–396, at pp. 374 and 394. A different view, by Patrick Glynn, cites Germany's calculated effort at the domination of Europe and sees the outbreak of war in 1914 as far from accidental. Glynn warns against the belief that the arms race drove the European powers to war and cautions against inferences about arms control as a means of preventing war. See "The Sarajevo Fallacy: The Historical and Intellectual Origins of Arms Control Theology," *The National Interest,* No. 9 (Fall 1978): pp. 3–32.

32. Richard Ned Lebow notes that the perceived "window of opportunity" was greater for Germany in 1905, 1909, and 1912 than in 1914 when that country actually went to war. "Windows of Opportunity," p. 184.

33. Jack Snyder, "Civil-Military Relations and the Cult of the Offensive, 1914 and 1984," *International Security* 9 (Summer 1984): 145–146.

chapter 8

A Glimpse into the Abyss: The Cuban Missile Crisis

. . . somewhere between one out of three and even.
—PRESIDENT JOHN F. KENNEDY'S
REPORTED ESTIMATE ON THE PROBABILITY OF NUCLEAR WAR[1]

We're eyeball to eyeball and I think the other fellow just blinked.
—SECRETARY OF STATE DEAN RUSK, OCTOBER 24, 1962[2]

If you have not lost your self-control, and sensibly conceive what this might lead to, then, Mr. President, we and you ought not now to pull on the ends of the rope in which you have tied the knot of war, because the more we pull, the tighter the knot will be tied. And a moment may come when the knot will be tied so tight that even he who tied it will not have the strength to untie it, and then it will be necessary to cut that knot; and what that would mean is not for me to explain to you, because you yourself understand perfectly of what terrible forces our countries dispose.
—SOVIET LEADER NIKITA KHRUSHCHEV,
LETTER TO PRESIDENT JOHN F. KENNEDY, OCTOBER 26, 1962[3]

The Cuban Missile Crisis illustrates . . . the insignificance of nuclear superiority in the face of survivable thermonuclear retaliatory forces. It also shows the crucial role of rapidly available conventional strength.
—STATEMENT OF DEAN RUSK, ROBERT MCNAMARA,
AND OTHER FORMER KENNEDY ADMINISTRATION OFFICIALS
ON THE TWENTIETH ANNIVERSARY OF THE CUBAN MISSILE CRISIS[4]

The Cuban missile crisis occurred in October 1962. Of all the post-1945 confrontations between the superpowers, it has captured the lasting attention of policymakers and scholars. The reasons for this prominence are not hard to fathom: the crisis presented not only the most direct and acute Soviet-American confrontation, but also the occasion on which the two superpowers came closest to the brink of nuclear war.

Beyond these dramatic aspects, the crisis has also provided a fruitful and seemingly endless source of inferences about the risks of war, crisis behavior, policymaking, and great power relations in a nuclear world.[5] The interplay between actual events and how people think about them has continued without interruption. Indeed, as old concerns have given way to new and different ones (nuclear and conventional arms races, Vietnam, third-world instability, efforts to reduce the risk of nuclear war, the end of the Cold War, nuclear proliferation), the Cuban missile crisis has been periodically reinterpreted for the lessons it is thought to offer on the most pressing questions of the time.

ORIGINS OF THE CRISIS

The Cuban missile crisis took place against the backdrop of growing tension in relations between the United States and the Soviet Union. The 1960 presidential election contest between Richard Nixon and John F. Kennedy had given rise to Democratic charges of a "missile gap." The outgoing Republican administration of President Dwight Eisenhower was blamed not only for allowing the Soviets to capture an early lead in space through the launching of the first space satellite, Sputnik, but also for permitting them to gain what was believed to be a significant advantage in intercontinental ballistic missiles.

By mid 1961, however, well into the first year of the new Kennedy administration, new satellite intelligence information revealed that the United States in fact maintained a considerable edge in both the quality and quantity of its strategic nuclear power. The Soviets had not been able to build new weapons at the rate anticipated and it was discovered that the first-generation Soviet ICBM had been a failure. Indeed, by October 1961, it appeared that there was a missile gap in reverse.

Cuba had become the subject of American concern after guerrillas led by Fidel Castro overthrew the Batista dictatorship in January 1959. The Eisenhower administration soon clashed with Castro over a number of issues, including the nationalization of American-owned businesses. For his part, Castro crushed the hopes of those who had anticipated that he would lead a non-Communist and democratic government. As Cuban-American tensions rose, Castro turned increasingly toward the Soviets for military and economic aid. In April 1961, matters came to a head with the abortive invasion of Cuba by CIA-trained and equipped Cuban exiles at the Bay of Pigs.

A June 1961 Vienna summit meeting between President Kennedy and the Soviet leader, Nikita Khrushchev, failed to ease the climate of superpower hostility. Although some accounts suggest that the Soviet leader came away with an impression of the new American leader as insufficiently resolute, the best available evidence indicates that this was not so.[6] In any case, the climate of relations was not improved.

Tensions had also begun to rise over the divided city of Berlin. In August 1961, the Communist government of East Germany had suddenly constructed a wall to keep East Berliners from fleeing their half of the city—an action that violated the four-power Berlin accords. Soon afterward, Soviet and American tanks came within a few hundred yards of each other in an East-West confrontation at "Checkpoint Charlie." Together with the Bay of Pigs fiasco, the Berlin crisis appears to have left the American president concerned about the need to demonstrate adequate resolve to deter future Soviet adventures.

During the summer of 1962, unsubstantiated rumors began to circulate that the Soviets were placing missiles in Cuba. At the beginning of September, President Kennedy issued both public and private warnings to the Soviets that the United States would not tolerate the stationing of offensive weapons there and that he would take action if this occurred. In response, the Soviet leader relayed a personal message to Kennedy, assuring him that missiles capable of hitting the United States would not be placed in Cuba.

Discovery of the Missiles

The crisis began on October 16, 1962, when President Kennedy was provided with evidence from military reconnaissance overflights of Cuba that the Soviets were actually in the process of installing missiles on the island. The president immediately convened a small working group of his highest foreign policy officials and closest advisors. This ad hoc body, subsequently designated as the "ExCom" (Executive Committee) of the National Security Council, was given the urgent task of weighing alternative courses of action and making crisis recommendations to the president.

The ExCom met under the chairmanship of Attorney General Robert Kennedy, the president's brother. Initially, its members were deeply divided over the best course of action. At first, a minority felt that the Soviet action could be viewed without undue alarm. As Secretary of Defense Robert McNamara put it, "A missile is a missile. It makes no great difference whether you were killed by a missile from the Soviet Union or Cuba." Indeed, he added that the missiles represented not a "military problem," but a "domestic political problem."[7] However, the dominant weight of opinion leaned toward an immediate military response, in the form of an air strike or invasion of Cuba. McNamara soon altered his own position, as did many of the key participants in response to their deliberations and the ongoing events of the crisis.

For the first several days, word of the missiles was kept secret so that the president and his advisors could decide on a thoroughly calculated course of action without letting the Soviets—or the American public—know of their discovery. The urgency of the crisis intensified, however, as American military experts determined that the missiles could become operational within one week. The missile warheads would equal roughly half the strength of the total Soviet ICBM force, and in a worst-case scenario, these weapons could kill 80 million Americans.[8]

Immediate American military action was backed by the chairman of the Joint Chiefs of Staff, General Maxwell Taylor, by former Secretary of State Dean Acheson, and initially even by Robert Kennedy.[9] However, the risks posed by this action appeared to become more serious as the ExCom considered the overall circumstances. While the United States enjoyed overwhelming military superiority in the Caribbean, an air strike would not by itself guarantee the destruction of all the missiles. The bombing would need to be followed by an actual American invasion of Cuba. In the meantime, there was deep concern that one or more surviving missiles in Cuba might be launched against the East Coast of the United States. By October 20, the CIA reported that 16 of the 24 Soviet medium-range ballistic missiles (MRBMs) were already operational.[10] A week later, and just one day before the resolution of the crisis, the total had risen to 20. Although the United States possessed overall nuclear superiority Secretary McNamara raised the spectre of "almost certain . . . chaos in part of the East Coast"[11] if a missile were launched.

A number of other factors also constrained the American response. For one thing, an invasion would be no simple matter. The island was some 700 miles in length, covered a land area the size of Pennsylvania, and was defended by sizeable Cuban forces likely to put up significant resistance. The resultant American victory would be likely to come at the cost of substantial casualties on both sides. Perhaps even more important, the Soviets were believed likely to retaliate in a region where they held local superiority. Berlin was thought to be the probable area for retaliation, and this posed the risk of escalation toward a wider war in Europe.

The Naval Quarantine of Cuba

Although some members of the ExCom continued to support immediate military action, the president and his advisors decided on October 20–21 to undertake a naval blockade (actually a "quarantine" of offensive weapons shipments) as the initial step instead. They saw this as a means of pressuring the Soviets and Cubans to withdraw the missiles. Meanwhile, the option of an air strike or invasion remained an immediate possibility if the quarantine did not succeed. On October 22, the president wrote Khrushchev demanding the removal of the missiles. On the same day, the United States formally raised the issue at the United Nations, in the Organization of American States, and within the NATO alliance. After briefing congressional leaders, President Kennedy delivered a dramatic speech to the American people, revealing the nature of the crisis and the initial response he had ordered.

In the following days, rapid construction activity continued at the missile sites, as did the uncrating and assembly of Soviet IL-28 bombers. Soviet ships in the region also continued their course toward Cuba. However, in order to give the Russian leadership more time to react, the president reduced the quarantine line from a radius of 800 miles around Cuba to one of 500 miles.

On Wednesday, October 24, tension at the White House mounted dramatically, as the confrontation with Soviet vessels approached. A sense of the drama—and danger—emerges in the words of Robert F. Kennedy's posthumously published memoir of the crisis:

> It was now a few minutes after 10:00 o'clock. Secretary McNamara announced that two Russian ships, the *Gagarin* and the *Komiles,* were within a few miles of our quarantine barrier. . . .
>
> Then came the disturbing Navy report that a Russian submarine had moved into position between the two ships. . . .
>
> I think these few minutes were the time of gravest concern for the President. Was the world on the brink of a holocaust? Was it our error? A mistake? . . . His hand went up to his face and covered his mouth. He opened and closed his fist. His face seemed drawn, his eyes pained. . . .
>
> We had come to the time of final decision. "We must expect that they will close down Berlin—make the final preparations for that," the President said. I felt we were on the edge of a precipice with no way off. . . .
>
> Then it was 10:25—a messenger brought a note to [CIA Director] John McCone. "Mr. President, we have a preliminary report which seems to indicate that some of the Russian ships have stopped dead in the water."[12]

In fact, some 20 Soviet ships approaching the quarantine line had halted or reversed course. The next day, October 25, the first Cuba-bound vessel (a Panamanian freighter under charter to the Soviets) was stopped and boarded without incident. More important, on October 26, the president also received an emotional letter from Khrushchev, urging a peaceful resolution of the crisis. A day later, a more formal and tougher letter arrived. However, the president and his advisors made the calculation that this had come not from Khrushchev personally, but from the Soviet politburo, and they decided to respond to the initial letter while ignoring the latter one.

In addition to almost daily messages between Washington and Moscow, behind-the-scenes ("back-channel") communications proved crucial. On October 26, an ABC diplomatic correspondent, John Scali, was approached by a Soviet embassy official, Alexander S. Fomin. Relying on Scali's connections to the State Department and White House, Fomin (himself believed by American analysts to be a KGB colonel and chief of Soviet intelligence within the United States) proposed terms for resolving the crisis. Its elements were the following: (1) the missiles would be removed and returned to the USSR under UN supervision; (2) Castro would pledge not to accept offensive weapons in the future; and (3) the United States would pledge not to invade Cuba.[13] The message seemed to convey Khrushchev's own course of action for resolving the crisis, in contrast to the position of the broader Soviet leadership.

Meanwhile, tension mounted. At a formal level, the Soviets had proposed trading the missiles in Cuba for comparable American Jupiter missiles stationed in Turkey—an offer Kennedy refused on the grounds that there could be no explicit trade for reversing the dangerous Soviet deployment, even though he had ordered a study on possible withdrawal of the missiles in August.[14] On October 27, an American U-2 surveillance plane was shot down by a Soviet SAM (surface-to-air missile) while photographing the continuing work on the missile sites. The President decided against immediate retaliation, but planning for an American air strike was intensified. The action was tentatively set for October 29, to be followed with an invasion by up to 100,000 American troops. This military response was broadly supported within the ExCom, even by Secretary McNamara and Robert Kennedy, who personally communicated the threat of an imminent invasion to Soviet Ambassador Anatoli Dobrynin. Large quantities of men and material were dispatched to the southeastern United States, in preparation for the assault. And, as a demonstration of resolve, American B-47 strategic bombers were dispersed to civilian airfields, so that they would not be vulnerable to a surprise Soviet attack.

Finally, on October 28, no more than one to two days before action was to be taken against Cuba, Khrushchev sent President Kennedy a message in which he announced the decision to withdraw the missiles, and made explicit the terms first suggested in the Scali-Fomin meeting. In the following days, construction activity ceased, the missiles were withdrawn (though without UN inspection, which Castro refused to permit), and the United States issued a noninvasion pledge. Ironically, it later came to light that the president had agreed to remove the missiles from Turkey after all, but not as a formal quid pro quo, and only after the rest of the crisis had been resolved.[15] The Soviets also accepted the administration position that removal of the United States missiles from Turkey would depend on the Soviets remaining silent about the arrangement.

THE CUBAN MISSILE CRISIS: CAUSES

A crisis necessarily involves the interaction of two or more major players. Any effort to make sense of what caused the Cuban missile crisis ought thus to begin by considering the outlooks of the Soviet and American leaders.

Soviet Calculations

The results of the crisis imposed serious costs on the Soviets. The economic burden of first establishing then dismantling and returning the missiles and bombers was considerable. The Soviets also risked mass destruction as a consequence of a high-stakes strategic gamble. In addition, the USSR suffered not only international political embarrassment, but political humiliation in being compelled to back down in the face of Kennedy's determination and American regional and strategic superiority. Indeed, the consequences of this episode contributed significantly to the ouster of Khrushchev from power two years later.

However, the crisis appeared to result from more than bungled risk taking on the part of the Soviet leader. At least three distinct objectives would have been served by the placement of missiles in Cuba.

First, the weapons offered a "quick fix" for the USSR's position of strategic nuclear inferiority vis-à-vis the United States. Contrary to expectations that followed the launching of Sputnik, problems in initial stages of the American space

Table 8.1 U.S. ESTIMATES OF SOVIET AND AMERICAN
STRATEGIC NUCLEAR FORCES
AT THE TIME OF THE CUBAN MISSILE CRISIS

	ICBMs	Missiles on Submarines	Strategic Bombers
United States	129	144	1300
Soviet Union	44	97	155

Source: American documents on Cuban missile crisis, cited in the Washington Post, 25 July 1985, p. A10.

program, and talk of the "missile gap," the United States maintained a position of strategic nuclear superiority. That is, although the continental United States had lost its invulnerability to Soviet attack in the mid to late 1950s, it was nonetheless to retain superior strategic nuclear forces until the late 1960s. (See Table 8.1.)

Indeed, Soviet inferiority in ICBMs was even worse than American intelligence estimated at the time. Although it was believed that the Soviets possessed some 44 land-based missiles capable of hitting the United States from Soviet territory (see Table 8.1), Soviet officials later revealed, in a January 1989 Moscow meeting with their American counterparts, that there had been only 20.[16] The attempted deployment of more than 40 missiles in Cuba thus would have tripled the number of Soviet land-based missiles able to strike the continental United States.

By deploying MRBM missiles and medium-range bombers to Cuba, the Soviets would thus find a shortcut in redressing the nuclear balance. Note, however, that these weapons would be relatively "soft" targets for the United States. That is, they would be visible and highly vulnerable to attack. Thus they would also be destabilizing: in a crisis situation, there was a risk that the Americans might seek to knock them out in a preemptive air strike before they could be used; conversely, the Soviets (facing a "use them or lose them" situation) might be tempted to employ the weapons early in a crisis or even in a first-strike situation if war seemed imminent.

Second, the missile deployment, together with the tangible evidence of Soviet commitment it signaled, might offer a means to underwrite the security of the Cuban regime of Fidel Castro. The memory of the Bay of Pigs invasion attempt remained fresh, and given the existence of covert CIA-directed operations to topple or assassinate Castro, the prospect of American intervention could not be ruled out. Soviet and Cuban officials were aware of covert infiltration teams sent to Cuba by the United States during 1962 under Operation Mongoose, and they anticipated an American invasion. In a January 1989 Moscow meeting held to discuss lessons of the crisis, Robert McNamara emphatically denied that the Kennedy administration had plans to launch a military operation to overthrow Castro. However, he found it possible that the Soviets and Cubans had misinterpreted Washington's intentions, and he added, "If I had been in Moscow or Havana at that time, I would have believed that Americans were preparing an invasion."[17]

Third, there was a political rationale for Soviet action. Contrary to Russian hopes, the consolidation of power in Eastern Europe, the recovery of the Soviet economy and industry from its wartime devastation, the coming to independence of vast areas of the third world, and an early but brief lead in space had not brought the hoped-for geopolitical gains. Rather than falling into a predicted crisis, Europe, Japan, and the United States had enjoyed vigorous economic growth and political stability. Indeed, the Russians had even experienced a major reversal in their deep and bitter rift with China—the world's other major Communist power.[18]

Under these conditions, Khrushchev might have hoped that a major bolstering of the Soviet strategic position would enhance the USSR's political and diplomatic standing across a range of issues, including Berlin. As President Kennedy observed, the nuclear weapons in Cuba would have "politically changed the balance of power; it would have appeared to change it and appearances contribute to reality."[19]

In any event, the Soviets were forced to withdraw the missiles. The United States not only possessed strategic nuclear superiority, but in the Caribbean region it held massive advantages in conventional (land, sea, and air) forces. The Kennedy administration clearly signaled that it considered removal of the weapons to be a matter of vital national interest. Both the specific American actions, as well as statements by U.S. leaders (supported by allies and much of Latin America), made it quite evident that the United States was determined to take forceful action if the Soviets did not respond immediately. This left Khrushchev and his colleagues with two unwelcome choices: either to experience the cost and embarrassment of backing down, or to take military action elsewhere (Berlin, or possibly Turkey), thus risking escalation toward general nuclear war.

American Calculations

Several key factors caused President Kennedy and his closest advisors to regard the Cuban missile issue as a major crisis and to respond as they did.

First, and arguably most important, was the matter of *credibility* in a nuclear age. As we have seen in Chapter 6, the strategic nuclear balance rests on a number of critical elements. One of these is credibility—that is, the clear understanding by each side of the meaning and determination in the positions taken and communicated by the adversary. Given the stakes involved in strategic nuclear deterrence, it is vital that neither side misunderstand the other's level of commitment and resolve. For one side to push the other too far is to court the risk of a nuclear conflict that can destroy both. In the summer of 1962, the Kennedy administration had already made it clear that it would regard the placing of offensive weapons in Cuba as a grave threat to its vital national interests. The message had been received by the Soviets, who had replied that no such activity would take place. In this light, the Soviet actions not only violated the rules of the game, but they also increased the risk of future conflict in that Khrushchev had failed to take the administration's position seriously.

Second, while the United States was already vulnerable to at least small-scale nuclear attack, the nature of Soviet strategic strength had been overstated, both at home and abroad. This is not to minimize the dire consequences for both sides in the event that a major war had broken out, but the Soviets had not yet attained the second-strike capability with which they were already credited. Thus, the administration was loath to acquiesce in a sudden leap by the Soviets to full nuclear parity with the United States.

Third, there were regional power issues at stake. The postwar confrontation between the superpowers had brought a de facto division of spheres of influence between the United States and the USSR. The United States had been unable to prevent Soviet domination of countries along its borders with Eastern Europe. And, while deploring the Soviet repression in the region, particularly in East Berlin in 1953 and Hungary in 1956, the United States had not sought to intervene forcefully and overtly in this area.° Meanwhile, the United States had assumed leadership of the Western alliance. While membership in this grouping was voluntary—rather than forced, as on the Soviet side—both superpowers were cognizant of Western Europe as an area of American vital interest.

In this sense, Latin America, and especially the Caribbean, were also seen as falling into an American sphere of interest and influence. Indeed, the United States' role here had roots going all the way back to the Monroe Doctrine in 1823. Recognition of these realities was simply part of the postwar balance of power. The fact of Soviet intervention in Cuba posed a symbolic challenge to the geopolitical status quo.

Fourth, and related to the above point, there were weighty domestic political considerations. The Cold War, together with the fate of China and Eastern Europe, had heavily impacted American politics. (These impacts, especially following the Communist victory in China and the rise of McCarthyism, are treated in Chapter 3.) The Kennedy administration was sensitive to avoiding the charge of being soft on the Soviets, which had been thrown at the Democrats in the late 1940s and early 1950s. Indeed, Kennedy's emphasis on restoring American strength, military as well as economic, was a key part of his election pledge to "get America moving again." Thus, even had the strategic implications been minimal, no Democratic administration at that time would have been in a position to take a relaxed view of the Soviet action in Cuba—particularly after the stunning debacle a year earlier at the Bay of Pigs. And, in the unfolding of the crisis itself, President Kennedy faced continual pressure, first within the ExCom and then from congressional leaders (on the eve of the November 1962 congressional elections), to take immediate military action even without waiting to see if the quarantine could produce the desired results.

°Very small and unsuccessful forms of covert action in Eastern Europe did take place in the early years of the Cold War. However, Anglo-American efforts to facilitate émigré return and resistance were penetrated and destroyed by Soviet double agents, for example in Albania. In the overall sweep of events, these episodes were no more than a footnote. They were also mirrored by various forms of covert Soviet activity in the West.

INTERPRETATIONS OF THE CRISIS: VICTORY, DEFEAT, OR RECKLESSNESS?

The events of the Cuban missile crisis were of great importance in themselves. However, they have given rise to sharply different interpretations. Students of the crisis have continued to derive very different meanings from it, even while examining the same phenomena. It is worth considering three sets of interpretations, not only for the contrasting perspectives they provide, but also because they demonstrate how thoughtful observers of the same facts may nonetheless draw differing conclusions about their meaning and lessons.

Interpretation No. 1: An American Victory

In the immediate aftermath of the crisis, the prevailing assessment depicted the outcome as a dramatic victory for the United States and the leadership of President John F. Kennedy. After all, the country had never been so directly threatened before, and the placement of missiles only 90 miles from American shores posed both a military and psychological challenge. The crisis had come little more than a year after a humiliating reversal at the Bay of Pigs. Had the United States backed down here as well, America's allies might have begun to question the country's will to protect them.

The leadership of President Kennedy also appeared to be at stake, both within the United States and on a global level. The Soviets had lied to him in denying they would ever place offensive weapons in Cuba, and failure to act might have jeopardized the president's personal credibility. Indeed, at one point during the crisis, Robert Kennedy remarked to his brother that he would have been impeached had he failed to act. The comment involves a good deal of hyperbole, but it nonetheless expresses the temper of the times.

And, as noted above, American credibility was thought to be at stake. In a nuclear environment, this was a matter of profound importance. If, by failing to act, President Kennedy had left the Soviets doubting American resolve, then there was increased risk of nuclear war through Soviet underestimation of U.S. firmness at a later date.

Moreover, in full view of allies and adversaries, the Soviets had been forced to back down after a reckless nuclear gamble. The United States had prevailed in a test of power and will. In the dramatic words of Secretary of State Dean Rusk, with the two sides eyeball to eyeball, it was the Soviets who had blinked.

Indeed, American behavior in the crisis had demonstrated brains as well as brawn. The president had resisted pressure for hasty or careless action. Deliberation within the ExCom had produced a successful response to the crisis, based on a carefully calibrated mix of force and diplomacy.[20] For example, after the Soviet UN ambassador had denied American charges, Ambassador Adlai Stevenson had scored a stunning diplomatic triumph in the Security Council by unveiling air-surveillance photographs of the missile sites. The president had employed a graduated series of measures to demonstrate American resolve. Yet the Russians had been given time and a means to withdraw without being forced into a corner from which there was no way out but to fight. The president had shown himself in charge throughout. His actions had neither been so reckless as to risk a possibly nuclear war, nor had they been so hesitant as to risk American credibility and thus show the country as unwilling to use force to defend its vital interests.

In sum, Kennedy had demonstrated good judgment, political savvy, determination, and strength. The American democracy was not so soft as to allow itself to be pushed around (the spectre of Munich), nor would it stagger blindly into nuclear escalation (the equivalent of 1914).[21] In the end, Kennedy's path had allowed the United States to prevail without firing a shot.

Interpretation No. 2: An American Defeat

The president had been under mounting pressure from right-wing critics during his first two years in office. They had been bitterly critical of his administration's failure to provide stronger backing for the Bay of Pigs invasion of Cuba. They also asserted that the president should have taken decisive action to prevent construction of the Berlin Wall in August 1961. Now, they offered a very different interpretation of the Cuban missile crisis, challenging the prevailing notion of it as a victory for the United States and for the president personally. In the words of a critic:

> It was what he [the President] could have done but did *not* do that will most strongly impress our Communist foes. He forced them to retract the move, and for a brief while aired their malice before the world. But he did nothing to penalize an action aimed at inflicting an almost mortal wound on us, and he even made a non-invasion pledge that had never been given before. To safeguard Berlin we needed a decisive victory in Cuba. We did not even get the *status quo ante*.[22]

In essence, this criticism focuses on the regional situation in the Caribbean. It asserts that by being forced to issue an assurance of noninvasion, President Kennedy was permitting the consolidation of a Communist dictatorship close to our shores. Indeed, this interpretation (which is not broadly shared by most analysts of the crisis) holds that the central purpose of the Soviet action may well have been to gain such a pledge from the United States.[23] Others have criticized President Kennedy for overestimating the risk of war or for not taking full advantage of America's massive strategic superiority at the time to drive a harder bargain with the Soviets.[24]

Interpretation No. 3: Recklessness or Lack of Necessity

Here we find a more diverse group of interpretations. In common, they reject the notion that the crisis resulted in either an unmitigated victory or a defeat for the United States. In often differing ways they emphasize the dangers involved and ask whether the crisis might have been avoided.

One such view criticizes the president for reckless impatience. In the view of journalist I. F. Stone, Kennedy's conduct reflected his immediate political interests at home and the impending 1962 congressional elections. The administration had learned that no missile or bomber gap actually existed. Stone contended that the Russians were actually weak strategically, and thus the threat to the United States was exaggerated. Stone also condemned the president for publicly rejecting the Soviet proposal to swap the withdrawal of Soviet missiles in Cuba for the American missiles in Turkey, and he charged that the president wanted unconditional Soviet surrender.[25]

A different view is not explicitly critical of President Kennedy, but does caution against euphoria and stresses the grave risk involved. In the words of an observer otherwise strongly sympathetic to the president and the aims of his administration, John Kenneth Galbraith:

> . . . In the Cuban missile crisis President Kennedy had to balance the danger of blowing up the planet against the risk of political attack at home for appeasing the Communists. This was not an irresponsible choice: to ignore the domestic opposition was to risk losing initiative or office to men who wanted an even more dangerous policy. But there is something more than a little wrong with a system that poses a choice between survival and domestic political compulsion. The missile crisis did not show the strength of our policy; it showed the catastrophic . . . pressures to which it was subject. We were in luck, but success in a lottery is no argument for lotteries. . . .[26]

Implicitly, this perspective is concerned with the risks of brinkmanship. Without necessarily asserting that Kennedy was incorrect in his assessment, it holds that the crisis involved a kind of global Russian roulette. Since the costs of a nuclear war were potentially cataclysmic, this view implies the necessity of finding ways to avoid repetitive trips to the brink of nuclear war. In short, the chief danger lies in repeated plays of a nuclear gamble.

An initial examination of the Cuban missile crisis might seem to suggest an advantage for the side willing to come closest to the brink of nuclear war. This lesson can be related to the game of "Chicken," in which two teenage drivers race automobiles toward each other and the one who swerves first earns the derisive label of "Chicken."[27] However, the Chicken game suffers serious flaws as a model for international conflict—especially in prescriptive terms. What Chicken (and, by analogy, brinksmanship) does is to prepare the player for no more than the lone crisis confrontation.[28] Yet superpower relations, and international relations more broadly, impose a predicament on their participants very different from that faced by teenagers driving stolen cars. Assuming that at least one of them has opted to swerve, the drivers will return home after having played the "game." But the players in world affairs do not have the luxury of playing only once, then quitting. In reality, world politics imposes a kind of survival game: the object is not simply to prevail in one lone contest, but to endure in order to face repeated engagements.

The risks of going to the brink thus become clearer if we consider it not as a one-time event, but as a repetitive problem. Imagine that there is a 90 percent probability of surviving a given contest unscathed. The odds would seem encouraging. However, the prospect of repeated games rapidly reduces the probability of survival. For example, the likelihood of being alive after two games of Chicken, each of which carried a 90 percent prospect of success, would not be 90 percent. Instead the figure would be the product of 90 percent times 90 percent, or 81 percent. Following this line of reasoning, the probability of a given individual surviv-

Table 8.2 THE CUMULATIVE RISKS OF PLAYING "CHICKEN" (INDIVIDUAL VS. CUMULATIVE PROBABILITIES OF SURVIVAL)

	Encounter						
	1	2	3	4	5	6	7
Probability of Survival On the Individual Encounter	.9	.9	.9	.9	.9	.9	.9
Cumulative (After *n*th encounter)	.9	.81	.729	.656	.590	.531	.478

Note: Calculations for cumulative figures assume probability of survival on individual encounter is 0.9. After second encounter it is $.9 \times .9 = .81$. After third encounter it is $.81 \times .9 = .729$, and so on.

Source: Adapted from Lieber, *Theory and World Politics*, p. 27.

ing seven successive encounters would be less than half (i.e., 47.8 percent). (See Table 8.2.)

To be sure, the probability of "success"—or of avoiding disaster—in any one crisis confrontation may be much better than 90 percent. (In those circumstances the cumulative chances of survival would still deteriorate, though at a slower rate.) However, it is worth bearing in mind the assessment of President Kennedy, quoted at the start of this chapter. In his words, the probability of nuclear war was "between one out of three and even."[29] Even allowing for a degree of exaggeration in these words, the risks of repeated crisis encounters at odds anything like these are daunting.

There is a third subset of views here, which focuses on longer-term or global implications. One such interpretation can be derived from the initial comment of Defense Secretary Robert McNamara that "a missile is a missile." Implicitly, since mutual vulnerability to strategic nuclear attack was perceived as close to becoming a fact of international life—with disagreements about the phenomenon based mainly on when it would take place—the nuclear weapons in Cuba did not represent such a radical departure after all. From this perspective, given the risks of nuclear confrontation, the United States could have afforded to view the missiles in Cuba with a lesser degree of concern—even though the deployment shortened the flight time and increased the probable accuracy of the Soviet weapons.

Finally, there is an outlook that emphasizes the longer-term consequences of the crisis. By and large, it identifies negative outcomes. For their part, it is widely believed, the Soviets reacted to geopolitical defeat by embarking on a massive, long-term effort to expand both their nuclear and conventional forces. The crisis had in fact been a blow to Soviet prestige, and as a leading Soviet official commented bitterly at the time, "You Americans will never be able to do this to us again."[30] Over the course of the 1960s and early 1970s, this Soviet force buildup led ultimately to much-enhanced power projection capabilities and a massive increase of Soviet nuclear weaponry.[31]

THE CUBAN MISSILE CRISIS: IMPLICATIONS

Each of the above views has been the subject of reexamination and criticism. Consider the first interpretation, particularly in its celebration of American skill and resolve in maneuvering through a grave crisis. One careful review of White House tapes of the ExCom meetings cautions against the praise heaped on policymaking during this event. It is particularly skeptical about the uncritical assessments appearing at the time, for example, in language referring to "this combination of toughness and restraint, of will, nerve and wisdom, so brilliantly controlled, so matchlessly calibrated, that dazzled the world."[32] In fact, this review argues that policies—though ultimately effective—were actually worked out in a "disorderly" and "unsystematic" manner.[33] Other careful studies of crisis behavior also suggest it is well not to exaggerate the elements of coolness, skill, and rationality in the actual conduct of decision-makers standing at the brink of war.[34] In essence, however, the outcome may be considered a "victory with compromise"[35] in the sense that the Kennedy administration did succeed in removing the Soviet missiles, while agreeing to eventual removal of the Jupiter missiles based in Turkey and providing a loose commitment that the United States would not invade Cuba.

As for the second interpretation, the stakes of the crisis and the method and costs of its resolution make it doubtful that the central purpose of the Soviet action was to install the missiles and then to withdraw them in order to gain a noninvasion pledge. The economic and political costs to the Soviets, especially the contribution the episode made to Khrushchev's downfall, were too great. And the scale of the offensive weaponry involved, together with more plausible alternative explanations (particularly the prospect of a quick fix in the strategic balance coupled with the Soviet leader's penchant for an impulsive gamble), make the explanation questionable. However, more than a quarter-century after the crisis, accounts by Soviet leaders suggest that strengthening the Cuban regime against a possible American invasion may have played a part in their calculations, even though American participants such as Robert McNamara emphasize that President Kennedy had no such intention prior to the Soviet missile deployment.[36]

Finally, there are the viewpoints in the third interpretation. Here the picture is mixed. Those that suggest deliberate recklessness on Kennedy's part do not give sufficient weight to the provocative and dangerous nature of the Soviet action. They do not reflect an appreciation of the president's specific efforts to delay a military response and the onset of the confrontation. Nor do they take into account the clear signaling of restraint by both sides in the midst of the crisis, including Kennedy's order that the Jupiter missiles in Turkey be immediately disarmed (an action he knew the Soviets would observe).

On the other hand, there were ways in which the crisis may have been even more dangerous, and more subject to uncontrolled events, than was understood at the time. For example, a high-placed Soviet official spying for the United States, Colonel Oleg Penkovsky, was arrested at the onset of the crisis. He managed to send a prearranged coded signal which was meant to indicate that the Soviets were on the verge of launching a nuclear attack. Fortunately, his CIA handlers opted to treat the signal as an act of desperation and ignored its content. Other especially risky features of the crisis included the downing of the American U-2 reconnaissance plane over Cuba (U.S. contingency plans had called for automatic retaliation in such an event); the conspicuous sending of an unprecedented Def-Con 2 alert by the head of the U.S. Strategic Air Command—in a manner bound to catch the attention of the Russians; the accidental violation of Soviet Siberian airspace by another U-2 on October 27; and actions by the U.S. Navy in using low-power depth charges to force Soviet submarines to surface.[37]

Here, it is also worth noting that the CIA found the Russians refrained from making specific preparations for war. In contrast to the Soviets' subsequent behavior during the 1973 Yom Kippur War, the CIA reported at the height of the crisis that it had not detected Soviet forces in any "significant redeployment."[38] The reasons for this Soviet caution are a matter for speculation, but may have reflected both their sense of the perils involved and the fact of American conventional and strategic superiority at the time.

Nonetheless, even beyond the perilous decision to place missiles in Cuba despite American warnings, it was later revealed that Soviets had taken a potentially catastrophic step. According to accounts and documents released in 1992, the Soviet military commander in Cuba had been given the authority to launch short-range tactical nuclear missiles against American invasion forces without receiving explicit authorization from Moscow. In the words of an order from the Soviet Defense Minister to the Commander of Soviet forces in Cuba:

> . . . in the event of a landing of the opponent's forces on the island of Cuba . . . and there is no possibility to receive directives from the U.S.S.R. Ministry of defense, you are personally allowed as an exception to take the decision to apply the tactical nuclear Luna missiles as a means of local war for the destruction of the opponent on land and on the coast with the aim of a full crushing defeat of troops on the territory of Cuba and the defense of the Cuban Revolution.[39]

Thus, had Khrushchev not agreed to withdraw all of the missiles when he did and had the Kennedy administration proceeded with an invasion, U.S. troops might well have been attacked with battlefield nuclear weapons and suffered thousands of casualties. Under these circumstances an American nuclear response would have been almost inevitable and the risks of nuclear escalation incalculable.

Regardless of the merits of the three sets of interpretations, each does reflect a different vantage point from which to try to make sense of the same events. The first perspective reflects an American viewpoint vis-à-vis the Soviet Union. The second emphasizes a local and regional viewpoint in which the focus is on Cuba itself. The third group of interpretations tends to rest on a more global and long-term set of criteria, and thus devotes less concern to regional or more immediate national priorities.

THE CUBAN MISSILE CRISIS IN RETROSPECT

Not only is the level of analysis thus a factor in shaping the interpretation of events, but the passage of time is also important. In this case, the crisis became the focal point for a debate over different kinds of military power. One viewpoint held that nuclear superiority such as the United States possessed in 1962—or at least the perception of it—conveyed tangible advantages. In the debate over American national security policies, this viewpoint argued for greater emphasis on the enhancement of strategic nuclear capability.

A contrasting position, taken explicitly by the surviving civilian members of the ExCom, de-emphasized the practical utility of nuclear force margins. It noted that the missile crisis occurred at a time when the United States did possess nuclear superiority, but that this had no crucial influence with Washington or Moscow. Instead, as Rusk and his colleagues put it, the crisis revealed the "insignificance" of nuclear superiority in the face of "survivable thermonuclear retaliatory forces." To these policymakers, the crisis underlined the crucial role of immediately available conventional forces instead.[40]

Yet another observer of the crisis has argued, however, that even if strategic superiority did not greatly influence American policy, the strategic inferiority of the Soviets appeared to have had a "profound effect" on their own crisis behavior.[41] However, this analysis does omit a crucial point: the asymmetry of vital interests between the two superpowers. In the case of Cuba, the region and the issues involved came to be seen by both sides as a matter of vital American national interest. With the urgency and stakes greater for the Americans, the Russians backed off rather than pursue a challenge that might well have led to war. In two other crises, one previous (Hungary, 1956) and one later (Czechoslovakia, 1968), the United States refrained from pressing the USSR more forcefully at a time when both sides saw Soviet national interests most at stake. This occurred even though the United States possessed clear nuclear superiority at the time of the 1956 crisis.

In retrospect, the Cuban missile crisis may have been even more dangerous than was understood at the time. Although President Kennedy and Secretary Khrushchev sought to find a negotiated way out, each risked losing control of events. Moreover, a growing accumulation of oral histories and documentation[42] has provided considerable evidence that leaders in Washington, Moscow, and Havana sometimes misunderstood or misinterpreted each other's calculations and actions, and did not always have accurate information to inform their crisis decision making.

Ironically, there may well have been a lesson with negative consequences for the United States. The Soviets, having been forced to back down in the crisis, embarked on a major, sustained buildup of both their conventional and nuclear weaponry. Over a period of years, they thus enhanced their own military weight vis-à-vis the Americans. On the United States' side, although the president himself cautioned against any exaggerated sense of triumph from the crisis, his warnings were not universally heeded. To some, the resolution of the crisis seemed to suggest the efficacy of careful, graduated escalation as a form of policy, as well as the lesson that, fortified by superior power and purpose, American resolve would always prove dominant. While there remain major differences of scholarly and political interpretation, it is at least arguable that some of the architects of America's policy in Vietnam derived a lesson from the October 1962 crisis that contributed to the making of a costly and painful debacle in Southeast Asia a few years later. Thus, we turn next to the subject of Vietnam.

NOTES

1. Theodore C. Sorensen, *Kennedy* (New York: Harper & Row, 1965), p. 705.
2. Comment after Soviet ships had stopped or changed course in response to the American naval blockade of Cuba. Quoted in Elie Abel, *The Missile Crisis* (New York: Bantam, 1966), p. 134.
3. Quoted in Abel, p. 161.
4. Former Secretary of State Dean Rusk; former Secretary of Defense Robert McNamara; former special assistant for national security affairs McGeorge Bundy, et al., joint statement on the twentieth anniversary of the missile crisis. *Time*, 27 September 1982, p. 85.
5. For an alternative view, see Eliot A. Cohen, "Why We Should Stop Studying the Cuban Missile Crisis," *The National Interest* 2 (Winter 1985/86): 3–13.
6. The eyewitness accounts of the Vienna summit convey only a frank and direct exchange of views, with neither leader giving ground. The contention that Kennedy showed weakness at Vienna was raised by *New York Times* columnist James Reston, and repeated by Elie Abel (*The Missile Crisis*, p. 37). However, Lebow notes that Reston presented no evidence for his conclusion, and books by those who were present (Arthur Schlesinger, Theodore Sorensen, Pierre Salinger, and Khrushchev himself) do not bear out the Reston position. See Richard Ned Lebow, "The Cuban Missile Crisis: Reading the Lessons Correctly," *Political Science Quarterly* (Fall 1983): 440–442.
7. "Documentation: White House Tapes and Minutes of the Cuban Missile Crisis," *International Security* 10 (Summer 1985): 164–203, at p. 168.
8. See the accounts in Arnold Horelick, "The Cuban Missile Crisis: An Analysis of Soviet Calculations and Behavior," *World Politics* 16 (April 1964): 363–389; Robert F. Kennedy, *The Thirteen Days: A Memoir of the Cuban Missile Crisis* (New York: Norton, 1971); Abel, *The Missile Crisis;* and Theordore C. Sorensen, *Kennedy.*
9. See, "Documentation," *International Security* (Summer 1985): 166.
10. Declassified Documents Collection, Kennedy Library, cited in Marc Trachtenberg, "The Influence of Nuclear Weapons in the Cuban Missile Crisis," *International Security* (Summer 1985): 142.
11. From transcripts of the ExCom, quoted in the *Washington Post*, 25 July 1985.
12. Kennedy, *The Thirteen Days*, pp. 46–49.
13. Abel, pp. 155–156.
14. See Trachtenberg, 145–146.
15. The information was conveyed by Robert Kennedy to Ambassador Dobrynin on the evening of October 27. See the account by Dean Rusk, Robert McNamara, et al., "The Lessons of the Cuban Missile Crisis," *Time*, 27 September 1982, p. 86; also ExCom transcripts for 27 October 1962, cited in *Washington Post*, 25 July 1985. President Kennedy's willingness to remove the Jupiter missiles from Turkey, rather than allow

them to become an obstacle to the withdrawal of Soviet missiles from Cuba, was also made public by Dean Rusk in a March 1987 letter to a meeting of former crisis participants. Kennedy secretly instructed Rusk to arrange for UN Secretary General U Thant to propose removal of the missiles in Turkey for those in Cuba, which the United States would then be prepared to accept publicly. However, Khrushchev agreed to withdraw the Soviet missiles before this occurred. See the accounts in the *Washington Post*, 29 August and 22 October 1987; also James G. Blight, Joseph S. Nye, Jr., and David A. Welch, "The Cuban Missile Crisis Revisited," *Foreign Affairs*, Vol. 66, No. 1 (Fall 1987): 170–188, at pp. 178–179.

16. *New York Times*, 29 January, 1989, pp. 1 and 10; also Joseph S. Nye, "Cuban Graffiti," *The New Republic*, 13 March 1989: 16–18. According to these accounts, American leaders at the time believed that the Soviets had 75 ICBMs—although the intelligence data in Table 8.1 indicate a figure of 44.

17. Quoted by Pierre Salinger, "Gaps in the Cuban Missile Crisis Story," *New York Times*, 5 February 1989. McNamara is similarly quoted in the *Washington Post*, 27 January, 1989, p. 14.

18. For an unconventional argument, which holds that the USSR sought to discouarge Chinese nuclear weapons development by demonstrating the efficacy of the Soviet nuclear umbrella, see Adam Ulam, *Expansion and Co-existence*, 2nd ed., p. 669.

19. Quoted in Horelick, 376. Note, however, that in their 1989 assessment, Soviet leaders cited only the first and second motives.

20. Graham Allison's widely cited work uses the Cuban missile crisis in order to explore three different frameworks for making sense of such events. These are the Rational Actor Model, Organizational Process Model, and Bureaucratic Politics Model. See *Essence of Decision: Explaining the Cuban Missile Crisis* (Boston: Little, Brown, 1971), especially pp. 4–7.

   However, serious reservations have been raised about applying the bureaucratic paradigm to the analysis of American foreign policy. See Robert J. Art, "Bureaucratic Politics and American Foreign Policy: A Critique," *Policy Sciences* 4 (1973): 467–490, at p. 486. Glenn H. Snyder and Paul Diesing do find the bureaucratic politics paradigm useful for explaining foreign policy decision making. However, they identify important limitations in applying the bureaucratic politics model to crisis behavior. Indeed, while they praise Allison's exposition of the model, they find its application to the missile crisis misleading, arguing instead that bureaucratic politics and organizational process are generally more applicable to noncrisis decisions. See *Conflict Among Nations: Bargaining, Decision Making, and System Structure in International Crises* (Princeton: Princeton University Press, 1977), pp. 511–513.

21. Note that prior to the crisis the president had read Barbara Tuchman's book, *The Guns of August*, and during the "thirteen days" he made explicit reference to the lessons of 1914. For a view that the fear of nuclear war was the controlling factor in the outcome of the crisis, see James G. Blight, *The Shattered Crystal Ball: Fear and Learning in the Cuban Missile Crisis* (Savage, MD: Rowman and Littlefield, 1990).

22. David Lowenthal, "U.S. Cuban Poilcy: Illusion and Reality," *National Review*, 29 January 1963, 61–63 at p. 63.

   More scholarly interpretations, for example that of Edward Crankshaw in his comments in *Khrushchev Remembers: The Last Testament* (Boston: Little, Brown, 1974), accept the Soviet leader's assertion that he shipped the missiles to protect Cuba. See Lebow, p. 436.

23. For another critical perspective, see Richard M. Nixon, "Cuba, Castro and John F. Kennedy," *Reader's Digest*, November 1964, 281–284ff.

24. For example, General Curtis LeMay, then head of the Strategic Air Command, stated in a 1984 interview, "in my mind, there wasn't a chance that we would have gone to war with Russia because we had overwhelming strategic capability and the Russians knew it." See Richard H. Kohn and Joseph P. Harahan, "U.S. Strategic Air Power, 1948–1962. Excerpts from an Interview with Generals Curtis E. LeMay, et al.," *International Security,* Vol. 12, No. 4 (Spring 1988): 78–95, at p. 95. General Maxwell Taylor and Paul Nitze were also critical of Kennedy for not driving a harder bargain with the Soviets.

25. See I. F. Stone, "The Brink," *New York Review of Books,* 14 April 1966. For other critical views, see, for example, Ronald Steel, "End Game," *New York Review of Books,* 13 March 1969; Barton Bernstein, "The Cuban Missile Crisis: Trading the Jupiters in Turkey?" *Political Science Quarterly* 95 (Spring 1980): 97–125.

26. "Plain Lessons of a Bad Decade," *Foreign Policy* 1 (Winter 1970–71): 32.

27. For a more comprehensive discussion of "chicken" in game theory and in relation to crisis behavior, see Robert J. Lieber, *Theory and World Politics* (Cambridge, MA: Winthrop, and Boston: Little, Brown, 1972), pp. 22–28. This discussion draws in detail from pp. 26–27.

28. This problem was identified by Karl Deutsch, in *Nerves of Government* (New York: Free Press, 1966), pp. 69–70. Deutsch also developed the argument about the consequent decreasing probabilities of survival.

29. Sorenson, *Kennedy,* p. 705.

30. Charles Bohlen, *Witness to History, 1929–1969* (New York: Norton, 1973), pp. 495–496.

31. This has been the prevailing view. However, a Soviet general at the 1989 Moscow conference stated in a private conversation that plans for a long-term buildup in the Soviet nuclear weapons program had originated in 1960 rather than in the aftermath of the October 1962 crisis. The account is from Nye, *The New Republic,* 13 March 1989, p. 17.

32. The words are from Arthur Schelsinger, Jr., *A Thousand Days* (Boston: Houghton Mifflin, 1965), p. 841. Schlesinger treats the resolution of the crisis on pp. 820–841.

33. Trachtenberg, p. 168.

34. Lebow, pp. 451–458.

35. See Barton J. Bernstein, "Reconsidering the Missile Crisis: Dealing with the Problems of the American Jupiters in Turkey," in James A. Nathan, ed., *The Cuban Missile Crisis Revisited* (New York: St. Martin's Press, 1992), p. 105.

36. In January 1992, former Secretary of Defense McNamara described a January 1989 Moscow meeting with the former Soviet Foreign Minister, Andrei Gromyko. In response to a question about why the Soviets had deployed missiles in Cuba, Gromyko responded that this had been done "to strengthen the defense of Cuba." While insisting that no such invasion had been contemplated, McNamara noted that, in view of the abortive Bay of Pigs operation, covert operations against the Castro regime, and calls for military action in Congress, "If I had been a Cuban or Soviet official, I believe I would have shared the judgment . . . that a U. S. invasion was probable." See Martin Tolchin, "U.S. Underestimated Soviet Force in Cuba During '62 Missile Crisis," *New York Times,* 15 January 1992, p. A11.

37. These incidents are recounted by Raymond L. Garthoff, *Reflections on the Cuban Missile Crisis* (Washington, DC: Brookings, 1987), pp. 40–41 and 108–109ff. Also see the 1989 revised edition of his book, and *Newsweek,* 26 October 1987, p. 34.

38. CIA memoranda prepared for the ExCom on 24, 25, and 27 October, quoted in Trachtenberg, p. 157.

39. The information on local control of tactical nuclear weapons in Cuba was revealed at a January 1992 Russian-American-Cuban meeting in Havana, by General Anatoly Gribkov, who had been head of operational planning for the Soviet General Staff. The tactical weapons were nine Luna missiles with ranges of approximately 25 miles and warheads of less than 100 kilotons. A document consistent with this account was subsequently released by the Russian Defense Ministry. This provided the text of an order from then Defense Minister, Rodion Malinovsky, issued in late September or early October 1962 to the Soviet commander in Cuba, General Issa Pliyev. Part of the text of the document, as well as an account of the Havana meeting, is quoted in Bruce J. Allyn and James G. Blight, letter to the editor, *New York Times,* 2 November 1992, p. A18.
40. Rusk, McNamara, Bundy, et al., *Time,* 27 September 1982, p. 85.
41. Trachtenberg, p. 161.
42. See, for example, Blight, *The Shattered Crystal Ball: Fear and Learning in the Cuban Missile Crisis;* Nathan, ed., *The Cuban Missile Crisis Revisited;* and Laurence Chang and Peter Kornbluh, *The Cuban Missile Crisis, 1962: A National Security Archive* (New York: The New Press, 1992).

chapter 9

Vietnam and the Limits of Intervention

Let every nation know, whether it wishes us well or ill, that we shall pay any price, bear any burden, meet any hardship, support any friend, oppose any foe, in order to insure the survival and success of liberty. This much we pledge—and more.

—PRESIDENT JOHN F. KENNEDY,
INAUGURAL ADDRESS, JANUARY 20, 1961

Yet everything I knew about history told me that if I got out of Vietnam and let Ho Chi Minh run through the streets of Saigon, then I'd be doing exactly what Chamberlain did in World War II. I'd be giving a big fat reward to aggression. And I knew that if we let Communist aggression succeed in taking over South Vietnam, there would follow in this country an endless national debate—a mean and destructive debate—that would shatter my Presidency, kill my Administration, and damage our democracy. I knew that Harry Truman and Dean Acheson had lost their effectiveness from the day that the Communists took over in China. I believe that the loss of China had played a large role in the rise of Joe McCarthy. And I knew that all these problems, taken together, were chickenshit compared with what might happen if we lost Vietnam.

—PRESIDENT LYNDON B. JOHNSON[1]

"You know you never defeated us on the battlefield," said the American colonel.

The North Vietnamese colonel pondered this remark a moment. "That may be so," he replied, *"but it is also irrelevant."*

—CONVERSATION IN HANOI, APRIL 25, 1975[2]

The concept of foreign military intervention has been indelibly affected by the Vietnam conflict and its legacy.Not only have subsequent American policies been debated in terms of avoiding future Vietnams, but the experience of the USSR in Afghanistan (1979–1989) came to be seen as the "Soviet Vietnam." With the passage of time, Vietnam has remained a watershed and its implications continue to shape contemporary understanding of international relations.

The vietnam conflict became the center of intense controversy during the years of American involvement. Yet ever since the U.S. withdrawal in 1975, the subject has been continuously reexamined and reinterpreted. At various times, the war has been described as embodying the overextension of American power, the continuation of a nationalist or anticolonial struggle by the Vietnamese against the Japanese and French as well as the Americans, a white man's war against Asians, a failure of nation building, a doomed effort to shore up a corrupt and unpopular South Vietnamese government, a civil war, a conflict shaped by the wrong kind of American weapons and military tactics, the capture of a genuine nationalist movement by Communist forces, the imposition of a harsh Marxist-Leninist dictatorship over an unhappy population, and a noble effort to aid the South Vietnamese people in achieving self-determination against aggression from the North.

Vietnam was by no means the only significant international problem with a major impact on America's role in the postwar world. Yet it has been the most traumatic and deeply felt. The United States committed combat troops to Vietnam in February 1965, at a time of national preeminence. The country stood at the pinnacle of its post–World War II power, wealth, and self-confidence. Observers could thus describe this as a time when American foreign policymakers exhibited a spirit of "benign invincibility." Yet a decade later, as helicopters lifted the last Americans off the roof of the Saigon embassy, the international role of the United States, along with its domestic consensus on foreign policy, had been dealt a severe blow. This would ultimately trigger a painful reassessment of the country's global position.

The United States approached Indochina from the perspective of its postwar global confrontation with the Soviet Union and in light of its experience with China. But whereas containment had succeeded in Western Europe—a region in which American economic and security assistance enabled viable polities to recover from the ravages of World War II and to withstand a political and military threat—the situation for Vietnam and its neighbors was very different. There the United States faced not Soviets but Vietnamese. Historic legacies including decolonization and the withdrawal of France, problems of nation building, the consolidation of control over Vietnamese nationalism by Ho Chi Minh and the Communists, and endemic instability within South Vietnam all made the effective application of containment extremely difficult.

The Vietnam war epoch was not only significant in terms of American involvement. It also incorporated elements of both the East-West and North-South conflicts. While important features of the war were indigenous to Southeast Asia, other aspects reflected broad problems of revolutionary nationalism and the playing out of superpower antagonisms in a regional setting.

At the time, world attention focused on the bloody events in North and South Vietnam, Laos, and Cambodia, with particular reference to the American role, though the Soviet Union and China also played significant parts. Ironically, despite the withdrawal of the United States, and the coming to power of Marxist-Leninist regimes in the countries of Indochina, the region experienced not the end of conflict but its redirection into more than a decade of savage and multilayered struggles involving Vietnam, China, and Cambodia.

In assessing the Vietnam era, this chapter begins by considering the origins of the war and of the American decision to intervene. Next, it examines the long process of de-escalation and withdrawal and the experience of Indochina in the years afterward. Finally, it analyzes the lessons of Vietnam.

ORIGINS OF THE VIETNAM WAR

France consolidated its control of Vietnam during a period stretching from the mid-nineteenth century until 1917. However, the region had a long history of national independence. Vietnam first revolted against Chinese domination in the year A.D. 40 and had maintained its autonomy with only brief interruptions from 967 until the arrival of the French.

Opposition to French rule grew slowly during the interval between World Wars I and II. Among various nationalist and revolutionary groups, the Communist party led by Ho Chi Minh made only modest progress. The outbreak of World War II and the defeat of France, however, brought drastic changes. In September 1940, Japanese forces took control of Indochina and proceeded to rule the area through arrangement with French colonial officials and the collaborationist Vichy regime. As in other regions, the military defeat of the colonial power was not only a blow to its physical control of territory, but also shattered the image of omnipotence through which the outside power had managed to rule a large population and land area with a relatively small contingent of troops and administrators.

The wartime experience brought Ho Chi Minh and the Communists their greatest opportunity. In 1941, Ho organized the "League for the Independence of Vietnam," or *Vietminh*. This Communist-dominated movement proved highly successful in gaining nationalist support. During the war years, Ho and the Vietminh even received backing from the Nationalist Chinese government of Chiang Kai-shek and from the American intelligence organization, the OSS, in the struggle against the Japanese.[3]

With the defeat of Japan, the Vietminh sought to take control of Vietnam. On September 2, 1945, in the northern capital of Hanoi, Ho Chi Minh, backed by an army of some 10,000 troops, proclaimed the country's independence. However, the effort was short-lived. A British-led Indian army division not only disarmed Japanese forces remaining in the southern half of the country, but restored that portion of Vietnam to French control. During the next six months, France and the Vietminh negotiated over the future of the entire country. On March 6, 1946, they reached agreement on limited self-government. France would accept a "Democratic Republic of Vietnam" as part of an Indochinese federation within the French union. The new state would have its own government and army, and a referendum would be held to determine whether three distinct parts of the country—the North (Tonkin), Center (Annam), and South (Cochin)—would become unified. In the meantime, 15,000 French troops would return to North Vietnam.

In the following months, however, an impasse developed that would lead to three decades of war. Disagreements between French and Vietnamese, political upheavals in Paris, French insistence on controlling the Vietnamese military and foreign relations, concerns about Communist power, and opposition by French colonial officials led to breakdown of the March agreement. On November 20, 1946, French forces attacked the Vietminh at the northern port city of Haiphong, leading to some 1,000 deaths. During the following month, fighting spread to Hanoi, forcing the Vietminh to withdraw to the countryside.[4] The Indochina war had now begun in earnest.

The forces fighting the French were by no means exclusively Communist. Large numbers of the Vietnamese were motivated by nationalism, and Ho Chi Minh was even criticized for failing to obtain total independence from France in the March 1946 agreement. Nonetheless, the Communists under Ho had seized a dominant position within the Vietminh. In the years to follow, though indigenous nationalism would provide the manpower and motivation, the Communists would be able to steer the movement in their own direction, and Ho himself would embody Vietnam's struggle for independence.

France, meanwhile, had been desperately weakened by the ravages of defeat and occupation in World War II and was not in a sound position to sustain the costs of a grinding colonial war. By the spring of 1950, the French government turned to America for assistance. While the United States had not encouraged the reassertion of French control in the region, the emerging global confrontation between East and West and the October 1949 victory of the Communists in the Chinese civil war caused the Truman administration to see the French request in a new light. Thus, in May 1950, Secretary of State Acheson agreed to send economic aid and military equipment to the French in Indochina.

Following the outbreak of the Korean War, the American government stepped up its support of France. In August 1950, it dispatched a group of 35 military advisors to provide assistance in the use of American military equipment. Within two years, this American commitment had assumed major proportions, and the United States was paying nearly half the cost of France's Indochina war.

The French struggle with the Vietnamese came to a head at the climactic battle of Dien Bien Phu.[5] In March 1954, France's regional military commander, General Henri Navarre, sought to lure the Vietminh forces, under General Giap, into a major battle in which the French superiority in conventional arms and experience could be brought to bear. To do so, he placed a garrison of 13,000 colonial troops (Vietnamese, North Africans, and Foreign Legionnaires, commanded by French officers) in an isolated valley outpost in the northwestern area of North Vietnam.

Events soon took an unexpected turn. Making use of mountainous terrain, a Vietminh force of 50,000 men managed to surround and cut off the French troops. They also succeeded in maneuvering heavy artillery onto the heights overlooking the French positions and installing it in concealed positions. The French artillery commander at Dien Bien Phu, taken by surprise and unable to destroy these guns, committed suicide. With the fate of the beleaguered garrison hanging in the balance, France appealed to the United States for help. The proposed measures included air strikes by planes from American aircraft carriers and possibly the use of nuclear weapons.

In hurried and intense consultations, the administration of President Eisenhower and Secretary of State John Foster Dulles conferred with military and congressional leaders and then with allied governments. Though Dulles and Admiral Arthur Radford, the chairman of the Joint Chiefs of Staff, supported intervention, others opposed it. Army leaders, notably Generals James Gavin and Matthew Ridgeway, feared that air strikes alone would not resolve the military issue, and as many as two million American troops might be needed. Congressional leaders, including the then Senate Democratic majority leader, Lyndon Johnson, also expressed opposition and feared that war with China could result. In the end, President Eisenhower decided against American military intervention.[6]

On May 7, 1954, Dien Bien Phu was finally overrun and the surviving French forces surrendered. A day later, negotiations began in Geneva on the future of Indochina. The participants included the French, British, Vietnamese, Russians, and Chinese. United States representatives were present but did not sign the agreement which was reached in July. The Geneva agreement provided for the independence of Laos, Cambodia, and Vietnam, and contained four principal elements: a military cease-fire, provisional division of Vietnam at the 17th parallel, national elections to be held in July 1956, and eventual reunification of Vietnam. (See Map 9.1).

The Geneva agreements left Ho Chi Minh and the Vietminh in control only of North Vietnam, although their military position might have enabled them to contest with the French for more of the country. South Vietnam, meanwhile, remained under the control of Emperor Bao Dai, who had been chief of state and a figurehead used by both the French and Japanese. More politically powerful in South Vietnam was the prime minister, Ngo Dinh Diem.

ORIGINS OF AMERICAN INVOLVEMENT

The Eisenhower administration faced difficult choices. In light of the loss of China five years earlier, it was loath to see Indochina fall under Communist control. Indeed, the president observed that in the event of such a loss, the remainder of Southeast Asia would topple very quickly, like a "row of dominoes," even driving Japan into the Communist camp. Eisenhower described the possible consequences of Indochina's fall as being "just incalculable to the free world."[7]

At the same time, the military picture remained difficult. Ho had a strong base of support in the North, and a direct challenge would require the use of American troops and also pose the risk of Chinese intervention, as in Korea some four years earlier. The Joint Chiefs of Staff remained divided over the American role, with army leaders opposing military intervention. President Eisenhower opted instead to support the South Vietnamese government with the objective of consolidating an independent and pro-Western state.

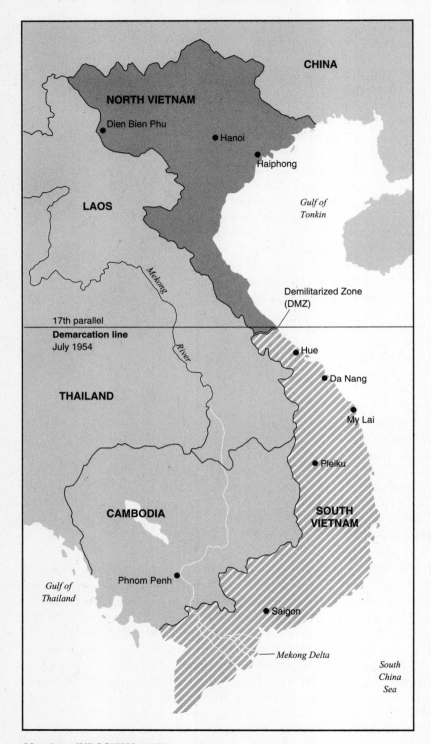

Map 9.1   INDOCHINA, 1965

Source: Adapted from Gary B. Nash and Julie R. Jeffrey, et al. (eds.), *The American People*, 3rd ed. (New York: HarperCollins, 1994), p. 990.

The task of nation building and of assuring a stable, non-Communist South Vietnam remained daunting. President Eisenhower even observed in his memoirs that had elections been held at the time of the fighting, "possibly 80 percent of the population would have voted for the Communist Ho Chi Minh as their leader rather than Chief of State Bao Dai."[8] In essence, by achieving popular support as leader of Vietnamese nationalism and the war against France, Ho and the Vietminh had achieved broader support than southern leaders at the time, even though he would soon consolidate a harsh, Marxist-Leninist dictatorship in the areas under Communist control.

In October 1954, President Eisenhower wrote to Ngo Dinh Diem, the aloof South Vietnamese prime minister, that American aid was being provided with the stipulation that his government would carry out necessary reforms as well as strengthen itself militarily. During the next year, the United States expanded its military advisory group to some 650 men and undertook training of the South Vietnamese army. Diem, who became president of South Vietnam in October 1955, responded during the following year with harsh measures against not only the Communists but also other opponents of his increasingly autocratic rule.

In July 1955, Diem announced that he would not comply with the Geneva provision for nationwide elections on the future of Vietnam, arguing that free choice would be impossible in the North. At the same time, events were hardening the separation between the two Vietnams. In the North, there was a peasant uprising in opposition to the collectivization of agriculture. In the process of quelling the rebellion and enforcing collectivization, Ho's regime killed more than 50,000 people. Ho consolidated control by repressing former nationalist or ideological allies, including North Vietnamese Trotskyists. During the two years following the Geneva accords, a population transfer also took place, with nearly one million persons (primarily Catholics or former military and administrative personnel and their families) moving South, and approximately 150,000 Vietminh supporters and their dependents heading North.

Although Diem succeeded for a time in consolidating his position and in blunting the Communist challenge to the South, he became increasingly isolated and unpopular. In mid 1959 he intensified the repression of both Communist and non-Communist opponents to his rule, causing many of the latter to move toward the Communists.

Meanwhile, a military challenge to South Vietnam was developing. Beginning in October 1957, guerrilla activity increased during the next two years. In the spring of 1959, North Vietnam launched a systematic effort to send men and arms into the South by means of the Ho Chi Minh trail (a circuitous jungle route extending through Cambodia). Then in December 1960, North Vietnamese leaders established the National Liberation Front (NLF). This Communist-led body, known as the *Vietcong*, aimed to establish control over South Vietnam. Like the Vietminh, it relied on appeals to nationalism and on a broadly based opposition to the government, but the key leadership positions were held by Communists. Many of the NLF combatants and officials were South Vietnamese, trained in the North, then infiltrated back into the South, where they drew on an often sympathetic rural population. Key command and control decisions were communicated from the North, however, where the ultimate political authority lay.

The Kennedy Administration's Response

The new administration of John F. Kennedy was immediately faced with the problem of Indochina in early 1961. Attention had initially centered on problems in the much smaller, more remote, and far less populous country of Laos. However, concern soon shifted to South Vietnam. There, Diem's regime appeared isolated and in the process of disintegration. The president and his brother, Ngo Dinh Nhu, controlled the police force and a restless military. The building of stable political institutions had not gone well, and political opposition to the government appeared to be growing. Many students opposed the repressive Diem regime, as did Buddhist monks, who resented the rule of the Catholic Nhu family and its associates over an overwhelmingly Buddhist population.

The Kennedy administration was initially hesitant over what course of action to take.[9] On the one hand, the language of the President's 1960 election campaign and his inaugural address promised an activist assertion of American power to promote the interests of the free world. Members of his administration were also fascinated with the possibilities of counterinsurgency warfare as a means of resisting Communist advances in the newly emergent countries of the developing world. Illustratively, the President's Deputy National Security Advisor, Walt W. Rostow, argued forcefully for a "maximum effort" in Vietnam. His reasoning can be found in a memorandum to other high officials of the Kennedy administration shortly after the Bay of Pigs debacle:

> There is one area where success against Communist techniques is conceivable and where success is desperately required in the Free World interest. That area is Vietnam. A maximum effort—military, economic, political and diplomatic—is required there; and it is urgently required.
> . . . a clean-cut success in Vietnam would do much to hold the line in Asia while permitting us—and the world—to learn how to deal with indirect aggression[10]

On the other hand, the difficulties were also apparent. The example of the French was sobering, as was the experience of the Eisenhower administration in seeking to cope with Indochina. In addition, the military and political situation appeared daunting.

Ultimately, the Kennedy administration acted as the previous administration had done—to ward off collapse. Although a few of his more liberal advisors urged an emphasis on political reform, most of the senior military and political advisors to the president advocated a military course of action. This became especially urgent after an October 1961 mission to the South Vietnamese capital by General Maxwell Taylor, the chairman of the Joint Chiefs of Staff, and Walt Rostow. Upon their return from Saigon, they and others called for the dispatch of a small American combat force.

In December, President Kennedy decided not to commit U.S. troops directly to the war effort. Expressing his caution about the Taylor-Rostow report, he observed:

> They want a force of American troops. . . . They say it's necessary in order to restore confidence and maintain morale. But . . . the troops will march in; the bands will play; the crowds will cheer; and in four days everyone will have forgotten. Then we will be

told we have to send more troops. It's like taking a drink. The effect wears off, and you have to take another.[11]

Kennedy added that the war in Vietnam was *their* war (i.e., South Vietnam's) to win or lose, and that if it were converted to a white man's war, the United States would lose as the French had a decade earlier. He thus continued to place responsibility for military performance on the Vietnamese themselves.

The administration did not commit combat troops, but it did undertake a major expansion of American military assistance. During the Kennedy presidency, the number of advisors grew to some 15,000. During the next two years, although fighting intensified, the military situation did improve at least slightly as a result of the influx of American arms and personnel. However, the political situation continued to deteriorate. Diem and his family encountered intensified popular hostility, and he resorted to the use of troops and police against Buddhist demonstrators. Two separate attempts by the military to oust Diem failed, but the South Vietnamese leader became more and more isolated and unpopular.

With civilian unrest growing, particularly on the part of Diem's non-Communist opponents, the South Vietnamese military successfully carried out a coup on November 1, 1963. In the uprising, Diem and his brother were assassinated. While the extent of American involvement in the coup has been a matter of dispute, American officials do appear to have had advance knowledge of it.

Although Diem and Nhu had been an obstacle to reform and to the building of a stable, non-Communist South Vietnam, the problem of stability and security in the country became worse. The Diem regime was replaced by a series of unstable and sometimes corrupt military governments. By mid 1964, unrest among non-Communist sectors of the population continued, and the military challenge from the North Vietnamese and the NLF intensified. As a result of the American military buildup and the overthrow of Diem, the United States became increasingly committed, yet the situation in Vietnam was once again deteriorating badly.

Lyndon Johnson, who had taken office after President Kennedy's assassination in November 1963, faced a series of unwelcome decisions. Although he had stated that American troops would not be sent to do what "Asian boys ought to be doing for themselves," he was even more determined not to be blamed for the loss of Vietnam. Here, the memory of the "loss of China" and of its impact on a Democratic administration and American politics weighed heavily on the president.

The Tonkin Gulf Incident

On August 2, 1964, three North Vietnamese torpedo boats fired torpedoes and machine guns at the USS *Maddox*, an American destroyer cruising in the Gulf of Tonkin some thirty miles off the North Vietnamese coast. The *Maddox* escaped harm, but American planes from the carrier *Ticonderoga* damaged the three attacking boats. Two days later, another attack was reported, this time on the destroyer USS *Turner Joy*, 65 miles off the coast. President Johnson retaliated with air attacks against torpedo boat bases and oil storage facilities. On August 7, at the administration's request, Congress passed a resolution authorizing the president to undertake "all necessary measures to repel any armed attack against the forces of the United States and to prevent further aggression." The vote carried in the House by 416 to 0, and in the Senate by 88 to 2.

Although in retrospect Tonkin Gulf was no more than an incident in a long and complex conflict, the dispute surrounding the events epitomized both the domestic controversy that would accompany the expanded American commitment to Vietnam and the problem of defining American objectives and interests in the Indochina conflict. On the domestic side, although the president had assured the Senate Foreign Relations Committee chairman, William Fulbright, that no commitment of American troops to Vietnam was contemplated, a leading administration official, Nicholas Katzenbach, later identified the Tonkin Gulf resolution as the "functional equivalent of a declaration of war." While the initial impulse among elected officials and the public was to rally around the president—and indeed the two senators who opposed the resolution, Wayne Morse of Oregon and Ernest Gruening of Alaska, were both defeated in the 1966 elections—a controversy would later arise over the manner in which the Johnson administration committed the United States to a land war in Asia.

Indeed, questions even arose over what had actually occurred in the waters off the North Vietnamese coast. According to information later made public in the Pentagon Papers, the destroyers had actually been associated with South Vietnamese boats carrying out attacks against Northern targets. Known as "34-A" raids,[12] the most recent of these missions had taken place just two days before the attack on the *Maddox*. Moreover, the details of the August 4 attack on the *Turner Joy* remain ambiguous. The incident took place at night and several eyewitness American accounts suggest there may not have been any contact. The most compelling of these was by James Stockdale, a Navy commander flying air defense over the destroyers. He concluded that only the two American destroyers were present, and that poor surface weather and mistaken sonar and radar readings caused the confusion. As he described it in his debriefing immediately after landing, there were no North Vietnamese boats in the August 4 incident:

> Not a one. No boats, no boat wakes, no ricochets off boats, no boat impacts, no torpedo wakes—nothing but black sea and American firepower.[13]

National Interest and the American Response

The issue, ultimately, was less a matter of how the United States should react to a specific incident than of what the long-term interests of the country required. However, policy appeared to take shape without sufficient consideration of whether national objectives could be accomplished at any acceptable cost. Nor was there evident appreciation of the difficulty of carrying out any policy (with its costs in money and lives) without full governmental credibility and sustained domestic support.

The crucial American escalation took place in February 1965. With the South Vietnamese war effort once again going badly and the political situation in the country highly unstable, the Johnson administration decided on a policy of continuous air strikes against North Vietnam and the commitment of large numbers of American troops to combat. By December 1965, the total of United States armed forces in Vietnam had risen to 200,000. The objective of this escalation, summed up in a July 1965 memorandum from Secretary of State Dean Rusk to President Johnson, was "to insure that North Vietnam not succeed in taking over or determining the future of South Vietnam by force."[14] However, administration policymakers assumed that they could achieve their objective by applying pressure on North Vietnam and thereby convincing the enemy of American resolve. As a group of officials involved in planning the air strikes put it in early 1965, six weeks of this punishment would drive North Vietnam to the conference table. When one participant reluctantly asked what would happen if the North Vietnamese did not in fact then seek peace talks on American terms, he was told that in that case, another four weeks of bombing would surely do the trick.[15]

However, the Vietcong and North Vietnamese proved able to match the American escalation and absorb a level of punishment they had not been expected to tolerate. North Vietnam, under the Marxist-Leninist rule of Ho Chi Minh and his party, had become a tightly disciplined and militarized society. During the following decade, it would withstand repeated and intense bombing, heavy military casualties, and the costs of continuing to infiltrate men and arms down the Ho Chi Minh trail into South Vietnam.

As the war escalated, the Johnson administration decided in 1966 to move the Army of the Republic of South Vietnam (ARVN) into a pacification role and turn over the bulk of the fighting to American troops. By the end of 1967, the United States forces numbered 500,000. Rusk and others had asserted that the interests of the entire free world were at stake: "the U.S. commitment is the principal pillar of peace throughout the world. If that commitment becomes unreliable, the Communist world would certainly draw conclusions that would lead to our ruin and almost certainly to a catastrophic war."[16] Nevertheless, America's allies were mostly reluctant to support the war effort. The only other countries to send troops were Korea (approximately 50,000—comparable to the number of American troops stationed in that country), Australia (some 5,000), and New Zealand (several hundred).

DE-ESCALATION AND WITHDRAWAL

The Johnson administration had sought to fight a war in Vietnam without jeopardizing the president's ambitious domestic programs (the Great Society) or disrupting established patterns of everyday life. The administration, in short, sought to follow a policy of both guns and butter. As a result, it was slow to raise taxes, thereby causing a large budget deficit and igniting inflation. It also agreed to limit military tours of duty in Vietnam to one year (and sometimes six months for officers), and was often less than wholly candid with the American public about the commitments, costs, and likely duration of the conflict. When casualties began to mount (ultimately leading to 58,000 American deaths), policymakers continued to respond with optimistic statements about the war. For example, the American ambassador to Saigon, Henry Cabot Lodge, observed on December 16, 1966, "By the end of 1967, there might be light at the end of the tunnel"; and the United

States military commander in Vietnam, General William C. Westmoreland, stated on November 15, 1967, "I have never been more encouraged in my four years in Vietnam."[17]

For the United States, and especially for the American public, however, the turning point toward eventual withdrawal came with the Communists' Tet offensive on January 31, 1968. On that day, large numbers of Vietcong and North Vietnamese launched attacks on cities throughout Vietnam. A Vietcong suicide squad even penetrated the American embassy compound in Saigon. After several weeks of heavy fighting, the offensive was decisively defeated. The Vietcong sustained especially heavy casualties in the fighting, and indeed, the role of the North Vietnamese in the war would henceforth become much greater. However, the Tet offensive had a significant political effect within the United States. Coming as it did after a wave of optimism on the part of military and civilian officials, the offensive suggested that there was not, after all, light at the end of the tunnel. After three years of combat, the commitment of half a million men, a sustained bombing campaign, and rising casualties, there was no end in sight. The North Vietnamese and Vietcong appeared to be willing to continue the war indefinitely.

PUBLIC OPINION AND THE VIETNAM WAR

Domestic opposition to the war, which had been growing during the previous year, began to spread and intensify. This was now less a matter of antiwar activism than of a change of heart by much of the general public. In essence, the mainstream of public opinion wished that the United States would win or get out. As winning appeared increasingly problematic, sentiment increasingly favored withdrawal.

Initially, with the expansion of the American combat role in 1965, public support for the war in Vietnam had actually increased. This phenomenon of "rallying around the flag" often occurs when a country at first becomes embroiled in a foreign conflict. In the Vietnam case, three times as many Americans approved of the war as opposed it during the latter part of 1965. However, this sentiment gradually eroded. At the beginning of January 1968 supporters and opponents of the war were roughly equal in number, and following the Tet offensive the trend levels of support and opposition for the war steadily diverged. By the middle of 1971, more than twice as many Americans opposed the war as supported it.[18]

Sentiment had also begun to shift among political leaders. For example, Secretary of Defense Robert McNamara, an early supporter of the war, resigned at the end of February 1968, amid reports he had privately concluded that American strategy was at a dead end. Others now focused their concerns on how to extricate the United States from the Vietnam quagmire with the least damage to the country's international role and national interests.

Matters came to a head with a request from General Westmoreland for an additional 206,000 American troops. The new secretary of defense, Clark Clifford, and his advisors studied and debated the issue, then recommended to President Johnson in late March 1968 that the United States not further escalate its commitment to Vietnam.[19] There was no assurance that the additional troops would prove decisive, nor that still further increases in troop strength might not be needed at a later date. President Johnson accepted their recommendation and in a surprise announcement on March 31 told the country that he was undertaking a partial cessation of the air war against Hanoi, making a renewed attempt at negotiations, and that he had decided not to seek reelection as president.

The Nixon Administration and Vietnamization

By the time of Richard Nixon's narrow election victory over Hubert Humphrey in November 1968, the United States had 550,000 troops in Vietnam. Negotiations toward a resolution of the conflict appeared unlikely, and the war had become a costly and bloody stalemate. Domestic opinion had turned against the war, and Nixon's administration and his national security advisor, Henry Kissinger, sought a means of reducing the American role without suffering adverse geopolitical consequences. Opponents countered that nothing was likely to be so harmful as continuation of an unending conflict that had already consumed 25,000 American lives—not to mention far larger numbers of Vietnamese on both sides—and had polarized the American political climate as well as distracting the country from other, more vital foreign policy priorities.

The Nixon and Kissinger strategy was Vietnamization, that is, the returning of principal responsibility for combat to the ARVN, coupled with continuation of a major United States role in advising and logistics. The air war would continue, and even at times be expanded, but at the same time there would be a steady withdrawal of American troops. The effort, coinciding with protracted negotiations in Paris between American and North Vietnamese officials, proved long and costly.

The administration contended that over the course of several years, its policies allowed the United States to disengage from a combat role (and from high levels of American casualties), to give the South Vietnamese time—"a decent interval"—to prepare to face the enemy on their own, and that it preserved American international credibility.

Critics of the Vietnamization program countered with several arguments. First, the war had expanded into Cambodia and Laos, causing frightful casualties and devastation. Second, if more than half a million American troops, plus air support and American political commitment had not enabled the South to prevail, how could it hope to sustain itself with the American combat role eliminated and the remaining presence sharply reduced? The United States, after all, had begun training the ARVN in 1954. Finally, American casualties in the years from 1969 to the cessation of a combat role and the signing of a peace agreement in 1973 were actually slightly higher than in the entire period of escalation.

For a time, it appeared that Vietnamization might actually succeed. On March 30, 1972, the North Vietnamese launched a major invasion that the South Vietnamese managed to repel with the aid of massive American air power. The United States' contribution included B-52 attacks on Hanoi and Haiphong beginning on April 15, and then the temporary mining of Haiphong harbor on May 8. While previously it had been feared that these steps could lead to a direct clash with China or the USSR, the détente initiatives of Nixon and Kissinger, the president's 1971 trip to Peking, and Soviet preference that the Nixon trip to Moscow proceed as planned, all helped to forestall a superpower confrontation.

With the North Vietnamese under pressure from China and the Soviet Union, and the South Vietnamese facing American desires to withdraw, the Paris peace negotiations finally produced a tentative settlement. On October 26, 1972, Henry Kissinger announced in a White House press conference, "We believe that peace is at hand."

Even before the Kissinger statement, completion of peace arrangements had hit a snag. South Vietnamese President Thieu feared being abandoned by the Americans and bitterly objected to terms of the proposed peace settlement. Although some two billion dollars' worth of new military equipment was quickly shipped to South Vietnam, including enough aircraft to give it the world's fourth largest air force, Nixon and Kissinger were unable to gain Thieu's agreement to the October peace terms. And although the United States and North Vietnam were close to a final agreement, Kissinger was unable to obtain changes in the draft agreement sought by President Nixon.

In response to this stalemate, and to the suspension of talks by the North Vietnamese and their chief negotiator, Le Duc Tho, President Nixon ordered the intensive bombing of military and logistical targets around Hanoi and Haiphong. The "Christmas bombing" lasted from December 18 to 30. In its aftermath, negotiations resumed on January 8, with Kissinger and Le Duc Tho reaching agreement the next day—on terms very close to what they had been in October. In turn, Nixon put pressure on the South Vietnamese to accept the terms, lest the United States proceed without them. With their concurrence, the Paris peace agreements were signed on January 27, 1973, and President Nixon proclaimed "peace with honor."

The Paris Peace Agreements

Until their negotiating breakthrough in October 1972, the two sides had sought each other's defeat at the conference table. North Vietnam had demanded dismissal of the South Vietnamese government and—in effect—the takeover of power by the Vietcong. The United States, in turn, had aimed at the withdrawal of the North Vietnamese from the South and the cessation of hostilities. Now, however, in an uneasy standoff, the North Vietnamese dropped their demand that the South Vietnamese government be replaced, and the United States accepted the continued presence of North Vietnamese troops in the South.

The principal provisions of the peace agreement[20] included the following:

Ceasefire agreement (essentially on an in-place basis).

Withdrawal of U.S. forces (the remaining American troops and military advisors were to depart within 60 days; there was to be no reinforcement or replacement of the approximately 150,000 North Vietnamese in the South;[21] both sides could replace existing equipment on a one-for-one basis).

Release of American prisoners of war (to be completed by the end of March).

Self-determination for South Vietnam (including free elections, to be decided on by the two South Vietnamese parties—the Saigon government and the NLF).

Respect for the demilitarized zone (DMZ) (the area on either side of the demarcation line between North and South Vietnam).

Neutrality and self-determination for Laos and Cambodia (including withdrawal of foreign troops and the prohibition of bases).

In practice, the Paris peace accords provided the means for the United States to withdraw from Indochina and obtain the release of its POWs without conceding the North Vietnamese objectives. The settlement took place on the basis of the status quo: that is, Hanoi remained in control of a portion of South Vietnam in order to have a basis for a Provisional Revolutionary Government. Saigon, meanwhile, retained control of more than three-fourths of the country's territory and population. Although American military forces completed their withdrawal, some 10,000 civilian personnel remained.

THE COLLAPSE OF SOUTH VIETNAM

The peace agreements provided for the extrication of the United States, but did nothing to resolve the bitter conflict between the Vietnamese parties. The prospect that the two sides could agree on the political shape of South Vietnam was almost inconceivable. Indeed, stalemate over the provisions for South Vietnam soon developed. Meanwhile, both sides took unilateral actions: Saigon in moving militarily against some of the Communist enclaves in South Vietnam, the North Vietnamese in systematically upgrading their logistics (including construction of a major highway and a fuel pipeline reaching deep into the South) in preparation for an eventual invasion.

Initially, President Thieu appeared to hold the advantage. His armed forces were equipped with large quantities of modern American weapons, the ARVN made successful inroads in Communist-controlled areas, and the North Vietnamese army was still reeling from the loss of between 50,000 and 100,000 men killed in its unsuccessful spring 1972 offensive. Indeed, according to one account, North Vietnam's leader, Pham Van Dong, met with discouragement when he sought support from China for a new offensive. The Chinese Premier, Zhou Enlai, told him that "it would be best for Vietnam and the rest of Indochina to relax for, say, five or ten years."[22]

However, two factors led to a reversal of fortunes. First, the American government was no longer in a position to provide air power and advisors to aid the South Vietnamese in repelling a major attack. President Nixon had made a confidential pledge to President Thieu that the United States would respond militarily if necessary. However, such action soon became nearly impossible. Congress and the American public had wearied of the Indochina conflict and of the manner in which the Johnson and Nixon administrations had waged it. Congress passed legislation effectively ending United States military action in Indochina as of August

15, 1973. At the same time, Nixon's power to act decisively as president was eroding as the details of Watergate became increasingly public.

A second crucial factor was the continuing disarray of the South Vietnamese
government and economy. The withdrawal of most of the 550,000 Americans left
the economy of the South in a badly weakened condition. Problems of serious corruption mounted, not least in the provision of wages, supplies, and ammunition
for the ARVN, thereby undercutting the viability of the long-trouble-plagued
armed forces. Meanwhile, the Thieu government failed to galvanize the loyalties
of its own population. That is not to say that there was a broad base of support for
the Communists, particularly among the large urban population which had expanded as a consequence of the decades of warfare, but morale was low and public support for the Thieu regime remained wanting.

By the beginning of 1975, the Communists had rebuilt their forces and were
prepared for a major assault, while the Thieu regime had deteriorated economically and politically. The North Vietnamese, using their main force army units
with heavy concentrations of tanks and artillery, launched a coordinated offensive
assault against the South. They achieved initial successes in January, seizing a
provincial capital less than 75 miles north of Saigon, and in early March, taking
the strategically located city of Banmethot in the central highlands. The latter action led to military disaster for the South Vietnamese. In mid-March, President
Thieu suddenly ordered his troops to withdraw from the entire northern section
of South Vietnam. Whatever the military rationale, this triggered massive civilian
panic in the north and the flight of ARVN units remaining in that part of the country.

While some South Vietnamese fought bravely under desperate conditions,
the military situation disintegrated with surprising speed. At the end of April the
remaining Americans were evacuated—many by helicopter from the roof of the
U.S. embassy in Saigon—amid mobs of Vietnamese frantically seeking to leave
ahead of the advancing North Vietnamese Army (NVA). On April 30, NVA troops
seized Saigon and completed their conquest of South Vietnam.

THE LESSONS OF VIETNAM

The meaning of important events is often subject to reinterpretation with the passage of time. Vietnam is no exception. In addition it is well worth asking: lessons
for whom? and about what? In the immediate aftermath of the fall of Saigon and
of the accompanying Communist victories of the Khmer Rouge in Cambodia and
the Pathet Lao in Laos, assessments often dwelt on the limits of American power
and the impetus of national liberation movements. Illustratively, initial judgments
frequently stressed the nationalist character of the Vietnamese conflict and were
highly critical of the purpose and character of America's intervention. They usually concluded with the exhortation, "No more Vietnams."

A decade later, in light of repressive rule by Hanoi, a wave of refugees (the
"boat people"), Pol Pot's genocidal slaughter in Cambodia, the Vietnamese invasion of Cambodia, and a border war between Vietnam and China, different con-

clusions were often voiced. These underlined the Communist character of the insurgencies and suggested that in light of the disastrous consequences for Indochina, American actions were justified or even noble and that they had failed chiefly because of domestic opposition and a lack of will, rather than for reasons of strategy or morality.

Conceivably, both these sets of judgments about the lessons of Vietnam have missed the point. At the time of its commitment of combat troops in 1965, the United States stood at the pinnacle of its power. Yet the objective of the American intervention was not only one of self-determination for the people of South Vietnam. In fact, there existed a welter of overlapping and sometimes contradictory purposes. These included maintaining the existence of an independent and non-Communist South Vietnam (as well as of Laos and Cambodia), deterring China, containing of communism, and demonstrating that Communist-dominated wars of national liberation could not succeed. Moreover, domestic imperatives were at least as important as international ones. Above all, the experience of the "loss of China" had proved traumatic, especially for the Democrats. The administration of Lyndon Johnson was loath to be saddled with responsibility for the possible "loss" of Vietnam.

Beyond the specific concerns of President Johnson, however, the dominant consideration for a series of administrations, Democratic as well as Republican, was to do whatever was necessary to avoid losing Vietnam. Ultimately, this would lead to an open-ended commitment. As one insightful analyst of the decision-making process had observed, Johnson was finally forced in 1965 to choose between accepting defeat or introducing American combat forces.[23]

What Went Wrong with U.S. Policy?

The foremost problem for the United States was that the basic political objective—securing a stable, independent, non-Communist Vietnam—was exceedingly difficult to achieve at a price Americans were willing to pay. Nation building is a difficult and often chaotic task, for which the United States was ill equipped in Indochina. Tragically, the Communists under Ho Chi Minh had succeeded in gaining control of the struggle against France. They did so through their appeals to land reform and Vietnamese nationalism, rather than to any broad-based support for a Marxist-Leninist dictatorship. Meanwhile, many of the leaders of South Vietnam had been compromised by their earlier involvement with the French.

To be sure, large sectors of the South Vietnamese population had no wish to fall under the domination of Hanoi, but a series of South Vietnamese governments had great difficulty in building a viable economy and society under wartime conditions. Meanwhile, as a leading figure in the NLF (who subsequently fled South Vietnam in disillusion after the North Vietnamese victory) has observed, many rank-and-file Vietcong were fighting for basic and often nonideological reasons:

After the war, one American writer declared that the average guerrilla couldn't have told dialectical materialism from a rice bowl. By and large this was true. As far as most of the Vietcong were concerned, they were fighting to achieve a better life for themselves and their families, and to rid the country of foreign domination—simple motives that were uncolored by ideological considerations.[24]

Military Problems

While American military power far exceeded that of the North Vietnamese and Vietcong, the United States nonetheless faced serious problems in bringing this power to bear. This reflected the fact that *power* in international politics is not a simple concept to measure but instead a complex phenomenon. Indeed, there are different kinds of power. For example, Karl Deutsch has contrasted one most common type, brute force and the ability to prevail over resistance, with a second type, the power to achieve precise results.[25] These two types of power are very different, and they have different uses.

In the case of Vietnam, the immense weight of nuclear weaponry could not be put to use in a war in which the adversary often blended in with the local population. The commitment of American troops to an active combat role, while the ARVN was relegated to pacification of the countryside, also appeared to bring about exactly what the State Department had warned against in the early 1960s: "a white man's war against Asians."

The intense use of American firepower and the difficulty of telling friend from foe exacerbated problems in the countryside. Rotation of American troops every twelve months, and of officers as often as every six months, worked against acquiring real familiarity with the situation on the ground. Indeed, one thoughtful military expert has argued that U.S. forces ought not to have been committed mainly to the fighting within South Vietnam, but should instead have been positioned so as to block the influx of North Vietnamese forces through the DMZ and Ho Chi Minh trail while leaving the struggle inside the South primarily to the ARVN.[26]

It is also important to note here the changing nature of the military conflict in the South. While the initial struggle against the French and a good deal of the fighting in the 1960s did involve guerrilla warfare, this pattern gave way to much more direct use of North Vietnamese forces. At first these were infiltrated into the South. Later, after destruction of large numbers of NLF cadres from South Vietnam in the 1968 Tet offensive,[27] and increasingly after the drawdown of American combat troops, the conflict became more and more conventional, with mainforce NVA units moving into the South, complete with their trucks, tanks, and artillery.

United States troops played major combat roles from 1965 through 1971, and in doing so they sustained substantial casualties. Indeed, American deaths during the Vietnamese conflict totaled more than 58,000. (During the years from 1961 to 1972, military casualties included more than 180,000 South Vietnamese dead and 921,000 North Vietnamese and Vietcong. Including civilians, more than 1.7 million Vietnamese are estimated to have been killed during this period.)[28] Yet, if the South Vietnamese, supported by half a million American troops plus 50,000 South Koreans and a few thousand Australians and New Zealanders could not prevail militarily, then their prospects *after* the American withdrawal were daunting. To avoid defeat would have required an open-ended American commitment to provide massive military assistance and the sustained use of American air power.

Vietnam, Grand Strategy, and the Limits of American Power

Much debate and analysis of the Vietnam War has often proceeded from a narrowly defined conception of the problem. However, given a perspective that identifies the United States as dwelling in a sometimes anarchic international environment, questions of priorities and of tradeoffs among objectives necessarily enter into any consideration of the American role.

From a Western—indeed from any non–Marxist-Leninist—perspective, it would have been desirable to prevent a Communist victory in Vietnam. But it is insufficient to pose the problem in these terms alone. It must also be asked, at what cost to other American objectives and purposes could the objective be achieved? In reality, the survival of an independent non-Communist South Vietnam would have required an open-ended American commitment. The costs, in manpower, resources, political capital, and domestic political support, exceeded the conceivable stakes involved in Indochina. Vietnam remained peripheral, not central, to American interests in maintaining an overall balance of power vis-à-vis the Soviet Union and protecting primary American and allied interests. The United States became committed in Vietnam for a series of reasons discussed earlier, and indeed, over a period of time the very commitment became the principal reason for which the United States continued to fight. But, given the obstacles to the South Vietnamese themselves maintaining a viable army and society, and the fact that the United States did not have infinite resources to expend, the outcome of the American commitment became problematic.

It was here that an expanded application of the containment doctrine played a key role. As historian John Lewis Gaddis notes, at the start of the Cold War George Kennan's original concept had emphasized distinctions between vital and peripheral interests and between levels of feasible response given available means. However, Gaddis argues that the Kennedy and Johnson administrations failed to make such distinctions. Instead, by 1965, "Johnson was relying almost exclusively on the use of military force in a theater chosen by adversaries."[29] Moreover, whereas Kennan had wished to use the force of nationalism, even where communist, to contain Soviet power, Johnson found himself opposing this force in Vietnam. Ironically, he and President Nixon ultimately found themselves seeking Soviet help in extricating the United States from this involvement. In contrast to the objectives of the flexible response strategy it embodied for the Johnson administration, Gaddis notes, "The war did not save South Vietnam, it did not deter future aggression, it did not enhance the credibility of United States commitments elsewhere in the world, it did not prevent recriminations at home."[30]

For reasons specific to Indochina, the North Vietnamese under Ho Chi Minh and his successors were in a position to fight an endless and bloody war. That is, the stakes for them were greater than those for the United States. They were prepared to fight on (not least because their repressive political system prevented effective opposition from war-weary sectors of their own population). They were then in a position to endure punishment and costs far greater than American policymakers had assumed a rational adversary could bear. By contrast, even though the United States Army did not lose a single important battle in Vietnam,[31] American forces could not continue to fight in that country indefinitely.

From the end of World War II to the mid 1960s, the United States enjoyed a position of international primacy: economic, political, and military. However, the economic recovery of Europe and Japan, the attainment of strategic parity by the Soviet Union, the achievement of independence by many countries in Africa and Asia, and the emergence of regional powers, all had the effect of diluting the *relative* power of the United States, even while its absolute power remained unequaled. This meant that if the United States were to preserve and advance its interests, its policymakers could not take individual decisions without regard to the costs involved and the resources required to achieve them.

Related to this problem of costs was that of the domestic base on which the exercise of American foreign policy rested. The bipartisan postwar consensus had allowed an active global role in security and economic policy. This may have reached its peak with the language of the Kennedy 1961 inaugural address that promised that America would "pay any price, bear any burden. . . ." However, by 1968, the Johnson administration was discovering that Congress and the media, together with the American public, were becoming increasingly restless over a foreign conflict the United States could neither conclude nor extricate itself from.

The inability either "to win or get out"[32] produced mounting frustration at home and then increasing political polarization. Eventually, this led to erosion of the domestic base on which continuation of the war depended. The Nixon-Kissinger strategy of Vietnamization was meant to end the American combat role and thus lessen the urgency of the Vietnam problem within the United States. However, sustaining the South Vietnamese government after American withdrawal was completed would have required the ability of an American administration to intervene again with force if necessary—at the least through massive use of United States air power, and it was this that neither Congress nor the American public were prepared to support after 1973.

In short, no American government has infinite resources of power and public support. At times these must be drawn on, but it is imperative that commitments be weighed against costs and priorities. The ultimate problem of the American involvement in Vietnam was that it posited an objective unattainable at a manageable cost and it jeopardized other interests of higher national priority. Indeed, the intellectual father of postwar foreign policy realism, Hans Morgenthau, acidly suggested that the conduct of the Vietnam War by the United States might be viewed as a kind of "pathology" of international politics. In this regard, he singled out five factors: (1) imposition of a "simplistic and *a priori* picture of the world derived from folklore and ideological assumption"; (2) "refusal to correct this picture . . . in light of experience"; (3) "the use of intelligence for the purpose . . . of reinterpreting reality to fit policy"; (4) "egotism of the policymakers"; and (5) "the urge to close the gap at least subjectively by action . . . that creates the illusion of mastery over a recalcitrant reality."[33]

The Tragedy of Indochina

American withdrawal in 1973 and the collapse of South Vietnam in 1975 did not end the Indochina conflict. Before the fact, it might have been imagined that the attainment of power by Communist-dominated national liberation movements in Vietnam, Laos, and Cambodia would have produced like-minded regimes which, along with their powerful Communist neighbor to the North, the People's Republic of China, would have much in common with one another. Instead, regional conflict continued and at times even intensified. Within Vietnam itself, the North Vietnamese consolidated their control of the South, disillusioning those South Vietnamese who had supported or even fought for the ouster of the French and Americans and the defeat of the Saigon government. Hundreds of thousands of refugees eventually fled from the South.

At the same time, the victorious Khmer Rouge movement in Cambodia immediately embarked on a massive emptying out of the cities, forcing entire populations into the countryside and deliberately murdering millions of people, including almost anyone with a formal education. This turmoil, coupled with intensification of the ancient animosity between ethnic Vietnamese and Cambodians, ultimately led to a Vietnamese invasion and occupation of Cambodia in 1978. The Vietnamese, while supporting establishment of a new (and pro-Vietnam) Cambodian government, soon found themselves facing renewed guerrilla opposition, not only from the remnants of Pol Pot's forces, but from smaller groups identified with the earlier government of the neutralist Prince Sihanouk as well as other nationalist forces Not until 1992 did the fighting in Cambodia come to at least a temporary halt, with a UN-brokered ceasefire and the dispatch of more than 15,000 UN peacekeeping troops. Ironically, UN-supervised elections in the spring of 1993 brought back to power the aging Prince Sihanouk, whose ouster had precipitated two decades of conflict.

For their part, in the years after American withdrawal, China and Vietnam clashed politically and then militarily. The Chinese, in 1979, launched a punitive expedition across their mountainous border with Vietnam in order to demonstrate to their Communist neighbor Chinese disapproval of the Cambodian invasion and of Hanoi's closer proximity to Moscow.

This stunning and deadly series of events suggests the limits to any simplified version of the lessons of Vietnam, in which the ouster of Westerners gives way to effective and popular self-government by national liberation movements. In practice, differences of ethnicity, regional power rivalries, and monopoly of political power by dictatorial regimes can prove to be deep-seated sources of brutal conflict.

Finally, although during the Cold War the East-West conflict sometimes came to be played out in a North-South context—often in ways that reflected poor outside understanding of local realities—the experience of Indochina suggests yet another serious lesson. It is that the sources of instability and war are sufficiently deep-seated within the developing world itself, so that conflict remains an all-too-frequent occurrence even in the absence of entanglement by global powers.

NOTES

1. Quoted in Doris Kearns, *Lyndon Johnson and the American Dream* (New York: Harper & Row, 1976), pp. 252–253.
2. Colonel Harry G. Summers, Jr., Chief, Negotiations Division, U.S. delegation, Four Party Joint Military Team, and Colonel Tu, Chief, North Vietnamese delegation, quoted in Summers, *On Strategy: A Critical Analysis of the Vietnam War* (New York: Dell, 1984), p. 21.
3. There is an account of this period in Theodore Draper, *Abuse of Power* (New York: Viking, 1968), pp. 17–20.
4. On this period, see the account by Stanley Karnow, *Vietnam: A History* (New York: Penguin, 1984), p. 155ff. Karnow's book provides a valuable and lucid history of the entire Vietnam conflict. Also see George C. Herring's useful book, *America's Longest War: The United States and Vietnam, 1950–1975* (New York: Wiley, 1979), p. 33.
5. The classic account of this battle is Bernard Fall's *Hell in a Very Small Place* (Philadelphia: Lippincott, 1966).
6. The most widely cited contemporary account of this debate is that of Chalmers M. Roberts, "The Day We Didn't Go to War," *Reporter* (14 September 1954): 31–35. Also see Ronald H. Spector, *Advice and Support: The Early Years,* Vol. 1 of Official U.S. Army History of Vietnam (Washington, DC: U.S. Army, 1984).
7. Dwight D. Eisenhower, *Mandate for Change* (Garden City, NY: Doubleday, 1963), pp. 346-347, and *Dwight D. Eisenhower, Public Papers, 1954* (Washington, 1955), pp. 382–384.
8. Eisenhower, *Mandate for Change,* p. 372.
9. See, for example, the account in Arthur M. Schlesinger, Jr., *A Thousand Days* (Boston: Houghton Mifflin, 1965), pp. 536–550.
10. Source: Memorandum from W. W. Rostow to the Secretary of State, the Secretary of Defense, Director of Central Intelligence, 24 April 1961. The memorandum was later declassified and published in Laurence Chang and Peter Kornbluh, eds., *The Cuban Missile Crisis, 1962: A National Security Archive Documents Reader* (New York: The Free Press, 1992), pp. 16–19, at p. 19.
11. Quoted in Schlesinger, p. 547.
12. For a brief description of the 34-A operations, see Leslie Gelb and Richard Betts, *The Irony of Vietnam: The System Worked* (Washington, DC: Brookings Institution, 1979), pp. 102–105.
13. James B. Stockdale and Sybil Stockdale, *In Love and War* (New York: Harper & Row, 1984), quoted in the *Washington Post,* 7 October 1984, p. D2. Stockdale was later shot down and was a prisoner of the North Vietnamese for eight years. The U.S. Navy's history of the Vietnam War draws a distinction between the August 2 and August 4 incidents, though its authors conclude that the latter left at least one North Vietnamese torpedo boat immobilized or sunk. See Edward J. Marolda and Oscar P. Fitzgerald, *The United States Navy and the Vietnam Conflict,* Vol. II (Washington, DC: U.S. Government Printing Office for the Naval Historical Center, 1987).

14. Quoted in U.S. Department of Defense study, the Pentagon Papers, as reported in the *New York Times*, 20 June 1971, p. 27. For an analysis of the memorandum, see Larry Berman, *Planning a Tragedy: The Americanization of the War in Vietnam* (New York: Norton, 1982), pp. 91–93. In addition, for an assessment of the Johnson administration during the key years from 1965 to 1968, including its official optimism and insufficient grasp of the Viet Cong and North Vietnamese resolve, see Larry Berman, *Lyndon Johnson's War: The Road to Stalemate in Vietnam* (New York: Norton, 1989).

15. James C. Thompson, Jr., "How Could Vietnam Happen?" *Atlantic*, (April 1968): 51.

16. In the Pentagon Papers, as quoted, *New York Times*, 20 June 1971. Also see, *The Pentagon Papers,* as published by the *New York Times* (New York: Bantam Books, 1971).

17. Quoted in the *Los Angeles Times*, 27 April 1975.

18. *Some Lessons and Non-Lessons of Vietnam* (Washington, DC: Woodrow Wilson International Center for Scholars, 1983), Appendix 1, based on data in John E. Mueller, *War, Presidents and Public Opinion* (New York: Wiley, 1973).

19. For an account of this policy reversal, see Townsend Hoopes, *The Limits of Intervention* (New York: David McKay, 1969).

20. These provisions were outlined in detail in a summary statement by Henry Kissinger; news conference, 24 January 1973, reprinted in *Department of State Bulletin* 68 (12 February 1973): 155–160. Also see "Texts of the January 1973 Vietnam Cease-Fire Agreement and Protocols," reprinted in Alan M. Jones, ed., *U.S. Foreign Policy in a Changing World* (New York: McKay, 1973), pp. 308–338.

21. CIA estimate, quoted in Karnow, p. 657.

22. Quoted in Karnow, p. 660.

23. Berman, p. 28. For a compelling account of Vietnam policymaking during the early years of the Johnson administration, also see David Halberstam, *The Best and the Brightest* (New York: Random House, 1972).

24. Truong Nhu Tang, *A Vietcong Memoir: An Inside Account of the Vietnam War and Its Aftermath* (New York: Vintage, 1986), p. 166.

25. Karl W. Deutsch, *The Nerves of Government: Models of Political Communication and Control* (New York: Free Press, 1966), pp. 110ff.

26. General Bruce Palmer, former commander of the U.S. Army in Vietnam, cited in Summers, pp. 170–171. (Palmer would also have positioned a limited number of U.S. troops in the central highlands and in the vicinity of Saigon.) For a more general critique of the manner in which U.S. forces have been employed, see Edward Luttwak, *The Pentagon and the Art of War: The Question of Military Reform* (New York: Simon & Schuster, 1984).

27. Chalmers Johnson estimates that by 1970, 80 percent of the combat in South Vietnam was being carried out by regular North Vietnamese troops, and only 20 percent by southern guerrillas. *Autopsy on People's War* (Berkeley: University of California Press, 1973), pp. 47–48.

28. Figures from International Institute for Strategic Studies, *Strategic Survey, 1972–1973* (London, Spring 1973), p. 48. Also see Milton Leitenberg, "America in Vietnam: Statistics of a War," *Survival* (London: IISS, November/December, 1972): 268–274.

29. John Lewis Gaddis, *Strategies of Containment: A Critical Appraisal of Postwar American National Security Policy* (New York: Oxford University Press, 1982), p. 239.

30. Gaddis, p. 237.

31. This point is emphasized by Douglas Pike and covers the period of direct American combat involvement from 1965 to 1973. See his book, *PAVN: People's Army of Vietnam* (San Francisco: Presidio Press, 1986). Among other treatments of U.S. involvement in

the war, see, for example, Leslie H. Gelb, with Richard K. Betts, *The Irony of Vietnam: The System Worked* (Washington, DC: Brookings, 1979); also Guenter Lewy, *American in Vietnam* (New York: Oxford University Press, 1978).

32. See in particular the analysis by William Schneider, "'Rambo' and Reality: Having It Both Ways," in Kenneth Oye, Robert J. Lieber, and Donald Rothchild, eds., *Eagle Resurgent? The Reagan Era in American Foreign Policy* (Boston: Little, Brown, 1987), pp. 41–72.

33. Morgenthau, *Politics Among Nations*, 5th ed. (1978), pp. 7–8. Also see Morgenthau, *Vietnam and the United States* (Washington, DC: Public Affairs Press, 1965). For a different assessment and one harshly critical of domestic opponents of the war, see Norman Podhoretz, *Why We Were in Vietnam* (New York: Simon & Schuster, 1982).

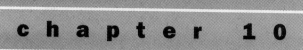

The Oil Decade—and After

And then one day the term "energy crisis" entered the vocabulary of international affairs. A developing-country poet might have written as William Wordsworth did of the French Revolution. "Bliss was it in that dawn to be alive; But to be young was very heaven. . . ."

—ALI MASRUI (IN THE AFTERMATH OF THE 1973 OIL SHOCK)[1]

. . . the global economic conditions necessary for another major unilateral price action by OPEC are not likely to reemerge for more than a decade—if ever.

—DAVID STOCKMAN, AUTUMN 1978 (SHORTLY BEFORE
THE ONSET OF THE IRAN CRISIS AND THE SECOND OIL SHOCK)[2]

Saddam Hussein's conquest of Kuwait . . . reminded us that security dilemmas, the use of force, and war remain endemic in the contemporary world and that the end of the Cold War has not fundamentally changed the international system, but only certain fissures and cleavages within it.

—K. J. HOLSTI[3]

A̲mong the watersheds in post-1945 international relations, the October 1973 outbreak of the energy crisis remains one of the most dramatic and important. Moreover, the date represents a divide between an initial postwar era of recovery, economic growth, and Western self-confidence, and an ensuing decade of economic and political disarray.

The oil decade also exemplifies the way in which different kinds of issues and geographic locales have moved to the center of world affairs. Thus, in contrast to the superpower conflict of the early Cold War and the Cuban missile crisis, the period brought to the stage a series of matters largely outside the arena of East-West confrontation. It made economic concerns especially critical and gave prominence to an agenda much more North-South in nature.

Initially, the oil shock led to widespread speculation about a profound shift in the lines of allegiance and conflict in world affairs. Indeed, it was sometimes identified (whether with foreboding or applause) as heralding a shift in wealth and power from the countries of the rich Northern world to those of the South. Much of this immediate assessment eventually proved to be (sometimes wildly) exaggerated. Nonetheless, the oil decade did have an enormous impact and thus merits careful attention.

In addition, the 1990–1991 crisis and war in the Persian Gulf following Iraq's invasion of Kuwait illustrated that oil and energy issues still have the potential to cause major international upheaval, and that instability and war remain intrinsic perils of the international system despite the end of the Cold War.

THE WORLD OIL REGIME ON THE EVE OF THE CRISIS

For half a century, the formal and informal rules of the game by which crude oil was extracted from the earth, transported, refined into petroleum products, and distributed were made by the large, multinational oil companies. The most important of these firms (the "seven sisters")[4] were Exxon, Socal, Mobil, Gulf, and Texaco (all American owned), plus British Petroleum, and Shell (which was Anglo-Dutch). Occasional challenges to this system, for example in 1951–1953 by the nationalist Iranian regime of Mohammed Mossadegh (who sought to nationalize the oil fields in his country) were unsuccessful. Indeed, Mossadegh himself was overthrown in a CIA-assisted coup.[5]

Through a network of oil concessions and cartel arrangements, the seven sisters maintained a dominant position in the world oil market. This enabled them to determine pricing and production policies. Indeed, as they consolidated their positions in the Middle East, initially in Iraq, Saudi Arabia, and Kuwait, and then in Iran, they were able to set prices as though the oil had originated in Texas. By 1947, these companies controlled 65 percent of non-Communist world crude oil reserves, 55 percent of actual production, 57 percent of refinery capacity, and 67 percent of privately owned oil tanker capacity.[6]

The seemingly unlimited supply of inexpensive oil helped to fuel a generation of unprecedented economic growth and rising living standards among the industrial democracies. During the 1950s and 1960s, Europe, Japan, and the United States found their economies shifting from reliance on coal (much of it domestically produced) to oil (mostly imported, except in the case of the United States). The change was both profound and rapid. For example, as late as 1960, Europe still relied on coal for 61 percent of its primary energy supply, as against 33 percent for oil. By 1970, however, the positions of the two fuels were reversed, with oil accounting for 60 percent and coal 33 percent.[7]

Throughout this period, the United States remained the leading force and largest producer in the world oil market.° While America actually became a net oil importer as early as 1948, its domestic oil reserves and ability to expand production, coupled with the existence of sizeable excess capacity elsewhere in the world, helped keep oil prices low and supplies ample. Consequently, Middle East wars in 1956 (the Suez crisis) and 1967 (the Arab-Israeli Six Day War) failed to have any sustained impact on the supply or price of oil, even though the Suez Canal was closed as a result of both wars and Arab oil producers briefly attempted an embargo in the aftermath of the 1967 conflict.

The formal and informal rules by which international activity proceeds in a given issue-area are known as "regimes."° In the case of oil, the prevailing international regime remained robust until 1970. Indeed, as measured in constant dollars, the price of Middle East oil actually declined by half during the course of two decades. Thus, as late as January 1970, the price of Saudi Arabian light marker crude oil was $1.39 per barrel.[9] By this time, however, the underpinnings of the existing system were beginning to weaken. One tangible sign was the peaking of American domestic oil production at 11.3 million barrels per day (mbd) in 1970.† From this time on, the balance between international demand for oil and the available world production capacity became progressively tighter.

A number of additional factors during the early 1970s also combined to bring about fundamental changes in economic and political power within the world oil system. In particular, the previously dominant role of the seven sisters began to erode as a result first of increased activity by smaller independent oil companies—thus making it harder for the companies to put up a united front—and then by the growing strength of OPEC (the Organization of Petroleum Exporting Countries). The emerging shift in power became visible in 1970, when the radical Arab government of Libya, under Colonel Muammar Qaddafi, was able to impose a price increase on one of the independent oil companies with limited alternative sources of production, the Occidental Petroleum Company. Some months later, at Teheran in February 1971, the OPEC countries as a group succeeded in negotiating a significant price increase with the major oil companies. In large measure, this occurred because of the narrowing margin of available excess production capacity in relation to demand.

Other accounts of this period suggest that the result of the Teheran meeting was due to indecisive American policy, or that the Shah of Iran may even have

---

°The concept of international regimes is discussed in Chapter 14.
†This figure includes crude oil plus natural gas liquids (petroleum recovered in extracting and processing natural gas).

been encouraged in this price increase by officials in the U.S. State Department. Indeed, not long afterward, President Richard Nixon—then presiding over the slow and painful liquidation of America's role in Indochina—had a meeting with the Shah. Nixon and Henry Kissinger, his national security advisor, had developed a concept (the Nixon Doctrine) whereby regional powers would exercise influence in areas where the full deployment of American political and military power now seemed too costly or impractical. Thus seeing the Shah as a guardian of Western interests in the Persian Gulf, the president leaned across the table at the end of the meeting and said to the Iranian leader, "Protect me."[10]

Whatever the cause, the balance of bargaining power had begun to shift decisively from the oil companies to the host countries. Consequently, the latter were increasingly in a position to set prices and production levels. As one tangible sign of this shift, it is worth noting the change in world oil prices *before* the October 1973 Middle East War. Although not widely noted by the general public, the selling price of Saudi crude oil had doubled between January 1, 1970 ($1.39 per barrel), and October 4, 1973 ($2.70 per barrel). (See Table 10. 1.)

OIL AND THE YOM KIPPUR WAR

In the early morning of October 6, 1973, Egyptian forces crossed the Suez Canal and Syrian forces attacked along the Golan Heights. The Yom Kippur War had begun. The onset of this Arab-Israeli conflict suddenly illuminated the shift in oil power that had been taking place less dramatically. The key decisions about oil now seemed to lie in the hands of the producing countries.

While intense fighting raged, dramatic events were taking place in the oil realm. On October 17, the Arab members of OPEC,* grouped in a separate body known as the Organization of *Arab* Petroleum Exporting Countries (OAPEC), announced a selective oil embargo. This measure divided the principal oil-importing countries into three different categories. One group was supposed to be excluded from receiving Arab oil altogether. This included the United States and the Netherlands, among a few other countries, for their support of Israel. A second group was to be exempt from the embargo because of their support for the Arab position. At first, this included France and Britain. Third, there were the remaining countries of Europe, plus Japan. These were to be squeezed through progressive reductions of 5 percent per month, in order to place political and economic pressure on them.

To implement these measures, Saudi Arabia announced a 25 percent production cut on October 19, as well as an embargo on shipment of its oil to the United States. A number of other Arab countries began small decreases in their oil pro-

---

*Saudi Arabia, Iraq, Kuwait, Libya, Algeria, United Arab Emirates, and Qatar. (Syria and Egypt belong to OAPEC but are not OPEC members.) The non-Arab OPEC countries are Iran, Nigeria, Venezuela, Indonesia and Gabon. Ecuador became an OPEC member in 1973 but later withdrew from the Organization.

Table 10.1 OFFICIAL SELLING PRICE OF
SAUDI ARABIAN LIGHT MARKER CRUDE OIL

Date	Dollars per Barrel
January 1, 1970	$1.39
October 4, 1973	2.70
March 1, 1974	10.46
January 1, 1977	12.09
January 1, 1979	13.34
June 1, 1979	18.00
November 1, 1979	24.00
January 1, 1980	26.00
April 1, 1980	28.00
July 1, 1980	30.00
November 1, 1980	32.00
October 1, 1981	34.00
March 14, 1983	29.00
February 1, 1985	28.00
February–March 1986 (approximately)	15–20.00[a]
July 1986 (approximately)	9.00[b]
1987 (average)	15.12[c]
1988 (average)	12.16[c]
1989 (average)	16.29[c]
1990 (average)	20.36[c]
1991 (average)	14.62[c]
1992 (average)	15.85[c]
1993 (average)	14.27[c]

[a]NB: Extensive Saudi use of "net-back" deals, beginning in late 1985, based per barrel price retroactively on value of refined products produced from a barrel of crude oil.

[b]Includes North Sea Brent, West Texas intermediate crude oil.

[c]FOB cost of crude oil imports from Saudi Arabia, U.S. Department of Energy.

Sources: Exxon Corporation, Middle East Oil, September 1980: 26; U.S. Department of Energy, Weekly Petroleum Status Report, 5 June 1981: 20; U.S. Central Intelligence Agency, International Energy Statistical Review, 22 December 1981: 21; New York Times, 31 January 1985, 26 February 1987; Economist, 24 January 1987; U.S. Department of Energy, Monthly Energy Review, June 1994: 112.

duction. In total, these reductions would ultimately amount to some 7 percent of world oil demand. In the months that followed, OPEC took advantage of the crisis atmosphere, shortfall in oil supply, and panic buying among consumers in order to put through a series of massive price increases. These drove the price of crude oil from $2.70 per barrel on October 4, 1973, to $10.46 on March 1, 1974—a fourfold increase.

This first oil shock damaged the economies of the industrial democracies. It also harmed the non–oil producing less developed countries (LDCs). Altogether, the Western allies and Japan—the members of the Organization for Economic Cooperation and Development (OECD)—lost the equivalent of 2 percent of gross national product.[11] In addition they experienced high inflation, rising unemployment, and balance of payments problems.

The United States, Europe, and Japan also found themselves in severe political disarray. Sharp differences emerged over Middle East policy, and individual European countries and Japan sought bilateral deals with oil-producing states rather than multilateral allied cooperation. Indeed, there were even suggestions that the time had come for an historic reorientation of Europe away from its Atlantic relationship with the United States and toward the countries of the southern Mediterranean and the emergent oil powers of the Middle East. Thus, at the height of the crisis, the Libyan prime minister urged establishment of an "Arab-European economic force" and told those attending a diplomatic dinner in Paris to accept the fact that, "If Europe's interests coincided with those of the United States in the 1940s and 1950s, that has no longer been the case in the 1960s and 1970s."[12]

Amid the economic and political disarray, there was one significant accomplishment on the part of the oil-importing countries. This was the creation of the International Energy Agency. This new body, established through the efforts of the United States and over the opposition of France, was designed to provide consumer country cooperation and oil sharing in the event a future crisis caused a serious oil shortfall.

The 1973–1974 oil shortage was dealt with by the major oil companies, which in effect allocated available oil on a pro rata basis. As a result, and regardless of their policies toward the Middle East, oil-importing states experienced roughly comparable reductions in their supplies during the crisis.

By itself, the oil embargo proved to be wholly ineffective. In large measure this resulted from the fact that oil is *fungible,* that is, that a given barrel of oil is more or less the same as any other.* Hence, if oil was not to be shipped directly from say, Saudi Arabia to the United States, then a large integrated oil company was in position to redirect its tanker traffic. The result was that oil previously bound from Nigeria to France could be redirected to the United States, while a comparable amount originally intended for shipment from Saudi Arabia to the United States would be sent instead to France. In the end, the Saudis could thus claim that they had maintained their embargo, yet both the Americans and French would have received the necessary oil.

While the above point may appear narrowly commercial or technical, it underlines a much broader issue concerning political power. The initial events in the oil crisis had given rise to massive exaggerations about the fundamental shift in wealth and power thought to be taking place on the world stage. While the events were of great importance, the passage of time would ultimately demonstrate that the shifts were less profound and more complex than initially assumed.

With time, the international oil problem began to ease. A serious economic recession in 1974–1975 caused reduced world oil demand. Oil price increases

---

*Technically, there are differences (specific gravity, light versus heavy crudes, sulfur content, paraffin and heavy metal concentrations, etc.), but the overall characteristics of crude oil nonetheless make for substitutability.

slowly began to stimulate conservation and energy efficiency, though the cumulative weight of these changes would not be felt until after the second oil shock. During the period from late 1974 to late 1978, the economic impact of the crisis was gradually absorbed. The improved supply and demand balance even began to produce a sense of complacency. Indeed, OPEC prices temporarily ceased to climb, and in real terms (i.e., after adjusting for the effects of inflation) declined by 13 percent between 1976 and 1978.

For the United States, however, the five years from the end of 1973 to the end of 1978 brought not a reduction in dependence on imported Middle East oil but an increase. These years saw a near stalemate over domestic energy policy. A few important steps were taken, such as legislation mandating long-term improvements in automobile gasoline mileage, and the decision to build a strategic petroleum reserve. However, oil and natural gas prices remained subject to broad price controls, and domestic oil consumption rose by nearly 12 percent. In addition, partly as a result of declining oil production within the United States and reductions in the amount of oil available from Venezuela and Canada, oil imports jumped by more than 28 percent and dependence on Arab oil soared (See Table 10.2). Illustratively, between 1973 and 1977, OPEC's share of American oil imports rose from 50 percent to 73 percent, while that of Arab OPEC states jumped from 15 percent to 38 percent.

REVOLUTION IN IRAN AND THE SECOND OIL SHOCK

Iran had continued to occupy a prominent place in American policy. And, as late as the end of 1977, President Jimmy Carter could offer a New Year's Eve toast to the Shah, in which he praised Iran as "an island of stability in one of the more troubled areas of the world." Indeed, the president added, "This is a great tribute to . . . the respect and the admiration and love which your people give to you. . . . We have no other nation on earth who is closer to us in planning for our mutual military security."[13] Notwithstanding the Carter endorsement, opposition to the Shah and increasing protests and civil unrest produced explosive instability during 1978. Iran had been OPEC's second largest oil producer after Saudi Arabia, accounting for 5.5 mbd as late as October, but political upheaval began to disrupt oil production in November. Production dropped by 2 mbd, and then fell an additional 1 mbd in December. With the Shah's departure from power in January, oil production came to a virtual halt. It then began to recover slowly; from April 1979 to the end of the year, it fluctuated at between three and four million barrels per day.

At first, much of the reduction was offset by increased oil production elsewhere. Saudi Arabia initially expanded its own output by a million barrels per day in November and December 1978. However, the Saudis then exacerbated the situation, reducing production by some 600,000 barrels per day in January—at the very point when Iran's own output was plunging to a mere 0.4 mbd. In April, the Saudis reduced production by an additional 1.0 mbd. The effects of these actions and other events touched off a panic in world oil markets.

Table 10.2 U.S. OIL IMPORT DEPENDENCE

Year	Total Oil Consumption (mbd)[a]	Net Import (mbd)	Imports as Percent of Consumption	Share of U.S. Oil Imports from			
				OPEC		Arab OPEC	
				mbd	%	mbd	%
1973	17.3	6.0	35	3.0	50	0.9	15
1974	16.7	5.9	35	3.3	56	0.8	14
1975	16.3	5.8	36	3.6	62	1.4	24
1976	17.5	7.1	41	5.1	72	2.4	34
1977	18.4	8.6	47	6.2	73	3.2	38
1978	18.8	8.0	43	5.8	73	3.0	38
1979	18.5	8.0	43	5.6	70	3.1	39
1980	17.1	6.4	37	4.3	67	2.5	41
1981	16.1	5.4	34	3.3	61	1.8	33
1982	15.3	4 3	28	2.1	49	0.9	21
1983	15.2	4.3	28	1.8	44	0.6	14
1984	15.7	4.7	30	2.0	43	0.8	17
1985	15.7	4.3	27	1.8	43	0.5	11
1986	16.3	5.4	33	2.8	53	1.2	21
1987	16.7	5.9	35	3.1	53	1.3	22
1988	17.3	6.6	38	3.5	53	1.8	27
1989	17.3	7.2	42	4.1	57	2.1	29
1990	17.0	7.2	42	4.3	60	2.2	31
1991	16.7	6.6	40	4.1	62	2.1	32
1992	17.0	6.9	41	4.1	59	2.0	29
1993	17.2	7.6	44	4.3	57	2.0	26

[a]mbd = million barrels per day

Source: Based on data from U.S. Department of Energy, Energy Information Administration, *Monthly Energy Review,* April 1990 (published July 1990): 13; and June 1994:17 (Includes imports for strategic petroleum reserve.)

At a time of unusually low world oil stock levels and disruption of established oil market patterns, fierce competitive bidding for oil erupted on international spot markets.° Prices surged upward, while oil-importing countries were unable or unwilling to cooperate effectively in restraining a runaway market. Over a 15-month period, prices rose 170 percent. Ultimately, the OPEC price reached a peak of $34 per barrel on October 1, 1981.

In fact, a relatively small reduction had taken place. In this case, a net shortfall of approximately 4 percent of world oil demand had occurred in the second

---

°The *spot market* in a term for oil that is bought and sold not on long-term contract basis, but to meet short-term supply and demand needs. At the time of the Iran crisis, only a fraction, perhaps 5 percent, of world oil supply was traded in this manner. In later years, however, spot markets became the basis for a much greater proportion of oil trading.

calendar quarter of 1979. Nonetheless, it was sufficient to stimulate an explosive price increase.

This phase of the oil decade was accompanied by other spectacular events. They included the seizure of American diplomats as hostages at the embassy in Teheran in November 1979, the Mecca mosque incident in Saudi Arabia (in which a group of fanatics sought to bring down the Saudi regime), and the Soviet invasion of Afghanistan in December 1979. None of the events directly caused interruption of oil supply, but they added to pervasive anxieties about Persian Gulf stability and the long-term reliability of oil supplies from the region. For example, the Soviet action led to fears that an impending peaking and then decline of its domestic oil production could cause the USSR to seek domination of Persian Gulf oil supplies.

In the end, the crisis triggered the most severe recession of the post-World War II world. The two oil shocks together cost the industrial democracies approximately $1.4 trillion in lost economic growth. The economic effects also contributed to the electoral defeats of Jimmy Carter in November 1980 and of French President Valéry Giscard d'Estaing in May 1981.

LESSONS AND NONLESSONS OF THE OIL DECADE

As a watershed event in international relations, the oil decade has proved subject to sharp differences of interpretation. In part, this is because of the broad array of economic, political, and regional questions involved. But it also reflects the dramatic and often unexpected events that occurred in the space of less than ten years. These encompass the Yom Kippur War, the Arab oil embargo, and the first oil shock; an interlude marked by a modest oil surplus; revolution in Iran, the second oil shock, Camp David and the Israeli-Egyptian peace treaty, the Teheran hostage crisis; outbreak of the Iran-Iraq War in September 1980; an oil glut beginning in 1982, and falling OPEC oil prices.

Consider some of the consequences widely believed to exist in the aftermath of the first and second oil shocks:

A fundamental shift of wealth and power from the rich countries of the North to the oil-producing states of the Middle East and Persian Gulf.

Continuing erosion of American power, due to increased dependence on imported oil; risks of future embargoes and oil blackmail.

Major benefit for the "have-not" countries as against the "haves."

Identification of the oil crisis, Middle East instability, and the Arab-Israeli conflict as nearly synonymous problems.

In reality, these lessons have proved more incorrect than correct. In each case, the initial assumptions failed to take into account both the nature of underlying power realities and the characteristics of the international oil system. Understanding also requires recognition that the rapid succession of oil crisis, glut, and crisis occurred in a highly integrated and dynamic world oil system, or "regime."

The continuing fluctuations within this system shape relations among producers and consumers of petroleum.

Oil Power and the Role of OPEC

In essence, the production or consumption of a barrel of oil, wherever it occurs, ultimately weighs in the balance of world supply and demand. World petroleum prices and availability are shaped *both* by political factors and by economic and market mechanisms. Prior to 1970, the role of the major oil companies was decisive in setting or influencing prices. Subsequently, the emergence of OPEC and especially Saudi Arabia as the source for meeting marginal changes in oil demand made those producers a decisive force. Nonetheless, it is the overall pattern of world oil supply and demand that sets the framework within which divergent forces contend. Above all, the larger the margin of spare petroleum production capacity and the more diversified among oil producing countries, the less vulnerable the system is to sudden oil shocks.

Wherever they occur, shifts in supply or demand affect the system as a whole. On the supply side, an increase in Saudi capacity, development of Alaskan, North Sea, and Mexican oil, and even small-scale increases in oil production among the LDCs all add to the potential world oil supply. Conversely, conflicts involving Iran or Iraq, decline in American and Venezuelan production, or disruptions of energy production in the former Soviet Union represent real or potential reductions in world supply.

On the demand side, fuel switching from oil to any other energy source (e.g., coal, natural gas, nuclear power, or solar energy), reductions in oil consumption, energy conservation and efficiency, the drawing down of energy stocks, or the effects of recession all result in decreased world oil demand. In turn, factors such as increased economic growth, development among the LDCs, and the wider spread of automobile ownership create increased demand pressure.

These forces shape a volatile international oil pattern. When there is little surplus production capacity available, the system becomes more vulnerable to oil shocks. These can result from any significant disturbance to routine supply patterns. Hence, after the outbreak of the October 1973 war, a shortfall of only 7 percent could create conditions for a 300 percent run-up in oil prices. Similarly, after the fall of the Shah, a 4 percent shortfall in the spring of 1979 provided the impetus for a 170 percent price increase.

Conversely, when substantial spare capacity and an excess of oil production in relation to demand exist, the system becomes far more resistant to disruption. The September 1980 outbreak of the Iran-Iraq War took place at a time of substantial surplus capacity and record high levels of world oil inventories. As a result, no oil shock occurred. Indeed, despite the continuation of the war, a series of other factors brought an increasing glut of oil and a softening of world oil prices. These included the growing impact of oil from the North Sea, Alaska, and Mexico, the cumulative weight of improvements in energy efficiency, a continued easing of the international supply/demand balance, and the drawing down of oil stocks by consumers.

The implications of this integrated world oil and energy system are thus profound. They impose a fundamental interdependence on the participants. Hence, the relative power of the players, whether they are oil producers or importers, is ultimately a function of the fluid international system in which they operate. As a result, the consequences of events will vary. Illustratively, the Yom Kippur War provided the catalyst for an oil shock, but the June 1982 Israeli invasion of Lebanon did not; the fall of the Shah triggered a new oil shock, but the outbreak of the Iran-Iraq War some twenty months later did not. Why did one set of events act as crisis catalysts but not the other? The answer is that they occurred at moments when the supply/demand system was tight, and therefore vulnerable to the effects of a political or military disturbance.

Similar criteria affect the power of the OPEC countries. Why did they possess the power to impose extraordinary oil price increases in 1973–1974 and again in 1979–1980, but not to prevent price declines in 1982–1986? The answer again lies in the broader contours of the international oil system. In 1973–1974 and 1979–1980, supply was perceived to be inadequate to demand, and a seller's market made it possible for oil exporters to take advantage of their power. In 1982–1986, however, a slack world demand picture and the presence of an oil glut created a buyer's market. Due to economic recession, improved energy efficiency, and the availability of some 6 mbd of new oil production from non-OPEC sources, OPEC production plunged from 30.9 mbd in 1979 to 22.6 mbd in 1981, and then to a low of 16.1 mbd in 1985 (see Table 10.3). As a consequence, although OPEC had produced more than half (55.8 percent) of the world's oil in 1973, its share fell to less than one-third (30.4 percent) by 1985. These results reflected an environment in which power was once again shifting: in this case away from OPEC and back toward the oil importing countries and companies.

Oil Power and The Role of Saudi Arabia

Of all the members of OPEC, Saudi Arabia stands out as the most important. With almost 260 billion barrels of proved crude oil reserves, the Saudis possess more than one-fourth of the world's entire supply (see Table 10.4). Moreover, by the beginning of the 1990s, Saudi Arabia possessed over half of OPEC's surplus oil production capacity. Yet it would be a mistake to exaggerate the political and military might of the country. In fact, Saudi Arabia is a land of approximately eight million people. Although it has spent heavily on expansion of its armed forces, weaponry, and military bases, it remains less powerful than other major players in the region: Syria, Iraq, Iran, and Israel.

Politically, Saudi Arabia has managed a difficult task in absorbing oil wealth and in modernizing a highly traditional and underdeveloped country in a few decades, without simultaneously undergoing severe destabilization. Despite the tensions inherent in the relationship between modernity and Islamic fundamentalism, the Saudi royal family has been able to maneuver through the turbulent decades since the 1973 oil shock.[14]

In general, the Saudis have behaved with considerable caution and have made large financial contributions to those who might otherwise have caused them trouble. At various times, particularly in the 1970s and 1980s, the recipients

Table 10.3 OPEC'S SHARE OF WORLD
CRUDE OIL PRODUCTION (MBD)

| Year | Oil Production | | OPEC Percent of World Production |
	OPEC	World	
1973	31.0 mbd	55.7 mbd	55.7%
1974	30.7	55.7	55.1
1975	27.2	52.8	51.6
1976	30.7	57.3	53.6
1977	31.3	59.6	52.5
1978	29.9	60.0	49.8
1979	31.0	62.5	49.6
1980	27.0	59.4	45.5
1981	22.8	55.8	40.9
1982	19.1	53.2	35.9
1983	17.9	53.0	33.8
1984	17.9	54.2	33.0
1985	16.6	53.6	31.0
1986	18.7	55.9	33.5
1987	18.8	56.3	33.4
1988	20.9	58.5	35.7
1989	22.6	59.5	38.1
1990	23.5	60.5	38.8
1991	23.7	60.2	39.4
1992	24.9	60.3	41.3
1993	25.7	60.1	42.8

Source: Calculated from data in U.S. Department of Energy, *Monthly Energy Review,* April 1990 (published July 1990), p. 111. Data for 1990–1993 from *Monthly Energy Review,* June 1994, p. 131.

of this largess included Syria, the PLO, and Iraq (which in the early phase of its war with Iran received as much as $1 billion per month). Subsequently, in reaction to Iraq's August 1990 invasion of Kuwait, the Saudi's halted payments not only to Iraq but to the PLO (which had supported the Iraqi action), and eventually made a $12.8 billion payment to the United States toward the costs of Operations Desert Shield and Desert Storm (the American-led military effort that ousted Iraq from Kuwait).

The Saudis have also sought to maintain the loyalties of their own military and emergent middle class through material incentives. They have subsidized creation of an expensive military infrastructure, an ambitious welfare state, costly urban services, and even the growing of wheat at a subsidized price five times world levels. Not surprisingly, the costs of these efforts have been substantial. Together with a trend toward lower world oil prices in the mid to late 1980s and early 1990s, and the cumulative $55 billion costs of the 1990–1991 Gulf crisis and war,

Table 10.4 ESTIMATED PROVED OIL
RESERVES (BILLION BARRELS, AS
OF JANUARY 1, 1992)[a]

Saudi Arabia	259
Iraq	100
United Arab Emirates	98
Kuwait	94
Iran	93
Venezuela	63
Commonwealth of Independent States	57
Mexico	51
United States	24
China	24
Libya	23
Nigeria	18
Algeria	9
Norway	9
Indonesia	6
India	6
Egypt	6
Canada	5
Oman	5
United Kingdom	5
Yemen	4

[a]Recoverable with present technology and prices, except for CIS.

Source: From data in Oil & Gas Journal, 27 December 1993.

Saudi Arabia has found its income and financial reserves much more constrained than during the oil decade.

In the years after 1981, in response to steadily declining world demand for OPEC oil, Saudi Arabia reduced its oil production (which had averaged 9.8 million barrels per day in 1981) to a low, in June 1985, of 2.4 mbd. It cut petroleum output in an effort to preserve OPEC and maintain a world price level for oil that might otherwise have collapsed. This led to an acrimonious debate with other OPEC states about burden sharing. The decline in production caused Saudi annual petroleum revenues to fall from $109 billion in 1981 to $19 billion in 1986.[15] The fall in oil revenues also ate into Saudi net foreign assets. These dropped from roughly $150 billion in 1982 to less than $80 billion by the end of 1985.[16]

In response, Saudi Arabia sought to discipline the other members of OPEC and some of the more important non-OPEC petroleum exporters. It did so by sharply increasing oil production in the autumn of 1985[17] and offering prices lower than those of other producers. The impact was dramatic. In the face of an oil glut, world oil prices plummeted from $28 per barrel a low of $9 in mid 1986 before beginning to recover. Only after a steep drop in their oil earnings and a series of acrimonious meetings did the OPEC countries finally renew their collective agreements. These committed the members to restrain production once more in an effort to maintain a higher price for oil. However, the willingness of the individual OPEC exporters to refrain from cheating (i.e., from producing more than their allotted quotas) remained a problem for OPEC.

Despite these efforts, from 1983 to 1991, Saudi Arabia ran a huge total foreign trade deficit. Altogether, the cost of imported goods and services exceeded the value of its exports (mainly oil) by $120 billion.[18] Combined with the costs of the Gulf crisis and war, this caused a sharp drop in foreign assets and currency reserves. Nonetheless, Saudi hard currency reserves still exceeded $35 billion in mid 1993, and the overall level of Saudi indebtedness as well as its infrastructure and oil wealth left it among the more creditworthy states in the international economy.

More broadly, Saudi Arabia's situation highlights the limitations on the OPEC countries' exercise of power. They are affected by the volatility and increased openness of world oil markets, as well as by their own propensity to import goods and services from the outside world. As a result, their overall balance of payments figures have been subject to stunning reversals. For example, in the space of just two years, the OPEC countries moved from a record surplus of $104 billion in 1980 to a collective annual deficit of $10 billion in 1982. More important, the experience of Saudi Arabia illustrates that notions of an unlimited pool of surplus petrodollars waiting to be spent at the whim of the OPEC countries had become a serious exaggeration. Indeed, throughout most of the 1980s and early to mid 1990s, they remained in an often substantial deficit.

Erosion in the wealth and power of the OPEC countries was a result of oil price increases during the previous decade. In this sense, OPEC's strength proved self-reversing. It is ironic that the consequences of these price increases for OPEC were foreshadowed in a speech by Saudi oil minister Sheik Ahmad Zaki Yamani in January 1981. Responding to students at the University of Petroleum and Minerals in Dammam, Yamani explained why the ultimate loser from further price increases could well be Saudi Arabia itself:

> If we force Western countries to invest heavily in finding alternative sources of energy, they will. This would take no more than seven to ten years and would result in reducing dependence on oil as a source of energy to the point that would jeopardize Saudi Arabia's interests. Saudi Arabia would then be unable to find markets to sell enough oil to meet its financial requirements. . . .
>
> Saudi Arabia's interests lie in extending the life span of oil to the longest period possible to enable us to build a diversified economy supported by industry, agriculture, and other endeavors. Unless we do that there will come a time when this developing country will receive a violent shock.[19]

Oil Power and the Role of the United States

The United States has continued to play a crucial role in shaping the international rules of the game (i.e., the international "regime") for oil. However, in the aftermath of the first oil shock and the United States' withdrawal from Vietnam, the recession of American political and economic power was widely regarded as well under way, particularly in contrast with the first two decades of the postwar period. The United States had, in the years after World War II, possessed hegemonic power. This had enabled America to preside over the creation of multilateral institutions that gave form to the Western economic and security order. The institutions thus created (the International Monetary Fund, the General Agreement on Tariffs and Trade, the Marshall Plan, NATO, *et al.*) helped make possible the cooperation among sovereign Western countries on which their postwar prosperity and security were based.

During much of the oil decade, however, it was sometimes argued that the United States lacked the power, influence, and ability to pay the costs of alliance leadership that would be necessary to maintain the existing international regimes or to create new vehicles for cooperation. In short, the "hegemonic stability" that had characterized the 1950s and 1960s was thought to be in the process of decay, and with it not only the leadership role of the United States, but also the ability of the Western countries and Japan to find means of cooperating in their mutual interests.[20]

Despite identifiable decline in the United States' share of world GNP, gold and hard currency reserves, trade, and the like, as well as the increase in American oil import dependence, the absolute levels of American power still remained considerable. Regardless of bitter disagreements among the Western countries, sharp divergences in policy toward the Middle East, and a *sauve-qui-peut* (every-man-for-himself) scramble for oil and export markets by the Europeans and Japanese, the United States nonetheless was able to preside over the creation of an organization meant to enable oil-importing countries to cope with the consequences of a future oil shock.

At the height of the 1973–1974 crisis, the United States, at the behest of Secretary of State Henry Kissinger, convened a meeting of allied countries. This February 1974 Washington Energy Conference took place despite the reservations of a number of European countries and the strong opposition of France. Ultimately, through political arm-twisting and the use of linkage strategies (especially in subtly threatening that America's continued commitment to the defense of Europe would depend on a positive allied response),[21] the administration succeeded in gaining agreement on establishment of the International Energy Agency.[22] This new body, formally established in November 1974 within the organizational framework of the OECD, provided a means for emergency oil sharing in the event a future oil shock caused a shortfall of 7 percent or more.[23] It also offered a means for exchanging information, for encouraging creation of oil stockpiles, and for other cooperation on energy matters. In effect, it provided a loose organizational umbrella for oil-importing countries, as a counterpart to the producing countries' own OPEC group.

America's power was also affected by its oil import dependence and relative vulnerability. However, during the course of the oil decade, between 1973 and the end of 1984, American consumption of oil actually fell by 9 percent while real GNP rose by some 31 percent.* In essence, the economy had become signifi-

---

*Calculations based on oil consumption figures in Tables 10.2.

cantly more efficient in its use of petroleum. The United States also diversified its sources of oil imports, so that by 1985 the Arab OPEC countries provided only 11 percent of oil imports, in contrast to a figure of 41 percent in 1980. In addition, by the 1990s, the United States had placed some 600 million barrels of crude oil into an underground strategic petroleum reserve. These developments, along with significant improvements in European and Japanese energy efficiency and a decline in oil imports, seemed to make the United States and its allies less vulnerable to the threat of a future oil crisis or embargo than they had been a decade earlier.

Nonetheless, the pattern of oil supply and demand remained volatile. During the last half of the 1980s, with world oil prices well below their oil decade peak, both U.S. and world oil consumption once again began to climb. In just five years, from 1985 to 1990, demand for OPEC oil surged by almost seven million barrels per day, equivalent to more than a 41 percent increase (see Table 10.3). The United States, with its declining oil production and increased consumption, accounted for almost 3 mbd of this growing demand. Indeed, American oil imports approached levels not seen since the late 1970s, both in terms of the volume of oil imported and the share of domestic consumption provided by foreign imports (see Table 10.2). These changes left the importing countries vulnerable to another crisis at the time of Iraq's 1990 invasion of Kuwait. Subsequent years appeared to bring renewed potential risk, although the American military role, in providing both deterrence and reassurance for Saudi Arabia and the oil-producing Gulf states remained important as well.

Oil Power and the LDCs

Contrary to the exhilaration expressed by Ali Masrui on behalf of the developing countries, in the quotation cited at the beginning of this chapter, the oil decade proved to be a mixed blessing for the developing countries. Although many LDC representatives initially acclaimed the first oil shock, the initial reaction soon gave way to second thoughts. In the first place, the costs of imported oil soared for *all* consuming countries, not just those located in Western Europe and North America. Thus the annual balance of payments deficit of the oil-importing LDCs climbed from $5 billion to $30 billion between 1972 and 1975. At first, Western banks proved willing and able to lend large amounts of funds to the LDCs to finance these debts. They did so as a means of recycling the large amounts of petrodollars they received from the OPEC countries, who sought to invest the vastly increased revenues from their oil production.

This recycling of petrodollars helped ease the effects of the first shock for many of the LDCs, but vicarious satisfaction over the North-South dimension proved short-lived, especially with the impact of the second shock and then the mounting debt crisis. Between 1978 and 1981, the combined annual balance of payments deficit of the non–oil-exporting LDCs soared from $27 billion to a staggering $85 billion (see Table 10.5). It became clear that an apparently inexhaustible source of bank lending was no longer available and that the accumulated debt was becoming difficult to repay.

At the same time, hopes for huge amounts of OPEC foreign aid were also disappointed. Although the oil-exporting countries, especially those with the largest

Table 10.5 BALANCE OF PAYMENTS ON CURRENT ACCOUNT
($ BILLION)

Year	OECD	OPEC	Non-Oil Exporting LDCs[a]
1972	8	1	−5
1973	10	8	−6
1974	−27	59	−23
1975	0	27	−30
1976	−15	36	−9
1977	−21	23	−14
1978	13	0	−27
1979	−27	61	−44
1980	−67	104	−65
1981	−26	49	−85
1982	−29	−10	−69
1983	−22	−21	−35
1984	−56	−9	−22
1985	−63	−1	−33
1986	−34	−33	−35
1987	−65	−13	−21
1988	−56	−24	−31
1989	−83	−4	−38
1990	−118	10	−33
1991	−30	−62	−35
1992	−36	−23	−52
1993	11	−25	−76
1994	13	−34	−83

[a]From 1985 on, based on data for non-OPEC countries of Asia, Latin America, and Africa. Excludes Asian newly industrializing economies (Hong Kong, South Korea, Singapore, Taiwan.)

Note: OECD data reflect "statistical errors and asymmetries," giving rise to "world totals (balances) that are significantly different from zero." OECD, December 1989, 145, note b.

Source: Adapted from OECD, *Economic Outlook,* July 1979, 78; and July 1987, 138; December 1989, 145; June 1994, A53. For non-OECD groups of countries, and for 1993–1994, the data are OECD estimates.

surplus revenues, did disburse a considerable volume of aid for a time, the pattern of these aid flows was highly skewed. Thus, most OPEC aid flowed to Arab and Islamic countries. For example, the top nine recipients of OPEC bilateral and multilateral aid in 1979 were Arab countries. Together they accounted for 73.8 percent of total OPEC aid.[24] While oil at below market prices was occasionally made available, this was the exception rather than the rule. In reality, the countries of sub-Saharan Africa, Latin America, South Asia, and the Caribbean mostly found themselves vulnerable to the direct and indirect effects of the oil shocks.

Many non–oil-exporting LDCs discovered that the international terms of trade were also turning against them. For example, while the dollar price of oil rose more than tenfold between 1972 and 1982, the price of commonly exported commodities such as coffee, sugar, and bananas roughly doubled. In effect, a typical LDC thus had to export five times the previous volume of its commodity exports in order to earn the dollars with which to buy a barrel of oil.[25]

In short, although the OPEC countries belonged to the South, the practical consequences of the oil decade imposed costs and burdens on most of the non–oil-producing LDCs, which belied not only their aspirations to third-world solidarity, but also worsened the everyday plight of many of their peoples. Indeed, when it came to oil, the "haves" versus "have nots" distinction proved to apply not just between North and South, but within the South as well.

The Oil Crisis, Middle East Instability, and the Arab-Israeli Conflict

Despite initial identification of the three sets of problems as virtually synonymous, the passage of time made it increasingly clear that the oil crisis, Middle East instability, and the Arab-Israeli conflict were at least as distinct as they were related. In fact, the Yom Kippur War had been the catalyst but not the cause of the first oil shock. The revolution in Iran five years later showed that other problems having nothing to do with that conflict could by themselves precipitate an oil crisis if they occurred at a time of tight oil supply/demand balances. Moreover, dramatic events such as the Iran-Iraq War from 1980 to 1988 and Iraq's invasion of Kuwait in August 1990 demonstrated some of the ways in which Middle East instability could occur irrespective of oil and Arab-Israeli dimensions.

The list of possible catalysts in the region thus remained long. In addition to threats to stability in the entire Persian Gulf region from both Iraq and Iran, it included numerous national rivalries (Iran-Iraq, Iraq-Egypt, Iraq-Syria, Syria-Jordan, Egypt-Libya, Algeria-Tunisia, to name but a few); ethnic and religious antagonisms; tensions between Islamic fundamentalism and modernizing or secular regimes; terrorism; the presence of missiles and chemical weapons; and grave problems of economic development.

In this light, even if resolution of the Arab-Israeli conflict and the Palestinian problem follows the September 1993 agreement between Israel and the PLO, many of the sources of Middle East instability will remain. At the same time, broader factors shaping the international oil system are likely to be only marginally affected.

THE OIL DECADE: RETROSPECT AND PROSPECT

Dramatic events during the early years of the oil decade gave rise to wildly exaggerated assessments about the consequences for international relations. Nonetheless, the oil decade does remain a watershed event and has had a lasting impact.

To grasp the significance of these events it is imperative to appreciate them as a problem in international political economy. In this sense, political *and* economic factors have interacted to shape international relations. As Robert Gilpin has observed, the role of markets is frequently neglected by political observers and political scientists, while the political setting of events and the importance of power are frequently overlooked by economists.[26]

In the case of the oil decade, an appreciation of both economic and political components is essential for understanding. Specifically, those who focused only on political dimensions and the statements of Middle East rulers failed to comprehend how market forces could shift the boundaries within which political choices are made. Thus it is worth bearing in mind that the cumulative effects of OPEC's price increases from $2.70 per barrel in 1973 to $34 in 1981 gave rise to market behavior (increased efficiency, fuel substitution, production of non-OPEC oil) which subsequently undercut the wealth and power of the OPEC countries. Conversely, those who dwelt only on the role of the market and the effects of impersonal supply and demand forces ignored important intervening variables. These included the role of OPEC and of Saudi Arabia within it, the impact of political and military events, the phenomenon of panic buying, the effect of market imperfections, and the consequences of unequal degrees of power among key regional and external actors.

In retrospect, we can assess some of the principal effects of the oil decade. Clearly, it demonstrated the impact that economic and resource issues can have on international relations and state behavior. It also interrupted a generation of unprecedented economic growth and full employment among the industrial democracies. In addition, the perceived economic vulnerability of Western Europe, both in terms of physical dependence on imported oil and then on Middle East oil-producing countries as export markets, shaped the behavior of these countries in reacting to Middle East events and in responding to terrorism, even when these events took place on their own territory. Thus, if Libya's primary export had been peanuts rather than petroleum, it is probable that governments in Rome, London, and Vienna would have adopted more assertive policies in response to Colonel Qaddafi's sponsorship of terrorism.

The start of the oil decade also signaled a major challenge to the relative power position of the United States. American frustration in grappling with issues of oil supply and price, with economic and financial consequences of the energy problem, and with events in Iran typified some of these problems.

West-West splits over "out-of-area" issues were an important product of the oil decade. The United States and its European allies frequently found themselves at loggerheads in responding to the multiple economic and political events of the time. These included not only the problem of collective response in dealing with the two oil shocks, but differences over sanctions policies toward Iran and Libya, Arab-Israeli issues, and even European purchases of Soviet natural gas.

Ultimately, the consequences of the oil decade were significantly less revolutionary than at first anticipated. Here, the long-term consequences of Western economic and even political power were fundamental. Not only did the market power of the OPEC countries prove self-reversing, but even when their role seemed more ascendant, they had little alternative to a constraining economic and technical interdependence with a Western-led international system. This was a matter not only of markets for oil exports. It also encompassed the means for investing and recycling petrodollar revenues, importing technology and expertise, and even cultural and educational ties. Indeed, this interdependence proved all the more entangling as the cyclical nature of oil power became increasingly apparent. With a few exceptions, the OPEC countries had not achieved the self-sustaining economic growth and diversified economic and technical base their oil had been expected to provide. Continuing dependence on petroleum economies and the volatile pattern of revenues from their primary export meant that, for many of them, their degree of usable economic and political power remained circumscribed.

The oil decade saw a dramatic series of upheavals in relative wealth and power. These provided a reminder that the international system is dynamic, not static. While the period in question later saw an undercutting of the OPEC countries' newly acquired wealth and power, such changes are rarely fixed in perpetuity. In the case of oil, huge price increases proved—within a decade—to be self-reversing. High prices gave rise to increased supplies of non-OPEC oil (in Alaska, Norway, Britain, Mexico, China, and elsewhere) as well as other forms of energy. These prices also stimulated more efficient use of oil. Thus, in the OECD countries, total oil consumption dropped by more than seven million barrels per day in a six-year period—from 41.6 mbd in 1979 to 34.3 mbd in 1985 (see Table 10.6). As a result, demand for OPEC oil fell by almost half in the same period, from a peak of 31 mbd in 1979 to 16.6 mbd in 1985. Taken together, these events contributed to the 1986 collapse in oil prices.

However, both the supply of non-OPEC oil and the demand for petroleum remain, in the long run, responsive to price. Thus, falling prices stimulated increased worldwide consumption of oil and undercut the provision of both non-OPEC oil supplies and nonpetroleum forms of energy.

This reflected the consequences of what one author has termed the "OPEC multiplier."[27] For economic and political reasons, oil importing countries prefer to rely on OPEC oil as a last resort. That is, they seek to depend as much as possible on domestically produced forms of energy and oil. To the extent that imports are required, the consuming countries turn next to non-OPEC sources of energy. Only when there is no other alternative do they rely on OPEC oil. As a result, when demand declines, the first source to be reduced is oil from OPEC. (The United States epitomized this pattern in 1980–1985, since domestic production continued to run at or near capacity, even while the amount of oil imported from OPEC plummeted.) Hence, OPEC bore a disproportionate share of the reduction in overall demand for oil.

The logic of the OPEC multiplier, however, works both ways. Thus, as demand for oil increased in the last half of the 1980s, the added production came from the OPEC countries. Given the fact that North American and North Sea (British and Norwegian) fields operated at or near capacity, as did production from non-OPEC producers such as Mexico, demand for OPEC oil rose almost as quickly as it had fallen.[28]

As a consequence, from its low point in 1985, demand for OPEC oil climbed by 7.7 mbd to a figure of 24.3 mbd by the spring of 1990. This represented the highest level since 1980. Although there remained several million barrels per day of unused production capacity, much of the surplus was concentrated along the

Table 10.6 WORLD OIL PRODUCTION (MAJOR PRODUCERS, MBD)

	1973	1979	1982	1985	1987	1989	1991	1993[b]
OPEC:	31.0	31.0	19.1	16.6	18.8	22.6	23.7	25.5
S. Arabia	7.6	9.5	6.5	3.4	4.3	5.1	8.2	8.2
Kuwait	3.0	2.5	0.8	1.0	1.6	1.8	0.2	1.7
Iran	5.9	3.2	2.2	2.3	2.3	2.9	3.3	3.6
Algeria	1.1	1.2	1.0	1.0	1.0	1.1	1.2	1.2
Iraq	2.0	3.5	1.0	1.4	2.1	2.8	0.3	0.5
Libya	2.2	2.1	1.2	1.1	1.0	1.1	1.5	1.4
UAE	1.5	1.8	1.3	1.2	1.5	2.0	2.4	2.3
Indonesia	1.3	1.6	1.3	1.3	1.3	1.4	1.6	1.5
Nigeria	2.1	2.3	1.3	1.5	1.3	1.7	1.9	2.1
Venezuela	3.4	2.4	1.9	1.7	1.8	1.9	2.4	2.4
Canada	1.8	1.5	1.3	1.5	1.5	1.6	1.5	1.6
Mexico	0.5	1.5	2.7	2.7	2.5	2.5	2.7	2.6
U.K.	nil	1.6	2.1	2.5	2.4	1.8	1.8	1.8
China	1.1	2.1	2.0	2.5	2.7	2.8	2.8	2.9
U.S.[a]	9.2	8.6	8.6	9.0	8.3	7.6	7.4	6.9
Former USSR	8.3	11.2	11.6	11.3	11.7	11.4	9.9	7.7
WORLD	55.7	62.5	53.2	53.6	56.3	59.5	60.2	60.0
OECD CONSUMPTION	39.6	41.6	34.5	34.3	35.9	37.5	38.1	39.2[c]

[a]Not including natural gas liquids (e.g., 1.6 mbd additional in 1985).

[b]6-month average

[c]4-month average

Source: U.S. Department of Energy, Monthly Energy Review (published July 1990): 110, 111, 115. Data for 1991 and 1993 from September 1993 issue; 132, 133, 137.

Persian Gulf, where two-thirds of the world's proved crude oil reserves are located.

THE PERSIAN GULF CRISIS

With the ending of the Iran-Iraq war in 1988, Iraq emerged as the dominant power in the Gulf region, but one burdened by wartime debts of as much as $80 billion. With a one-million-man army equipped with missiles and chemical weapons, and led by its ruthless President-for-life, Saddam Hussein, Iraq began to put pressure on its oil-producing neighbors, especially Kuwait. Ultimately, on August 2, 1990, Saddam's forces invaded and occupied the Persian Gulf sheikdom and thus placed an additional 95 billion barrels of oil reserves under Iraqi control. Moreover, Iraq's forces appeared to threaten Saudi Arabia as well.

In reaction both to this lawless attack against a United Nations member state and in recognition that Saddam Hussein was in a position to dominate the oil reserves of the entire region, President George Bush sent American forces to Saudi Arabia at the request of its leaders. These land, sea, and air forces, dispatched as part of Operation Desert Shield, grew over the next six months to a strength of more than 500,000. Over a period of months, they were joined by an additional 200,000 troops and support personnel from some 40 countries, including Britain, France, Italy, Egypt, Kuwait, Saudi Arabia, and even Syria.

At the same time, a series of United Nations Security Council resolutions provided an unprecedented degree of international legitimacy and support for the American-led effort to oust Saddam Hussein from Kuwait. The end of the Cold War now saw cooperation between the Soviet Union and the United States. On the very day of the invasion, this made possible Security Council Resolution 660, condemning the Iraqi conquest and demanding immediate withdrawal, and on the following day Secretary of State James Baker and Soviet Foreign Minister Shevardnadze issued an unprecedented joint condemnation of the Iraqi action. Subsequently, Resolution 661, on August 6, ordered a far-reaching trade and financial boycott against Iraq. When Iraq continued to defy the international community, the Security Council passed resolution 678 on November 29. This established January 15, 1991 as the deadline for withdrawal from Kuwait and authorized the use of force ("all necessary means") after that time.[29]

In the face of Saddam Hussein's intransigence, coalition forces launched Operation Desert Storm, beginning with massive air strikes against Iraq on January 16, 1991. Weeks of these attacks inflicted massive damage on Iraq's military forces and infrastructure, but did not prevent Saddam from unleashing Scud missile attacks against civilian targets in Israel's largest city, Tel Aviv, and against Riyadh, Saudi Arabia. Ultimately, the American-led forces launched a massive ground attack on February 23, as shown in Map 10.1 on pages 230-231. This offensive overwhelmed Saddam's forces within 100 hours and was called to a halt by President Bush on February 27, with the liberation of Kuwait.[30]

In the initial days and weeks of the crisis, there were fears of a major oil crisis. As a result of Saddam's invasion and UN sanctions, some 2.1 mbd of oil from Iraq and an additional 2 mbd from Kuwait were excluded from world oil markets. In reaction, world oil prices, which had been as low as $13 per barrel in May 1990, briefly tripled to over $40 per barrel in early October.[31] However, it soon became apparent that increased production from Saudi Arabia, amounting to nearly 3mbd, along with modest additional quantities from Iran, Libya, Venezuela and Mexico, would provide sufficient oil to offset the shortfall. This, combined with the mounting evidence that the military challenge from Saddam could be dealt with effectively, caused oil prices to settle back into the $20 per barrel range as the crisis moved toward its resolution.

The Persian Gulf crisis thus did not precipitate a major oil shock. However, it is sobering to understand that its outcome could have had much more disruptive consequences. Had Saddam Hussein sent his forces into Saudi Arabia in early August 1990, they would have been able to seize strategic oil-producing areas as well as deny bases, ports, and airfields to the coalition forces. In consequence, the

American-led military effort would have been far more difficult and costly in terms of allied lives. Moreover, Saddam's destruction of Kuwaiti oil wells during the Gulf War could have foreshadowed similar destruction in Saudi Arabia. In addition, the crisis itself unfolded in ways that were almost ideal from the standpoint of the international community. Cooperation proved effective not only in military terms, but also in its diplomatic, economic, and oil dimensions, aided by the intransigence of Saddam Hussein and the blatant and brutal character of his actions. Had any of these matters evolved differently, had the military effort proved less effective, or had Saddam delayed the crisis for another 18 months until Iraq had brought its nuclear weapons effort to fruition, the outcome of the crisis could well have been far more dangerous.

The crisis thus illustrated, once again, that oil retained its potential for economic and political upheaval. The invasion of Kuwait had come after a decade in which the oil shocks of the 1970s appeared to be receding into history. The reemergence of the oil issue was not the result of chance, but reflected intertwined economic and political dimensions that remain a potential source of conflict in the post–Cold War world.

NOTES

1. Quoted in Walter Laqueur, "Containment for the 80s," *Commentary*, Vol. 70, No. 4 (October 1980): 38.
2. "The Wrong War? The Case Against a National Energy Policy," *Public Interest* (Fall 1978): 3–44, at p. 20.
3. K. J. Holsti, "Farming, Ranching, and Accounting: Perspectives on Change in International Relations," in Holsti, *Change in the International System: Essays on the Theory and Practice of International Relations* (Aldershot, England and Brookfield, Vermont: Edward Elgar Publishing Company, 1991), p. 4.
4. Anthony Sampson provides a comprehensive treatment in *The Seven Sisters: The Great Oil Companies and the World They Shaped* (New York: Bantam, 1975).
5. See, for example, the account in Barry Rubin, *Paved with Good Intentions: The American Experience in Iran* (New York: Oxford University Press, 1980).
6. Dankwart Rustow, *Oil and Turmoil: America Faces OPEC and the Middle East* (New York: Norton, 1982), pp. 95–96. Rustow's book provides a concise and lucid treatment of this subject.
7. Organization for Economic Cooperation and Development, *Oil: The Present Situation and Future Prospects* (Paris, 1973), p. 265.
8. For discussion of America and the international oil system, on which part of this chapter is based, see Robert J. Lieber, "International Energy Policy and the Reagan Administration: Avoiding the Next Oil Shock?" in Oye, Lieber, and Rothchild, eds., *Eagle Resurgent? The Reagan Era in American Foreign Policy* (Boston: Little, Brown, 1987), pp. 169ff.
9. Data from Exxon Corporation, *Middle East Oil* (September 1980), p. 26.
10. Quoted in Gary Sick, *All Fall Down: America's Tragic Encounter with Iran* (New York: Random House, 1985), p. 14. The meeting took place in Teheran, on 30 May 1972.
11. OECD, *Economic Outlook* (Paris), No. 27 (July 1980): 114.
12. Salam Jalloud, quoted in the *New York Times,* 17 February 1974.

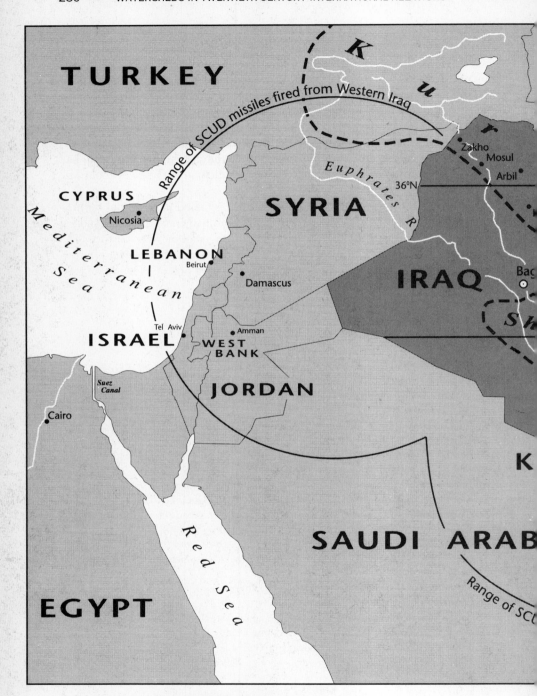

Map 10.1   IRAQ AND THE MIDDLE EAST
Source: John O. Loughlin, et al. (eds.), *War and its Consequences* (New York: HarperCollins, 1994), p. xii.

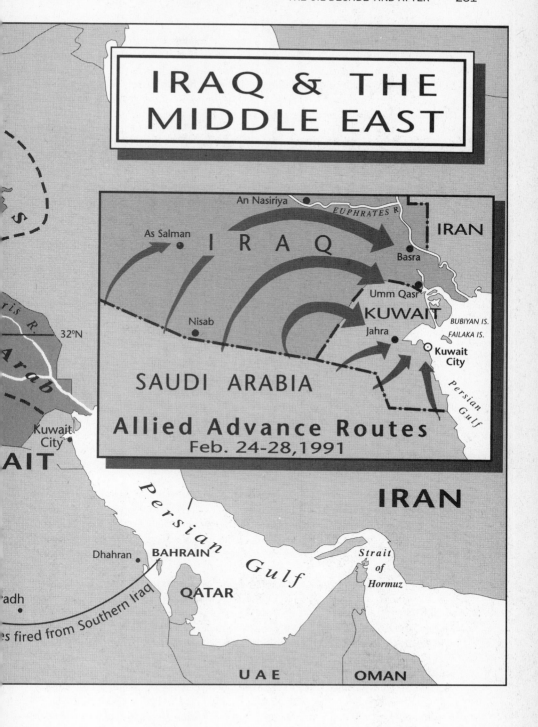

IRAQ & THE MIDDLE EAST

An Nasiriya

EUPHRATES R.

IRAN

As Salman

I R A Q

Basra

Umm Qasr

KUWAIT

BUBIYAN IS.

FAILAKA IS.

32°N

Nisab

Jahra

Kuwait
City

*Persian
Gulf*

SAUDI ARABIA

Allied Advance Routes
Feb. 24-28, 1991

Tigris R.

Shatt al Arab

Kuwait
City

KUWAIT

IRAN

Persian Gulf

Dhahran

BAHRAIN

*Strait
of
Hormuz*

Riyadh

QATAR

...es fired from Southern Iraq

U A E

OMAN

13. Quoted in Lewis H. Lapham, *Harper's* (March 1979): 46.
14. Mark Heller and Nadav Safran identify a strong challenge from the middle classes and anticipate increasing problems of regime stability. See *The New Middle Class and Regime Stability in Saudi Arabia,* Harvard Middle East Papers, No. 3 (Cambridge, 1985). William Quandt finds that the monarchy has been relatively successful in managing a difficult transition. See *Saudi Arabia in the 1980s: Foreign Policy, Security and Oil* (Washington, DC: Brookings, 1981).
15. Source: International Monetary Fund, in *New York Times,* 29 October 1984; and the *Economist,* 13 July 1985, p. 67. Also *New York Times,* 12 February 1987.
16. Estimates for Saudi and OPEC foreign assets are from OECD, as reported in the *Economist,* 4 January 1986, p. 54.
17. Saudi oil production surged from a low of 2.3 mbd in August 1985 to as high as 6.4 mbd in August 1986. Data from U.S. Department of Energy, *Monthly Energy Review,* October 1986 (published February 1987), p. 110.
18. IMF Study, cited in "Saudi Stability Hit by Heavy Spending Over Last Decade," *New York Times,* 22 September 1993, pp. 1 and 12. Also see response by Mohammad Abalkhail, Saudi Minister of Finance and National Economy, *New York Times,* 1 September 1993.
19. The text of Yamani's speech is printed in Quandt, pp. 167 and 169.
20. The theory of hegemonic stability holds that "order in world politics is typically created by a single dominant power," and that "the maintenance of order requires continued hegemony." Robert O. Keohane, *After Hegemony: Cooperation and Discord in the World Political Economy* (Princeton: Princeton University Press, 1984), p. 31. See Robert Gilpin, *War and Change in World Politics* (New York: Cambridge University Press, 1981), pp. 144–145; Charles P. Kindleberger, *The World in Depression, 1929–1939* (Berkeley: University of California Press, 1973), p. 305; and Keohane, "The Theory of Hegemonic Stability and Changes in International Economic Regimes," in Ole Holsti *et al., Change in the International System* (Boulder: Westview Press, 1980), pp. 131–162.
21. For a remarkable account of the use of American power and influence at the Washington meeting, see Henry A. Kissinger, *Years of Upheaval* (Boston: Little, Brown, 1982), especially pp. 915–916.
22. Note that this creation of the IEA through the use of American power contrasts with the interpretation of Robert Keohane, who implies that cooperation in establishing this regime took place in the absence of hegemony: "As hegemony erodes, the demand for international regimes may even increase, as the lack of a formal intergovernmental oil regime in the 1950s, and the institution of one in 1974, suggest." *After Hegemony,* p. 244.
23. For analysis of the International Energy Agency's operation and the dynamics of its possible functioning in a crisis, see Lieber, *The Oil Decade: Conflict and Cooperation in the West* (Lanham, MD: University Press of America, 1986, and Westport, CT: Praeger, 1983), pp. 123–126; also Richard Scott, "The International Energy Agency," *Hastings International and Comparative Law Review* (Spring 1977), especially p. 39; Robert O. Keohane, "International Agencies and the Art of the Possible: The Case of the IEA," *Journal of Policy Analysis and Management* 1 (1982): 469–481; Mason Willrich and Melvin Conant, "The International Energy Agency: An Interpretation and Assessment," *The American Journal of International Law* 71 (1977): 199–223; Edward N. Krapels, *Oil Crisis Management: Strategic Stockpiling for International Security* (Baltimore: Johns Hopkins University Press, 1980).

24. Syria and Jordan received more than half of total OPEC aid in 1979, followed by the Sudan, Arab regional recipients, the Yemen Arab Republic, Somalia, Oman, Egypt, and Mauritania. See H. Askari, in the *SAIS Review*, (Winter 1981–82): 146.

25. See Helmut Schmidt, *A Grand Strategy for the West* (New Haven: Yale University Press, 1985), pp. 69–81.

26. *U.S. Power and the Multinational Corporation: The Political Economy of Direct Foreign Investment* (New York: Basic Books, 1975), pp. 4–5.

27. Bijan Mossavar-Rahmani, "The OPEC Multiplier," *Foreign Policy* 52 (Fall 1982): 136–148.

28. For a view that the OPEC countries will find it very difficult to boost prices and restrain supply through the Saudi-led petroleum cartel, see Eliyahu Kanovsky, *Another Oil Shock in the 1990s? A Dissenting View* (Washington, DC: Washington Institute for Near East Policy, 1987). Kanovsky identifies the revenue needs of oil exporters and their competition for market share as the most powerful forces holding down the price of oil for the foreseeable future. He also cites the end of the Iran-Iraq war, energy efficiency, and improved oil exploration and recovery technology. See also Kanovsky, *OPEC Ascendant? Another Case of Crying Wolf* (Washington Institute for Near East Policy, 1990).

29. The texts of the UN Security Council Resolutions can be found in Joseph S. Nye, Jr., and Roger K. Smith, eds., *After the Storm: Lessons from the Gulf War* (Lanham, Maryland: Madison Books, 1992), pp. 357–398.

30. For an excellent comprehensive account, see Lawrence Freedman and Efraim Karsh, *The Gulf Conflict, 1990–1991: Diplomacy and War in the New World Order* (Princeton: Princeton University Press, 1993).

31. Robert J. Lieber, "Oil and Power After the Gulf War," *International Security*, Vol. 17, No. 1 (Summer 1992): 155–176, at p. 157.

PART 4

Order and the "Anarchical Society"

chapter 11

The Causes of War

For the last two or three centuries major war—war among the developed countries—has gradually moved toward terminal disrepute because of its perceived repulsiveness and futility.

—JOHN E. MUELLER[1]

The prudent reader will check that his air raid shelter is in good repair.

—SIR MICHAEL HOWARD (REVIEWING JOHN E. MUELLER'S BOOK)[2]

As long as there are sovereign nations possessing great power, war is inevitable.

—ALBERT EINSTEIN[3]

The international system has always been anarchical and oligarchical: anarchical because of the absence of a monopoly of legitimate violence, oligarchic (or hierarchic) in that without civil society, rights depend largely on might.

—RAYMOND ARON[4]

The question is: If international relations can approximate both a Hobbesian state of nature and a Lockean civil society, why does cooperation emerge in some cases and not in others?

—KENNETH A. OYE[5]

W hy does war occur?[6] This age-old question has given rise to numerous and contradictory explanations and hypotheses. We have been told that war is a universal human trait or that wars are planned by decision-makers; that wars are the result of impersonal historical forces or the consequences of the ambitions of individual national leaders; that violence inheres in the nation-state or that violence results from errors of judgment on the part of decision-makers. Nor has the analysis of international conflict been confined to a small coterie of political scientists. Sigmund Freud, the father of psychoanalysis, lamented the nature of man, which he viewed as likely to make the abolition of war impossible. On the other hand, President Richard Nixon, who presided over the United States withdrawal from the Vietnam War, ventured a very different judgment in observing: "I seriously doubt if we will ever have another war. This is probably the very last one."[7]

The question of why conflict and war occur is by no means the only important subject of inquiry in international relations. Thus, one observer criticizes political theorists who have uncritically accepted the Hobbesian conception of international relations as a state of nature. He argues that by committing themselves to the notion that international relations is primarily concerned with national rivalries and war, they neglect other pressing questions about contemporary international relations and world order.[8]

Notwithstanding this complaint, conflict and war do remain the most important phenomena with which the study of international relations must deal. Conflict, that is, the competition for limited resources among different individuals and groups, is a pervasive feature of politics at all levels. However, it is the occurrence of war, the use of mass, organized violence as a method for resolving conflict among states, that concerns us here. The phenomenon of warfare can and does end the lives of large numbers of people, civilians as well as combatants.

While the Cold War era did not lead to a catastrophic World War III among the nuclear powers, a succession of bloody conventional wars has nonetheless taken the lives of more than 20 million people since 1945. Indeed, even early twentieth-century conflicts caused huge casualties. For example, in 1916 the Battle of Verdun took the lives of some 800,000 French and Germans in a matter of months, even though the outcome did not ultimately prove decisive for the course of the war. World War I itself caused 10 million deaths in the years from 1914 to 1918. In turn, World War II killed more than 50 million people between 1939 and 1945. Half of those killed were civilian victims of the war, including the six million Jews who perished in Hitler's genocide.

The list of contemporary armed conflicts is long—and similar lists can be compiled for earlier periods. To cite only a number of the more important post-1945 cases, there have been wars pitting China against India, China against Vietnam, Israel against Egypt and Syria, India against Pakistan, North Korea against South Korea, Iran against Iraq, Vietnam against Cambodia, and internal or civil wars in Afghanistan, Algeria, Angola, China, Cuba, Cyprus, Nicaragua, Nigeria, Vietnam and the former Yugoslavia.[9] (See Table 11. 1.)

Table 11.1 WARS SINCE 1945 (PARTIAL LIST)

Countries	Dates
Indonesia v. Netherlands	1945–1946
Greece (c)	1945–1949
China (c)	1946–1950
India (c)	1947–1948
Indochina (France v. Vietminh)	1946–1954
Israel v. Egypt, Iraq, Jordan, Lebanon, Syria	1948–1949
Colombia (c)	1949–1962
Philippines (c)	1950–1952
Korea (S. Korea, U.S., UN v. N. Korea, China)	1950–1953
Algeria (France; c)	1954–1962,1993-
China v. Tibet	1956–1959
Russia v. Hungary	1956
Suez (Israel, France, Britain v. Egypt)	1956
Cuba (c)	1958–1959
China v. India	1962
Yemen (Egypt v. Royalists)	1962–1967
Sudan (c)	1963–1972, 1984–
Dominican Republic (c)	1965
Vietnam (U.S., S. Vietnam v. N. Vietnam, NLF)	1965–1975
India v. Pakistan	1965 & 1971
Six Day War (Israel v. Egypt, Jordan, Syria)	1967
Nigeria (c)	1976–1970
El Salvador v. Honduras	1969
Guatemala (c)	1954 and 1966–1991
Pakistan (E. Bengal)	1971
Zimbabwe (c)	1972–1979
Yom Kippur War (Israel v. Egypt, Syria)	1973
Ethiopia v. Eritrea	1974
Cyprus (c)	1974
Angola (c)	1975–
Indonesia (E. Timor)	1975–
Lebanon (c)	1975–1990
Ethiopia (c)	1976–1991
Morocco (Western Sahara)	1976–1990
Ethiopia v. Somalia	1977–1978
Uganda, Libya v. Tanzania	1978–1979
Nicaragua (c)	1978–1979, 1981–1988
Vietnam v. Cambodia	1978–1988
China v. Vietnam	1979
El Salvador (c)	1979–1992
Afghanistan (USSR; c)	1979–1988,1988–
Iran v. Iraq	1980–1988
Mozambique (c)	1981–1992

(continued on next page)

Table 11.1 *(continued)*

Countries	Dates
Falklands (Britain v. Argentina)	1982
Syria (c. v. Moslem Brotherhood)	1982
Sri Lanka (c)	1985–
Armenia v. Azerbaijan	1988–
Liberia (c)	1990–
Serbia-Croatia-Bosnia	1991–
Georgia (c)	1991–
Gulf War (Iraq v. U.S. and coalition)	1991
Rwanda (c)	1994

(c) = civil war or insurrection

Source: Adapted, in part, from data in Melvin Small and J. David Singer, *Resort to Arms: International and Civil Wars, 1816–1980* (Beverly Hills: Sage, 1982), pp. 92–95, 98–99, 229–232; and Ruth Leger Sivard, *World Military and Social Expenditures, 1989* (Washington, DC: World Priorities, Inc., 1989), p. 22.

WAR: DIVERSE EXPLANATIONS

Can we present valid generalizations about why war occurs? Are there insights that go beyond either detailed and narrow treatments of individual disputes or obvious and uninteresting generalizations? Certainly, diverse interpretations of war are almost as numerous as the different wars themselves. In the twentieth century alone, the range of explanations has been remarkable. For example, in the years before World War I, President Woodrow Wilson identified the cause of war as the absence of self-determination and democratic government. In his view, wars occurred at the behest of dictatorial governments, whereas a government responsive to the will of its people would not be likely to embark on aggressive action.

Marxist-Leninists took a very different view. Lenin held that international conflict was caused by the dynamics of imperialism, as the highest stage of capitalism. The notion that Communist states would therefore enjoy harmonious relations of international proletarian solidarity was, however, contradicted repeatedly, as in the Soviet invasions of Hungary in 1956, Czechoslovakia in 1968, and Afghanistan in 1979. Soviet conflict with China (1969) and wars between China and Vietnam and between Vietnam and Cambodia provided additional contradictions to this view.

Conversely, there were views that blamed *all* conflict on the Communists. For example, William Randolph Hearst, Jr., the editor-in-chief of the Hearst newspapers, wrote:

> Wherever you go, whomever you talk to, the important world problems all have a common denominator: Communism.
> The world's troubles would become relatively inconsequential if it were not for the everlasting conniving and trouble-making of the Reds.[10]

Similarly, Richard Nixon once observed:

If it weren't for the Communist threat, the free world could live in peace.[11]

These political explanations come nowhere near exhausting the range of explanations. Illustratively, the English philosopher Bertrand Russell commented that just as children run and shout from impulse and dogs bay at the moon, so grown men quarrel, boast, beat at each other, and murder.[12] And, from yet another perspective, a president of the American Psychological Association once proposed the development of a drug that national leaders could take in order to decrease their propensities to react to some future world crisis by starting a nuclear war; he also suggested that this "psychological disarmament" might be negotiated among nations much in the way that military disarmament has been the subject of contemporary negotiations.[13]

Still other explanations for conflict and war have been offered. They are based on widely diverse factors, for example, population pressure, economics, rigidifying balances of power, individual political and personal ambition, technological change, various types of imperialism, and even a mythical international Zionist conspiracy. Most of these are single-factor explanations, yet the dimensions of conflict seem far more complex than any one factor can encompass.

Consider how just a few of the twentieth century's past and more recent wars cut across these diverse explanations. For instance at the outbreak of World War I in 1914, the major combatants (France, Russia, and Britain versus Germany and Austria-Hungary) were not opposed along Communist/non-Communist or democratic/nondemocratic lines. Instead they were mostly nonrevolutionary constitutional monarchies that had in common their private enterprise economic systems and the Christian religion. Indeed, the most democratic of the belligerent states, France and Britain, were allied with the most autocratic one, czarist Russia.

Among post–World War II armed conflicts, there exist a wide array of causal factors. The Korean War began with an attack by Communist North Korea against non-Communist South Korea. Subsequent conflicts have been based on religion, ethnicity, and territory (Israel versus the Arabs, India versus Pakistan), colonialism (France in Algeria), ethnicity or tribalism (Hausas versus Ibos in Nigeria, Tamils versus Sinhalese in Sri Lanka, Serbs versus Croats and Muslims in the former Yugoslavia), maritime power (Britain versus Argentina in the Falkland Islands), or a combination of factors (Iraq's war with Iran and its invasion of Kuwait).

In view of this diversity of historical experience and the plethora of explanation, how can we begin to make sense of the phenomenon of war? The problem is not merely one of choosing among contradictory explanations at different conceptual levels, but also of determining whether *any* systematic approach may be worthwhile. Indeed, the author of one of the most ambitious quantitative efforts to explain international war, J. David Singer, has observed that, "A . . . discouraging fact is our failure to achieve any significant theoretical breakthrough."[14] And another scholar, John Vasquez, reviewing a series of studies by Singer and others concedes that:

The scientific study of war began with the hope and promise that the collection of reproducible evidence and its systemic analysis would result in a major breakthrough in

our understanding of general factors associated with war and peace. That breakthrough has not occurred.[15]

With such limitations in mind, it is most useful to search not for single causes, but
for systemic patterns or groups of explanations.

Here an effective point of departure for the analysis of conflict is suggested
by the scheme Kenneth Waltz employs in his book, *Man, the State and War*.[16] In
this widely cited work, Waltz has identified three divergent "images" or sets of explanations for the occurrence of war. The first image finds in man himself the lo-
cus of important causes of war. Second-image explanations dwell on the nature of
individual states. The third image finds the effective cause of war inherent in the
nature of the nation-state system itself. While most explanations for the causes of
war, and thus for its mitigation or even prevention, fall into one of these three categories, the insight provided by third-image explanations is most valuable for
comprehending the systemic causes of conflict. Before considering the implications of this systemic perspective, however, it is useful to consider the first and
second images in more detail.

First-Image Explanations

These explanations rest on the assumption that the causes of war are to be found
in the nature and behavior of man. Thus in the seventeenth century, the philosopher Spinoza explained violence by reference to human imperfections, whereby
passion displaced reason. He held that out of self-interest men ought to cooperate, but instead they engage in deadly quarrels. Writing at nearly the same time as
Spinoza, the English poet John Milton held that war was inevitable because men
were irrevocably evil. Although very different in perspective, the views of
Bertrand Russell also can be grouped within this first-image category since they
place the onus of responsibility on the character of policymakers.

Explanations of war that focus on the nature of man actually encompass two
different versions of the causes of war. One interpretation emphasizes the problem of human nature, that is, of qualities common to all humans. The other places
greater weight on the role of specific individuals, as in the case of Adolf Hitler.

Both optimists and pessimists, as Waltz observes, are subsumed within the
first image. Pessimists find the real nature of man to be essentially flawed and beyond correction, so that little can be done to prevent the recurrence of war. By
contrast, optimists characterize man as at least potentially good and society as essentially harmonious, provided that certain prescriptions are followed so that humanity will be uplifted or enlightened.

Psychological conflict theories also fit within the first-image category. Some
of these analyses focus on individual leaders; others assume that because war represents aggressive behavior by nations, an understanding of its causes can be ob-
tained by examining the determinants of aggressive behavior in individuals. However, many psychologists and other social scientists have concluded that
psychological and anthropological research results do not support the assumption
that war is rooted in human nature and is thus inevitable. Efforts to determine the
causes of war that proceed from individual psychology rather than from analysis of

relations between nations are thus of dubious relevance.[17] Psychology does have contributions to make, for example, on the psychology of aggression, the motivation of decision-makers, and the distortion of perception under conditions of stress, but there cannot be a self-contained psychological theory of international relations.

First-image explanations, in some cases, lead to prescriptions for the mitigation of conflict. The more optimistic approaches have sought to end warfare by enlightening or improving humans in their knowledge and behavior. Pacifists, for example, have sought to oppose war by refusing to bear arms and encouraging others to refuse as well. Other illustrations can be found in antiquity. For example, in his play *Lysistrata,* written in 412 B.C., the classical Greek playwright Aristophanes depicted a situation in which the women of Athens refuse to engage in sex with their men until peace is achieved.

On the whole, although first-image explanations sometimes provide useful emphasis on the responsibility of specific individuals for precipitating war, they nonetheless tend to fall well short of providing comprehensive explanations of why war occurs. They cannot, for the most part, explain why warfare has been endemic in some regions and historical periods and rather infrequent in others. Human beings possess capacities for both cooperation and conflict, and explanations that concern themselves exclusively with individual human behavior are likely to be incomplete. Analysis of conflict must thus proceed at the state and systemic level within which human drives are channeled.

Second-Image Explanations

Second-image explanations assume that war depends on the type of national government or the character of a society. The implication here is that while human nature may not be changeable, social and political institutions are. The perspectives of Woodrow Wilson and of Lenin fall within this category, but neither seems to withstand the test of experience. During the Cold War, Communist countries were by no means more peaceful in their international behavior than capitalist ones. Indeed, during the post-1945 era, relations among the countries of Eastern Europe were much *less* peaceful and stable than those among the industrial democracies of Western Europe.

Wilson's formulation that democracies are more peaceful, while authoritarian and monarchical states are aggressive, fares better, but still falls short of providing a comprehensive explanation. Argentina's experience with Britain in the Falkland Islands, Indochina's and Algeria's experience with France in the 1940s and 1950s, and the encounters of Mexico and Spain with the United States in the nineteenth century provide cases in point. During the 1960s and 1970s, a number of ambitious studies of war sought to identify patterns based on the propensity of certain types of countries to become involved in warfare. Yet one historical study of warfare in the century from 1865 to 1965 found little evidence that any particular kind of government (whether authoritarian or liberal, communist or democratic, military or civilian) was more prone to undertake armed attack than any other kind.[18]

Diverse studies by philosophers and historians have also tried to connect the type of state with the propensity to engage in international conflict. Two nineteenth-century philosophers, August Comte and Herbert Spencer, held that military conquests were typical of the behavior of backward agrarian societies. By contrast, they characterized industrial countries as exhibiting less aggressive international behavior because international stability created conditions conducive to economic production and increased wealth.[19]

These views, however, were disputed in the work of L. F. Richardson. In his research, much of it published posthumously, Richardson demonstrated that the connection was not supported by actual historical data. He found that although the *destructiveness* of wars had increased greatly since the early nineteenth century (which also coincided with the expansion of the industrial revolution in Britain), the actual *frequency* of war had not decreased significantly. As a result, Richardson could find no confirmation for the argument that industrialized countries were less conflict prone.[20] Subsequent studies have suggested, however, that societies undergoing transition to industrialization, particularly when experiencing rapid economic, population, and technological growth, may be more likely to become involved in international conflicts.[21]

A more recent study returns to the proposition that the progress of civilization will bring an end to war. John Mueller holds that war has become increasingly obsolete, and pays less attention to why wars occur—asserting, for example, that World War I "should never have happened" because "there was not really a great deal to fight about. . . ."[22] Mueller notes that there have been no wars between the 44 richest countries since 1945 (with the exception of the 1956 Soviet attack on Hungary), and he prophesies that as the poorer countries become more developed, they will place greater value on prosperity rather than military strength and will also resort less to war.

Another author also sees the progress of civilization as leading to the end of international war. James Lee Ray draws an analogy with the abolition of slavery, noting that both it and war were once considered inevitable consequences of human nature. Ray takes note of the absence of war between major powers since the end of World War II, strong norms against colonialism, and the lack of war between democratic states. While qualifying his argument, he concludes that war has not only become obsolete between the world's richest and most powerful states, but that international norms also inhibit some forms of depredation by the powerful against the weak.[23]

A different approach can be found in a broad-ranging historical and philosophical analysis by Francis Fukuyama. He argues that the Western idea of economic and political liberalism has triumphed over alternatives such as fascism, Marxism-Leninism, and Islamic fundamentalism. The author holds that the world may be witnessing "not just the end of the Cold War, or the passing of a particular period of postwar history, but . . . the universalization of Western liberal democracy as the final form of human government."[24] Fukuyama's "end of history" envisages a reduction in major wars because "large-scale conflict must involve large states still caught in the grip of history, and they are what appears to be passing from the scene."[25] Fukuyama is careful not to imply the end of international conflict. He concedes the possibility of war between what he terms states "still in history" and those "at the end of history" (i.e., East-West conflict cannot be ruled out), and sees a high and even rising level of nationalist and ethnic violence. Citing such groups as Palestinians, Kurds, Sikhs, Tamils, Irish Catholics, Belgian Walloons, Armenians and Azeris, he finds it likely that "terrorism and wars of national liberation will continue to be an important item on the international agenda."[26]

Among larger quantitative studies, conclusions about the relationship of a nation's attributes to the likelihood of its involvement in war have produced modest or contradictory results.[27] Indeed, a number of methodological problems may well limit the practical and theoretical value of mathematical correlations based on historical experience. It has been argued that some nations or ethnic groups or types of political systems are (or have been at times) more warlike than others. In data provided by Melvin Small and J. David Singer from their ambitious Correlates of War project, the country that emerges as having been involved in the greatest number of international wars is France, with 22. (England comes second with 19, then Turkey and Russia with 18 each.) Yet as the authors themselves observe, the fact of frequent involvement in war may or may not indicate something significant about the character of the country in question:

> Many have argued that some nations . . . are more aggressive than others, or that some ethnic groups are naturally warlike whereas others are naturally pacific. At the same time, *repeated involvement in war may not necessarily relate to any innate characteristic but merely to the misfortune of being geographically proximate to predatory powers.*[28]

What does seem to be the case is that democracies do not fight wars with each other. The reasons for this are the subject of debate, but Michael Doyle—drawing on the philosophy of Immanuel Kant—has suggested several key explanatory factors. First, voters provide a restraint on government because it is they who ultimately must pay the human and material costs of war. Related to this, war against another democracy is unlikely to be seen as legitimate, and the rotation in office of national leaders helps insure that personal animosities between heads of governments do not act as a cause of war. Second, democracies are accustomed to free speech and the rule of law internally, and are thus presumed to be more cooperative internationally in respecting international law, and to anticipating that other democracies will behave in a similar fashion. Thus, mutual expectations make cooperation easier. Third, the "spirit of commerce" encourages states to promote peace and avoid war because they are better off economically if they can trade freely, rather than taking refuge in narrow, self-contained, autarkic economies under conditions of conflict. Fourth, in the economic interchange among democratic states with market economies, the international market, rather than specific states, makes decisions about production and distribution, so that states do not appear directly responsible for outcomes.[29]

A more recent empirical study also finds that democratically governed states rarely go to war against one another. Its authors, Bruce Russett and his colleagues, offer a series of propositions to explain this: (1) decision-makers in democratic states will try to follow internationally the same norms of conflict resolution that have developed in domestic politics; (2) decision-makers will expect their counterparts in other democratic states to act likewise; (3) democratic decision-makers expect to resolve conflicts by compromise and nonviolence; (4) democracies will thus follow norms of peaceful conflict resolution in relations with other democracies and will expect that others will do so; (5) the more stable the democracy, the more likely that democratic norms will guide its behavior with other democracies and the more other democratic states will anticipate this; and (6) if violence occurs between democracies, at least one of them is probably politically unstable.[30]

For a wide variety of reasons, however, democracies do become involved in wars with *non*democratic states. In explaining this, the Russett study, for example, notes that these violent conflicts will still occur because leaders of nondemocracies may use and expect others to use violence to resolve conflict; other states will anticipate this; and democratic states may resort to nondemocratic norms in dealing with nondemocracies.[31]

In essence, second-image explanations of the causes of war are incomplete. While one important conclusion is evident—that democracies rarely, if ever, make war on one another—democracies historically have nonetheless been involved in numerous wars involving nondemocracies. There are thus two analytical limitations involving explanations for the causes of war that are based at the state level. One is that there is only a limited relationship between the type of nation and the incidence of international conflict. The other is that while first- and second-image explanations can provide important insights, the pattern of the international system in which countries find themselves shapes their behavior in profound ways. Hence, it becomes imperative to consider third-image explanations.

Third-Image Explanations

The essence of the third image is that the ultimate cause of warfare inheres in the very condition of the international system, which Waltz and others have identified as one of international anarchy. That is, states exist in an international milieu that lacks effective means for peaceful resolution of conflicts because of the absence of any accepted overall authority or sense of community. Unlike the position of individuals within an ordered nation-state, the security and interests of countries are not by and large protected by some established authority with a monopoly of the means of violence or by a judicial system for the authoritative resolution of disputes. Instead, states exist in an environment where each is substantially dependent on its own efforts for its security, and where the ultimate means of conflict resolution or settlement of disputes is often one of power, coercion, or force. This perspective on the nature of the international system and the way in which it differs from the political system that exists *within* states is lucidly expressed by George Modelski:

> States . . . are political systems possessing community, consensus, and a monopoly of the means of violence; by contrast, international systems lack these characteristics. Hence the basic difference between domestic and international politics is most strikingly manifested in the fact that while peace is the rule in domestic politics, war is the distinguishing feature of international relations. The state of war is the direct result and the unavoidable consequence of the lack of community, consensus, and monopoly of the means of violence in the world at large. Thus war, the expectation of war, and the diplomatic and strategic behavior consequent upon it become the *explicanda* of international relations.[32]

This insight is important, but it is by no means novel. Identification of the international system problem can be found in the writing of the historian Thucydides (460–400 B.C.), describing the Peloponnesian Wars among the Greek city-states. Notable treatments of the problem include the writing of the English philosopher Thomas Hobbes (1588–1679). Hobbes's widely cited work contrasts the existence of civil society at the national level with the state of nature at the international level. For Hobbes, individuals in a state of nature fear for their own safety and are driven to attack others for fear that others might injure them. As Hobbes describes their predicament, "during the time men live without a common power," they are in a condition of war. Finding life in this condition "solitary, poor, nasty, brutish and short," men turn to civil society, or the state, for the security on a collective basis that they lack individually. In effect, this Hobbesian state of nature is said to characterize relations among states in the international environment.

A paradigm for the predicament of man in the state of nature, and by implication for nations in the international environment, was offered by the French philosopher Jean Jacques Rousseau (1712–1778). Rousseau's story of the stag hunt depicts a small group of primitive hunters who have gathered to trap a stag. If all of them cooperate, they can succeed, but if one of them defects to catch a rabbit, he will have something to eat while the others go hungry. Although each hunter would be better off with a share of the meat from a stag, each is nonetheless tempted to chase the rabbit because he fears that if he does not do so, one of the others will. Rousseau summarizes the predicament as follows:

> If a deer was to be taken, every one saw that, in order to succeed, he must abide faithfully by his post: but if a hare happened to come within the reach of any one of them, it is not to be doubted that he pursued it without scruple, and having seized his prey, cared very little, if by so doing he caused his companions to miss theirs.[33]

The lesson of this tale is that self-interest may make cooperation impossible even when all parties have an interest in the enterprise, and the same conditions may also create a propensity toward conflict or war even though none may wish it.[34]

THE SECURITY DILEMMA AND THE INTERNATIONAL SYSTEM

Owing to the quasi-anarchic, or "self-help," environment in which states exist, they are said to face a *security dilemma*. In the words of Glenn Snyder:

> Even when no state has any desire to attack others, none can be sure that others' intentions are peaceful, or will remain so; hence each must accumulate power for defense. Since no state can know that the power accumulation of others is defensively motivated only, each must assume that it might be intended for attack. Consequently, each party's power increments are matched by the others, and all wind up with no more security than when the vicious cycle began, along with the costs incurred in having acquired and having to maintain their power.[35]

In short, states must rely on themselves to protect their own security and independence. However, in doing so, their search for security becomes a cause of insecurity for others.[36] As each state arms itself against its neighbors, they respond by increasing their own armaments. Arms races take place, and states find themselves in continuing jeopardy. Thucydides relates the manner in which the rise in the power of Athens caused fear among the Spartans and made war inevitable:

> In these years the Athenians made their empire more and more strong, and greatly added to their power at home. . . . So finally the point was reached when Athenian strength attained a peak plain for all to see and the Athenians began to encroach upon Sparta's allies. It was at this point that Sparta felt the position to be no longer tolerable and decided by starting this present war to employ all her energies in attacking and, if possible, destroying the power of Athens.[37]

In the twentieth century, comparable considerations of power have contributed to the outbreak of major wars. Thus, as the strategist Michael Howard observes, many Germans in 1914, and most British in 1939, felt themselves justified in going to war, not so much over a particular issue but to maintain their power. In Howard's analysis, they did so while it remained possible and before they would become isolated or weakened in a way that would require them to acquiesce in an international system their opponents dominated.[38]

The security dilemma exists because of the absence of any broader international body with the authority to provide authoritative settlement of disputes or offer protection for individual states. Although all states exist in this condition of formal international anarchy (in the sense of absence of formal authority), the fate of individual states differs, depending both on their relative power and on the external circumstances in which they exist. Indeed, the security policies of states tend to be determined more by the circumstances of their international situation than by their domestic systems. As Michael Mandelbaum argues, "Two states that are similarly situated in the system but have different domestic orders will tend to pursue similar security policies. In contrast, states that are alike in domestic terms but different in their relationship to the international system will carry out different security policies."[39]

As a consequence of formal anarchy, the resultant system of "self-help," and the security dilemma, the circumstances in which states find themselves can make them more inclined toward the use of force than might otherwise be the case or can actually draw them toward war.

The Case of the Falkland Islands

The 1982 Falklands War between Britain and Argentina provided an unusually clear example of the manner in which the international system can create a propensity toward conflict. The case is worth considering not so much in order to examine the legitimacy of the respective British and Argentine claims to the islands, but because of the dynamics that led the two countries toward war.

The Falklands (known as the Malvinas by the Argentines) are a small group of islands located in the South Atlantic, approximately 400 miles off the Argentine coast, and populated by some 1,800 people (mostly sheep farmers of British descent). The islands were discovered by an Englishman in 1592 and later claimed and occupied at different times by the English, French, Spanish, and Argentines. Indeed, in 1771 Britain and Spain came close to war over the Falklands. In the late eighteenth century Spain held the islands, and after Argentina achieved its independence from Spain in 1816, it laid claim to the territory. In 1833 Britain regained control, and over the next 150 years the Falklands were the subject of intermittent British-Argentine dispute.

On April 2, 1982, after 18 years of periodic but largely undramatic controversy, the Argentine armed forces suddenly seized the Falklands. Britain immediately took its case to the United Nations Security Council. There, on April 3, the council passed a resolution demanding immediate Argentine withdrawal. The measure was supported by a ten-to-one vote, with only Panama in opposition and the Soviet Union abstaining.[40] Notwithstanding the fact that Britain also received overwhelming support in the European Parliament, along with Common Market sanctions against Argentina, and that the action of the Argentine junta in seizing the islands violated the Rio Pact of 1947, in which 19 Western hemisphere states undertook "not to resort to the threat or use of force in any manner inconsistent with the provisions of the Charter of the United Nations," the British were left with little practical alternative other than self-enforcement of their case.

In other words, although rudimentary international and regional institutions attentive to the Falklands dispute had, in effect, supported the British position, the vote of the United Nations Security Council was not self-enforcing. Unlike a domestic judicial or legal decision, no external authority was in a position to implement the British claim. The military ruler of Argentina, General Leopoldo Galtieri, was not about to telephone his garrison commander to order withdrawal because of the UN resolution.

Britain reacted by dispatching a naval force some 8,000 miles to assert its claim. While the British received invaluable assistance from the United States in logistics and intelligence, they were essentially on their own in their bid to regain control of the Falklands. On May 21, British troops landed in the islands to do battle with the Argentines. (This effort to retake the islands was promptly condemned by the Organization of American States, by a seventeen-to-zero margin, with four abstentions.) After several weeks of sometimes heavy fighting, the British prevailed. On June 15, they completed the recapture of the islands and took 15,000 prisoners of war.[41] Before the fighting ended, however, some 250 British soldiers, sailors, and airmen were killed, as were some 750 Argentines.

System-Induced Conflict: The Case of the Six-Day War

The way in which the international system may actually induce conflict is evident not only in the Falklands case, but also in an area of far greater consequence and involving hostilities on a much more deadly scale. Specifically, Israel's conflict with Egypt and Syria in June 1967 provides apt illustration of behavior compelled by systemic imperatives.

Since Israel's inception as a state in 1948, its overriding concern has been preservation of its own existence. Israel has been unable to rely on external international bodies for its security. In November 1947, the United Nations voted to partition the British Mandate of Palestine into Arab and Jewish states. However, when the British Mandate expired in May 1948, the surrounding Arab countries launched a military effort to obliterate Israel. In this instance the Israelis were compelled to fight for their survival, while the role of the UN was restricted to facilitating an eventual cease-fire.

After eight years of tension and mounting hostilities, a crisis led to the 1956 Suez war. The outcome left Israel momentarily in possession of the Sinai Peninsula and the Gaza strip. Israel withdrew in 1957 on the basis of a guarantee from the United States, Britain, and France that her ships would have freedom of navigation through the international waterways of the Straits of Tiran.* However, on May 18, 1967, President Nasser of Egypt demanded the removal of UN forces from Sinai and from Sharm el Sheik, a vital strategic point overlooking the straits.

The immediate compliance of then UN secretary-general U Thant with Nasser's request provided a stark example of the international state of nature problem as far as Israel was concerned. Specifically, the weak embodiment of international community in the United Nations proved quite unable to assert itself as an arbiter between the two main parties: Egypt and Israel. Nasser's announcement that he was closing the Straits of Tiran not only failed to evoke an effective response from the world community (despite a violation of international law, which created a *casus belli*), but was also followed by indications that the pledges to preserve Israel's right of navigation made by the United States, the United Kingdom, and France would not or could not be implemented.

The Israeli predicament at this point exemplified Rousseau's vision that no authoritative international arbiter exists with the means of imposing order. Existing international guarantees had been vitiated, Egyptian armor had moved into the Sinai, and speeches of Arab leaders promised to drive the Israelis into the sea. Israeli decision-makers were thus faced with two possible and unwelcome choices. Either they could do nothing, in the hope that the Egyptians and Syrians would not attack (or that if war broke out, their own defense efforts and the response of the international community would prevent the destruction of Israel) or they could seek to preserve Israel's own security by means of a preemptive strike.[42]

The nature of the international system here created a propensity for Israel to choose the second alternative. (In game theory terms, discussed below this involved what is termed a "mimimax" strategy, or the choice of the least bad outcome.)[43] Given the international environment, Israeli calculations would appear to have been as follows. If they chose the first option (to wait), a sudden Arab onslaught might succeed in overwhelming the Israelis, who had little room for tactical retreat and maneuver on dry land. By contrast, if the Israelis chose the second alternative (preemption), they would in effect play it safe. At worst they would fight a (possibly unnecessary) war from an initially favorable position and conceivably stand to occupy additional territory as a buffer. Given the fact that the Israelis had no room for retreat or mistake, that to await absolute certainty of an Egyptian attack might mean enormous casualties and—as a worst case—the possible de-

---

*Between 1956 and 1959, Israeli goods were permitted to traverse the Seuz Canal in ships not flying the Israeli flag. However, in 1959, Egypt blockaded this route by detaining a number of ships and seizing their cargoes.

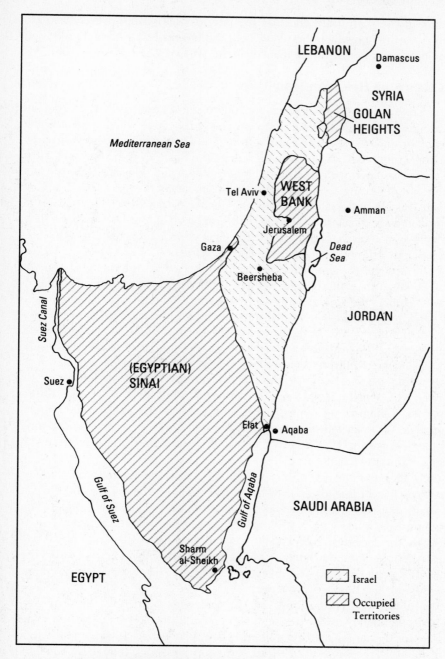

Map 11.1 ISRAEL FOLLOWNG THE 1967 WAR

Source: Federick H. Hartmann and Robert L. Wendzel, *America's Foriegn Policy in a Changing World* (New York: HarperCollins, 1994), p. 399.

struction of the state itself, and that the international system provided no real means of security on which they could rely, the Israelis had a strong inducement to launch the preemptive attack that began the Six-Day War on June 5, 1967.[44]

The Case of the Iran-Iraq War

Two powerful states contend for domination in the Persian Gulf area. Iran and Iraq are the heirs of Persian and Arab empires and peoples who have confronted one another since the seventh century. In 1975 the two states concluded an agreement concerning their disputed border along the Shatt al Arab waterway. However, five years later, with Iran racked by revolution and domestic upheaval, and in the midst of soaring animosity between the leaders of the two states, President Saddam Hussein and Ayatollah Ruhollah Khomeini, Iraq launched a massive air and ground assault against its neighbor. This outbreak of hostilities on September 22, 1980 began a war that was to last nearly eight years, inflict great damage on the cities and industries of both countries, and consume one million lives.

In the absence of voluntary agreement by both parties, international or multilateral bodies such as the United Nations or the Arab League, as well as outside powers including the United States and the Soviet Union, were unable to provide either an avenue for settlement of disputes between Iran and Iraq or an effective means of ending the war. In the early years of the conflict a UN-sponsored mediation effort by Prime Minister Olaf Palme of Sweden failed to achieve results. Later in the war, with the balance of advantage having seesawed back and forth between Iraq and Iran, and with the two belligerents increasingly war weary, the UN Security Council sought to end the conflict. On July 20, 1987, it passed Resolution 598, calling for an immediate cease-fire and withdrawal to international boundaries. Yet even with the support of the superpowers and the other permanent members of the UN Security Council, this outside effort was ineffective in bringing the war to a halt.

Only after another year of bloody fighting, marked by missile attacks against the capital cities of Baghdad and Teheran and the use of poison gas, did the conflict finally move toward an end. Iran, reeling from a series of costly battlefield defeats, punished by clashes with U.S. naval forces in the Gulf and damage to its vital oil export facilities, increasingly isolated internationally, and faced with growing demoralization at home, finally signaled its willingness for a cease-fire. Only at this point did the self-help approach of the belligerents finally make way for international action to end the war.

On July 18, 1988, Iran's President, Ali Khamenei, notified UN Security-General Javier Pérez de Cuéllar that Iran was prepared to accept a cease-fire under the terms of Resolution 598. The following day, Ayatollah Khomeini told the Iranian people that the decision to end the war was necessary, though he lamented that it was "more deadly than taking poison." Even then, with the Iranians having accepted the cease-fire in principle and both the UN and the world powers supporting it, it took more than a month for a formal halt to hostilities. In the days after Iran's announcement, Iraq's Saddam Hussein took the occasion to launch air attacks on Iranian industrial targets. Iraq followed this with a ground offensive on the central front that employed chemical weapons, while advancing some 40 miles into Iranian territory. Only on August 20, 1988 did the cease-fire officially begin. At that point, the symbolic international presence of the United Nations was finally introduced into the region as a 350-member UN peacekeeping force, drawn from 25 member countries, took up positions on the border between Iran and Iraq.

War in the Former Yugoslavia

In the case of Yugoslavia,[45] the absence of an external authority able to resolve disputes or maintain order meant that local conditions were conducive to military conquest by Serbia after the republics of Slovenia and Croatia declared independence in 1991, and Bosnia-Herzegovina in 1992. The remnants of the Serb-led central government and army, together with Serbian groups in the republics, could embark on the conquest of large areas of Croatia and Bosnia, as well as threaten action against Kosovo and Macedonia.

The conflict took place against the background of a long and bloody interethnic history, including the legacy of World War II in which a fascist regime in Croatia had slaughtered as many as a half-million Serbs and members of other ethnic groups. Moreover, local Serbian militias often took initiatives within Croatia and Bosnia. The Serbian government, under Slobodan Milosevic, was able to pursue a deliberate policy of conquest and "ethnic cleansing" in the belief that no international power or organization was likely to have the ability or the will to intervene decisively. In the process, amid the worst brutality and bloodshed seen in Europe since 1945, large numbers of innocent people were uprooted, with widespread human rights abuses including pillage, rape and torture, and the loss of some 200,000 lives.

In the face of the slaughter in Yugoslavia, the European states remained divided and uncertain. The institutions of the European Community provided no practical basis for collective action. The Conference of Security and Cooperation in Europe (CSCE), with its diffuse membership of more than 50 countries and the absence of effective institutions, was too weak and unwieldy. NATO lacked the internal agreement necessary for it to act decisively in a conflict for which it was not designed.

The involvement of UN forces for humanitarian purposes was slow and of modest scale, although some 27,000 troops were eventually deployed. The forces lacked the authority and numbers to impose order, the cease-fires they negotiated were fragrantly violated, and their earnest measures to feed starving populations in cities such as Sarajevo did not prevent the Serbian regime from carrying out its bombardment of civilian populations and its deliberate campaign to force vast numbers of Croats and Muslims from their homes.

UN sanctions efforts against Yugoslavia also had only limited effect. Although the largely Serbian population of Belgrade suffered considerable hardship, the embargo was widely flaunted by Serbia's Eastern neighbors, particularly Romania, whose own precarious economic and political situations made them indifferent to UN policies. Moreover, the weapons embargo had the unintended effect of favoring the Serbs over their victims in Bosnia. Local Serbian forces were amply supplied with heavy weapons from the central government, while the Bosnians had

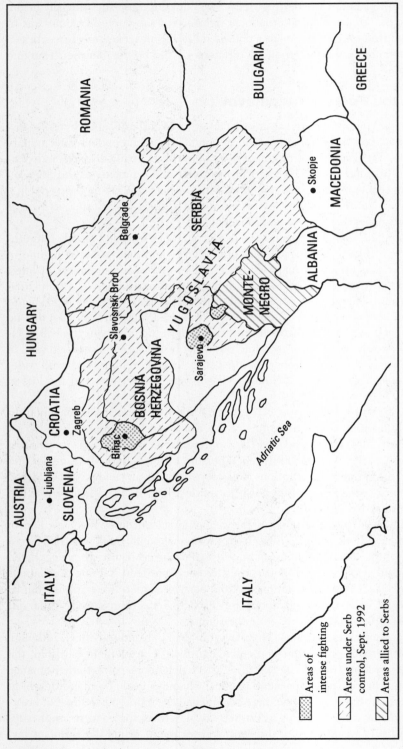

Map 11.2 YUGOSLAVIA'S BREAKUP

Source: Frederick H. Hartmann and Robert L. Wendzel, *America's Foreign Policy in a Changing World* (New York: HarperCollins, 1994), p. 321.

only light weapons with which to defend themselves against the Serbian on-slaught.

Ironically, the limited UN measures may have actually worsened the situation on the ground. In the absence of the international community's arms embargo, it is at least conceivable that the Bosnians (who substantially outnumbered the Serbs within the borders of their republic), might have been able to procure sufficient arms to defend themselves and achieve a rough balance of power. Had this not been sufficient to cause the Serbs to end their onslaught and seek to negotiate, it might have allowed the Bosnians to protect their people from the worst bombardments, starvation and human rights abuses, as well as to halt the massive population exodus which contributed to the worst refugee crisis in Europe since the end of World War II.

One small incident illuminates the broader problem of order and of the incapacity of outside actors such as the United Nations. It took place in January 1993, as a Bosnian Deputy Prime Minister was being escorted by French United Nations troops from the Sarajevo airport to the city. En route, the UN armored personnel carrier in which he was riding was halted at a Serbian roadblock. During the encounter, and over the ineffectual protests of the UN troops, Serbian soldiers opened the doors of the armored vehicle and shot the Serbian official dead.[46] Here, as in the cases of system-induced conflict discussed above, the weakness of effective international authority is not just a metaphor but a deadly fact of life. The contrast with domestic authority is evident. It is difficult to imagine that authorities in any normal city would allow a criminal gang to stop a police vehicle and execute one of its occupants while the police made impotent protests.

The Arab-Israeli conflict, the Falklands, the Iran-Iraq War and the Yugoslav conflict are among the many cases that demonstrate the problem of the international system. Evan Luard's study indicates that since 1945 most wars have arisen not out of deliberate policies of aggrandizement or aggression—though important instances of this have taken place—but from specific incidents and disputes.[47] This type of conflict would be susceptible to resolution in a more ordered international environment, but in the absence of such a framework, international dynamics propel the parties in the direction of war. War thus occurs not so much because of desires or disputes—though at times, these can and do provide necessary and sufficient cause—but because of the absence of anything that would curb or settle them. As Waltz observes, the immediate (or efficient) causes of war may lie to some extent in the nature of men and states, but the permissive cause is to be found in the inability of the international system to prevent war. The conclusion is that war is a necessary consequence of the state system.

A Domestic Contrast: The Case of the Colorado River

The nature of the international system stands out in vivid contrast when we compare cases such as those of the Falklands, the Six-Day War, or Bosnia with an incident drawn from American domestic politics. The case involves a 1964 U.S. Supreme Court decision that allocated a large share of Colorado River water to the state of Arizona, despite the claims of the state of California, where San Diego County had been utilizing huge volumes of the water for its own needs.

The issue takes on broader significance if we imagine that rather than existing within the United States of America, Arizona and California were instead separate countries, as is the case among the states of Central and South America. Given a dispute over valuable waters and the claim of the smaller and weaker state to the larger share, it is by no means improbable that the state/country of California might have resorted to self-help to assert its own claims. It may be fanciful to imagine a California governor in the late 1960s (Ronald Reagan) mobilizing his National Guard and sending the troops across the Arizona border (perhaps to seize adjacent territory and imprison leaders of the neighboring state/country— e.g., Senator Barry Goldwater and the Udall brothers). Of course, no such events occurred. The Supreme Court decision was taken as definitive by all parties. But in the international environment, this kind of routine and peaceful settlement of a dispute cannot be taken for granted. The Colorado River case illustrates the very different dynamics that underlie relations among participants in domestic political systems as opposed to international ones.

System-Induced Conflict: The Game of Prisoner's Dilemma

Game theory, and in particular the game of Prisoner's Dilemma, offers an intriguing approach to understanding the dynamics of conflict. Game theory itself is a special kind of analysis of bargaining and conflict.[48] It provides for analysis of social situations while taking the existence of conflict into account as an often inevitable accompaniment. It also facilitates the understanding of decision making in which each side has incomplete control of the final outcome owing to the presence of other independent decision-makers or "players."

The abstract nature of game theory offers a number of advantages in analyzing international relations. It requires the observer to approach decision making and conflict situations by considering the utilities and disadvantages that alternative courses of action offer to each participant. It thus provides a means of viewing one's antagonist as something other than an incompetent swine or omniscient superman. To be sure, the precision and analytical power of a mathematical model do require a narrow focus and the omission of important complexities that invariably exist in the real world. Nonetheless, the use of game theory facilitates a line of reasoning that would otherwise be difficult to follow.

Among its simplifying assumptions, game theory posits a special kind of rationality in which players can always make a decision when faced with alternatives, are able to rank their preferences precisely, and always choose the alternative that ranks highest.[49] The players may be persons or even countries and always confront two or more possible outcomes that offer different values or *payoffs*. Each player seeks to maximize payoffs while bearing in mind that he or she must act in the presence of other players with conflicting or at least divergent interests who are seeking to maximize their own payoffs, and whose choices will partially determine

Figure 11.1 PRISONER'S DILEMMA

	Cooperate (silence)	Defect (confession)
Cooperate (silence)	B gets 1 yr (−10) CC both silent A gets 1 yr (−10)	B gets 3 mos (−3) CD A gets 10 yrs (−100)
Defect (confession)	B gets 10 yrs (−100) DC A gets 3 mos (−3)	B gets 5 yrs (−50) DD both confess A gets 5 yrs (−50)

B is shown above the columns; *A* is shown to the left of the rows.

the outcome of the game. Th[...]
displayed in a chart called the [...]

Prisoner's Dilemma has [...]
with various numerical values [...]
main largely consistent. In on[...]
arated. The prosecutor believ[...]
cient evidence for conviction [...]
alternatives: to confess to the [...]
ted, or not to confess. If neith[...]
them on a lesser charge such [...]
get relatively minor punishm[...]
prosecuted, but he will reco[...]
prisoners will each be sent [...]
doesn't, the confessor will r[...]
(three months' imprisonmen[...]
sentence (ten years).

Prisoner's Dilemma is set out in a matrix (Figure 11.1). Looking at the situation from the vantage point of the two prisoners, we see that each has two choices:
silence (i.e., *cooperation* with his fellow prisoner, represented in the payoff matrix
by the letter *C*), or confession (i.e., *defection*, represented by the letter *D*). Although the optimal outcome would be for both prisoners to remain silent, that is,
to cooperate, so that each received only a one-year sentence, that is not in fact the

dominant outcome. Instead, both prisoners confess, that is, defect (the *DD* outcome), and both get five years. By examining how this "rational" outcome occurs, and by thinking of each of the players as a country, we can begin to gain an insight about the way in which the international environment induces conflict.

Obviously, Player *A* does not deliberately seek an outcome leading him to spend five years in jail when he could have gotten away with just one year behind bars. But *A* calculates as follows:

He does not know what *B* will do.

If *A* chooses silence (cooperation), his worst possible outcome would be ten years in jail (which has a utility value of −100) in the event that *B* defects.

If *A* confesses (defection), his worst possible outcome is five years in jail (−50) in the event *B* defects.

Player *A* finds himself drawn toward confessing. Rationality (and the minimax strategy) require that he make a choice that will guarantee the least damaging of the worst possible outcomes.

A can look at the situation another way, but this also leads him to defect:

If he is silent (cooperates), his possible payoffs are one year if *B* remains silent, or ten years if *B* confesses.

If he confesses (defects) he faces payoffs of three months if *B* is silent, or five years if *B* confesses.

Since *A* prefers three months to one year, and five years to ten years, and since he has no control over *B*'s choice, he is better off to choose to confess (defect) regardless of what *B* does.

Unfortunately for *A*, Player *B* makes precisely the same calculations and also chooses to confess. This outcome of mutual defection (*DD*) dominates.* Both players spend five years in prison despite the fact that had both remained silent (*CC*), both would have spent just one year in jail.

The broader lesson of Prisoner's Dilemma is that circumstances exist in which the most rational competitive calculation for each side leads to harm for both, despite the existence of a different and mutually preferable alternative. The lesson is immensely revealing when applied to international relations because it suggests how a situation may lock two participants into conflict regardless of their individual wishes or intentions.

A wide array of international relationships can embody the prisoner's dilemma. To some extent, Israeli calculations on the eve of the Six-Day War reflect the problems of "cooperation" versus "defection" vis-à-vis Egypt. A closer approximation can be found in some arms races. Consider the following example (Figure 11.2).† Country *A* faces virtually the same calculations as Player *A* in Pris-

---

*In game theory terms, this is known as the unique *saddlepoint*.
†It is left to the imagination of the reader what countries to insert in the matrix to represent Country *A* and Country *B*.

Figure 11.2 AN ARMS RACE AS A PRISONER'S DILEMMA

	Cooperate (low arms spending)	Country B	Defect (high arms spending)
Cooperate (low arms spending)	CC arms limitation B (−10) A (−10)		CD Country B advantage (+50) Country A serious disadvantage (−100)
Defect (high arms spending)	DC Country B serious disadvantage (−100) Country A advantage (+50)		DD arms race B (−50) A (−50)

(Country A label is on the left side)

oner's Dilemma. If it chooses low arms spending, the worst possible outcome for it is that Country B will continue high arms spending and thus obtain a strong military and political advantage. The outcome of this CD situation, in which A cooperates while B defects, is represented in the matrix as −100 for A and +50 for B.[51] If A opts for high arms spending, its payoffs are a strong international advantage (+50) if Country B does not pursue the same course of action (outcome DC), or a mutually costly arms race (outcome DD, equivalent to −50). By this calculation, A would choose a strategy offering the least harmful of two undesirable outcomes, and so would choose high arms spending (defection).

Looking at the situation another way, Country A still defects (opts for high arms spending). Its calculations are as follows:

If it cooperates (keeps arms expenditures low), its possible payoffs are arms limitation if B cooperates (outcome CC), or a serious disadvantage if B undertakes high arms spending (outcome CD).

If A defects (chooses high arms spending), its payoffs are a strong international advantage if B spends little, or an arms race if B spends much.

Since A prefers gaining an international advantage (+50) to arms limitation (−10), and an arms race (−50) to international disadvantage (−100), the model suggests that Country A will have a propensity to choose high arms spending (defection) regardless of what B does.

The problem, of course, is that within the confines of the model, Country B makes precisely the same calculations; it too opts for high arms spending. Once more the dominant outcome is mutual defection, *DD,* hence an arms race. Each country spends huge sums yet derives no definite advantage over the other. By contrast, both would have benefitted from outcome *CC,* mutual cooperation: neither side would possess an advantage and both would save substantial resources for other national needs.

Prisoner's Dilemma does not imply that conflict is desirable or that countries should opt for defection—with its mutual costs—when mutually preferable outcomes are at least theoretically available from cooperation. What it does do is shed light on the structural properties of situations in which two countries follow a course of action that benefits neither but has a grim rationality of its own. Prisoner's Dilemma also possesses more complex ramifications. It has been developed as a computer simulation as well as an experimental game, with players choosing alternative courses of action and receiving small monetary payoffs after each trial. The experimental results suggest that the players' ability to communicate increases the possibilities for cooperation. Additionally, a learning process takes place, and more cooperation occurs if the players realize that the game will be repeated indefinitely.[52]

THE MITIGATION OF CONFLICT

Prisoner's Dilemma provides a valuable stimulus to our understanding of circumstances in which two players can find themselves propelled toward conflict regardless of their intentions. It is also valuable in demonstrating how the parties to a conflict may have interests that are simultaneously competing *and* cooperative. Both players may do better or both may do worse from different sets of outcomes, rather than each obtaining a benefit exactly equal to the other party's loss. In other words, international relationships are not necessarily zero sum games. These insights, coupled with the results from simulations of Prisoner's Dilemma, offer evidence not only on the occurrence of conflict, but also on how it may be possible to mitigate conflict.

In examining this problem, Kenneth Oye suggests three sets of circumstances that favor the emergence of cooperation under anarchy.[53] The first of these dimensions concerns altering the payoff structure. By increasing the gains from mutual cooperation (*CC*) as contrasted with those from defection (*DC*), Prisoner's Dilemma games can be alleviated or actually changed into less conflictual classes of games.[54] For example, one analysis suggests that the diffusion of liberal economic ideas has led to an increase in the perceived benefits of mutual economic openness (a *CC* outcome in terms of the international economy). These rewards are greater than those anticipated from a strategy of closure (a *DD* outcome). On the other hand, the matrix can also be altered in a negative direction: under some circumstances, the spread of offensive military technology can increase potential rewards for defection.[55]

A second set of measures for increasing cooperation concerns enhancing the players' awareness that the game will be repeated indefinitely (a situation termed *iterated prisoner's dilemma*) rather than played for a small, finite number of encounters. Oye terms this "lengthening the shadow of the future.[56] Under competitive but one-time situations, a player has an overwhelming temptation to defect. However, if he knows that the game will continue and that the payoff structure will not be altered substantially by the outcome of a particular play, the prospects for cooperation can improve since the payoffs from *CC* are potentially greater than for other outcomes.

Strategy also enters into consideration here. Robert Axelrod has demonstrated that "tit-for-tat" behavior can provide higher payoffs over the long run and can increase the chances of *CC* outcomes. That is, in repeated experimental plays of Prisoner's Dilemma, a strategy of reciprocity, in which cooperation is responded to by cooperation and defection met with defection, after which cooperation is again offered, seems to provide optimal payoffs. By contrast, strategies that emphasize defection tend to elicit similar behavior in the opponent and hence lower payoffs for both sides. Further, strategies emphasizing cooperation regardless of the other side's behavior will tend to bring out the worst in the other player as he realizes that he can exploit the opponent's action to his own benefit.[57]

The application of these lessons, especially reciprocity, to international relations is by no means automatic. Important obstacles exist, but real-world comparisons can be found. For example, the "live-and-let-live" system during periods of trench warfare in World War I embodies the "tit-for-tat" experience.[58] In other applications, favorable conditions of play can be enhanced by explicitly defining the norms or rules of conduct, by providing the means to verify compliance with agreements (whether in trade or arms control), and by sharing information.[59]

A third general set of measures for mitigating the conflict embedded in prisoner's dilemma situations is to alter the number of players. In game theory terms, the prospects for cooperation appear to erode as the number of players increases. Oye points out that the presence of more players makes it harder for the actors to identify and realize common interests or to negotiate agreements. In addition, with more players the chances of defection and the difficulties of recognition and control increase. (Concerns about nuclear proliferation leading to a breakdown of deterrence provide an illustration here.) Finally, it becomes more difficult to impose sanctions on defectors and to implement a strategy of reciprocity. (The unwieldy nature of alliances on the eve of World War I embodies this problem.)[60]

The remedies here involve efforts to create international regimes, with agreed-upon rules of the game for all players in specific issue areas, such as trade or monetary policy. Establishment of institutions also may provide mutual advantages in specifically defined areas, as in the case of NATO, the General Agreement on Tariffs and Trade (GATT), or the International Monetary Fund.[61] Finally, countries may negotiate as blocs—as in the case of NATO and the former Warsaw Pact, or the European Community and a large group of African countries in the Lome Agreement.

The Case of Postwar Europe

This chapter has put forward the case that conflict is inherent in international relations because of its anarchic and self-help characteristics. In such an environment, the search for security by each country exacerbates the fears of other countries. The consequent security dilemma can foster conflict and warfare, even when the participants do not intend to be aggressive and expansionist. Yet as a practical matter, this propensity toward conflict is often mitigated. Postwar Western Europe provides a case in point. There, the security umbrella provided by the United States as a result of the need to deter the Soviet Union also eliminated the imperative for the Western Europeans to pursue their own national defense needs vis-à-vis one another.

The American commitment thus had the side effect of dispelling conflict among the principal prewar powers (Britain, France, Germany, Italy). In these terms, the systemic pattern of interstate relations within Western Europe shifted from the Hobbesian anarchic environment to one in which states no longer anticipate the possibility of war versus one another (a "security community").[62] In addition, the creation of the European Common Market in 1957 and its subsequent development and expansion provided an institutional means for addressing economic problems and for dealing with disagreements. The relative success of the European Community or European Union (as it came to be called in 1993) has brought significant payoffs for the participants and provided another means to mitigate conflict.

In a very different way, relations among the smaller and medium-sized countries of Eastern Europe were also altered and conflict among them dampened during the Cold War. However, in this case, the change in environment was unilaterally and sometimes brutally imposed by the Soviet Union, in terms of compulsory membership in the Warsaw Pact as well as in the imposition of Communist regimes throughout the region.

There was also a Cold War stability between Eastern and Western Europe—albeit an armed one based on deterrence. Indeed, Anton DePorte argued that by submerging the German problem through the forced division of Germany—and at considerable human cost—the Cold War had the effect of removing one of the prime sources of European instability.[63] Ironically, the end of the Cold War left Eastern Europe facing increased instability as an unintended consequence. This was evident not only in the warfare that erupted among Serbia, Croatia, and Bosnia, but also in tensions elsewhere in the Balkans and Southeastern Europe as well as in conflict within and among a number of former Soviet republics.

IS THE ANARCHY PARADIGM EXAGGERATED?

International relations involves conflict *and* cooperation. Both are intrinsic. Theoretically and empirically, it would be a mistake to conceive of relations among states as little more than a Hobbesian war of all against all. A number of international relations scholars have underscored this point. The late Hedley Bull, for example, emphasized the ways in which forms of order do exist in world politics, through such means as diplomacy, alliances, international law, the balance of power, and the role of the great powers.[64] Moreover, James Rosenau and Ernst-Otto Czempiel see a changing global environment eroding the role of individual states and thus the applicability of concepts that describe the post-1648 Westphalian system. They suggest shifting the focus of attention in international relations from a preoccupation with such features as power and deterrence in the relationship among states to interdependence, cooperation, global institutions, and world order.[65] Despite these arguments, it would be erroneous to assume that cooperation is the natural condition of world affairs and that conflict is mainly an aberration rather than something intrinsic.

Insofar as *conflict* is concerned, the competition of national interests, including power, ethnicity, ideology, and the characteristics of individual leaders and regimes, provides an impetus toward conflict, but—as we have seen above—the lack of a coherent international order or arbiter generates the security dilemma and allows these diverse factors to culminate in war. Appreciation of the anarchic international environment is also useful in explaining conflict because it discourages an obsession with the traits of individual countries or leaders at the expense of more systemic factors.

Cooperation, too, is intrinsic. The record of world history includes not only conflict and war but also international order, trade, and communications, as well as institutions or regimes that embody rules of the game in a wide range of issue areas. Historically, cooperation and order have sometimes been imposed by a dominant (or hegemonic) power. Illustratively, the Roman Empire enforced a Pax Romana for a thousand years. By contrast, the late twentieth-century world is one in which the relative power of the dominant countries has eroded to some degree. This diffusion of power, along with an increase in trade, economic interdependence, and the like, has created a climate in which many states (as well as individuals and firms) enter into cooperative endeavors, particularly in economic and technological exchange, in order to achieve their own objectives. For the most part, the higher payoffs—or at least the avoidance of negative ones—available through cooperation motivate their behavior, not altruism or idealism.

Nuclear weapons also make cooperation—or at least the mitigation of conflict—more salient in relations among the most powerful states. Given the perils of a major nuclear war, they find it in their self-interest to seek means of alleviating the risks of war. The extensive arms control agreements between Russia and the United States (as discussed in Chapter 6), embody this impulse.

IMPLICATIONS

These insights about conflict are not meant to convey the simple message that some kind of world government is both necessary and inescapable. While the "third-image" problem suggests a profound difference between domestic and international politics, it is important to bear in mind that within some domestic political systems, a Hobbesian environment can also exist. The deadly examples of Cambodia after 1975, of Lebanon after 1976, of Uganda under Idi Amin, and of Bosnia and Somalia in the early 1990s, provide recent tragic illustrations of the ways in which civil society can break down. Consequently, a prescription suggesting that the 184 members of the United Nations ought to call a constitutional convention (analogous to the 13 American colonies meeting in Philadelphia some two centuries ago) would be pointless. Given the inevitable conflicts over values, material resources, and governance, not even a minimal degree of consensus would be available, and hence any supranational scheme would unravel in acrimony or even a global "civil war."

By implication, therefore, it is imperative to see both conflict and cooperation as intrinsic to international relations. For policymakers, and for all who would seek effective understanding, it remains valuable to recognize these features. Prudence—and an accompanying recognition of conflict as inherent in a quasi-anarchic international environment—dictates awareness of the need for countries to take measures to safeguard their individual and collective security. At the same time, recognition of the imperatives for cooperation as a means of meeting national interests (as well as a historical phenomenon) suggests that efforts to facilitate cooperation in the mutual interest of the relevant "players" is an act neither of utopianism nor of raw idealism. Instead it is but a reasoned response to the international environment in which countries exist.

With these considerations in mind, we now turn to an examination of the search for order in the global, regional, and economic realms.

NOTES

1. *Retreat from Doomsday: The Obsolescence of Major War* (New York: Basic Books, 1989), p. 4.
2. *New York Times Book Review,* 30 April 1989, p. 14.
3. *Atlantic Monthly,* November 1945.
4. *Progress and Disillusion: The Dialectics of Modern Society* (New York: Praeger, 1968), p. 160, quoted in Robert W. Tucker, *The Inequality of Nations* (New York: Basic Books, 1977), pp. 3–4.
5. "Explaining Cooperation Under Anarchy: Hypotheses and Strategies," *World Politics* 38 (October 1985): 1.
6. Portions of this chapter are adapted from Lieber, *Theory and World Politics* (Boston: Winthrop Publishers and Little, Brown, 1972), Chaps. 2 and 5.
7. Interviewed by C. L. Sulzberger, *New York Times,* 10 March 1971.
8. Charles R. Beitz, *Political Theory and International Relations* (Princeton: Princeton University Press, 1979), p. vii.
9. This listing includes civil wars. The distinction between this type of conflict and an interstate war is not always clear, particularly once outside countries come to the aid of the combatants (as they often do), because the ferocity and casualties in such wars (e.g., in China, Nigeria, Pakistan) are often greater than in wars between states. The list of wars compiled by Melvin Small and J. David Singer for the period between 1945 and 1980 includes 30 which they term interstate, 12 extrasystemic, and 44 civil wars. See *Resort to Arms: International and Civil Wars, 1816–1980,* 2nd ed. (Beverly Hills: Sage, 1982), pp. 92–99, 229–232.
10. *San Francisco Sunday Examiner and Chronicle,* 22 December 1968.
11. *New York Times,* 19 November 1953, quoted in Kenneth N. Waltz, *Man, the State and War* (New York: Columbia University Press, 1959), p. 157.
12. Bertrand Russell, *Why Men Fight* (New York: Century, 1916), p. 8, cited in Donald A. Wells, *The War Myth* (New York: Pegasus, 1967), pp. 177–178.
13. Address by Dr. Kenneth B. Clark to the annual meeting of the American Psychological Association, and interview as reported in the *New York Times,* 5 September 1971.
14. J. David Singer, "Introduction," in Singer and Associates, *Explaining War: Selected Papers from the Correlates of War Project* (Beverly Hills: Sage Publications, 1979), p. 14.

For a more recent presentation of the data, see Singer and Paul F. Diehl, eds., *Measuring the Correlates of War* (Ann Arbor: University of Michigan Press, 1990). Also see the critique by David Dessler, "Beyond Correlations: Toward a Causal Theory of War," *International Studies Quarterly,* Vol. 35, No. 3 (September 1991): 337–355.

15. John A. Vasquez, "The Steps to War: Toward a Scientific Explanation of Correlates of War Findings," *World Politics* XL (October 1987): 108–145, at 108. The author does, however, argue that these studies have contributed "a new body of evidence and insight separate from those provided by history, traditional discourse, and political philosophy" (p. 108). And he describes the difference between the approaches of Singer and Kenneth Waltz in the following terms:

   "Singer does not profess to know what regularities of behavior pervade world politics, and therefore he has nothing to explain until he has documented the regularities that do in fact exist. Waltz, on the other hand, knows what the regularities are . . . and sees his main purpose as explaining why they occur, and how and why they might change" (p. 113).

16. *Man, the State and War: A Theoretical Analysis* (New York: Columbia University Press, 1959).

17. This point is made by Herbert C. Kelman, ed., *International Behavior: A Social-Psychological Analysis* (New York: Holt, Rinehart & Winston, 1966), pp. 5–7.

18. Evan Luard, *Conflict and Peace in the Modern International System* (Boston: Little, Brown, 1968), p. 66.

19. Michael Haas, "Social Change and National Aggressiveness, 1900–1960," in J. David Singer, ed., *Quantiative International Politics* (New York: Free Press, 1968), p. 216.

20. See L. F. Richardson, *Statistics of Deadly Quarrels*, Quincy Wright and C. C. Lineau, eds., (Pittsburgh: Boxwood, 1960).

21. See Nazli Choucri and Robert North, *Nations in Conflict: National Growth and International Violence* (San Francisco: W. H. Freeman, 1975). The study dwells on the period from 1870 to 1914, culminating in the outbreak of World War I.

22. Mueller, p. 51.

23. "The Abolition of Slavery and the End of International War," *International Organization* 43 (Summer 1989): 405–440.

24. Francis Fukuyama, "The End of History," *The National Interest* 16 (Summer 1989): 3–18, at p. 4.

25. Fukuyama, p. 18.

26. *Ibid.*

27. See, for example, Rudolph J. Rummel, "The Relationship Between National Attributes and Foreign Conflict Behavior," in Singer, *Quantitative International Politics,* pp. 187–214; and Rummel, "Dimensions of Foreign and Domestic Conflict Behavior: A Review of Empirical Findings," in Dean G. Pruitt and Richard C. Snyder, eds., *Theory and Research on the Causes of War* (Englewood Cliffs, NJ: Prentice-Hall, 1969), pp. 225–226. Rummel finds little relationship between national attributes and involvement in war. Another study, however, did find modest relationships. See Jonathon Wilkenfeld, "Some Further Findings Regarding the Domestic and Foreign Conflict Behavior of Nations," *Journal of Peace Research* 2 (1969): 155.

28. Melvin Small and J. David Singer, "Patterns in International Warfare, 1816–1980," in Small and Singer, eds., *International War: An Anthology and Study Guide* (Homewood, IL: Dorsey Press, 1985), p. 14. Italics added. Another ambitious study, while arriving at the conclusion that when conflicts break out, the stronger belligerent is more likely to be the initiator of war, has also encountered comparable limits in arriving at any significant conclusions concerning the *causes* of war. See Bruce Bueno de Mesquita, *The War Trap* (New Haven: Yale University Press, 1981).

29. Michael Doyle, "Kant, Liberal Legacies & Foreign Affairs," in *Philosophy & Public Affairs*, Vol. 12, Nos. 3 & 4 (Summer, Fall, 1983): 205–235 and 325–353. Doyle particularly draws on Immanuel Kant's 1795 work, *Perpetual Peace*, citing, for example "Perpetual Peace," in Carl J. Friedrich, ed., *The Philosophy of Kant* (New York: Modern Library, 1949). Also see Doyle, "Liberalism and World Politics," *American Political Science Review*, Vol. 80, No. 4 (December 1986), especially pp. 1162–1163.

30. Bruce Russett, with the collaboration of William Antholis, Carol R. Ember, Melvin Ember, Zeev Maoz, *Grasping the Democratic Peace: Principles for a Post-Cold War World* (Princeton: Princeton University Press, 1993), p. 35.

31. *Ibid.*

32. George Modelski, "The Promise of Geocentric Politics," *World Politics* 22 (July 1970): 617.

33. Jean Jacques Rousseau, *Discourse on the Origin of Inequality*, in Rousseau, *The Social Contract and the Discourses*, trans. G. D. H. Cole (New York: E. P. Dutton, 1950), p. 238. Kenneth Waltz provides a longer and more detailed summary of the stag hunt parable in *Man, the State and War*, pp. 167–168.

34. Kenneth Oye suggests that Rousseau's original use of the stag hunt parable actually illustrates the possibility of cooperation during man's first period of primitive social interdependence. By contrast, he observes that Waltz uses the story to illustrate the infeasibility of achieving mutual interests under conditions of international anarchy. Oye, citing a different translation of Rousseau, holds that "the temptation to defect to protect against the defection of others is balanced by the strong universal preference for stag over rabbit." See "Explaining Cooperation Under Anarchy: Hypothesis and Strategies," in Oye, ed., *Cooperation Under Anarchy* (Princeton: Princeton University Press, 1986), p. 8.

35. Glenn H. Snyder, "The Security Dilemma in Alliance Politics," *World Politics* 36 (July 1984): 461. The use of the concept originates with John H. Herz, in *Political Realism and Political Idealism* (Chicago: University of Chicago Press, 1951). Also see his book, *International Politics in the Nuclear Age* (New York: Columbia University Press, 1959). In addition, see Herbert Butterfield, *Christianity, Diplomacy and War* (London: Epworth, 1953), and *History and Human Relations* (London: Collins, 1961).

36. See Robert Jervis, "Cooperation Under the Security Dilemma," *World Politics* 30 (January 1978): 167–214, at p. 169.

37. Thucydides, *History of the Peloponnesian War*, trans. Rex Warner (Baltimore: Penguin, 1954), p. 77.

38. Michael Howard, *The Causes of War* (Cambridge: Harvard University Press, 1983), p. 16.

39. Michael Mandelbaum, *The Fate of Nations: The Search for National Security in the Nineteenth and Twentieth Centuries* (New York: Cambridge University Press, 1988), p. 2.

40. China, Poland, and Spain also abstained. For more information on Security Council Resolution No. 502, see, for example, *New York Times*, 4 April 1982.

41. For an account of the fighting see Max Hastings and Simon Jenkins, *The Battle for the Falklands* (New York: Norton, 1984). The legal issues are treated in Alberto R. Coll and Anthony C. Arend, eds., *The Falklands War: Lessons for Strategy, Diplomacy and International Law* (Boston: Allen & Unwin, 1985).

42. See also the treatments of this case as anticipatory self-defense in Michael Walzer, *Just and Unjust Wars* (New York: Basic Books, 1977), pp. 82–85; and Williaam V. O'Brien, "International Law and the Outbreak of War in the Middle East, 1967," *Orbis* 11 (Fall, 1967): 692–723.

43. The notion of *minimax* was put forward by John Von Neumann and Oskar Morgenstern, who were the authors of the original work on game theory, *The Theory of Games and Economic Behavior* (Princeton: Princeton University Press, 1944). Also see Anatol Rapoport, *Two-Person Game Theory* (Ann Arbor: University of Michigan Press, 1969); and Robert J. Lieber, *Theory and World Politics*, pp. 18–37.

44. For an insightful analysis of how the security dilemma has shaped Israel's strategy of conventional deterrence, see Avner Yaniv, *Deterrence Without the Bomb: The Politics of Israeli Strategy* (Lexington, MA: Lexington Books, 1986). The 1981 Israeli attack on the Iraqi nuclear reactor, Osiraq, near Baghdad also reflects the security dilemma.

45. Portions of the Yugoslav case here are drawn from Lieber, "Existential Realism After the Cold War," *The Washington Quarterly*, Vol. 16, No. 1 (Winter 1993): 157–158.

46. For an account of the incident, and the killing of Bosnian Deputy Prime Minister Hakija Turajlic, see, John F. Byrnes, "Bosnian Muslims Criticize UN Over Official's Killing," *New York Times*, 10 January 1993, p. A8.

47. Luard, *Conflict and Peace*, p. 316.

48. For valuable treatments of game theory, see Thomas C. Schelling, "What Is Game Theory?" in Schelling, *Choice and Consequence: Perspectives of an Errant Economist* (Cambridge: Harvard University Press, 1984), pp. 213–242; also Martin Shubik, *Game Theory in the Social Sciences* (Cambridge: MIT Press, 1982).

49. In other words, each player has consistent preferences. See the formulation in Anthony Downs, *An Economic Theory of Democracy* (New York: Harper & Row, 1957), p. 6, as abstracted by Downs from Kenneth J. Arrow, *Social Choice and Individual Values* (New York: Wiley, 1951), Chaps. 1 and 2.

50. The version here is essentially that presented by Robert D. Luce and Howard Raiffa in *Games and Decisions* (New York: Wiley, 1967), p. 95. Also see Anatol Rapoport and Albert. M. Chammah, *Prisoner's Dilemma: A Study in Conflict and Cooperation* (Ann Arbor: University of Michigan Press, 1965), and Robert Axelrod, *The Evolution of Cooperation* (New York: Basic Books, 1984).

51. The corresponding entries in the Prisoner's Dilemma matrix (Figure 11.1) were −100 (*A*'s loss) and −3 (*B*'s far smaller loss). However, assigning a utility for *B* of +50 seems more appropriate here given the political-military implications of any profound advantage in an arms race. Both sets of figures are arbitrary, but their relative significance in the two matrices is comparable. The rational choices and basic structure of the two games also remains comparable, although under some kinds of changes in the payoff matrix the nature of Prisoner's Dilemma can shift decisively. See Luce and Raiffa, *Games and Decisions*, pp. 94–104; also Axelrod, passim; and Kenneth A. Oye, ed., *Cooperation Under Anarchy* (Princeton: Princeton University Press, 1986), discussed later in this chapter.

52. For more detailed treatment of experimental results, see Rapoport and Chammah, *Prisoner's Dilemma*, pp. 204–227; also Luce and Raiffa, *Games and Decisions*, pp. 100–101.

53. See "Explaining Cooperation Under Anarchy: Hypotheses and Strategies," in Oye, ed., *Cooperation Under Anarchy* (Princeton: Princeton University Press, 1986), especially pp. 3–22.

54. For a discussion of how Prisoner's Dilemma can be transformed into the less conflictual "Stag Hunt" game, see Oye, pp. 9ff., and Robert Jervis, "Cooperation Under the Security Dilemma," *World Politics* 30 (January 1978).

55. See John Ruggie, "International Regimes, Transactions, and Change: Embedded Liberalism in the Postwar Economic Order," in Stephen D. Krasner, ed., *International*

Regimes (Ithaca: Cornell University Press, 1983); and Jervis, "Cooperation Under the Security Dilemma."

56. Oye, p. 12. Also see Luce and Raiffa, *Games and Decisions,* pp. 100–101.

57. The original idea here stems from Rapoport and Chammah, in *Prisoner's Dilemma.* The systemic formulation and testing of "tit-for-tat," as well as the discussion of historical parallels, is that of Axelrod in *The Evolution of Cooperation.*

58. This live-and-let-live system involved mutual restraint on the part of small British and German units facing each other along quiet sections of the Western front. Their cooperation was based on the reality that intensification of sniping, shelling, raiding parties, etc., would lead to retaliation in kind and thus make life in the trenches even more difficult for those on both sides. See Axelrod, *The Evolution of Cooperation,* pp. 73–87, based on Tony Ashworth, *Trench Warfare 1914–1918: The Live and Let Live System* (New York & London: Holmes & Meier, 1980).

59. See Oye, pp. 16–17.

60. Note that there exists a separate and much older debate among international relations theorists over the stability of multipolar versus bipolar systems. Karl Deutsch and J. David Singer have argued that increased multipolarity tends to mitigate conflict and enhance stability. See "Multipolar Systems and International Stability," *World Politics* 16 (April 1964): 394. By contrast, Kenneth Waltz asserts that bipolarity is more conducive to stability, on the grounds that the two superpowers are prone to conduct themselves more cautiously and responsibly. See "The Stability of a Bipolar World," *Daedalus* 93 (Summer 1964): 892–907. For additional discussion of this controversy, see Lieber, *Theory and World Politics,* pp. 113–116.

61. Oye, p. 20.

62. The term "security community" is that of Karl W. Deutsch et al., *Political Community and the North Atlantic Area* (Princeton: Princeton University Press, 1957), p. 5. The notion of Western European stability discussed above is similarly put forward by Josef Joffe, *The Limited Partnership: Europe, the United States and The Burdens of Alliance* (Cambridge, MA: Ballinger, 1987).

63. Anton DePorte, *Europe Between the Superpowers: The Enduring Balance* (New Haven: Yale University Press, 1979).

64. See Hedley Bull, *The Anarchical Society: A Study of Order in World Politics* (New York: Columbia University Press, 1977). Also see Beitz, *Political Theory and International Relations.*

65. James N. Rosenau and Ernst-Otto Czempiel, eds., *Governance Without Government: Order and Change in World Politics* (New York: Cambridge University Press, 1992). Note that in a review of their work, Richard Falk offers a different kind of criticism. In his view, the book fails to engage major normative issues such as oppression, the global environment, poverty, civic disorder, and ethnic intolerance. See *American Political Science Review,* Vol. 87, No. 2 (June 1993): 544–545.

chapter 12

The Search for Global Order

A steadfast concert for peace can never be maintained except by a partnership of democratic nations. . . .

The world must be made safe for democracy. Its peace must be planted upon the tested foundations of political liberty. . . .

—WOODROW WILSON
(REQUESTING A DECLARATION OF WAR, 1917)[1]

. . . if the League [of Nations] was created to prevent the outbreak of World War I, the French Maginot Line was also built to win the battles of World War I. . . . The United Nations may with some justification be described as a device for nipping World War II, rather than World War III, in the bud. . . .

—INIS L. CLAUDE, JR.[2]

The great majority of the rules of international law are generally observed by all nations without actual compulsion, for it is generally in [their] interest. . . .

The problem of enforcement becomes acute, however, [when it has] . . . a direct bearing upon the relative power of the nations concerned. In those cases . . . considerations of power rather than of law determine compliance and enforcement.

—HANS J. MORGENTHAU[3]

If, in a world of shaky regimes, contested borders, ethnic upheavals and religious revivals, every act of aggression requires the mobilization of three-quarters of a million troops, many sent across the seas, to face well-armed troublemakers and obtain their unconditional surrender, there will be very few cases of collective security.

—STANLEY HOFFMANN[4]

Previous chapters have dealt with the East-West and North-South conflicts; nuclear weaponry; watershed events including two world wars, the Cuban missile crisis, Vietnam, the oil decade, the Gulf crisis; and the causes of war. Their subject matter has thus concerned actual or potential conflict stemming in large measure from the quasi-anarchic international environment and the security dilemma. Yet there is a great deal more to international relations than conflict and war. Indeed, efforts to instill order in relations among states are as old as international relations itself. Not coincidentally, new initiatives have often emerged in the aftermath of the deadliest conflicts.

The purpose of this chapter is to examine the most important twentieth-century efforts to achieve global order. It thus considers the experience of the League of Nations (established in the aftermath of World War I), the United Nations (born out of the ashes of World War II), and contemporary international law. This examination provides evidence of the inability of these undertakings to meet the universal goals for which they were established. While rudimentary forms of organization and law do exist, and in the post–Cold War environment there have been some successes in conflict resolution and peacemaking, it is also evident that formal mechanisms of global order have only limited impact on disorder and war in relations among states.

FAILURE OF COLLECTIVE SECURITY: THE LEAGUE OF NATIONS

The devastation of World War I prompted the victorious powers to seek a world order in which so deadly and unexpected a conflict could not recur. The century ending in 1914 had seen no general war (despite a number of lesser conflicts), and prevailing opinion held that Europe had blundered into a disastrous and preventable bloodletting. The idea for a world organization to prevent war, the League of Nations, thus flowed from a profound reaction to the experiences of 1914–1918.

A second source of inspiration came from the beliefs of the League's founders, especially of the American president, Woodrow Wilson. Here, Wilson and others drew on ideas such as those of the German philosopher Immanuel Kant. In his essay *Perpetual Peace,* written more than a century earlier, Kant had conceived of establishing world peace by means of agreement among democratic countries.[5] Wilson believed the problem of war to be caused by the absence of democratic government and self determination. The American president, with strong support from influential figures in Britain and a number of other Allied countries, in effect sought to apply to the relations among nations the kind of democratic government that existed in domestic politics among many of the most advanced countries of the time.

The actual drafting of the League of Nations Covenant was carried out by a committee established at the Paris Peace Conference, and chaired by Wilson himself. Work began in January 1919, and the Covenant (essentially the constitution for the League) itself became part of the Versailles peace treaty. The League of Nations came into existence in 1920.[6]

To preserve peace, as well as to protect the new states that had come into existence after the collapse of the Russian, German, Austro-Hungarian and Ottoman (Turkish) empires, the League adopted the principle of *collective security*. The previous network of alliances and a balance-of-power system had come crashing down in 1914. Thereby discredited, this system was to be replaced with one in which all countries would act together, employing economic and even military sanctions in order to oppose any state that violated the peace. The heart of this collective security concept lay in Article 10 of the League Covenant, which required members "to respect and preserve as against external aggression the territorial integrity and existing political independence of all members of the League." However, Article 10 embodied a potentially disastrous loophole: in effect, the decision on whether and how to meet this obligation was left to the discretion of each member state.

The organizational structure of the new body foreshadowed that of the United Nations a generation later. There was a Council, on which the most powerful states sat as permanent members, along with four smaller states elected for fixed terms. However, both the Council and the Assembly, in which all member states were represented, operated on a unanimity rule. The League of Nations also included a Secretariat, located in Geneva, Switzerland, as well as bodies for implementing the League's work with disarmament, territorial mandates, and social and economic welfare. Closely associated with the League were a Permanent Court of International Justice and the International Labor Organization.

While the League was established through the impetus of the major Allied powers—particularly the United States, Britain, and France, and to a lesser extent Italy and Japan—smaller states and the defeated powers from World War I were brought into the organization. At its maximum size, the League encompassed 58 member countries.[7] While only a handful of states failed to join the League (e.g., Afghanistan, Nepal, Yemen), there was one major exception to the near-universality of membership: the United States.

President Wilson's idealism, his actions in committing the United States to the Allied cause in 1917, and his advocacy of democracy and self-government had won him immense acclaim among the peoples of Europe. However, in both style and substance he clashed repeatedly with the leaders of the Senate. Ultimately, and despite a number of changes in the Versailles treaty aimed at eliciting American support, the Senate failed to provide the necessary two-thirds margin required for ratification of the treaty. Wilson thereupon launched an ambitious campaign to rally support for the treaty and for membership in the League. But the overburdened president (Wilson had even typed his own correspondence at Versailles) soon suffered a stroke. With Wilson's health failing and the climate of isolationist and virulently antiforeign sentiment burgeoning within the country, the United States was destined never to enter the League.

For a time, the League and its collective security machinery captured idealistic attention as a means for ending war. Even into the mid 1930s, this faith

remained considerable. For example, a prominent American scholar of international relations could write of his beliefs as a graduate student at the time:

> ... along with other budding young international relationists I continued to parse
> clauses in the Covenant of the League of Nations as if that document were as central
> to world politics as the United States Constitution is to American politics.[8]

Although the League did achieve a number of successes in dealing with minor disputes in the 1920s, it ultimately failed in coping with the threats that
emerged in the following decade. The details of these events are less crucial than
the reasons for failure. In retrospect, some of these reasons were present from the
very inception of the League. These included the unanimity rule, the loose organizational framework of the League, and the absence of the United States.

Other problems facing the world organization reflected the political dynamics
of the 1920s and 1930s, over which the League had little influence. Most important was the fact that collective security was not the foremost priority of the member states. In effect, the League of Nations had been established by the victorious
allied powers to preserve the post–World War I status quo. However, each member state had its own national interests and priorities, among which the obligations
of League membership rarely took precedence. Under these circumstances, it was
difficult for the League to deal with the threat posed by those countries pushing
for revision of the post–World War I international status quo. Germany, Italy, and
Japan all sought territorial adjustment or expansion, and did so with increasing vir-
ulence as their fragile postwar democracies gave way to more militarist and even
Fascist regimes (Italy in 1922, and Germany in 1933). Meanwhile, the revolutionary leadership of the Soviet Union had its own territorial claims and ambitions,
and even after Russia's belated admission to the League, the USSR and the other
powers regarded one another with deep mutual suspicion.

The democratic and status quo powers within the League were unable to sustain a consistent and forceful stance. The absence of the United States deprived
them of the power and leadership that America's role had provided from 1917 to
1919, and France and Britain had difficulty in agreeing on a coordinated policy of
resistance. The problem of Allied response was exacerbated by increasing political
instability within France, as well as by French fears of being left to face Germany
without full support from Britain.

Given these organizational and political impediments, the League was ill
equipped to deal with the worsening international situation from 1931 on. In that
year, it failed to act forcefully in response to the Japanese attack against China in
Manchuria. In 1935 the League did impose economic sanctions on Italy for its aggression against Ethiopia. These measures were limited, however, and failed to include an oil embargo. They did little to prevent Mussolini's successful completion
of his conquest.

In the aftermath of these failures in Manchuria and Ethiopia, there were others. With the United States, Britain, France, and the Soviet Union unable or unwilling to agree on common measures to counter the actions of Germany, Italy,
and Japan, the pace of the Axis powers intensified. The League was unable to act
against Italian and German intervention in Spain in 1936, the Japanese attack on
Shanghai in 1937, Hitler's annexation of Austria in 1938 and of Czechoslovakia in

1938–1939. The League's failure helped to usher in World War II, with its 50 million deaths. (Ultimately, the League would quietly expire in 1946, handing over its remaining assets to the newly emergent United Nations.)

LIMITS OF GLOBALISM: THE UNITED NATIONS

The embodiment of post-World War II aspirations for international order is the United Nations. Disappointment over its shortcomings has been all the more acute because the hopes for the institution were initially so high. As in the case of the League, this world body grew out of the ending of a worldwide conflict and was shaped by the victorious allied powers. Indeed, the term *United Nations* originally gained currency as a designation for the coalition of Allied countries battling the Axis powers in World War II.

The UN emerged from a conflict that exhibited the worst features of international anarchy and of man's inhumanity to man on a scale unprecedented in human history. The war, with its devastation of large portions of Europe and Asia, vast civilian and military casualties, and genocidal slaughter, gave rise to a sense that something had to be done to provide a more durable world order, not only to prevent another such conflict, but also to combat the economic and social conditions that had contributed to the rise of fascism and the coming of war.

Initially, President Franklin D. Roosevelt and Secretary of State Cordell Hull conceived of the UN as a means by which the Big Three powers (the United States, Great Britain, and the Soviet Union—later expanded to include China and France) could preserve the peace by acting as the policemen of the postwar world. Agreement in principle emerged from a series of wartime conferences (Moscow in October 1943, Dumbarton Oaks in August 1944, and Yalta in February 1945). Roosevelt died in April 1945, shortly before the defeat of Hitler's Germany and the subsequent August surrender by Japan. However, many provisions in the United Nations Charter reflected the American president's aims. The United Nations Charter itself emerged from a conference in San Francisco, in which some 50 countries took part, and was signed there on June 26, 1945.

The new organization was pledged, through the preamble to its Charter, to seek four important objectives:

1. To save future generations from the scourge of war.
2. To reaffirm faith in fundamental human rights.
3. To establish conditions under which justice and respect for international law can be maintained.
4. To promote social progress and better living standards in larger freedom.

The organizational structure of the UN included a General Assembly, in which all member states were represented and which was to operate on the basis of majority voting (with two-thirds majorities required on important questions); the Security Council, on which the five great powers sat as permanent members, each with a right of veto, along with ten other nonpermanent members; and a Secretariat, run by a Secretary-General and charged with the day-to-day operation of the UN.

In addition, the International Court of Justice in The Hague (established as the successor to the Permanent Court of International Justice) was designated (under Chapter 14 of the UN Charter) as the "principal judicial organ" of the UN. A wide array of specialized agencies also were linked to the UN. Among these agencies were such bodies as the World Health Organization, the Food and Agricultural Organization, the International Monetary Fund, and the International Bank for Reconstruction and Development (the World Bank).

While the United Nations did not represent a radical effort to restructure the international system by imposing a world authority (the Charter explicitly recognized the "soverign equality" of all its member countries), it nonetheless aimed to provide a far greater degree of order in relations among the countries of the world. One means for doing this was to create an organization whose membership would be virtually global; that is, all countries were potentially eligible for membership. Second, agreement among the great powers, institutionalized through the Security Council, was to provide the means for preventing war and even for using force against aggressor nations.

This notion of preserving peace through agreement among the powers was made explicit in a memorandum by the secretary of state to President Roosevelt:

> The entire plan is based on two central assumptions:
> First, that the four major powers will pledge themselves . . . not to go to war against each other or against any other nation, and to cooperate with each other . . . in maintaining the peace; and
> Second, that each of them will maintain adequate forces and will be willing to use such forces as circumstances require to prevent or suppress all cases of aggression.[9]

The logic of this position rested on the assumption that if the big powers were to agree, they had the capacity to halt wars or aggression. On the other hand, if any of the permanent members were not in accord, each was too powerful to be coerced into agreement. Great-power dominance was embodied in the Security Council of the UN. The Charter provided this organ with the power to act in identifying threats to the peace and in taking actions including the interruption of economic and communication links and even the use of force. Members were to keep military forces available for collective UN actions.

In fact, agreement among the major powers had become tenuous even before the end of the war. As a consequence, throughout the Cold War and except in largely technical and specialized matters, the effective functioning of the United Nations was obstructed. Indeed, the problem of great-power disagreement was later exacerbated by the emergence of important regional powers. These would be increasingly difficult to coerce even in those circumstances where the Americans and Russians did find themselves in accord.

The United Nations and the Security Dilemma

The UN was not created as a supranational world authority meant to impose its sovereignty over a quasi-anarchic world. In fact, the Charter is quite explicit in recognizing the autonomy of member states in their domestic affairs. Thus, in the words of Article 2:

Nothing contained in the present Charter shall authorize the United Nations to intervene in matters which are essentially within the domestic jurisdiction of any state or shall require the Members to submit such matters to settlement under the present Charter. . . .°

The UN cannot, therefore, be judged by the standard of an incipient world government. All the same, it can and should be assessed in terms of the criteria for which it was established. By this standard the record is promising in a number of areas, modest in some, and dismal in others.

War Prevention and Peacekeeping

By the single most important criterion, that of preventing aggression and war, UN performance has been weak. Since 1945, between 25 and 30 million people have lost their lives in wars. Given the need for great-power unanimity in the Security Council, it is not surprising that the UN was often unable to respond during the Cold War. Exercise of the veto by the Soviet Union, and occasionally by the United States, was sufficient to block action whenever an East-West dimension was involved in some way. The one significant exception to this stalemate occurred with the outbreak of the Korean War in June 1950. Because of Soviet absence from the Security Council (their representatives had walked out earlier in a dispute with the Western countries), the United States initially succeeded in obtaining the Council's condemnation of the attack by the Communist regime of North Korea and in gaining UN support for the defense of South Korea. With the Soviets' return, American representatives managed to transfer the issue to the General Assembly, where no Soviet veto could be cast, and to obtain the necessary majority there under the "Uniting for Peace Resolution." As a result, American and other forces fought under the UN flag during the Korean War.

The shift in UN membership during the 1950s and 1960s brought a dramatic change in numbers and political composition of the UN and the General Assembly. The 50 original signatories to the Charter in June 1945 came overwhelmingly from Europe and from North and South America, and the United States enjoyed a comfortable voting majority among them. But the expansion of membership, accommodating the newly independent countries of the developing world, more than tripled the UN's membership, and with the rise in numbers came a geopolitical shift as well. Of the 159 member countries at the end of the 1980s, 120 came from the developing world, 99 belonged to the "nonaligned" group, 50 were from Africa, 33 from Latin America, and only 22 from Western Europe.[10] As a result, during the latter years of the Cold War, the United States found itself regularly outvoted. According to a study released by the U.S. Mission to the UN, member countries in the General Assembly during 1985 voted with the United States only 22.5 percent of the time on issues where there was a roll call vote and which were not adopted by consensus.[11]

Subsequently, the end of the Cold War brought important changes. These included another increase in UN membership as a result of new states emerging

---

°The text of Article 2 does continue with the words: "but this principle shall not prejudice the application of enforcement measures under Chapter VII."

from the breakup of the Soviet Union and Yugoslavia, and participation by other new or small states. By 1993, with the addition of Eritrea (which had separated from Ethiopia) and the European principalities of Monaco and Andorra, total UN Membership grew to 184 countries. In addition, the end of the Cold War and the discrediting of Marxist-Leninist forms of political and economic organization enhanced the legitimacy of democracies and market economies. These developments combined to reduce significantly the level of ideological confrontation in both the Security Council and the General Assembly.

From the time of its inception until the end of the Cold War, the United Nations undertook more than a dozen peacekeeping operations. A number of these, carried out with the support of the major powers and of the local combatants, and involving a reasonably clear demarcation of the warring parties, were relatively successful. The Golan Heights (Syria versus Israel) and Cyprus (Greeks and Turks) are cases in point. Roughly half these efforts were in the Middle East; other noteworthy interventions involved India and Pakistan, as well as Zaire (formerly the Congo). Two of these peacekeeping bodies were more than 40 years old, dating back to the late 1940s. Thus UNTSO (the UN Truce Supervision Organization, located in Beirut and the Sinai) originated as long ago as June 1948, and UNMOGIP (the UN Military Observer Group in India and Pakistan) dated from January 1949. Other UN forces were far newer, for example, the UN Iran-Iraq Military Observer Group (UNIIMOG) established in August 1988 to monitor the cease-fire between the two major Persian Gulf adversaries after the bloodiest conflict since World War II.

The end of the Cold War created opportunities for a huge increase in UN peacekeeping operations. With the end of the East-West conflict, a number of regional conflicts were brought to a halt either because of direct involvement by the superpowers or because local actors no longer had the support of external patrons to continue hostilities. In Afghanistan, a small UN mission (UNGOMAP) was established in April 1988 to observe Soviet troop withdrawal. In Central America, a UN observer group (ONUCA) was established in November 1989 to monitor borders, discourage movement of guerrillas and weapons supplies, and oversee the disarming of Nicaraguan Contra rebels in Honduras. Other missions followed with increasing rapidity in Angola, Kuwait, El Salvador, Western Sahara, Cambodia, the former Yugoslavia, Somalia, Mozambique, and Rwanda. (See Table 12.1)

A number of these operations had considerable success, but they were large and very expensive. For example, in Cambodia, at a cost of over $2 billion, more than 21,000 UN personnel were sent to act as a buffer and observer force and to monitor national elections. Other operations were also costly, but less successful in terms of peacekeeping. For example, in the former Yugoslavia, some 27,000 troops provided observers and humanitarian assistance, at an annual cost of $1 billion. And in Somalia, a force of up to 26,000 members, costing $1.5 billion, helped to prevent a disastrous famine, but found itself in armed conflict with local groups and was unable to reestablish political stability.

Other UN operations were much more modest in scope, as in the case of a small observer force of 78 members, with a budget of $10 million, sent in June 1993 to monitor a cease-fire and peace accord on the Rwanda/Uganda border in East Africa. There was also a 83-member observer force sent to reactivate a peace

Table 12.1 LOCATION OF ACTIVE UNITED NATIONS PEACEKEEPING OPERATIONS

Operation	Place	Purpose	Number of Personnel	Annual Cost $*	Established
UNOMSA (UN Observer Mission in South Africa)	South Africa	Observe free nonracial elections (does not include a security component)	1800	34 million	January 1994
UNMLT (UN Military Liaison Team in Cambodia)	Cambodia	Monitor security incidents	20	1.1 million	November 1993
UNAMIR (UN Assistance Mission in Rwanda)	Rwanda	Buffer, observer and humanitarian operation, monitor peace accord	1180	96 million	October 1993
UNOMIL (UN Observer Mission to Liberia)	Liberia	Implement peace accord	325	90 million	September 1993
UNOMIG (UN Mission in Georgia)	Georgia	Observer force, facilitate negotiated settlment	24	5–30 million	August 1993
UNOMUR (Rwanda Observer Force)	Uganda/Rwanda border	Monitor ceasefire and peace accord (incorporated into UNAMIR)	78	10 million	June 1993
ONUMOZ (UN Operation in Mozambique)	Mozambique	Buffer, monitor election, civil administration	6574	330 million	December 1992

(continued on next page)

Table 12.1 (continued)

Operation	Place	Purpose	Number of Personnel	Annual Cost $*	Established
UNOSOM II (UN Operation Somalia II)	Somalia II	Buffer, limit hostilities, humanitarian assistance	25,747	1.5 million	March 1992
UNTAC (UN Transitional Authority in Cambodia)	Cambodia	Buffer and observer force, monitor national elections	21,100	2 billion (1993) no longer a current operation)	March 1992
UNPROFOR (UN Protection Force)	Former Yugoslavia	Buffer, humanitarian operations, observers	26,947	1 billion	February 1992
ONUSAL (UN Observer Mission in El Salvador)	El Salvador	Monitor cease-fire and maintain public order	310	30 million	May 1991
UNA VEM II (UN Angola Verification Mission II)	Angola	Observer force to reactivate peace plan	83	24 million	May 1991
MINURSO (UN Mission for the Referendum in Western Sahara)	Western Sahara	Buffer and monitoring of plebiscite	347	27 million	April 1991

Operation	Location	Function	Personnel	Annual Cost	Date Established
UNIKOM (UN Iraq Kuwait Observation Mission)	Iraq-Kuwait	Observer force and buffer	700 (increasing to 1200)	75 million	April 1991
UNIFIL (UN Interim Force in Lebanon)	Southern Lebanon	Observe Israeli troop withdrawl and restore security in region	5247	153 million	March 1978
UNDOF (UN Disengagement Observer Force)	Golan Heights	Supervise Israel-Syria cease-fire	1027	43 million	May 1974
UNFICYP (UN Peacekeeping Force in Cyprus)	Cyprus	Separate Greek and Turkish areas and prevent renewal of fighting	1221	25 million	March 1964
UNTSO (UN Truce Supervision Organization)	Beirut, Sinai	Truce supervision, assistance to UNDOF and UNIFIL	216	31 million	May 1948
UNMOGIP (UN Military Observer Group in India and Pakistan)	India-Pakistan border	Monitor cease-fire in Jammu-Kashmir region	39	5 million	April 1948

*All annual cost figures as of 1994 unless otherwise indicated

Sources: Based on data from United States, Central Intelligence Agency, Directorate of Intelligence, *Worldwide Peacekeeping Operations, 1994* (Springfield, VA: National Technical Information Service, EUR 94-10001, Feb. 1994); and *The Economist* (London), 12 June 1993, p. 21.

plan for Angola. But set against the vast size of the country and the severity of the conflict, the operation was of too small a scale to be effective.

The first several years after the end of the Cold War saw a remarkable upsurge in UN peacekeeping operations. In the aftermath of the American-led and UN-sanctioned Operation Desert Storm, which successfully drove Saddam Hussein's Iraqi forces out of Kuwait in February 1991, the United Nations became a focus of world attention. Overall, in the five-year period from 1988 to 1993, the world body undertook more peacekeeping operations than during its prior 43 years of existence. The contrast in numbers and costs was striking. From operations in 1988 involving 10,000 troops, at an annual cost of $233 million, UN forces increased to approximately 80,000 troops, at a cost of more than $3.5 billion.[12]

Moreover, a series of obstacles and problems became increasingly evident, and together these had the effect of limiting what initially had appeared to be an extraordinary opportunity for UN peacekeeping in the post–Cold War international environment. First, there remained a crucial distinction between *peacekeeping* and *peacemaking*. The most successful operations were in those areas where parties to a conflict could be brought to some kind of agreement and the UN could provide forces to legitimize, monitor, reassure, and sometimes enforce an agreed cease-fire. However, when one or more of the local adversaries have been bent on war, UN forces have been ineffective (as in Yugoslavia and earlier in Southern Lebanon) or likely to be withdrawn (as in Somalia in 1993–1994 or the Sinai Peninsula in 1967). The problem involves both the weakness of the UN as an institution, which can rarely if ever impose itself forcefully on the parties to a conflict, and the capabilities of local forces, which can be difficult to overcome except with the application of the kind of military force that the UN does not command.

The experience of Operation Desert Storm and the role of the American-led international effort to oust Iraq from Kuwait (discussed in Chapter 10) is a case in point. Although the UN Security Council played a vital role in providing international legitimacy and support, the operation, involving more than 40 countries, was led not by the UN but by the United States, which provided more than half a million troops. Had the United States not played that role, neither the UN as an institution, nor any of the regional organizations, would have been in a position even to attempt to undertake the effort. By contrast, it is sobering to note that existing UN operations are often modest in terms of force capabilities and are often limited in their authority to use force. For example, UN guards initially sent to Kurdish areas of Northern Iraq were unarmed.[13] Though this deployment came in the aftermath of Iraq's decisive defeat by the American-led coalition forces, the UN personnel were nonetheless facing the forces of Saddam Hussein who had previously slaughtered between 100,000 and 180,000 Kurds in the *Al Anfal* operation.[14] In another instance, in October 1992, the Security Council banned Serbian flights over Bosnia, but was silent on the means of enforcing the ban.[15] In this case, as in others, local Serbian forces repeatedly violated cease-fires and local agreements, taking military action with knowledge that the UN was in no position to enforce peace.

In addition, during some of the bloodiest conflicts of the past four decades, the regional parties have been hostile to intervention and the UN has been absent altogether. Examples include Vietnam, which experienced three decades of warfare beginning in 1946; Cambodia, where the Pol Pot regime murdered millions of its own subjects in the late 1970s; Uganda, where in the 1970s some 300,000 people perished under the murderous regime of Idi Amin and an additional 200,000 during the rule of his successor, Milton Obote, and in the 1985 civil war that followed; and the bloody Iran-Iraq war in which more than a million men died between 1980 and 1988.[16]

Second, there remain problems of political agreement among the five permanent members of the Security Council. Unless they achieve a consensus, the UN is usually ineffective, or even powerless to act. Illustratively, Russia, which has traditionally had close ties to Serbia, has been reluctant to support more forceful actions against Serbia despite the latter's actions in Bosnia. France and Russia have resisted imposing tougher measures against Libya for its support of terrorism, thus weakening sanctions resolutions. And China, which has long-standing ties with North Korea, has been hesitant to support strong measures aimed at halting that country's covert nuclear weapons program.

Third, there have been limits on the UN's own institutional capabilities. With more than a dozen separate operations in progress and 80,000 UN personnel in the field as "Blue Helmets," the UN headquarters in New York has simply lacked the organizational capabilities to provide timely political direction, intelligence, and administrative support. The organization's long-standing reputation for bureaucratic inefficiency has grown as the tasks of peacekeeping have expanded. In reaction to the difficulties that peacekeeping operations experienced, especially in Somalia, modest efforts were undertaken to enhance the organizational capacity at UN headquarters.

Fourth, there are problems of cost. The escalation in peacekeeping operations brought a comparable leap in expenses, and it has become increasingly difficult to raise the necessary sums of money from member states. The United Nations has no formal taxation powers, and while contributions are in many cases based on previously agreed-upon formulas, they remain essentially voluntary. Some states, including the United States, have been substantially in arrears on their contributions. This is a matter both of the domestic unpopularity of such expenditures and of antiquated cost-sharing formulas, which have required the United States to contribute 31.7 percent of peacekeeping costs—a proportion far higher than the country's 20 to 25 percent share of world economic activity.

It is worth putting the cost issue in perspective. While the expenses of peacekeeping have escalated, the sums are tiny when set against the amounts that individual countries spend for their own national defense and the numbers of personnel in their armed forces. For example, in 1991, the total assessment for UN peacekeeping amounted to $491 *million*. By comparison, member states spent $921.5 *billion* on their own military forces. The ratio of these national expenses to peacekeeping costs was 1,877 to 1.[17] Even with the large increase in peacekeeping costs in subsequent years, with the figure for 1993 on the order of $3.5 billion, the ratio of national military to UN peacekeeping costs was still in the range of 200–300 to 1.

In different ways, each of these problems reflects the international realities that limit the capability of the UN and the international community in keeping the peace.[18] The relative strength of local forces and the intractability of some of their conflicts, the problem of gaining political agreement within the Security Council, weak institutional capabilities, and the difficulty of raising sufficient funds all reflect the fact that human society remains organized on the basis of distinct national states. Despite the fact that a great deal of international life takes place across or even without regard to formal national boundaries, the sources of political legitimacy, armed forces, and funding remain essentially national, and the limited capabilities of the United Nations reflect this reality.

Human Rights

Here, too, the UN record has fallen far short of the organization's original goals. On the one hand, the UN has adopted a series of impressive declarations and conventions concerning guarantees of human rights, prevention of genocide, and opposition to discrimination based on race, sex, and belief. Most notable among these is the General Assembly's adoption of the Universal Declaration of Human Rights (December 10, 1948).

However, the gap between rhetoric and practice has been immense. Indeed, according to a major human rights study in the late 1980s, more than half the countries of the world still held political prisoners and more than one-third practiced systematic torture.[19] A large proportion of member states from the developing world do not themselves adhere to basic human rights practices within their own borders. As a consequence, they are usually reluctant to support forceful policy standards that would be applied to all cases, rather than wielded selectively in the service of more limited political agendas. Moreover, until the latter part of the 1980s the Soviet Union frequently invoked the principle of nonintervention in internal affairs whenever its own practices were challenged, and it collaborated with repressive regimes in the developing world to weaken or prevent more assertive UN positions on human rights.

While criticisms of grave human rights abuses in, for example, South Africa, prior to the ending of *apartheid* and then during the transition to majority rule in 1993–1994, were very much to the point, a wide array of other major cases (Afghanistan, Argentina, Cambodia, Cuba, Ethiopia, Guatemala, Iran, Iraq, Sudan, Syria, and Uganda, to name just a few) were minimized or ignored during the latter years of the Cold War. Moreover, the most extensive and severe human rights violations (not only of political rights but of rights of individuals to be free of physical abuse, torture, and murder) were often overlooked or cited only in passing, even while a torrent of criticism was unleashed against a handful of generally Western-oriented members. For example, Arab-Israeli and Palestinian issues were subject to repeated and disproportionate overemphasis, culminating in the notorious November 1975 General Assembly resolution—opposed by the United States and most of the countries of Western Europe—that "Zionism is racism." Not until December 1991, in the aftermath of the Cold War, the successful effort to oust Iraq from Kuwait, and the opening of Arab-Israeli peace talks on a broad scale, was the resolution finally repealed.

Several specific cases illustrate the human rights problem at the United Nations. The private voluntary organization Amnesty International, which investigates and criticizes human rights abuses among all forms of political systems, and lobbies for the release of political prisoners provided only that they have not been involved in the use of violence, has submitted large numbers of documented cases of persecution to the UN Human Rights Commission without receiving action on them. In the mid 1970s, the same organization, which was later awarded a Nobel Peace Prize for its activity, actually had facilities withdrawn from its use by UNESCO (United Nations Educational, Scientific, and Cultural Organization) lest a conference concerning torture offend UN member governments. Shortly thereafter, the UN Human Rights Commission saw a behind-the-scenes agreement reached to minimize the issue of torture in Chile in exchange for avoiding the subject of Soviet treatment of dissidents.[20] Even requests to investigate human rights violations in Uganda, a country whose domestic polity was disintegrating to the point of anarchy, were rejected by the Commission.

Another important instance of the UN's inability or unwillingness to act involved the killing of an estimated 5,000 Kurdish civilians in the Northeastern Iraqi town of Halabja. On March 16–17, 1988, in the final weeks of the Iran-Iraq war, government forces attacked the town with chemical weapons. In addition to the large numbers of civilians killed, Amnesty International reported that an additional 1,000 people, some wounded in the gas attack, were summarily executed and buried in mass graves. (Iraqi government spokesmen maintained that the area had been the scene of military operations and that Iranian troops had carried out the attacks.) Subsequently, a UN-sponsored report agreed that a gas attack had taken place but declined to blame Iraq.[21]

Indeed, even a Dutch resolution introduced in the UN General Assembly calling for member states to promote their people's freedom of expression and assembly was defeated. Though Articles 55 and 56 of the UN Charter specifically call for the signatories to promote "human rights and freedoms," representatives from the developing world claimed that the resolution entailed improper interference in their internal affairs. China even proposed to restrict the UN's right to criticize human rights violations by its member states on the grounds that "the principle of noninterference in the internal affairs of its members should also apply to the issue of human rights."[22]

These radically different conceptions of human rights were especially visible in the years after the end of the Cold War. Thus, in April 1993, a group of 34 Asian and Arab governments issued the Bangkok Declaration, in which they asserted the cultural relativity of human rights, claiming that human rights are a relative concept and "must be considered in the context of . . . national and regional particularities and various historical, cultural and religious backgrounds."[23] This kind of position, fostered by notorious human rights violators such as China, Cuba, Iran, Syria, and Vietnam, as well as by states such as Indonesia, Malaysia, Pakistan, Singapore, and Yemen,[24] has been an obstacle to more effective international activity. Related to this, opponents of a more forceful stand on human rights have resorted to invoking Article 2 of the UN Charter (cited earlier in this chapter) to support their long-standing insistence that domestic affairs are to remain outside the scope of international attention.

Despite these efforts to dilute the meaning of human rights and their significance for the UN, there has been some increase in attention and support. A 161-country World Conference on Human Rights, held in Vienna in June 1993, the largest such international gathering in a quarter-century, rejected the restrictive position of the Bangkok Declaration. Instead, it upheld the immutability of human rights despite attempts to subordinate them to national or cultural considerations.[25] Moreover, in December 1993, the UN General Assembly agreed to create a position for a UN High Commissioner for Human Rights. While the High Commissioner would lack the means to force governments to change their behavior, he or she would be able to publicize their abuses and report these to the UN Human Rights Commission (UNHCR) in Geneva or to the General Assembly itself. Moreover, the text of the resolution establishing the post omits restrictive provisions sought by China, Indonesia, and others, which would have required confidentiality or a mandate from the UNHCR prior to acting. In addition, it gives the Commissioner duties to promote and protect "civil, cultural, economic, political and social rights" and to prevent "the continuation of human rights violations throughout the world."[26]

Justice and Respect for International Law

The subject of international law is treated later in this chapter; however, it is useful to consider here the fate of one of the key provisions of the UN Charter, Article 2(4). This provides for a particularly stringent restraint on the use or threat of force:

> All members shall refrain in their international relations from the threat or use of force against the territorial integrity or political independence of any state, or in any other manner inconsistent with the purposes of the United Nations.

In practice, this stipulation has been repeatedly violated. Under the Charter, force may only be employed under one of two specific circumstances. One of these is an enforcement action ordered by the UN Security Council in response to a threat to the peace. However, until the 1990–1991 measures against Iraq, this had not been voted because of lack of agreement among the permanent members. The other avenue is that of individual or collective self-defense, under Article 51 of the Charter:

> Nothing in the present Charter shall impair the inherent right of individual or collective self-defense if an armed attack occurs against a Member of the United Nations, until the Security Council has taken the measures necessary to maintain international peace and security. Measures taken by members . . . shall be immediately reported to the Security Council. . . .

In the absence of effective enforcement machinery, the self-defense justification becomes a blanket rationale, or else the officially sanctioned justifications are overlooked altogether in a world where much contemporary conflict (civil wars, violence in the developing world, terrorism, guerrilla wars) has little to do with the kind of formal declared wars the framers of the UN Charter had sought to prevent.

Less dramatically, however, internationally agreed-upon rules and norms are widely adhered to in a host of functional, technical, and economic spheres (such as health, aviation, and monetary affairs). Some of these matters involve the oper-

ation of specialized UN agencies; many others lie outside the UN realm altogether.

In any case, the effort to enact significant new international legal agreements
has been halting. The UN Law of the Sea Conference is a case in point. After conferences in 1958 and 1960, the UN brought together a third conference, which
took place from 1973 through 1982. This produced the UN Convention on the
Law of the Sea, aimed at addressing not only the issues of territorial waters, freedom of transit, and coastal resource jurisdiction, but also of deep seabed mining.
Although signed by 159 states, only 26 ratified the convention within the next four
years. The stumbling block concerned deep seabed matters, where the United
States, backed by Britain and the Federal Republic of Germany, objected to a
number of provisions for international control and refused to sign.[27] In successive
years, however, the number of states ratifying the Treaty slowly increased until in
November 1993 it reached the required figure of 60. This had the effect of
putting the Treaty in force one year later—though its provisions remained binding
only on those countries adhering to the document. Under these circumstances,
the United States entered into negotiaions with a group of developing countries in
order to revise the provisions dealing with deep seabed mining. Tentative agreement to meet western concerns meant that the U.S., Britain and Germany would
ultimately sign and ratify the treaty more than a dozen years after the original document had been negotiated.

Clearly, the codification of accepted international law has proved difficult.
Major powers have been reluctant to accede to international jurisdiction when
they have believed their vital interests to be at stake. This refusal has taken the
form of claiming a privileged status for internal matters—as in the practice of the
Chinese (and of the pre-Gorbachev Soviets), even when this directly contravenes
existing international agreements (e.g., the Universal Declaration of Human
Rights).

The substantial relaxation of East-West tensions at the end of the 1980s did,
however, create improved opportunities for using international legal mechanisms.
For its part, the Soviet Union proposed a treaty obliging signatory states to submit
disputes to the International Court of Justice (ICJ) in the Hague for binding arbitration. The Court is available because it serves as the judicial organ of the UN.
Together, in 1989, the United States and USSR also agreed to accept binding ICJ
arbitration in disputes involving a series of treaties on terrorism and drugs.[28] By
contrast, long-standing arrangements have meant that the Court can only adjudi-
cate disputes in which governments specifically accept its jurisdiction.

While steps such as these can enhance the role of international law, as well as
play a part in resolving disputes among states, it remains clear that such measures
have been dependent on changes in the political relationships among states.

Moreover, the role of important countries other than the superpowers is by
no means automatically assured. For example, in 1979 the United States sued Iran
in the World Court over the seizure of its Teheran embassy and the holding of 55
American diplomats as hostages. Although the Court upheld the U.S. position, the
Iranian government simply refused to comply with the decision. Ultimately, the
hostages were not released until January 1981, and then only after difficult ad hoc
negotiations mediated by the government of Algeria.

Social Progress and Better Living Standards

Here, the record of UN specialized agencies and of other bodies much more loosely associated with the United Nations reveals some areas of substantial achievement. Notable successes have been reached by the World Bank, the International Monetary Fund, the International Civil Aviation Organization, the World Health Organization (WHO), and the children's fund (UNICEF). Other agencies have provided effective technical assistance on agriculture, the environment, and aid to refugees. The picture has been more mixed in the case of bodies such as the International Atomic Energy Agency (IAEA).

In other instances, however, the results have been quite poor. As one example, UNESCO exhibited so abysmal a record of extreme politicization and gross fiscal irresponsibility that the United States in 1984 and Britain in 1985 opted to withdraw from membership. Although the Director General, Amadou Mahtar M'Bow of Senegal, was replaced in 1987, his successor, Federico Mayor of Spain, was also criticized for problems in management and for inefficiency. In his first four years in office, he spent a disproportionate share of his time making 168 official visits, and critics in the United States and elsewhere argued that there was little to show for the agency's $720 million biennial budget.[29] Another illustration of wasteful organizational behavior concerns the UN Economic Commission for Africa. During the height of the Ethiopian famine in 1984, with hundreds of thousands or even millions of people facing starvation and death, the agency committed $73.5 million, not for essential roads or water supply systems, but to construct a conference center for itself in the capital city of Addis Ababa. Eight years later, the projected cost had reached $107 million, yet there was only a huge hole in the ground to mark the site.[30]

A Balance Sheet on the United Nations

The UN's record is not wholly negative. Even those governments most severely critical of its failings have remained within the organization. The criterion of universal membership has been nearly approximated, despite exceptions such as Switzerland and Taiwan. In addition to the successful operation of a number of its specialized agencies, the UN provides an avenue for dispute settlement and peacekeeping in those circumstances where the parties to the conflict are willing to seek such an avenue. On occasion, it can provide a face-saving way out of a confrontation for a country that would prefer to avoid more overt entanglement or even war.

The UN also provides, however imperfectly, a forum for regular meeting and communication among widely diverse and sometimes bitterly antagonistic countries. And, despite serious abuses, its existence does force countries to justify and explain their actions in front of a wider audience than would otherwise be the case. (The Suez crisis and the Soviet invasion of Hungary in 1956, the Cuban missile crisis of 1962, and the Soviet shooting down of a Korean Airlines plane in 1983 are all cases in point.) By no means does the organization eliminate the problems of the quasi-anarchic international environment, nor of the security dilemma, but it does slightly alleviate the anarchic characteristics of the international system by creating at least a faint shadow of an international community in which countries exist.

On the other hand—and it is quite a caveat—the UN exhibits debilitating limitations. Many of these have been enumerated above. In addition, the organization itself has become bloated and overstaffed, a source of international patronage and secure employment for a class of diplomats and former diplomats—many of whom prefer living in the headquarters city of New York (or in the locales of the specialized agencies, such as Geneva, Vienna, Rome, and Paris) to returning to their home countries. Less mundane is the organization's selective morality. At its worst, this results in spokesmen for countries with records of behavior that grossly contradict the most basic UN ideals arising to denounce other countries. International standards are applied selectively and capriciously, with some of the worst infringements of human rights escaping condemnation altogether.

The climate of institutionalized hypocrisy was reflected in the belated revelation that a former two-term (1972–1981) UN Secretary-General, Dr. Kurt Waldheim, had lied about his World War II years and in fact served as intelligence officer for a notorious Nazi general. Waldheim's unit operated in Yugoslavia where it was involved in the infamous Kozara roundup and massacre of Yugoslav civilians as well as the deportation of Jews, Serbs, and others to Nazi concentration camps. Waldheim's commanding general, Alexander Lohr, was later executed for war crimes. Indeed, in April 1987, because of his wartime role, the U.S. Department of Justice placed Waldheim's name on a "watchlist" of person's excluded from entering the United States. That an international civil servant could serve for ten years as head of the world organization, with a claim to speak on behalf of the international community, and do so without his past coming to light—or being divulged by those individuals and countries that had some prior knowledge—testifies in some measure to the very limits of the UN itself.

To be sure, the organization is not static and changes do occur. The dramatic improvement in United States-Soviet relations during the latter part of the 1980s and the subsequent end of the Cold War made possible much greater cooperation within the Security Council on a number of important regional issues. More importantly, Soviet-American cooperation permitted an unprecedented degree of UN action after Iraq invaded Kuwait on August 2, 1990. On the same day, with all five permanent members in agreement, the Security Council voted 14 to 0 (with only Yemen abstaining) to adopt Resolution 660, condemning the invasion and demanding immediate withdrawal of all Iraqi forces. Subsequently, it adopted resolutions ordering a trade and financial boycott of Iraq, declaring Iraq's annexation of Kuwait null and void under international law, and demanding that all detained foreigners be released. On August 25, with only Cuba and Yemen abstaining, the Council voted 13 to 0 to give the United States and other member states the right to use force in order to carry out the economic embargo. Most dramatically, on November 29, after Iraq continued to defy the United Nations and the international community, cooperation between the United States and the Soviet Union made it possible for the Security Council to pass Resolution 678. This unprecedented measure set January 15, 1991 as the deadline for Iraq's withdrawal from Kuwait and authorized "all necessary means" (i.e., the use of force) to ensure withdrawal after that date.[31]

These Security Council resolutions significantly enhanced the international legitimacy of the American-led effort to oust Iraq from Kuwait. They also facilitated creation and maintenance of the large multinational coalition organized to implement sanctions and the use of force against Iraq, lessened regional opposition to condemnation of Saddam Hussein's action and the military measures which followed, and even played a contributory role in shaping public and congressional opinion within the United States.

Based on the original 1945 Roosevelt conception, improved Russian-American cooperation, along with broader agreement among the five permanent members, creates important opportunities for a more effective UN role. However, the passage of half a century has brought important changes in international relations. The increasingly global diffusion of power, enhanced weight of regional actors (who are very difficult to coerce), and the fact that a substantial majority of UN membership now comes from the developing world means that the opportunity for the Security Council, and especially its most powerful permanent members, to act decisively—let alone as "world policemen"—faces significant obstacles.

In view of these limitations, there exist a number of possible means for enhancing the capabilities of the United Nations. One is to expand the number of permanent members of the Security Council. In recognition of their greatly increased importance, proposals have been made to provide seats for both Japan and Germany. However, there are difficulties with this. One is that both countries have deep-seated political and institutional inhibitions against deploying their armed forces abroad, even as part of peacekeeping operations. This constraint stems from the appalling legacy of World War II. Another problem concerns the absence of representatives from the developing world, other than China. As a consequence, interest has been expressed in permanent seats for a number of major regional powers, such as Nigeria, India, Brazil, and Indonesia. However, this proposal evokes concern that enlargement of the Security Council could make it so unwieldy as to cause paralysis, especially if these countries were afforded the same veto privileges as the original five permanent members.

In sum, although it is the one world organization with nearly global membership and the mission of addressing the widest array of international concerns, the United Nations has so far had only a modest role in mitigating the anarchic international environment. Important possibilities for a more effective role do exist, but the causes of many of its institutional shortcomings lie beyond the reach of the UN. In that sense, the organization's limits reflect the problem of the international system itself. All the same, the United Nations has fallen short of fulfilling the purposes for which it was created.

INTERNATIONAL LAW

If the United Nations does not provide the framework of international order that would significantly alleviate conflict, what about the role of international law?[32]

The phenomenon itself has existed among different types of civilizations and regions, and it antedates by many centuries the operation of the United Nations. It also merits examination since it contrasts with the conflictual characteristics of world politics that have been emphasized in the preceding chapters.

Contemporary international law rests on a long Western tradition. Other civilizations have had their own versions, but the prevailing form is largely the product of a Western inheritance with its roots in ancient Rome. Two concepts stem from antiquity. One is *jus naturale* (natural law), or the assumption that there is a natural order of things that people share by virtue of their common humanity. The Romans believed that jus naturale was reflected in the practices of the various peoples whom they ruled, and that it was applicable across different cultures. The other is *jus gentium* (the law of peoples), which Rome developed to regulate the extensive trade and commerce carried on throughout the empire.

The Roman natural law tradition underlies Western international law, which became increasingly codified in the seventeenth century. During the Thirty Years War, the Dutch jurist Hugo Grotius invoked this tradition. His 1625 book, *On the Law of War and Peace (De Jure Bellis ac Pacis)*, bases much of its argument on a common human nature and a self-evident law stemming from it. With the Peace of Westphalia in 1648 and the subsequent spread of the contemporary nation-state system, Grotius' concepts of international law, sovereignty, and restraints in the conduct of war took on added weight.

International law was further elaborated on by a series of Western jurists and philosophers during subsequent centuries. In this process, a distinction began to grow between those who emphasized what states should do (the *ought*) and those who focused on what states actually do (the *is*). This split between naturalists and positivists has continued virtually to the present day. While the influence of the natural law school diminished considerably in the nineteenth century, it gained renewed currency in response to twentieth-century horrors. The influence of natural law is apparent in the Nuremberg trials of Nazi war criminals, the UN Genocide Convention (adopted in 1948), and the International Court of Justice.

In a broad sense, international law, based on Western ideas of higher law, became established during the period from the seventeenth century on. It spread outward to much of the world, especially during the nineteenth century, as a consequence of the growing global influence of Western countries. The foundations of this law are diverse, however, given the crucial fact that there is no single sovereign authority in international relations with the power of enactment or enforcement. Indeed, this fundamental characteristic sharply differentiates international law from domestic law. Overall, the sources of international law include the following:

Treaties and conventions
Custom and expectation
General principles
Judicial decisions
Opinions of text writers

Those sources most often cited—formal treaties and judicial decisions of the World Court—provide a type of law that is frequently transgressed or has little enduring effect. The Briand-Kellogg Pact to outlaw aggressive war provides an apt illustration. Signed in 1928 by 44 countries (including the United States), it stipulated that the signatories would renounce war and seek to resolve disputes only by peaceful means. In fact, the pact quickly became a dead letter and later a subject of ridicule. On the other hand, there have been areas in which international conventions are adhered to because they serve the practical convenience of states. The treatment of diplomats° is a case in point, as are customary laws and a series of understandings concerning the use of the sea.

As another embodiment of formal international law, the International Court of Justice (ICJ) at The Hague has so far compiled a lamentable record. It takes few cases, commonly deals with modest subjects, produces decisions with limited reach (often after long deliberation), and is frequently ignored. For instance, the World Court spent five years considering the status of Namibia (formerly Southwest Africa). In the end the court rejected the case, which had been put by Liberia and Ethiopia against South Africa, on the grounds that the two black African countries lacked standing on the issue. In an Atlantic fishing rights case, the court issued guidelines for the countries involved—which Iceland promptly defied. During the Iran hostage crisis of 1979–1980, the ICJ ordered the immediate release of American diplomats whom the Iranians had seized. The Iranians simply ignored the court. In still another prominent case, the court in June 1986 issued a judgment on behalf of Nicaragua in a complaint brought by it against the United States for supporting armed intervention against the Sandinista government. In its opinion (neither binding nor enforceable) the court ruled that the United States had violated international law and was "under an obligation to make reparations" to Nicaragua for damages caused by American activities.[33] However, two years earlier, the United States had announced its refusal to accept the court's jurisdiction, and despite a flurry of newspaper headlines, the court opinion was simply ignored.

A more successful instance involving use of the Court can be found in the September 1992 settlement of a long-standing territorial argument between Honduras and El Salvador. Their dispute, which originated in the nineteenth century, had been the basis for a 1969 war in which thousands lost their lives. However, in 1986 the two countries agreed to bring the case to the World Court. After years of reviews and deliberation, in what the presiding judge termed the most complicated case ever heard by the Court, the ICJ handed down a verdict awarding Honduras approximately two-thirds of the disputed border territory and stipulating that the two countries must share the Gulf of Fonseca with Nicaragua.[34] The international legitimacy and stature of the Court allowed both sides not only to agree to submit the case for a decision, but also to accept the verdict of the Court without facing insurmountable domestic opposition.

°The 1961 Vienna Convention on Diplomatic Relations codified long-existing custom in the treatment of diplomats.

If international law rested only on these weak, formal foundations, there would be little to it. In fact, the sources inherent in custom and expectation, as well as in general principles, give it a wider applicability than is commonly assumed. In essence, international law is less a matter of what jurists term formal or "black letter" law than it is a matter of custom and expectation—a rudimentary international common law.[35] As a consequence, the efficacy of international law on a subject such as diplomatic immunity is relatively high (notwithstanding the Iran hostage crisis). Similarly, and in the interest of the parties who find it a matter of mutual convenience, a great deal of regularity and adherence to international law exists in such routine and undramatic areas as communications, laws involving innocent passage of air and sea routes, and questions of legal jurisdiction. As the late Hans Morgenthau observed, it is generally in the interests of countries to comply voluntarily with international law. For example, the rights of foreign diplomats in a country's capital and its obligations under commercial treaties carry reciprocal privileges, and states may lose more than they gain by failing to comply. Voluntary compliance is thus frequent and commonplace, and Morgenthau noted that the "great majority" of the rules are not affected by the weakness of the enforcement system. Nonetheless, in a limited but important and "generally spectacular" number of cases, criteria of national power and interest prevail over those of law.[36]

The expectation that international law will be adhered to on matters in which the vital interests and sovereignty of states are at stake is thus low, particularly on questions of war and peace. Doctrines of morality concerning war do exist, however. These are rooted in the just-war doctrine of Scholastic writers such as St. Augustine and St. Thomas Aquinas. The subject matter concerns permissible recourse to war, *jus ad bellum,* which is based on proper authority, just cause, right intent, and peaceful end. A closely related doctrine concerns prescriptions for the actual conduct of war, *jus in bello.* The criteria here include proportionality, discrimination in means, and prohibited means, among others.[37]

We can say that the absence of international authority means that international law has a very limited effect on high-priority political and security issues. Conversely, on more technical and routine aspects of their relations, states find it in their mutual interest to adhere to certain types of rules and regimes. These patterns of order and restraint exist because it is not generally beneficial or desirable for states to live in a condition of perpetual hostility with their neighbors. As the English jurist James L. Brierly observed, "it is a principle of nature that this world should be a system of order and not chaos, and that therefore states, despite their independence, can be no exception to this universal rule."[38]

The wider effect of this established practice and of the spread of international law as understood in its Western sense is evident in the stance taken by Communist countries prior to the end of the Cold War and by states of the developing world. For the Soviet Union, an orthodox Marxist-Leninist approach would theoretically have ruled out any generalized international law. After all, law was postulated as reflecting the economic substructure of society. Hence, if countries had different substructures (capitalist, state-socialist, etc.), no commonly grounded superstructure of international law would have been applicable. However, the Soviet approach was more pragmatic. Stalin, for example, perceived international law as a means to deal with outside pressures at a time of Soviet weakness.

In practice, the Soviets made use of international law for a variety of purposes. Thus, where it was useful to them, they followed the conservative, nineteenth-century state-oriented approaches, with an emphasis on custom, legality, state sovereignty, and diplomatic immunity. On other occasions, especially when they could gain politically by doing so, the Soviets made more assertive references to general principles such as nonintervention in internal affairs and denunciation of threats to the peace, for example, involving Article 2(4) of the UN Charter. Nonetheless, and despite the Soviet penchant for legalisms, the rudiments of international law did not stand in their way when they regarded their greater interests as at stake. The invasions of Hungary in 1956, Czechoslovakia in 1968, and Afghanistan in 1979 were all transgressions of international law, but were justified either by a contrived "fraternal" request for assistance (as asserted in 1979), or through invoking the Brezhnev Doctrine, which—until Gorbachev abandoned it in the late 1980s—was essentially a unilateral Soviet assertion that countries with pro-Moscow Communist regimes would not be allowed to change their form of government. However, the reorientation of foreign policy under Gorbachev led to an increasing Soviet emphasis on the importance of international law in the relations among states.

The countries of the developing world have also displayed an ambivalence regarding international law. For some, a wariness of traditional order rests on the proposition that international law serves an imperialist or neoimperialist system, or—in less ideological terms—that it serves the interests of the "haves" at the expense of the "have-nots." There is also suspicion of international law for its concern with order rather than with justice. Notwithstanding these reservations, countries of the developing world have frequently sought to use or have simply accepted the precepts of international law. Less powerful states have often invoked international norms about nonaggression or noninterference in internal affairs when they have been threatened by outside powers or when their own internal practices have come under criticism for abuses of human rights. They have also made extensive use of international organizations and conferences, both in voting procedures in the UN General Assembly (for example, where the rule is one country one vote) and in advocating policies critical of the international status quo. In addition, even though many of their boundaries (especially in Africa) were determined arbitrarily by the great powers, the developing countries have for the most part accepted existing borders as given, if only to avert ubiquitous challenges.

In practice, and because international law does provide a degree of regularity in relations among states, this order comes far less from formal written stipulations or from the operations of the World Court than it does from custom and tradition. It also pertains much more to everyday matters of interchange than to grand matters of war and peace. The actual practices of states, far more than codified treaties and agreements, thus do constitute a rudimentary but nonetheless real body of international law.

The international law of war provides an illustration. Here, the concept of *jus in bello*[39] derives from custom and internationally agreed-upon legal codes, based on The Hague Convention IV of 1907, the Geneva Conventions of 1949, and two 1977 Geneva Protocols. These agreements concern the conduct of war. Among their central provisions are the principles of *proportionality,* relating military means to political and military ends; *discrimination,* prohibiting intentional attacks on noncombatants and nonmilitary targets; and *prohibited means,* that is, means of war which are by definition disproportionate (e.g., chemical and biological warfare). Other provisions stipulate the duties of belligerents, for example, in the treatment of prisoners of war. Although these rules of conduct are not universally applied, especially in civil wars, their applicability has become a matter of convention and mutual convenience in many conflicts. Insofar as international law is concerned, this is a modest success in a world in which the kind of overarching principles enshrined in the League Covenant and the UN Charter are honored far more in the breach than the observance.

As a practical matter, one other area deserves attention. This concerns procedures for the *pacific settlement of international disputes.* While we have seen the limitations of formal judicial efforts through the World Court—a form of dispute resolution known as *adjudication*—this is just one (and the most formal) of several customary methods available for seeking to resolve conflicts. The others, in ascending order of rigor, are negotiations, good offices, mediation, and arbitration.

Of these methods, *negotiation* is the simplest form of peaceful settlement. It entails exactly what the term suggests: discussion of a dispute by the parties involved in an effort to resolve their differences. Rather than being a formal and judicial proceeding, negotiations are essentially political in nature. A second method (and it should be noted that two or more means may be employed simultaneously) entails the use of *good offices.* This requires the presence of a third party or state. Its role is simply to bring the parties together, but not to participate in the actual negotiations. *Mediation* comes next. In it, the third party actually participates in the negotiations. Examples here include Secretary of State Henry Kissinger's role in the Israeli-Egyptian and Israeli-Syrian talks after the 1973 Yom Kippur War, and President Jimmy Carter's participation in the Camp David negotiations leading to the Israeli-Egyptian peace treaty of March 1979. Finally, there is *arbitration,* usually involving binding settlement of a dispute by a third party, but carried on outside existing international judicial or legal institutions. A form of this procedure was used in resolving financial claims between Iran and the United States during the 1980s.

There is thus a spectrum of possibilities for peaceful settlement of disputes. While they have not generally been applicable in the most serious conflicts between states, they nonetheless have had a modest and comparative success in lesser disputes. On the whole, while the applicability of international law is often greatly constrained, it does suffice to mitigate conflict and to provide a far greater degree of regularity in international relations than would exist if there were little more to relations among states than anarchy.

THE PROBLEM OF GLOBAL ORDER

Efforts at international order on a global scale fall far short of the aspirations of their architects and proponents. The ambitious international and multipurpose effort represented by the League of Nations was a failure. Its successor, the United

Nations, has been quite limited in its achievements. In the realm of international law, formal and overarching efforts have also met with frustration. The International Court of Justice in The Hague has not remotely approximated a "World Court." Efforts to outlaw war have failed utterly, and a meaningful system of collective security remains out of reach.

Practical achievements do exist. The specialized agencies of the UN have tangible accomplishments to their credit; the Security Council played a significant role in the Gulf crisis; and the world body has not only survived as an institution but has gained increased attention and importance in the post–Cold War world. International law has also attained a degree of legitimacy and presence, not only in custom but in technical and commercial realms as well. Moreover, despite great difficulties and an exceptionally slow process, broader agreements have been achieved, for example, the Law of the Sea. The transformation in East-West relations, along with efforts to resolve a number of regional conflicts, may result in somewhat greater scope for both the UN and the World Court, though the weakness of the UN and its institutions and the intractability of local wars have been evident simultaneously. Nonetheless, aspirations for global and general purpose regimes to provide authoritative and overarching order have been largely disappointed.

With this experience in mind it is therefore useful to turn to an examination of international bodies which, though they fall well short of the universal applicability once sought for the League, the UN, or the World Court, have nonetheless achieved tangible cooperation and order well beyond the confines of the nation-state. Such bodies are organized on a *regional* rather than a global basis to address specific *functional* areas more than to cover general and grandly political purposes. The following chapter thus turns to the search for regional order.

NOTES

1. Address to Congress Asking for a Declaration of War, 2 April 1917.
2. *Swords into Plowshares: The Problems and Progress of International Organization*, 4th ed. (New York: Random House, 1984), p. 46. The texts of the League Covenant and the United Nations Charter can be found in appendices to Claude's book, pp. 453–462 and 463–489.
3. *Politics Among Nations: The Struggle for Power and Peace*, 5th ed., rev. (New York: Knopf, 1978), p. 299.
4. Stanley Hoffmann, "Avoiding New World Disorder," *New York Times*, 25 February 1991, p. A19.
5. For a lucid discussion of the Kantian and Lockean roots of Wilson's beliefs, see Claude, *Swords into Plowshares*, pp. 49–54.
6. F. S. Northedge's history of the League identifies the institution's ultimate failure as due to the inherent irreconcilability of collective security with international realities. See *The League of Nations: Its Life and Times, 1920–1946* (New York: Holmes & Meier, 1986).
7. The maximum number of members at any given time was 58, though 63 states belonged to the League at one time or another. See Jack C. Plano and Roy Olton, *The International Relations Dictionary*, 3rd ed. (Santa Barbara: ABC-Clio, 1982), p. 323. See

also, on U.S. Senate disagreement with President Wilson's approach to the League of Nations, William C. Widenor, *Henry Cabot Lodge and the Search for American Foreign Policy* (Berkeley: University of California Press, 1980.)

8. William T. R. Fox, "Isolationism, Internationalism, and World Politics: My Middle Western Roots," *International Studies Notes* 12 (Spring 1986): 34. See also Roland N. Stromberg, *Collective Security and American Foreign Policy* (New York: Praeger, 1963.)

9. Cordell Hull, Memorandum for the Pesident, 29 December 1943 (referring to the draft plan of 23 December 1943), *Postwar Foreign Policy Preparation, 1939–1945*, Department of State Publication 3580 (Washington, DC: Government Printing Office, 1949), p. 577, quoted in Claude, *Swords into Plowshares*, p. 74.

10. See Thomas M. Franck, *Nation Against Nation: What Happened to the U.N. Dream and What the U.S. Can Do About It* (New York: Oxford University Press, 1985).

11. Data as reported in *New York Times*, 4 July 1986. Note that countries abstaining or not taking part in votes were treated as though they had voted against the United States. This methodology was later criticized by supporters of the UN in the U.S. Congress and even by a former U.S. ambassador to the UN, Vernon Walters, on the grounds that it gave an overly negative picture of UN voting patterns. See, for example, *New York Times*, 16 May 1989, p. A10.

12. Figures from U.S. Department of Defense, Pentagon Joint Staff, as reported in *Washington Post*, 5 August 1993, pp. A1 and A22; also *New York Times*, 12 December 1993. For thoughtful assessments of UN peacekeeping, see Anthony Clark Arend, "The United Nations and the New World Order," *Georgetown Law Journal*, Vol. 81, No. 3 (March 1993): 491–533; and William J. Durch, ed., *The Evolution of UN Peacekeeping: Case Studies and Comparative Analysis* (New York: St. Martin's, 1993).

13. *Washington Post*, 21 May 1991.

14. Kanan Makiya, *Cruelty and Silence: War, Tyranny, Uprising, and the Arab World* (New York: Norton, 1993), p. 152. For documentation of Iraq's mass killings of Kurds, see staff reports to the Committee on Foreign Relations of the U.S. senate, *Kurdistan in the Time of Saddan Hussein* (Washington DC, November 1991), and *Chemical Weapons Use in Kurdistan: Iraq's Final Offensive* (Washington DC, October 1988).

15. *New York Times*, 10 October 1992, p. 3

16. For a thoughtful treatment of the UN's efforts to deal with the Iran-Iraq war, see Anthony Arend, "The U.N. Role in the Iran-Iraq War," in Christopher C. Joyner ed., *The Persian Gulf War: Lessons for Strategy, Law and Diplomacy* (Westport, CT: Greenwood Press, 1990). For a broad study of the UN's conflict management performance in 137 disputes referred to it in the years from 1945 to 1984, see Ernst B. Haas, *Why We Still Need the United Nations: The Collective Management of International Conflict, 1945–1984* (Berkeley: University of California, Institute of International Studies, Policy Papers in International Affairs, No. 26, 1986).

17. *Financing an Effective United Nations: A Report of the Independent Advisory Group on U.N. Funding* (New York: Ford Foundation, 1993), pp. 30–33.

18. Adam Roberts has provided a thoughtful analysis of the wide range of problems facing the UN in attempting to address the issue of international security. These include: an overload of security issues; the changing character of conflict, particularly the large number of cases of civil war and interethnic struggle; limited agreement among the major powers; the problematic structure of the Security Council; problems of organizing enforcement actions under UN command; difficulties of controlling actions at long distance; application of the laws of war; and inherent limitations of any collective security system. See "The United Nations and International Security," *Survival*, Vol. 35, No. 2

(Summer 1993): 3–30, especially p. 5. Also see, on the need for the UN to define the area between peacekeeping and enforcement, John Gerard Ruggie, "The U.N.: Wandering in The Void," *Foreign Affairs*, Vol. 72, No. 5 (November/December 1993):26–31.

19. Statement by the Deputy Director of Amnesty International, quoted in the *Washington Post*, 14 December 1988. For detailed country reports see *Amnesty International Report 1989* (New York and London: Amnesty International Publications, 1989). According to an annual report from the US Mission to the UN, resolutions on the Middle East and southern Africa made up 63 percent of the General Assembly's business in the 1986–1987 session. (*New York Times*, 15 July 1987, p. A9.)

20. See Shirley Hazzard, "The UN, Where Governments Go to Church," *New Republic*, 1 March 1975, p. 14. The phenomenon of deals between representatives of the Soviet Union and Latin American right-wing dictatorships was also confirmed by a French member of the Human Rights Commission (in a confidential interview with the author).

21. Reports of the chemical weapons attack and of other government attacks on Kurdish civilians in Iraq can be found in *Amnesty International Report 1989*, pp. 257–260. The UN report is cited in *Foreign Affairs*, "America and the World, 1988/89," Vol. 68, No. 1, p. 234. And see Makiya, *Cruelty and Silence*, p. 153.

22. Statement by China's UN representative, Li Luye, quoted in *New York Times*, 17 December 1989, p. 34.

23. *Washington Post*, 15 June 1993, and Charles Krauthammer, "Human Rights Shell Game," *Washington Post*, 18 June 1993, p. A25.

24. *New York Times*, 14 June 1993, p. A3.

25. *Washington Post*, 26 June 1993, p. A18.

26. *New York Times*, 14 December 1993, p. A7.

27. For an analysis of the Law of the Sea controversy and U.S. policy, see Leigh S. Ratiner, "The Law of the Sea: Crossroads for U.S. Policy," *Foreign Affairs* 60 (Summer 1982): 1006–1021; also Bernard Oxman, et al., eds., *Law of the Sea* (San Francisco: Institute for Contemporary Studies, 1983.)

28. *New York Times*, 9 October 1989.

29. *New York Times*, 22 September 1992.

30. *The Economist* (London), 2 December 1989, p. 23; *Washington Post*, 20 September 1992, p. A26.

31. One important by-product of this experience was renewed attention to the UN by American policymakers. See, for example, the analysis by Robert W. Gregg, *About Face? The United States and the United Nations* (Boulder: Lynne Rienner, 1993).

32. O'Brien. See also his book, *The Conduct of Just and Limited War* (New York: Praeger, 1981); and "The Law of War, Command Responsibility and Vietnam," *Georgetown Law Journal* 60 (February 1972): 605–664.

33. See, for example, the *Washington Post*, 28 June 1986. Note that the Reagan administration might have had some initial grounds for its support of the Contras, based on "collective self-defense" against Nicaraguan aid to guerrillas in El Salvador, but this argument was not presented to the court. See Richard N. Gardner, "A Reagan Fiasco in the World Court," *New York Times*, 2 July 1986.

34. "World Court Settles a Latin Border Dispute," *New York Times*, 13 September 13 1992, p. 10.

35. The point is made by O'Brien. Also see, for example, Myres S. McDougal and Florentino P. Feliciano, *Law and Minimum World Public Order* (New Haven: Yale University Press, 1961).

36. Morgenthau, *Politics Among Nations,* 5th ed., p. 299.

37. There is a rich literature on these subjects. See O'Brien, *The Conduct of Just and Limited War,* pp. 13–69; James T. Johnson, *Ideology of Reason and Limitation of War: Religious and Secular Concepts* (Princeton: Princeton University Press, 1975); and Michael Walzer, *Just and Unjust Wars* (New York: Basic Books, 1977), p. 21ff.

38. J. L. Brierly, *The Law of Nations,* 6th ed., ed. Sir Humphrey Waldock (New York: Oxford University Press, 1963), p. 43.

39. See O'Brien, *The Conduct of Just and Limited War,* pp. 37–56.

chapter 13

The Search for Regional Order

Dante, Goethe, and Chateaubriand belong to Europe only insofar as they are respectively and eminently Italian, German, and French. They would not have served Europe very well had they been men without a country, or had they written some kind of Esperanto or Volapuk.

—CHARLES DE GAULLE[1]

Today I am the governor of a central bank who has decided, along with his nation, to follow fully the German monetary policy without voting on it. At least, as part of a European central bank, I'll have a vote.

—JACQUES DELAROSIERE (FRENCH CENTRAL BANK GOVERNOR)[2]

Citizenship of the [European] Union is hereby established.

—THE MAASTRICHT TREATY

It is not surprising that so many Europeans find it difficult to identify with a "Europe" that remains a purely economic and bureaucratic construction and shows few signs of becoming a nation.

—STANLEY HOFFMANN[3]

Conflict, as previous chapters have shown, is inherent in international relations. Efforts to overcome the problem of anarchy by introducing rules and institutions for a global order have fallen far short of their objectives. An observer given to world-weary cynicism might therefore conclude that no lasting achievements toward greater order and reduced conflict will ever be possible.

Yet between the stark alternatives of unmitigated conflict on the one hand, and institutionalized and general purpose world order on the other, there exists a significant range of alternatives. The experience of Western Europe in the post-1945 world provides a striking illustration. In this region, profound changes have in fact occurred. While they are limited geographically as well as functionally (i.e., they concern just the member countries of the European Union and are applicable to a series of specific issue areas, rather than to all forms of interstate relations), their achievement deserves close attention.

Although much of the development of regional integration in Western Europe is taken for granted, and sometimes has been the object of criticism for its failure to achieve far more lofty objectives, consider how far Europe has come since the end of World War II. For three centuries following the Peace of Westphalia in 1648 and the consolidation of the European state system, Europe experienced repeated conflict and warfare. Even in those periods in which general war was averted (especially the years from 1815 to 1914), states routinely contemplated and prepared for the possibility of war against one another. This perennial rivalry among the principal European powers reached its culmination in the two disastrous world wars of the twentieth century. Meanwhile, the brief interwar period of the 1920s and 1930s had seen the disillusion of hopes for a peaceful, prosperous, and democratic evolution on the Continent, and instead witnessed the Great Depression, the collapse of newly established democracies, and the rise of both fascism and Stalinism.

Yet since 1945, the intervening decades have brought not renewed warfare, but an unprecedented degree of both formal and informal integration among the countries of this region. More important—and it is an achievement that dwarfs other considerations—these states no longer seriously contemplate or prepare for the possibility of war against one another. In other words, they have achieved a *security community*.[4] In this context, the elimination of the seemingly permanent antagonism between France and Germany (the key Western European belligerents in World Wars I and II) merits special attention.

The ending of this centrally important European rivalry demonstrates that major world conflicts are not necessarily permanent. Change—sometimes for the better—is not an impossibility. To be sure, the achievements in Western Europe have not been easily accomplished, and they fall far short of the full-fledged European unity that was sought in the aftermath of World War II. In addition, it is well to be cautious in drawing theoretical conclusions. While France, Germany, Britain, Italy, and their smaller and medium-sized neighbors have established a security community, causes other than regional integration require attention. Chief among these was the division of Europe in the aftermath of the war and the embedding of Western Europe in an American-led Western order as a reaction to Soviet hegemony in Eastern Europe (analyzed in Chapters 3 and 4). In effect, the American role and the creation of a network of economic, political, and military institutions in the West provided the means for resolving the Hobbesian international order problem as it shaped relations among the Western Europeans themselves.[5]

ORIGINS OF UNITY IN WESTERN EUROPE

World War II proved a cathartic experience for the Western Europeans. Coming only two decades after the end of World War I, it left European leaders and publics willing to seek new means for preventing the recurrence of war and to question previous assumptions about national sovereignty. (By contrast, it is significant that the only major European country neither occupied nor defeated during the conflict, Great Britain, remained wary of major European initiatives.)

By 1945, national institutions had been badly shaken or wholly discredited throughout the European continent. In its more assertive and aggressive forms, nationalism was associated with the outbreak of the first world war and—in its most virulent and pathological embodiment—with the fascism and Nazism that brought the devastation of World War II. This was especially the case for Germany and Italy. Elsewhere, even in those countries that had managed to maintain democracy, national identity was shaken by the inability of sovereign institutions (national governments, national armies, and geographic borders) to protect their populations against defeat and occupation by the Axis powers in the early years of the war.

Nor was the discrediting of national institutions solely a legacy of World War II. The individual economic initiatives of European states during the interwar period, including economic nationalism, protectionism, competitive devaluations, and efforts at autarky, had largely failed. For the most part, they tended to worsen rather than mitigate the effects of the Depression of the 1930s. From these experiences of national rivalry, war, and depression, the leading political forces and the anti-Nazi resistance movements (Socialists, Christian Democrats, and others) emerged in 1945 with a broadly shared recognition that traditional ways of doing things had failed, and a determination that steps toward a more unified Europe were essential if the continent were ever to achieve peace and prosperity. Indeed, new constitutions in France (Fourth Republic, 1946), Italy (1947), and the Federal Republic of Germany (1949) provided for the possibility of transferring sovereign powers to a United States of Europe.[6]

The immediate postwar years saw a flurry of activity.[7] This included widely heralded European conferences at Zurich in September 1946 and at The Hague in May 1948. The first of these meetings featured a call by Winston Churchill (then out of office, but appearing as leader of the British Conservative Party) for a United States of Europe. Churchill's grand declaration, however, portrayed

Britain's role as a "friend" and "sponsor" but not a member. Ultimately, the Zurich meeting proved a disappointment and had little lasting effect.

The subsequent Hague Congress led to a more tangible result. This was the creation of the *Council of Europe.* Here too, however, the actual accomplishment was less substantial than the language of the participants would have suggested. In this case, the quid pro quo for British participation was a watering down of the organization's authority. Instead of exercising any supranational power (that is, authority above that of the participating Western European states), the new body was given no significant responsibilities and functioned on exclusively intergovernmental lines. Indeed, unanimous approval by all fifteen member countries was required for any action. The institution amounted to little more than a forum for general discussion of European affairs. Its chief contribution was symbolic. This was the pattern of cross-national seating established in its parliamentary assembly, where representatives of national parliaments sat not as Germans, French, or Dutch, but on the basis of political identity as Christian Democrats, Socialists, Liberals, and so forth. The precedent would be widely followed in later European assemblies.

During this initial postwar period of the late 1940s, efforts to create a coherent and powerful organization to unify the countries of Western Europe failed to make headway. However, more narrowly focused measures did meet with success. In the realm of defense, Britain and France signed the Treaty of Dunkirk in March 1947, a 50-year pact aimed against any renewed German threat. This was expanded a year later, with the signing of the Brussels Treaty, to include the Benelux countries (Belgium, the Netherlands, and Luxembourg). Although the signatories appear to have had Germany partly in mind, their timing was also responsive to the Czech coup of February. The growing Cold War confrontation and the Berlin blockade of June 1948 moved them increasingly toward a greater emphasis on the Soviet threat. The most far-reaching defense integration was, however, Atlantic rather than European. It was achieved through the commitment of the United States and the signing of the North Atlantic Treaty in April 1949. This led to the establishment of NATO (the North Atlantic Treaty Organization) and the eventual military integration of West Germany in 1955.

The Cold War and the greatly increased American peacetime role in Europe also produced major economic steps, though once again on an Atlantic rather than strictly European basis. At a time of grave economic and political disarray in Western Europe, American Marshall Plan aid was linked to a requirement that the Europeans themselves coordinate the use of this assistance.[8] Accordingly, in April 1948, 16 countries of Western Europe established the *Organization for European Economic Cooperation.* Although the new body did not break new ground institutionally, in that there was no supranational transfer of formal sovereign powers, this intergovernmental organization nonetheless gave Western Europeans practical experience in far-reaching economic coordination.

THE EUROPEAN COAL AND STEEL COMMUNITY

By 1950, five years after the end of the war, little significant progress had been made in building distinctly *European* institutions, let alone in moving toward a substantive European integration or unity. The bodies established within Europe—for example, the Council of Europe—were intergovernmental and disposed of no real power. More important organizations such as NATO were Atlantic in composition.

A dramatic break came with a May 1950 proposal by Robert Schuman, the French foreign minister, for the creation of a European Coal and Steel Community (ECSC). Although the industries involved have since dwindled greatly in their importance, coal and steel were at the time the sinews of the European economy. The objective of the Schuman Plan was political as well as economic. By binding together the key industries of France and Germany, the ECSC would make it nearly impossible for them to prepare again for war against each other, as they had done three times in a period of 75 years.

In essence, the plan called for pooling French and German coal and steel production in a common market, controlled by a joint High Authority. Its members would be appointed by national governments, but they would exercise sovereign powers. That is, their decisions would have the force of law in member countries. The new body, which would be open to membership from other European countries, would be run by new European institutions. For example, the High Authority would be responsible to a parliamentary assembly. In addition, there would be a court of justice to resolve legal matters within the community. National governments, meanwhile, would be represented by a council of ministers, but individual governments would not necessarily be able to block policies with which they alone disagreed. In all, the new body would supersede the decision powers of its component governments in matters pertaining to coal and steel. The ECSC was thus to be the first truly supranational European body.

The Schuman Plan was the brainchild of a remarkable backstage actor, Jean Monnet. This former French official, banker, and negotiator was determined to spur the creation of a united Europe, which he believed governments would not achieve if left to business as usual. Monnet created a network of influential European political, business, and labor elites, operating through a small but highly influential pressure group. For Monnet, the ECSC was to be the first step toward an eventual European federation.

This time, British objections were not allowed to dilute the coherence of the new organization, and indeed, the proposal was presented in a manner that made British involvement less likely. Ultimately, France and Germany were joined by Italy and the Benelux countries in signing the ECSC Treaty in May 1951. With strong American backing, the community began operation in July 1952. The member countries (known as "the Six") achieved considerable success in cooperating to modernize their coal and steel industries.

THE EUROPEAN DEFENSE COMMUNITY

Meanwhile, other unification efforts were being pursued. The June 1950 outbreak of the Korean War, just one month after the ECSC proposal, led to growing concern about a possible war in Europe and to increased American pressure for German rearmament. Monnet responded with a dramatic new initiative, which was formally put forward by French Prime Minister Pleven in October 1950. This called for establishment of a European Defense Community (EDC). In what amounted to a European army, national contingents would be merged into a unified force with a single General Staff. The EDC would have an institutional framework similar to that of the ECSC, and it was proposed that a European Political Community be created to provide governance of these new bodies.

The EDC faced grave obstacles, however. Bitter wartime memories made many Europeans extremely reluctant to cooperate in rapid rearmament of their former enemy. Opposition also came from nationalist political leaders, who disliked such a significant inroad on national sovereignty, as well as from powerful Communist parties in France and Italy, which rejected measures aimed against the Soviet Union. External events also played a role. Britain again refused to take part in a meaningful unification measure. Without the weight of the United Kingdom as a counterbalance, many Europeans feared being tied to a rearmed and potentially powerful Germany. Formal negotiation of the EDC Treaty was not completed among the Six until May 1952. Ratification proceeded slowly, with major political controversies in the member states. Meanwhile, Stalin died in March 1953 and the Korean War came to an end a few months later—both events seeming to suggest that the Soviet challenge had become less urgent. Finally, more than four years after the initial proposal, the French National Assembly defeated the ratification measure, and the effort to create EDC died.

Ultimately, the rearmament of the Federal Republic went ahead. This took place within the integrated military command structure of NATO and via an organization established to succeed the Brussels Treaty Organization, a loosely structured grouping called *Western European Union*. Ironically, Britain now agreed to maintain troops on the Continent, even though a similar commitment had been denied to EDC. The arrangements for rearmament contained treaty provisions precluding German acquisition of nuclear weapons, but the kind of force integration stipulated by EDC was omitted.

The failure of EDC was noteworthy for several reasons. First, it touched off strong recriminations from the United States. Secretary of State John Foster Dulles threatened an "agonizing reappraisal" of America's commitment to Europe—in what foreshadowed a recurrent pattern of crises in Atlantic relations over successive decades. Second, the experience suggested that progress toward greater European unity would not be smooth or continuous, but that periodic reversals were likely. Third, the rejection of the European army, and with it the ambitious project for a European political community, demonstrated that direct creation of a formal federal structure would be very difficult.

THE EUROPEAN COMMON MARKET

Operating behind the scenes, Jean Monnet and his collaborators moved to re-launch the European effort. Monnet, then president of the ECSC High Authority, worked closely with the Belgian Socialist foreign minister, Paul Henri Spaak, and a number of other key European leaders. A decade had passed since the defeat of Hitler, yet progress in building Europe had been modest. It was clear to Monnet that political unity could not be accomplished by proposing an overarching frame-work acceptable to all key decision-makers within the member countries. Unlike North America of the 1780s, Western Europe did not consist of weak and newly independent entities sharing a common colonial past and bound by a shared language and a successful revolutionary war. The nation-states of Europe possessed unique histories, and each had its own language, customs, institutions, and deep-seated political memories. Monnet thus chose to emphasize an indirect route, by means of economic integration of the type that had begun with the Schuman Plan.

In June 1955, representatives of the Six convened in Messina, Italy, to discuss these initiatives. Their efforts eventually led to the signing of the Rome Treaties in March 1957, establishing an Atomic Energy Community (*Euratom*) modeled after the ECSC, and a European customs union and common market to be known as the *European Economic Community*. As in the earlier endeavors, Britain re-mained aloof. Indeed, the United Kingdom established a parallel body known as the *European Free Trade Association*. This group ("the Seven") consisted of Scan-dinavian countries (Norway, Sweden, and Denmark), European neutrals (Austria and Switzerland), plus Portugal and Britain. Although it promoted increased trade among its members and to some extent with the Common Market countries, its overall reach remained strictly limited. It did not encompass agriculture, nor did it provide for broader economic integration among its members or the kind of supranational institutions and objectives the Six explicitly shared.

The drive to establish the Common Market gained added force from a num-ber of outside factors. One of these was the British-French debacle in the Suez crisis of November 1956. The experience provided painful confirmation that the ability of these two major colonial powers to act on their own in world affairs had been drastically curtailed. In addition, it showed them to be deeply vulnerable to pressure from the United States and the Soviet Union. By implication, there was more reason than ever to find means for enhancing the economic and political weight of the countries of Europe. With strong political support from Christian Democratic leaders, especially in Germany and Italy, and from some leading So-cialists, Spaak in Belgium and Prime Minister Guy Mollet in France, the EEC and Euratom came into existence on January 1, 1958.

European political and economic elites generally recognized that the *raison d'être* of the European Economic Community was political, even though its means were overwhelmingly economic at first. Very quickly, the EEC became the most vital of the various European organizations. Unlike the ECSC, its range en-compassed a far wider scope of activity, and in marked contrast to most other organizations, it exhibited elements of supranationality—even though these were less extensive than had been hoped, and even less advanced than institutions within the ECSC. However, by the late 1950s, the Coal and Steel Community had begun to face difficulty, both because of the growing challenge to coal from imported oil, and because national governments faced large surpluses of coal. In turn, Euratom also fell far short of original expectations. Its problems were exacerbated by the fact that key areas remained under national control, and because the then most advanced nuclear power in Europe, Great Britain, remained outside the community.

The three European communities (the EEC, ECSC, and Euratom) were merged in 1967, to create the "European Communities." However, the organization continued to be labeled with the name of its most important constituent part, the Common Market, and was frequently referred to as the *European Community*. Subsequently, on November 1, 1993, after ratification of the Maastricht Treaty, its name became the *European Union*.*

EUROPEAN INTEGRATION: ACHIEVEMENTS

Assessments of the European Community often suffer from hyperbole: the Common Market is treated either as a potential United States of Europe on the one hand, or a narrow bureaucratic and commercial arrangement on the other. The reality is more complex. In any case, an early indication that the Common Market encompassed far more than a restricted economic agenda was evident from an event that occurred in 1971.

On March 23 of that year, some 80,000 European farmers traveled to Brussels for a protest march. They sought major changes in agricultural policy, and in demonstrating their anger they clashed with police. During the ensuing riot, 50 police and 100 demonstrators suffered injuries and one person was killed. What is significant about this event is that it occurred not in a national capital such as Rome, Paris, or Bonn, but in Brussels, the headquarters of the European Community. The farmers were demonstrating where they believed significant authority lay for determining agricultural policy in Europe. The partial transfer of sovereignty from the national to the European level, at least in this particular issue area, was thus evident.

To be sure, full authority for agricultural policy has not been completely transferred to Brussels, and farm protests continue to be directed at national governments as well. Even so, it is at meetings of the Council of Ministers in Brussels that European farm prices are broadly set.†

Another tangible manifestation of the Community's impact has been its expansion of membership (see Table 13.1). The number of countries taking part has

---

*The terms *Community* and *Union* are used interchangeably throughout this chapter, with *Union* being emphasized for the post–November 1993 period.
†Technically, currency fluctuations and a series of adjustments intended to insulate farmers from the effects of these changes mean that prices for agricultural products are not identical in all of the European Community countries.

Table 13.1 EXPANSION OF THE EUROPEAN COMMUNITY

Date	Countries	Total
July–August 1952	(European Coal and Steel Community) France, Germany, Italy, Begium, Luxembourg, Netherlands	6
1 January 1958	(European Economic Community and Euratom)	
1 July 1967	(Merger of Community Institutions)	
1 January 1973	Britain, Denmark, Ireland	9
1 January 1981	Greece	10
1 January 1986	Spain, Portugal	12
1995	Scheduled entry of Austria, Finland, Norway and Sweden	16

increased from the original six to a total of twelve. In addition, seven countries have formally applied for admission. Among them Austria, Finland, Norway, and Sweden, are scheduled to become members in 1995. Three others (Cyprus, Malta, Turkey) face difficulties and are unlikely to enter before the year 2000, if at all. A number of East European countries are potential candidates for entry over the longer term. They include Poland, Hungary, and the Czech Republic.

During the years since its creation the Community has gained great importance across a wide array of economic and commercial matters. Its objectives for integration have included the following:

Customs union and common external tariff; these provide the member states with standardized tariffs toward imports from the outside world

Common agricultural policy (CAP)

Social policy harmonization (working conditions and social benefits)

Regional policy

Transportation policy

Competition policy

Trade policy, especially in negotiations with other countries and groups of countries

Services and professional credentials

European Monetary System (EMS), begun in 1979 to coordinate exchange rate policies among the member currencies (although not all EC countries take part)

Foreign Policy (voluntary coordination)

To carry out its tasks, the Community has established an elaborate—some would say overly elaborate—institutional framework. The heart of these institutions is the *Commission*. It oversees the daily functioning of the Community and has the right to initiate policies. Its 17 members (two each from the largest states—Britain, France, Germany, Italy, Spain—and one from each of the other countries) are appointed for four-year terms by agreement among the member governments. However, the commissioners are expected to function autono-

Table 13.2 EUROPEAN PARLIAMENT

By Political Group[a]		By Country	
Socialists	198	Germany	99
European People's Party	157	France	87
(Christian Dems & Conservs)		Britain	87
Liberals	37	Italy	87
European Unitarian Left	28	Spain	64
(ex-Communists)		Netherlands	31
Forza Europa (Berlusconi	27	Belgium	25
Party, Italy)		Greece	25
European Democratic Alliance	26	Portugal	25
(Gaullists & others)		Denmark	16
Greens	23	Ireland	15
Radical Alliance	19	Luxembourg	6
(Independent Left)			
European Union of Nations	19		
(anti-European Union)			
Non-attached	33		
(including far-right)			
TOTAL SEATS	567	TOTAL SEATS	567

[a]As of July 1994.
Source: Delegation of the European Commission, Washington, DC, July 1994.

mously, and once in office are independent of their governments. Indeed, they take an oath to discharge their responsibilities as Europeans.

The Commission presides over a very large staff in Brussels; together, the Community institutions employ more than 20,000 European civil servants. The budget for the operation of the Community and its institutions does not come directly from member governments. Instead, the Community relies on its own resources, which derive mainly from customs duties and a percentage of the Value Added Tax each member state levies.

The *Council* remains the Community's chief decision-making body. It is the institution in which the member governments are directly represented. Usually, it is made up of the foreign ministers of the individual states, but on more specialized matters it includes ministers responsible for finance, agriculture, or other areas. The Council has the power to implement community treaties, and accept or reject the proposals put to it by the Commission. Member states rotate the chairmanship of the Council every six months. The country chairing the group is referred to as holding the presidency of the Council. Three times a year, the heads of state or government of the 12 member states meet, as the European Council, to address major policy questions.

The *European Parliament* possesses a consultative and supervisory role. Direct elections for the parliament first occurred in 1979 and take place every five years. The 567 members, drawn from the 12 member states, sit by political party rather than by nationality (see Table 13.2). The parliament has the authority to consider Commission proposals before the council takes action. It also has a role in the budget process. By a vote of censure the parliament can require the Commission to resign, but this power has never been used, and in any case the parliament would not have the power to appoint a new commission. In July 1987, its powers were increased giving it a role in approving international agreements and expanding its ability to amend legislation proposed by the Commission and the Council. Under the Maastricht Treaty, which took effect on November 1, 1993, the Parliament gained additional powers. These include the right to approve members of the European Commission, to veto most international agreements, and to veto Community measures involving a wide range of matters (consumer affairs, the environment, education, health, culture, and other aspects of the single market).

The *Court of Justice* is composed of 13 judges, who are appointed for six-year terms through agreement among the member states. Their responsibility is to interpret the treaties and the huge body of regulations, directives, and decisions issued by the Commission and Council. While the court has discharged this role effectively and is the final authority in doing so, it has not attempted to establish the kind of independent judicial power the Supreme Court exercises within the American political system. Even so, the European Court of Justice possesses the legal authority to order governments that have not met their obligations under the Treaty of Rome to bring themselves into compliance.

The Community also plays a rudimentary role in foreign policy. In the foreign trade realm, it has an important international agreement in the Lomé Convention, which is the basis for economic cooperation between the Community and 66 developing countries in Africa, the Caribbean, and the Pacific. As a result of the Lomé IV Convention, which came into force in September 1991, the Europeans have committed some $13.8 billion in foreign assistance for the period from 1990 to 1995.[9] In addition, negotiating on behalf of its 12 member countries, the European Union reached agreement with the United States for completing the Uruguay Round under the General Agreement on Tariffs and Trade (GATT). Although the European negotiators had to overcome internal differences, particularly by France over agriculture, movies, and television, the accord with the United States made possible the wider and highly important multilateral agreement. Altogether, the EC has trade agreements with more than 100 countries.

The 12 Common Market countries seek to coordinate their foreign policies in international organizations and multilateral negotiations. This effort began with an arrangement known as *European Political Cooperation (EPC)*. Efforts at a common foreign policy by means of the EPC grew out of European summits in 1969 and 1970. Until 1987, EPC functioned outside the Rome treaty, and was based on consultations and the exchange of information. To implement their work, foreign ministers of the member countries meet at least four times per year and the political directors of their national foreign ministries convene at frequent intervals. However, the practical extent of this cooperation has been modest. With the expansion of the Community from nine to ten and then twelve members, the degree of consensus at first declined. For example, Greece was often at odds with the other Community countries in UN votes and on regional issues—as in the case of the Middle East.[10]

As a result of the Single European Act of July 1987, the Community governments for the first time committed themselves to foreign policy cooperation within the formal provisions of their Treaties. They pledged "jointly to formulate and implement a European foreign policy," and agreed to coordinate more closely on the political and economic aspects of security.[11] Although this step had symbolic significance, the commitment remained one of voluntary cooperation, rather than a formalized institutional requirement. Under the Maastricht Treaty there is a commitment to pursue a common foreign and security policy "to enable the Union to speak with a single voice." Although the Treaty provides for certain foreign policy issues to be decided by majority vote, this represents less of an achievement than might appear to be the case. The provision affects only less important matters and the majority vote rule applies only if all members agree.

THE SINGLE EUROPEAN MARKET AND THE MAASTRICHT TREATY

In reaction to a long series of frustrations, and in anticipation of the entry of Spain and Portugal, the European heads of state and government agreed in March 1985 to seek completion of a "single market by 1992," without frontiers, and with free movement of goods, persons, services, and capital.[12]

The objective of economic union had been periodically reaffirmed, yet never achieved. The leaders of the Common Market countries thus undertook a major new initiative aimed at completing the Community's single internal market by December 31, 1992. The prospect of a unified European market of 324 million people promised to provide Europe with a dynamism it had long lacked. Moreover, an official estimate put the benefits to be derived from removing internal obstacles at between $2\frac{1}{2}$ and $6\frac{1}{2}$ percent of GNP, and another study suggested that the actual benefits could be up to five times greater.[13]

To achieve the internal market objective, the European Council in June 1985 formally endorsed a Commission "White Paper" listing some 300 specific measures to be taken. They followed this in 1986 by signing the Single European Act (SEA). This measure, which took effect in July 1987 after being ratified by each of the 12 member countries, amended the original Community treaties. It provided for majority voting in the Council on issues affecting the internal market, as well as on the environment, worker health and safety, and consumer protection. The Act also increased the powers of the European Parliament and gave formal recognition to foreign policy cooperation.

Major obstacles remained, however. These included harmonization of taxes; arrangements to establish a European monetary system, a central bank, and a common currency; and the complete abolition of frontier controls among all the Community's individual countries. Moreover, key policy areas—defense, foreign policy, and the expensive agricultural programs—remained largely outside the scope of the Europe 1992 agenda.

Unresolved issues also affected the Community's ability to move toward closer integration. These included harmonization of labor conditions and social policy, regional differences between the most and least prosperous parts of Europe, and fundamental questions of political authority that pitted national versus Community control. Indeed, support for far-reaching measures of unity was far from universal. Just as France under General De Gaulle had been a major impediment to progress in the 1960s, so too were a series of British governments after the United Kingdom gained entry in 1973. For a decade, this took the form of battles over the share of the Community's budget to be paid by Britain. Especially under Prime Minister Margaret Thatcher (1979–1990), British governments remained reluctant to see the transfer of sovereign authority to Brussels.

As Thatcher expressed this concern:

"We have not successfully rolled back the frontiers of the state in Britain, only to see them reimposed at a European level within a European superstate exercising a new dominance from Brussels."[14]

In December 1991, governmental leaders of the 12 European Community countries met in the Dutch city of Maastricht to approve the Treaty on European Union. The agreement, widely known as the Maastricht Treaty, was designed to take effect with the onset of the single European market on January 1, 1993, and to amend the Rome Treaty which had established the Common Market in 1957. Maastricht's ambitions appeared far-reaching. The Treaty renamed the Community as the "European Union" and proclaimed a European citizenship, with the right of people to live and to work anywhere within the Community and to vote in local and European (though not national) elections wherever they resided. It proposed to enhance the authority of the Community in a broad range of existing areas. The most notable of these was to be economic and monetary union, including establishment of a European Central Bank on or after January 1, 1997 and—for all countries except Britain—a single currency by January 1, 1999. Social policy (again, with the exception of Britain) was to come under European jurisdiction, including provisions for working conditions, health and safety, equal pay, social security, and labor-management relations. The Treaty also sought to establish a common foreign and security policy—though with decisions requiring unanimity among the members—and looked toward an eventual common defense policy. In institutional terms, the powers of the Parliament were enhanced, and there was agreement to make greater use of majority voting within the Council of Ministers.

To alleviate concerns over extensive centralization in Brussels, Maastricht adopted the principle of "subsidiarity." This complex, even opaque term meant that decisions were to be taken at the lowest appropriate local, regional, or national level, and were to be dealt with by Brussels only if they could not be managed effectively by those authorities.

In the immediate aftermath of the signing of the Maastricht Treaty, and with the single market for free movement of people, capital, goods, and services due to take effect just one year later, there was widespread expectation in Europe and elsewhere that the Community had achieved real momentum toward a far more unified and internationally important role. However, as with previous "relaunchings," Maastricht too proved more complex and less formidable than initially appeared to be the case.

First, many hopes (and fears) about the Treaty were exaggerated. Most provisions of this long and complex document actually entailed little significant change. For example, European citizenship was largely symbolic, and the subsidiarity concept was not likely to have much impact on the daily operation of the European Union. While Maastricht did create two new arrangements separate from the Community to deal with foreign affairs and with domestic matters including immigration and police cooperation, the initiatives were in fact limited and did not significantly enlarge the scope of European powers.

On the other hand, the Treaty did include a number of potentially significant measures, particularly the commitment to economic and monetary union and the eventual creation of a central bank and common currency—though the obstacles to their implementation remained daunting. In addition, institutional changes promised to give the Union greater coherence. The Parliament, though still weak, was given the right of "co-decision" with the Council on matters related to the internal market. (These powers did not, however, include the major areas of foreign and defense policy, economic and monetary policy, nor judicial cooperation.) In addition, the Council was to make more use of "qualified majority voting" on policies related to the internal market, thus lessening national veto power. In areas such as capital movement, the environment, education, transportation, and regional aid funds, the new procedures meant that it would take the combined opposition of at least two of the larger states and one of the smaller ones to block a measure favored by all the other members.[15]

A second problem pertained not to the Community or Union itself, but to the lack of public involvement and identification with its institutions. This was evident in the difficulties and delays that the ratification process faced. Thus, Danish voters first rejected the Maastricht Treaty in a June 1992 referendum, approving it in a new vote the following year; and French voters only very narrowly voted in favor of Maastricht, with just 51 percent endorsement in a September 1992 referendum. In Germany, legal challenges were not resolved by the courts until October 1993. And in Britain, which had opted out of key monetary and social provisions of the Treaty, ratification by Parliament took place only after a bitter and divisive debate, amid suspicion of the Brussels bureaucracy and fears of foreign control over the English way of life.

Public opinion polls showed that while 73 percent of the public in the 12 European Community countries supported European integration and the Community, only a 41 percent plurality described themselves as "for" the Treaty.[16] Indeed, only 42 percent said they would be very sorry if the Community were scrapped altogether.[17] More broadly, this weakness in public support reflected what has been termed the "democratic deficit," and the lack of accountability of emerging European institutions. By a margin of 47 percent to 41 percent, Europeans described themselves as not satisfied with democracy in the Community.[18]

As a consequence of these sentiments, and the national debates over ratification, the coming into force of the European Union Treaty was delayed from its originally scheduled January 1, 1993 date to November 1, 1993.

Third, the arrangements for economic and monetary union proved far more difficult to sustain than anticipated. Economic, commercial, and trade policy had long been at the heart of efforts to achieve integration in Europe, and the Maastricht Treaty called for far-reaching convergence of economic policy in the 12 member countries. In this case, however, the tensions between national priorities and Community needs led to a serious crisis.

The problem began after German unification in 1990, with the former German Democratic Republic (East Germany) and its 16 million people being absorbed by the Federal Republic. At the time, the West German authorities decided to exchange the almost worthless East German currency at a one-to-one ratio with the West German mark. They also committed to rebuilding the decrepit infrastructure of the East and to phase in Western levels of wages and social benefits. Even for the wealthy and powerful West German economy, the costs of unification were immense, and the net transfer of funds from West to East soon amounted to more than $100 billion per year. The Bonn government of Chancellor Helmut Kohl had promised that no German would be worse off after unification and thus was reluctant to raise taxes in order to cover these costs. In effect, it sought to pay for unification by borrowing rather than raising taxes. As a result, and reacting to soaring budget deficits as well as historic fears of inflation, the German central bank (the Bundesbank) stepped in to raise interest rates sharply in July 1992.

At this point the conflict between national and European priorities came into the open. Under the Exchange Rate Mechanism (ERM) of the European Monetary System, exchange rates for 11 of the Community countries had long been tied together in order to fluctuate within a band of no more than 2.25 percent from a central value. However, the sudden rise in German interest rates caused funds to flow toward Germany for the higher returns available there. Given the Bonn government's refusal to raise taxes and the Bundesbank's reluctance to reduce interest rates, Germany's partners in the ERM found themselves facing difficult choices.

In the absence of agreement to revalue the mark upward or to suspend the ERM so that exchange rates could float, European countries committed to the ERM were forced to raise interest rates in order to keep their own currencies from depreciating below the agreed values, and to keep the system from collapsing. However, high interest rates discouraged business investment, and the changes brought on a serious recession. As a result, unemployment (which was already high) rose to levels not seen in four decades, for example reaching 12 percent in France. Meanwhile, speculators bet that governments would ultimately be forced to devalue their exchange rates in order to be able to lower interest rates and revive their economies and they sold these currencies while buying marks. At vast expense, European central banks intervened in exchange markets in an effort to support the weaker currencies.

In September 1992, Britain and Italy withdrew from the ERM, and Britain lowered its interest rates in order to stimulate its economy. In November, the Irish, Danish, and French currencies came under pressure, and the Portuguese and Spanish currencies were devalued by 6 percent. By the late spring and early summer of 1993, amid growing resentment in Europe over the recession and interest rates, another wave of speculation occurred. The Bundesbank undertook modest interest rate cuts, but the currencies of Denmark, Belgium, Spain, and Portugal were seriously weakened, and the French Franc came under severe pressure. Finally, in August, at the height of the currency crisis, an agreement was reached allowing currencies to fluctuate by a huge margin of plus or minus 15 percent, thus preserving the ERM in name only.[19]

Not only did this crisis prove costly and disruptive, it damaged the partnership between France and Germany that had long been the driving force behind the European Community. From the French perspective, the Bonn government had given priority to Germany's national interest over its responsibilities to Europe and to its close ally, France. Moreover, the crisis had proved very costly. In the words of a leading German economist, ". . . the French threw some $60 billion out of the window" in the Banque de France's futile attempt to defend the franc.[20] Assessing the debacle, France's Prime Minister, Edouard Balladur, blamed high German interest rates for the crisis. France's leading newspaper, Le Monde, accused Germany of a "diktat," and another leading paper's headline read, "Europe Broken?"[21]

At a time of intense crisis, national priorities had taken precedence over European ones, and the weakness of common European institutions thus became painfully evident. In assessing the problems of sustaining European monetary cooperation, Benjamin J. Cohen has observed that economic variables and organizational characteristics are secondary. The main conditions necessary for success are either the existence of a local hegemon willing and able to sustain the arrangement or the ultimate political will of those involved to sustain their common endeavor.[22] In the case of the ERM crisis, these conditions were clearly absent.

Fourth, and finally, foreign policy represents a kind of litmus test for the emergence of a real European identity in the international system, but the Community has repeatedly failed the test. To be sure, the Maastricht Treaty seemed to suggest otherwise, in stating the European Union's aim "to assert its identity on the international scene, in particular through the implementation of a common foreign and security policy including the eventual framing of a common defence policy." In practice, however, despite common statements and policy coordination on lesser matters and a significant degree of integration for international trade negotiations, the European Community has not been able to achieve effective foreign policy cooperation on the most important problems, nor even to begin on defense issues.

The most traumatic case of the Community's failure concerns Yugoslavia. Nearly two decades earlier, the Community had found itself in disarray in responding to the October 1973 Middle East war and subsequent oil shock. Yet those events had been outside Europe. The passage of time, the deepening and enlarging of the Community, the mandate of Maastricht, and the end of the Cold War division of Europe all suggested that the time for a European foreign policy was at hand. With the disintegration of Yugoslavia, the Community had an opportunity to take the lead in addressing a major European crisis. The weakening and breakup of the USSR seemed to remove one of the superpowers from an active

Table 13.3 COMPARISON OF EUROPEAN COMMUNITY, UNITED STATES, AND JAPAN

	EC	United States	Japan
Population (mil. 1991)	345	253	124
Area (mil. sq. miles)	.870	3.619	.146
GDP ($bil. 1992)	6.9	5.9	3.7
Exports 1992 ($bil. merchandise)	565[a]	448	330
Armed Forces (mil., 1992)	2.2	1.9	0.2

[a]Exports to rest of world.
Source: OECD, International Institute for Strategic Studies, Eurostat, as reported in *The Economist,* 3 July, 1993, Survey p. 19.

role, and in the aftermath of the Gulf War, the United States appeared willing to see the Europeans take the lead. Instead, the Community countries abdicated their responsibility.

Thus, in August 1991, European Community foreign ministers failed to reach agreement on steps to halt bloody fighting between Serbs and Croats. They rejected a German proposal to send a peacekeeping force and instead asked that other organizations such as the Conference on Security and Cooperation in Europe (CSCE) or the UN act to halt the bloodshed. Disarray was also apparent over diplomatic recognition. In early 1992, Germany stirred resentment among other members of the Community by announcing recognition of the breakaway Yugoslav republics of Slovenia and Croatia, without waiting for the Community to reach its own decision. Subsequently, and despite the dispatch of a small observer group, the activities of peace negotiator Lord David Owen, and the dispatch of 11,000 mainly French and British troops to provide humanitarian relief, the Europeans were incapable not only of bringing peace to Yugoslavia but also of stopping the worst human rights abuses in Europe since 1945.

The causes of this foreign policy failure were complex, but they were not the fault of public opinion, which actually favored the Community's military intervention by a margin of 55 percent to 28 percent.[23] Instead, the difficulties lay in the absence of any common European military force, a political decision-making process and sovereignty which remained national rather than European, and historic and constitutional constraints on sending German troops abroad. The consequences were summarized by a leading French intellectual, Andre Glucksmann, who lamented that "even a tiny gesture showing the will to use force could have stopped war and saved many lives," and by an American observer who added a bitter indictment of Europe's failure:

> The dream of a united Europe, powerful contributor to a better world, is dead. It died when the European Community refused to act against Serbian aggression—when it would not lift a finger to stop mass racial murder on its own continent.[24]

THE LIMITS OF EUROPEAN INTEGRATION

Measured in the aggregate, the Community has achieved both considerable coordination among its member states and a significant international stature. As Table 13.3 indicates, the 12 countries of the European Community, when compared with the United States, and Japan, represent a formidable force in terms of population, gross national product, and share of world trade. Indeed, the Community is the world's leading exporter.

Throughout the Community's history, however, there have been major limitations to the extent of European unity. Despite the indirect approach toward integration through economic and technical means rather than direct political and federal efforts, the core of sovereignty has generally been resistant to serious encroachment. In 1965–1966, for example, President de Gaulle caused French representatives to boycott Community institutions until agreement was reached (the "Luxembourg compromise"), severely curtailing arrangements for majority voting that would otherwise have gone into effect.[25]

As evident in the post-Maastricht difficulties cited above, there exists a continuing tension between national sovereignty and integration, in which national priorities tend to prevail. In crisis periods, sharp political differences have often characterized the interplay among countries of the European Community. Illustratively, the 1973–1974 oil shock led to a situation in which the Netherlands became the target of an Arab oil embargo for its ostensible support of Israel. For a brief time, France and Britain appeared willing to comply with the terms of the boycott, in the hopes of avoiding trouble for themselves, even though this would have violated the provisions of the Rome treaty. The controversy proved short-lived, but it illustrated how external events could prove bitterly divisive within the Community. Community countries periodically found themselves at loggerheads over external political issues. In the mid 1980s, for example, Greece opposed a tougher stand against Libyan involvement in terrorism. On the other hand, in response to the East European revolutions of 1989, despite differences of emphasis, the Common Market countries did display considerable cooperation.

Nor has integration itself been an unmixed blessing. The Community has been criticized for the creation of a mammoth bureaucracy. And more than half of its budget goes to just one area: the Common Agricultural Policy, which subsidizes huge agricultural surpluses. The evolution of these costly policies has had less to do with logic and overall European interests than with the political power of farmers inside a number of key European countries, and with the ability of governments such as that of France to maneuver its partners into accepting its point of view in order for the Community to continue functioning.

As an illustration of the way in which national priorities and narrow domestic interests can prevail over Community priorities and broader purposes, France at one point blocked a major trade agreement between the Community and the emergent East European democracies of Poland, Hungary, and Czechoslovakia. In September 1991, the foreign ministers of the 12 EC countries met to approve an agreement which the Community had spent eight months negotiating, and which would have granted access for East European products to the European market. Even though other EC countries had agreed to relinquish preferences for their own products such as steel, textiles, and agricultural products, France objected because of a proposed tiny increase in beef imports, amounting to less than one one-hundredth of one percent of total European consumption. The position not only ran counter to the widespread interest of encouraging successful economic and political transformation in Eastern Europe, it also contradicted the proclaimed internationalism of France's Socialist government. However, it clearly reflected the domestic political fervor of French farmers and the government's anxiety over forthcoming elections. In reaction, the Danish foreign minister described the French position as a "disgrace," and Jacques Delors, the President of the Commission and himself a French Socialist, commented bitterly, "It is no good welcoming the independent countries of Eastern Europe with tears of joy if we do not allow them access to our markets."[26]

IMPLICATIONS OF THE EUROPEAN EXPERIENCE

The Community matches or even surpasses the United States and Japan in terms of aggregate measures such as population and economic strength, however its potential power is undercut by two limitations. The first of these is the absence of common foreign and defense policies. Without a more explicit ability to organize its own foreign relations and external security, the Community is unlikely to attain the international stature its population and wealth would otherwise suggest. Second, and equally important, despite Europe's impressive economic integration, the continuing predominance of national priorities and institutions insures that the full weight of its wealth and power cannot be brought to bear on the world stage.

In important realms, European Community decisions can and do take precedence over national policies and laws. Regional integration in Western Europe has brought an unprecedented (for the modern world, at least) degree of order and stability for the countries of that area. One of the founding fathers of this new Europe, Jean Rey, once remarked that he and his colleagues were engaged in building a "Gothic cathedral." The final form would not be seen in their lifetimes, but the scope and design were on a grand scale. By any broad reckoning, the interim results of this effort—even were they not to progress much beyond their late twentieth-century form—represent a remarkable achievement. Despite its limitations, the European Union's regional cooperation and the fact that its member states no longer prepare for even the possibility of war against one another demonstrate that the Hobbesian problem of the international system, along with the security dilemma, may not be fixed for all time.

The European states continue to maintain their sovereign national institutions. Yet as nonsuperpowers they find it difficult to provide effectively for their own prosperity and security on a strictly national basis. As a result of the constraints within which they operate, they have found that to accomplish their own national goals it becomes advantageous to pursue cooperation with their neighbors.

To some extent, the European case is unique. In its formative years, the existence of a stable nation-state pattern, the experiences of two world wars, the role of the Soviet Union (in posing a security threat) and of the United States (in fostering security and encouraging European unity) were all specific to the Western half of the European continent.

In comparison with global organizations such as the League of Nations and the United Nations, the European Community has achieved relative success where the global organizations have not. This seems to suggest that—other things being equal—it is more feasible to build regional order. *Regionalism,* in which a group of states in a geographic area seek to form a distinct political entity of some kind, may therefore be more attainable because of its limited scale and the possibility of greater commonality among its participant countries. One reason for this is that international cooperation may be more difficult to accomplish as the number of states involved increases. In an important theoretical analysis bearing on this problem, Kenneth Oye has identified three means by which the number of players affects the likelihood of cooperation.[27]

First, the larger the number of actors, the harder it becomes to identify and achieve common interests. With a larger number of participants, transaction and information costs increase, making it harder both to identify opportunities for mutually beneficial cooperation and to coordinate policies for achieving these results. Second, with a larger number of players, the opportunities for defection increase, as do problems of control and recognition. Here, "free-riding" may become an impediment to cooperation.[28] There may also be problems of compliance from states too weak domestically to pay the costs. Also, the larger the number of actors, the more likely it is that some will not meet even the most basic standard of rationality. Third, with increasing numbers of actors, the practicality of imposing costs on, or punishing, those who defect lessens. The threat to retaliate against those who break the rules of the game becomes harder to carry out.

This analysis suggests that endeavors such as regional integration, as well as attempts such as restraining the proliferation of nuclear weapons, are likely to be more practical with a limited number of states participating than if the effort is sought at the global level. It may also suggest greater obstacles to European cooperation as membership in the Community increases.

Of course, the advantages of regionalism are far from automatic. Despite their geographic and cultural affinity, the states of Western Europe have had a history of deadly conflicts among themselves, and other regions of the world (Southeast Asia, the Middle East) provide evidence of endemic local animosity and warfare. Actual regional organizations, such as the Organization of African Unity (OAU), Organization of American States (OAS), and the Arab League have had little substantive success.

Ironically, some observers remain critical of European regionalism, not because of its limited progress, but because it may go too far. Thus one critic has worried whether the European Community would become an imperialist superpower, creating greater division within the world and harming the interests of the poorer countries.[29] Notwithstanding this criticism, the cooperative and internationalist impulses conducive to regional integration are not likely to foster the aggressive regional nationalism that such criticism implies. For the most part, the Community's record in aiding and trading with developing countries demonstrates a practical record of responsiveness toward poorer regions of the world.

Another aspect of the European experience concerns the limits of *federalism* as opposed to the possibilities of *functionalism*. Federalism is an approach to political community through the creation of formal institutions. In both theory and practice it aims to unite peoples who live in nearby states or who share common attributes such as culture or ethnicity. Advocates of federalism have maintained that the creation of institutions will lead to the development of common attitudes and a sense of community among their members. A federation can be said to exist when diverse political entities are united in an overall order but retain their own existence.[30]

The most commonly cited examples of successful federalist arrangements are the United States of America, Switzerland, and the Federal Republic of Germany. However, each of these arrangements has had a unique history in which relations among the participating units were already extremely close. In addition, with the exception of Germany (where national government had already existed and where the purpose of federalism was actually to lessen the authority of too strong and dictatorial a central authority), these federations were established in a preindustrial era. Postwar efforts to establish federal arrangements among existing states have mostly failed—sometimes disastrously—as in the case of Rhodesia, the British West Indies, and the United Arab Republic of Egypt and Syria. And in Europe itself, the more ambitious attempts at federal and supranational institution creation (as in the case of the European Defense Community) have not succeeded.

Functionalism, however, enjoyed widespread scholarly attention during the period of the Common Market's early development and consolidation. Its basic logic held that whereas federalism, and the grandiose designs with which it was often put forward, could not supersede the impulses of nationalism, peaceful world order could be achieved through a different means. This could be accomplished by organizing international cooperation in specific functional necessities such as health, transportation, science, culture, trade, and other economic activities.[31] If countries could cooperate successfully in these endeavors without there being an overarching political authority, the activity would nonetheless bring them closer together and foster peaceful relationships. The experience of effective conduct of these common tasks would encourage governments to delegate more of their authority for practical matters to international bodies. Ultimately, the resulting economic and functional integration[32] would promote not only peace but the attainment of wider political understandings.

The practical experience of the European Coal and Steel Community led scholars such as Ernst Haas to emphasize the utility of functional institutions on a regional (rather than global) basis. Their conception, sometimes termed *neofunctionalism*, held that decisions taken on a step-by-step basis offered advantages over strictly political decisions. Beginning with a common interest in their own welfare, states would find it advantageous to see economic integration spill over from one specific area into adjacent sectors of their activity. This view held that economic self-interest of the actors, as well as the activity of domestic pressure groups pursuing the interests of their own sectors, would lead toward ever closer ties.[33] Incremental actions aimed at closer functional cooperation would ultimately have important and unintended consequences as they led the participating countries toward establishment of new supranational regional authority. In Haas's words, "the determinism implicit in the picture of the European social and economic structures is almost absolute. Given all these conditions, . . . the progression from a politically inspired common market to an economic union, and finally to a political union among states is automatic."[34]

Functionalism and neofunctionalism thus assumed the primacy of economics over politics. However, two sets of problems intervened. One of them concerned the nature of the integration process itself. Here, it was one thing to dismantle barriers to commercial and other interchange among the countries of Western Europe; it was quite another to agree on the positive steps required in building new institutional arrangements. More important, a political core remained against which the "expansive logic of functionalism" made comparatively few inroads. Almost invariably, major new undertakings or the expansion of existing arrangements have required overt political initiatives—or have been vulnerable to negative political intervention.[35] They have not simply proceeded as the result of an ongoing process of functional integration.

A compendium of some of the more visible political issues and interventions makes this point quite clearly. These have included the following:

Chancellor Konrad Adenauer's actions in bringing Germany into the new EEC in 1958.

Prime Minister Harold Macmillan's political decision in late 1960 to seek British entry into the Common Market.

President de Gaulle's vetoes of Britain in 1963 and 1967.

De Gaulle's successful blocking of the scheduled onset of majority rule in 1965–1966.

Agreement by Prime Ministers Edward Heath of Britain and Georges Pompidou of France leading to Britain's Common Market entry in 1973.

Political agreement among EEC heads of state and government for admission of Greece in 1981 and Spain and Portugal in 1986.

Decision by the European Council in 1985 to complete the internal market by December 31, 1992.[36]

Agreement by European heads of state and government on the Maastricht Treaty, December 1991.

Crisis of Exchange Rate Mechanism in aftermath of German unification and interest-rate policies, August 1993.

The tenacity of the political dimension in relationship to neofunctionalism is conceded by Robert Keohane and Stanley Hoffmann, in an analysis which otherwise sees a good deal of merit in Haas's original approach. The authors find Haas's notion of supranationality the "most appropriate label for the political process" of the European Community.[37] Supranationality here is understood by Haas as a process of decision making "in which the participants refrain from unconditionally vetoing proposals and instead seek to attain agreement by means of compromises upgrading common interests."[38] However, Keohone and Hoffman make a distinction concerning supranationality in recognizing that the Community's key decision-making body, the Council of Ministers, "is not a supranational entity in the sense of being an authoritative decision-maker above the nation-state, nor has loyalty been transferred from the nation-state to the Commission."[39] Thus in reaching their conclusion about the Single European Act, Keohane and Hoffmann have, in effect, described another in a series of key political decisions. Specifically, they note that "successful spillover requires prior programmatic agreement among governments expressed in an intergovernmental bargain"; and that spillover does not adequately account for the decisions leading to the SEA. While they argue that a state-centric perspective by itself does not provide a satisfactory explanation for the SEA, they agree that explanation must begin with governmental actions, and that "interstate bargains remain the necessary conditions for European integration and must be recognized as such."[40]

Not only does the political component sometimes pose a real obstacle to the functionalist process, but there remain serious questions about the applicability of the European example in other regions. The combined presence of well-developed governmental administrative machinery (allowing national compliance and smooth operation of the Community's institutions), the specific impact of World War II, and the unique—and antithetical—roles played by the United States and the Soviet Union may explain why integration efforts succeeded in Western Europe but have failed in Latin America, the Caribbean, East Africa, and elsewhere.

Many of these problems caused functionalist writers to reconsider their initial appraisals. Haas, for example, noted that functionalist theory erred in assuming the end of ideology as well as in minimizing the significance of the external world.[41] Indeed, Haas later concluded that as a result of these and other limitations, the theory of regional integration had become obsolete. It had experienced significant problems of both explanation and prediction. While better theories could be developed, Haas argued that "the effort is probably not worthwhile." Instead, he urged exploration of other themes, in which aspects of regional integration theory could nonetheless be useful. These different realms include systems change and especially *interdependence*,[42] and it is the latter, and the related search for economic order, to which the next chapter will turn.

NOTES

1. The quotation by the then French president can be found in Merry and Serge Bromberger, *Jean Monnet and the United States of Europe* (New York: Coward-McCann, 1969), p. 175.

2. Quoted in Hobart Rowen, ". . . Of European Unity," *Washington Post*, 25 October 1990.

3. Stanley Hoffmann, "Goodbye to a United Europe," *New York Review of Books*, 27 May 1993, pp. 27–31, at p. 31.

4. The term is that of Karl W. Deutsch et al., *Political Community and the North Atlantic Area* (Princeton: Princeton University Press, 1957), p. 5.

5. In different ways, this theme is developed by Anton DePorte, *Europe Between the Superpowers: The Enduring Balance,* 2nd ed. (New Haven: Yale University Press, 1986); and by Josef Joffe, "Europe's American Pacifier," *Foreign Policy* 54 (Spring 1984): 68–69, and *The Limited Partnership: The United States and the Burdens of Alliance* (Cambridge, MA: Ballinger, 1987).

6. See Roger Morgan, *West European Politics Since 1945: The Shaping of the European Community* (New York: Capricorn Books, 1972), p. 5. Morgan also provides a useful treatment of this early period.

7. For a more detailed treatment of this period and the subsequent measures taken to create the European Communities, see Lieber, "The European Community," in A. Groth, R. Lieber, and N. Lieber, *Contemporary Politics: Europe* (Boston: Winthrop Publishers and Little, Brown, 1976), pp. 365ff. Also see John Pinder, *European Community: The Building of a Union* (New York: Oxford University Press, 1991); and Derek Unwin, *The Community of Europe: A History of European Integration Since 1945* (New York: Unwin, 1991).

8. On the American role in fostering the integration of Western Europe during the initial decade and a half after 1945, see Max Beloff, *The United States and the Unity of Europe* (New York: Vintage, 1963).

9. Leigh Bruce, "Europe's Locomotive," *Foreign Policy,* No. 78 (Spring 1990): 68–90, at pp. 73–74. For details, see also *From Lomé III to Lomé IV: Review of Aid From the Lomé Conventions at the End of 1991,* Report prepared by the Directorate-General of the Commission of the European Communities in Collaboration with the European Investment Bank (Brussels: Commission of the European Communities, DE 75, November 1992).

10. There was actually a lower percentage of common EC positions in UN voting in 1981 (the first year of Greek membership) than in 1975. See *Economist,* 4 December 1982, p. 52.

11. UK Office of the European Parliament, *Europe's Parliament and the Single Act,* (London: May 1989), p. 5. Also see Press and Information Office, Federal Republic of Germany, *European Political Cooperation,* 5th ed. (Bonn, 1988).

12. For a detailed official treatment of the blueprint for 1992 and the specific measures required for its implementation, see Commission of the European Communities, *Completing the Internal Market: White Paper from the Commission to the European Council, June 1985* (Luxembourg: Office for Official Publications of the European Communities, 1985). For thoughtful assessments of the Community's renewed impetus, see Stanley Hoffmann, "The European Community and 1992," *Foreign Affairs,* Vol. 68, No. 4 (Fall 1989): 27–47; Colin Crouch and David Marquand, eds., *The Politics of 1992: Beyond the Single European Market* (Oxford and Cambridge, MA: Basil Blackwell, 1990); and Alberta M. Sbragia, ed., *Euro-Politics: Institutions and Policymaking in the "New" European Community* (Washington, DC: Brookings, 1992).

13. The original study, known as the Cecchini Report, was done for the European Community in 1988. The higher estimate is by Richard Baldwin, in "The Growth Effects of 1992," *Economic Policy,* No. 9 (October 1989), cited in *The Economist,* 18 November 1989.

14. Speech in Bruges, Belgium, September 22, 1988, quoted in *New York Times*, 14 March 1989, p. 36.

15. For assessments of the Maastricht provisions, see *The Economist*, 1 May 1993, p. 54; and *Europe* (Washington, DC: The European Community), December/January 1993–1994, No. 332; also *From Single Market to European Union* (Brussels: Commission of the European Communities, 1992).

16. 35 percent were undecided and 24 percent opposed. Data from *Eurobarometer*, No. 39, June 1993, (Brussels: Commission of the European Communities), pp. 10 and 31.

17. 38 percent would have been indifferent and 11 percent "relieved." *Ibid.*, p. 9.

18. *Ibid.*, pp. 8–9.

19. For lucid accounts of the crisis, see *The Economist*, 23 October 1993, p. 25; and Robert J. Samuelson, "Europe's Economic Insanity," *Washington Post*, 5 August 1993.

20. Kenneth Courtis, economist at Deutsche Bank, quoted in Hobart Rowen, "Germany Needs to Loosen its Credit Reins," *Washington Post*, 31 October 1993.

21. The headline is from *France Soir*. Both quotations from *Washington Post*, 3 August 1993, p. A11.

22. Benjamin J. Cohen, "Beyond EMU: The Problems of Sustainability," *Economic and Politics*, Vol. 5, No. 2 (July 1993): 187–203, at pp. 200–201.

23. Respondents were asked if, "in the framework of a common foreign and defense policy, the European Community should intervene militarily in former Yugoslavia, in order to establish peace." Among the population of the 12 member countries, 55 percent were in favor, 28 percent against, and 17 percent did not know. Only in Denmark, Greece and East Germany were pluralities of respondents opposed. *Eurobarometer*, June 1993, p. A25.

24. Anthony Lewis, "Death of a Dream," *New York Times*, 29 March 1993, also includes the Glucksmann quote.

25. The Luxembourg compromise permits a member government to employ a veto if its "vital interests" are at stake. This determination is at the discretion of the individual country. See, for example, John Newhouse, *Collision in Brussels: The Common Market Crisis of 30 June 1965* (New York: Norton, 1967).

26. The proposed increase in the East European beef quota amounted to 550 metric tons, while total annual European consumption was 7 *million* metric tons. The incident and quotations are reported in *New York Times*, 7 September 1991, pp. 35 and 38.

27. "Explaining Cooperation Under Anarchy," in Oye, ed., *Cooperation Under Anarchy* (Princeton: Princeton University Press, 1986), pp. 18–19.

28. There is a substantial literature on the problems of "free-riding" and on collective action dilemmas. In addition to Axelrod's *The Evolution of Cooperation* (discussed in Chapter 11), see Mancur Olson and Richard Zeckhauser, "An Economic Theory of Alliances," *Review of Economics and Statistics* 48 (August 1966): 266–279; Charles Kindleberger, "Dominance and Leadership in the International Economy: Exploitation, Public Goods and Free Rides," *International Studies Quarterly* 25 (June 1981): 242–254; Mancur Olson, *The Logic of Collective Action* (Cambridge: Harvard University Press, 1965); and Russell Hardin, *Collective Action* (Baltimore: Johns Hopkins University Press for Resources for the Future, 1982).

29. Johan Galtung, *The European Community: A Superpower in the Making* (London: Allen & Unwin, 1973).

30. For a discussion of federalism, see Lieber, *Theory and World Politics*, pp. 39–41. A strong presentation of the argument for federalism can be found in Carl J. Friedrich, *Trends of Federalism in Theory and Practice* (New York: Praeger, 1968).

31. The seminal statement of functionalism is the 1943 work by David Mitrany, *A Working Peace System: An Argument for the Functional Development of International Organization* (London: Oxford University Press and the Royal Institute of International Affairs). For a more detailed analysis of functionalism, neofunctionalism, and their limits, see Lieber, *Theory and World Politics*, pp. 41–50.

32. The integration process is defined as one in which "political actors in several different national settings are persuaded to shift their loyalties and political activities toward a new center whose institutions possess or demand jurisdiction over the pre-existing national states." Haas, *The Uniting of Europe: Political, Social and Economic Forces, 1950–1957* (Stanford: Stanford University Press, 1958), p. 16. For a subsequent and more comprehensive treatment, see Haas, *Beyond the Nation-State: Functionalism and International Organization* (Stanford: Stanford University Press, 1969).

33. One of Haas's most important assumptions was that as pressure groups began to organize themselves across international borders as a means of influencing decisions that had previously been made only by national governments, group pressures would "spill over into the federal sphere and thereby add to the integrative impulse." See *The Uniting of Europe*, 1968 ed., p. xxxiii.

34. See "The 'Uniting of Europe' and the 'Uniting of Latin America,'" *Journal of Common Market Studies* 5 (June 1967): 327.

35. For a systematic treatment of the British case, see Lieber, "Interest Groups and Political Integration: British Entry into Europe," *American Political Science Review* 66 (March 1972): 53–67. On the broader argument against "painless transcendence" of the nation-state see Stanley Hoffmann, *Gulliver's Troubles, or the Setting of American Foreign Policy* (New York: McGraw-Hill, 1968), pp. 404–405.

36. Wayne Sandholtz and John Zysman identify the Europe 1992 initiative as a dramatic new start. They see this as having been caused by changes in international structure (a shift in the distribution of economic power resources, involving relative American decline and Japanese ascent), which caused European elites to rethink their roles and interests in the world, and by the policy leadership of the European commission. At the same time, they consider but reject an hypothesis that the internal dynamics of the integration process (described by functional or neofunctional theory) can account for the change. See "1992: Recasting the European Bargain," *World Politics*, Vol. XLII, No. 1 (October 1989): 95–128, at pp. 95–97.

37. Robert O. Keohane and Stanley Hoffmann, "Institutional Change in Europe in the 1980s," in Keohane and Hoffmann, eds., *The New European Community: Decisionmaking and Institutional Change* (Boulder: Westview, 1991), p. 15.

38. Ernst B. Haas, *Technocracy, Pluralism and the New Europe,*" in Stephen R. Graubard, ed., *A New Europe: Political, Economic and Social Forces, 1950–1957* (Boston: Houghton Mifflin, 1964), pp. 64 and 66, quoted in Keohane and Hoffmann, p. 15.

39. Keohane and Hoffman, p. 16.

40. Keohane and Hoffmann, pp. 17 and 19.

41. *The Uniting of Europe* 1968 ed., pp. xiii–xv. Haas also noted a certain disillusion toward the European experience:

> Regional integration in Western Europe has disappointed everybody: there is no federation, the nation-state behaves as if it were both obstinate and obsolete, and what once appeared to be a distinctive "supranational" style now looks more like a huge regional bureaucratic appendage to an intergovernmental conference in permanent session.

The Obsolescence of Regional Integration Theory, Research Series No. 25 (Berkeley: Institute of International Studies, University of California, 1975), p. 6.

42. Haas, *The Obsolescence of Regional Integration Theory*, p. 1.

chapter 14

The Search
for Economic Order

The notion of the state as a sovereign unit, dependent in the final analysis only on itself, has largely captured intellectual fashion. But today, no state can aspire to the degree of independence that such concepts have entailed.

—RICHARD ROSECRANCE[1]

Seldom has the discrepancy been wider between the homogeneity suggested by "interdependence" and the heterogeneity of the world we live in. . . . Logically it is wrong, and politically it is obscurantist to consider the world a unit and call it "interdependent."

—KENNETH WALTZ[2]

But the key reality of the post-1945 period is that states play in two arenas. The first is the traditional strategic and diplomatic one, in which there is no broad international consensus, and in which power tends to be used in ways it has always been, usually as a contest in which my gain is your loss. The second is the economic arena. . . . Here the logic of "anarchy" . . . is checked by the logic of, and a broad consensus on, an open global economy.

—STANLEY HOFFMANN[3]

This book has emphasized the way in which a formally anarchic environment shapes state behavior in international relations. The sometimes bitter realities of the international system have a great deal to do with the historical propensity toward conflict and war. In various ways, the problem has existed since antiquity, though in its present form it has more or less prevailed since the Peace of Westphalia in 1648.

This emphasis on the way in which harsh international realities condition behavior does, however, require qualification. First, a great deal of international activity does not involve conflict and war. As the previous chapters have demonstrated, the search for order is very much an intrinsic component of world politics. Efforts at creating or advancing international law and both global and regional forms of international order are a part of reality. Second, the practical aspects of state interaction have undergone important changes in the past half-century.

This chapter assesses the nature of international order in the economic realm. In doing so, it also examines whether a pattern of increased interdependence reflects a significant evolution in the realities of international relations.

THE INTERNATIONAL POLITICAL ECONOMY

Since the late 1960s, world events have stimulated a surge of attention to the impact of economic phenomena on international relations (and vice versa). For example, the dramatic August 1971 economic measures taken by President Richard Nixon severed the link of the U.S. dollar to gold and marked a break with an entire generation of postwar American economic leadership.[4] Subsequently, the oil shocks of 1973–1974 and 1979–1980 seemed to suggest major changes in global patterns of wealth and even of power. At the end of the 1980s, severe economic problems played a fundamental role in bringing about the collapse of the Soviet Union and profound changes in Eastern Europe.

More recently, problems of international competitiveness have come to the fore as the most prosperous economies have found themselves in an intensive international competition not only with each other but with emergent developing world economies such as that of China. Moreover, controversial but ultimately successful negotiations over the North American Free Trade Agreement (NAFTA) and the General Agreement on Tariffs and Trade (GATT) have illustrated the political importance of trade issues. Longer-term developments also contributed to this redirection of attention. These have included the increasingly rapid spread of high technology and global communications, the growth of multinational corporations, the rise of Japan as an economic superpower, the extraordinary success of newly industrializing countries in East Asia, problems of trade and debt in the developing world, and the impact of international monetary and economic trends on the advanced industrial states.

The term *international political economy* itself denotes a subject matter in which political and economic factors interact to shape relationships on an international scale. As Robert Gilpin has observed, whereas political scientists have tended to neglect the role of markets, economists often ignore the political context of events and in particular the importance of power.[5] Illustratively, the need to consider both economics and politics is crucial in making sense of the international politics of energy. To focus solely on the market mechanism and the effects of supply and demand results in the exclusion of key intervening variables: political and military events, the role of multinational actors such as OPEC, security considerations, and market imperfections. On the other hand, analysts who consider only political power fail to appreciate the means by which market forces shape the constraints within which policy choices are made.[6]

All the same, it would be well not to exaggerate the novelty of this approach. Economic phenomena often have been of vital importance in international relations. Thus the European discovery of the Americas, and the subsequent growth in gold and silver mining and trade in raw materials had an enormous impact on Europe of the sixteenth and seventeenth centuries. In addition, serious study of these matters is by no means new. For example, major thinkers of the eighteenth and nineteenth centuries—Adam Smith, David Ricardo, Thomas Robert Malthus, Karl Marx, John Stuart Mill, and others—based their work on the relationships between politics, economics, and moral philosophy.[7]

For a more recent era, Kenneth Waltz has noted that the share of exports plus imports as a percentage of gross national product was sometimes greater in the late nineteenth and early twentieth centuries than as recently as the mid 1970s. For example, in the half-decade before World War I, some 50 percent of Great Britain's GNP was accounted for by exports plus imports, compared with just 41 percent in 1975. For Japan, the respective figures were 33 percent and 23 percent. And even in the case of the United States, the 14 percent share of imports plus exports in GNP was the same in the decade from 1879 to 1898 as nearly a century later in 1975.[8]

On the other hand, the importance of foreign trade has increased enormously for the advanced industrial states, especially when compared with the lower levels of the mid 1940s to the mid 1960s, and in some cases of the 1920s and 1930s as well. Indeed, the importance of trade has grown since the mid 1970s. Moreover, there exist other important ways to measure interdependence beyond calculating trade as a percentage of GNP. Economists, for example, emphasize the integration of markets, as indicated by the comparable movement of prices in different regions. In addition, many economic and environmental phenomena make themselves felt far beyond the national borders within which events occur. Diverse elements of interdependence include inflation, balances in the production of manufactured goods or supply of raw materials, balance of trade and payments deficits, air and water pollution, population pressures, and a host of other factors.

In essence, international economics, foreign trade, and other facets of interdependence have gained greatly increased significance in recent decades. They constitute a realm in which traditional power politics criteria alone do not provide a sufficient basis for understanding. Illustratively, for Hans Morgenthau, economic matters were of secondary importance. He did depict economic strength as a vital component of state power, but by and large Morgenthau downplayed the autonomous importance of these issues in contrast to the high politics concerns of power and conflict.

The relationship of international political economy to problems of world order is particularly important. In realms such as trade, money, technology, communications, transportation, investment, and the like, a vast amount of interaction does take place on a daily basis. This interchange reflects extensive practical cooperation and order, the importance of which is not well grasped within the Hobbesian paradigm, and it requires specific attention.

MODERNIZATION AND THE TRANSFORMATION OF THE WORLD ECONOMY

While fundamental characteristics of the modern nation-state system can be traced back to 1648, and other basic dynamics of state-to-state relations can be observed among the city-states of Renaissance Italy or of Greece in the fifth century B.C., profound transformations have taken place in the twentieth century, especially in the postwar world. In particular, a series of economic and social transformations have reshaped the patterns of relations among nations. Their effect has been to make most countries increasingly interdependent. States have typically become much more sensitive to influences from outside their own borders as well as subject to greater constraints on their ability to act unilaterally in determining their own fate.

A number of authors argue that national economies have become extensions of a global and integrated world system with a logic of its own.[9] In this view, the notion of a closed national economy that still governs much thinking about international relations is outdated. Instead, there is now a "worldeconomy,"[10] characterized by far-reaching and complex transactions in money, trade, investment, technology, and other sectors, and whose elements extend far beyond the simple national interactions commonly thought of, for example, under the subject of free trade.

For example, in a period of a quarter-century, the value of world exports surged from $187 billion to more than $3.3 trillion per year, substantially exceeding the increase in gross domestic product.[11] Trade among the industrial democracies has been increasing at almost twice the rate of economic growth. Among developing countries, the expansion of trade has been even greater in relation to GNP. (See Table 14.1.) Moreover, for East Asia, the growth has been extraordinary, with exports rising by an average 10.2% percent per year between 1980 and 1991, and GNP per capita increasing by 6.1 percent.[12]

As another confirmation of the international economy's greatly increased importance to the industrial democracies, it is useful to compare the average of imports and exports as a proportion of gross domestic product over a 20-year period. From 1965 to 1985, this nearly doubled for many countries. For example, Belgium saw its foreign trade climb from 36 percent to 76 percent of gross domestic product, West Germany from 18 percent to 33 percent, Japan from 10 percent to

Table 14.1 GROWTH IN EXPORTS AND GROSS NATIONAL PRODUCT PER CAPITA

Country Group	Average 1980–1991
Industrial Market Economies:	
Export Growth	4.1%
GNP Growth (per capita)	2.3%
Developing Countries:	
Export Growth	4.1%
GNP Growth (per capita)	1.0%

Source: Adapted from the World Bank, *World Development Report 1993,* (New York: Oxford University Press, 1993), pp. 239 and 265.

15 percent.[13] What emerges is a pattern in which the smaller the country, the more open it is to international trade, in the sense that its economy is more deeply penetrated or interdependent. On the whole, the relative involvement of all the advanced economies has grown dramatically.

Nor is trade the only significant measure by which we can say that the world economy exhibits greatly increased interdependence. Monetary and financial relations have also become more important. For example, fluctuations in the exchange rates of national currencies have immense importance for the economic well-being of individual countries. Thus France and Britain, for example, have repeatedly encountered problems when they sought to expand their domestic economies. Their efforts to do so have triggered a surge in imports, balance of trade and payments deficits, a speculative outflow of capital, and severe downward pressure on their exchange rates.*

Monetary relationships have also had an increasing impact through large loans made by banks in the developed world to the developing countries. This capital flow took on vast dimensions after the 1973 oil shock, as developing countries borrowed huge sums to pay the quadrupled price for oil and to continue their economic growth. In that decade, they spent $350 billion to import oil—nearly three-fourths of the $460 billion increased indebtedness they incurred in this period.[14] At the same time, Western banks, flush with petrodollars (money deposited by the OPEC countries, which temporarily enjoyed hugely increased revenues), were more than glad to lend abroad.

However, a number of factors combined to create a growing problem between the borrowing countries and the banks making the loans.[15] Among these elements were a massive rise in total indebtedness, steep increases in interest rates (and hence in the burden of debt service) after 1979, the fall in oil revenues be-

---

*Other things being equal, a fall in its exchange rates makes a country's exports more competitive. However, this positive effect can be offset through other adverse economic consequences, including imported inflation (through higher prices for imports of raw materials, energy, and manufactured goods), as well as the need to raise domestic interest rates.

ginning in 1981–1982, and the severe recession of the early 1980s. In this emerging global debt crisis banks faced the risk of bankruptcy from loan defaults. At the same time major countries of the third world (Mexico, Brazil, Argentina, Egypt, the Philippines) were confronting the risks of insolvency.

Banks and international institutions thus encountered the problem of whether to write off bad loans or to lend new money to restructure the existing debt and provide for the developing countries to make their interest payments. Not only was the solvency of the banks a potential issue—and some of them faced severe risks in the event major debtors were to default—but the problems reverberated far more widely. These linked third-world governments, which feared massive political protests (e.g., in Egypt in reaction to attempts at reducing bread subsidies), and exporters from the developed world, who found their markets painfully affected because of the reduced ability of developing countries to purchase their goods with hard currency.

Throughout much of the world, social, political, and economic modernization has ushered in an increasingly globalized economy. The above illustrations in trade, exchange rates, and loans to the developing world provide examples of a pervasive web of interdependence. These relationships have not taken place at random, let alone under circumstances of near anarchy. Instead, they reflect the existence of a series of formal international institutions created during the early postwar period.[16] Many of these bodies were given impetus through the initial leadership of the United States. Among the most important of these have been the following:

The General Agreement on Tariffs and Trade (GATT), established in 1947 among the industrial democracies; provides the organizational basis for regulations governing trade, and for promoting negotiations aimed at reducing international tariff barriers; membership of more than 100 countries.

The International Monetary Fund (IMF), created at the 1944 Bretton Woods conference, and expanded to more than 150 member states; promotes international financial stability, provides short-term loans to countries in temporary balance-of-payments difficulties, often on the basis of stringent conditions for reforms in domestic economic policies.

The World Bank, institutional partner of the IMF, originally called the International Bank for Reconstruction and Development; makes long-term loans to promote infrastructure and economic growth in developing countries.

Through these and other institutions, public and private, networks of transactions link governments, firms, and individuals. Economic interdependence is also evident in a huge volume of related activities. These include foreign investment, the operation of multinational corporations, the diffusion of technology, extensive communications links, transportation (particularly inexpensive air travel), tourism, and educational and cultural exchanges. On the whole, this activity provides vivid evidence that interdependence has become a practical reality. The broader implications of interdependence, however, together with the manner in which it is understood, require closer attention.

ECONOMIC PENETRATION OF THE NATION-STATE

The policies and actions of individual countries are often discussed as though each was a wholly self-contained entity. This portrayal extends to the operations of states in the international environment as well as to their domestic policies. Yet most states are penetrated in ways that contradict any simple "billiard ball" conception. Other things being equal, this penetration is relatively greater for smaller states than for larger ones, and for those with market economies than for those with nonmarket (i.e., Communist and state-controlled) economies.

Consider the case of the steel industries within the advanced industrial countries. These had long been considered the very basis of national industrial capacity, yet since the late 1970s they have been in dire trouble, with plant closings, bankruptcies, and massive unemployment. Moreover, these troubles have caused severe dislocation for steel-producing regions. The United States, the European Common Market countries, and Japan have each sought to grapple with their difficulties nationally, but the origins of the problem lie mostly beyond their borders. As late as 1970, some 85 percent or more of these countries' steel capacity was being utilized. However, the pace of global economic development has caused the rapid expansion of steel capacity in Latin America, Asia, Eastern Europe, and elsewhere. As a result, world steel capacity doubled between 1960 and the early 1970s, growing from 420 million tons per year to 835 million tons.[17] By 1983, global capacity had risen to over one billion tons per year, well beyond the demand for steel. Thus, by the mid-1980s, only 65 percent of world capacity was being utilized—and well under 60 percent in the United States and Europe—leaving huge portions of the industry shut down or else subjected to fierce price competition from cheap foreign steel in a glutted world market. As a consequence, by 1991 American steel production had fallen by 30 percent compared with the level a decade earlier. In short, layoffs and plant closings in the Ruhr area of Germany, in Pittsburgh, in Northern France, or even in Japan, resulted as much or more from actions taken in Taiwan, Brazil, and South Korea, as they did from decisions of local firms or of governments in Bonn, Washington, Paris, or Tokyo.

These problems of foreign competition exist not only in steel, but in many other manufacturing sectors, such as textiles, petrochemicals, automobiles, and electronics. Agriculture provides yet another example of how decisions in one country impact directly on people far beyond its borders. For example, in the mid 1970s, the European Community was a net importer of grain, since it produced only 94 percent of its domestic consumption. However, a decade later, through the expansion of subsidy programs, it produced 105 percent[18] of its grain needs, thus becoming a major net exporter. By encouraging a grain supply glut, and thus helping to cause a fall in world prices, European agricultural subsidies have affected farmers as far away as Iowa, Argentina, and Australia. Indeed, by 1992 European farmers earned as much from subsidies as from farming.[19] Of course, such policies are by no means confined to Europe. Through different means, the United States and Japan also provide significant subsidies and protection for their own domestic agriculture.

Interest rates, currency parities, inflation, foreign debt, trade competition, oil prices, and a wide range of other economic phenomena often originate with or are shaped by external events. In the post–World War II era, most governments among the industrial democracies have assumed responsibility for successful management of both a welfare state and a partially managed economy. They are held accountable for the economic well-being of their population, and are judged by their electorates on the basis of criteria that include their performance in dealing with economic growth, inflation, and unemployment. Yet the expanded scope of international interdependence has caused the levers of control over many of these outcomes to be shaped as much or more by decisions and events taking place externally as by those within a country's own borders. As the experience of the oil decade has vividly illustrated, inflation, unemployment, industrial dislocation, and even political instability can be dramatically affected by events that a government does not control and can scarcely even influence.

While interdependence imposes constraints, most countries derive major economic benefits from this involvement. Moreover, there are potential political benefits as well, not least in providing influence vis-à-vis other countries with which a nation interacts.

During the past generation it has become increasingly clear that a country's ability to insure the military security of its population is jeopardized by the enormous risks posed by a major conflict or a hypothetical nuclear war. Yet the realities of interdependence are bringing about an analogous development in the economic realm. In essence, national ability to ensure economic security has become subject to major constraints owing to both interdependence and the economic penetration of individual societies. As evidence of this, the case of France is instructive. This important but middle-sized European power has consistently sought to achieve the maximum degree of autonomy in its foreign and domestic policies, yet the record of recent decades shows that even France has found its room for maneuver increasingly confined.

CONSTRAINTS ON NATIONAL POLICY: FRANCE

The pattern of economic constraint is greatest for those countries that are smallest and most open. By contrast, it is relatively lower for the largest states, since they tend to have correspondingly greater resources and opportunities for self-sufficiency. Yet interdependence causes even a substantial middle-sized power such as France to find its freedom of action restricted in key realms such as economics, energy, and security.

For France, as for other medium-sized countries, the evolution of a postwar international role and of the limits on room to maneuver have been shaped by long-term changes in the international environment. Among these shifts the following developments have been fundamental.[20]

First, there has been a decline in the relative power of the countries of Europe. Initially, this stemmed from Soviet-American hegemony in the immediate post–World War II world. Subsequently, however, an increasing global diffusion of power has resulted in growing importance for other states and regions. In more recent decades, countries in the developing world and among the NICs have become significant international actors. While Western Europe's importance remains enormous, the area no longer possesses the role it held in the pre–World War II era. For France, a leading player in balance-of-power coalitions on the eve of both world wars, the relative decline has been evident.

Second, military power of a "world class" variety has come to rest on massive continental resources and population bases as well as on strategic nuclear forces. While successive governments have positioned France adroitly in terms of the acquisition and development of effective nuclear forces, these are not of the same magnitude as those possessed by the United States and Russia. In addition, the costs of developing national nuclear weapons have caused tradeoffs vis-à-vis conventional forces. Choices in resource allocation have also limited the amounts available for domestic purposes. Here, the contrast between France and Japan is striking. During the 1970s and 1980s, France devoted approximately 4 percent of its annual GNP to defense and even in the early 1990s was still spending some 3.5 percent. By comparison, Japan typically has spent about 1 percent, thus preserving a greater proportion of its resources for investment and economic expansion.

Third, there has been a globalization of the international economy. France has struggled to compete with other industrialized democracies of its size and stature, as well as with newer players. Although French performance has been impressive for much of the postwar period, the country still does not possess the overall economic weight and power of the United States, Japan, or Germany.

Finally, there has been France's growing participation in the European and international economy, particularly during and after the presidency of Charles de Gaulle (1958–1969). The increased opening of the French economy to a Western-dominated but global market oriented economic system represented a major shift away from the more sheltered economy of the interwar years. While the reorientation was essential as part of the effort to provide a broader basis for French strength in the postwar world, it made France more interdependent and thus more sensitive to changes in the international environment. The impact of these changes ultimately constrained the freedom of maneuver available not only to de Gaulle, but also to his neo-Gaullist, conservative, and Socialist successors.

Despite economic success, French governments have repeatedly experienced restrictions on their freedom of action resulting from the international environment. These limits are all the more striking in view of the fact that states such as France with strong traditions of political centralization are in a better position to pursue effective policies than are states with more fragmented institutions or authority, even when the latter possess greater power.[21] The dimensions of the

French experience are evident in specific issue areas such as energy and economics.

Consider the case of oil—a strategic commodity, the price of which is denominated in dollars. Long after the twin shocks of the 1970s, France continued to be affected. During the years from 1981 to 1984, and despite a decline in the world price of oil from $34 to $29 per barrel, the simultaneous appreciation of the dollar caused the cost in French francs to increase painfully. By one estimate, the real price paid by France per barrel of imported oil climbed 22.5 percent from the fourth quarter of 1980 to the first quarter of 1985. By contrast, the cost for the United States actually fell by 24.9 percent.[22]

France only began to experience significant reductions in the cost of oil imports as the result of two developments—both of which originated outside its borders and over which it had very little influence. The first of these was a decline in the exchange rate of the dollar in 1985 and 1986. The second was a plunge in world oil prices. The lower dollar and falling oil prices, along with the cumulative effects of the changes in economic policy adopted by the Mitterrand government in 1982–1983, contributed to easing France's balance-of-payments constraint and stimulating noninflationary economic growth. However, the long-term course of the dollar and of world oil prices continued to be dictated by forces external to France.

Partly as a consequence of this vulnerability, French policies on terrorism and Middle East matters have sometimes been affected. For example, in December 1993, the French government released and expelled two Iranians being held for the murder of an Iranian dissident in Geneva. Switzerland had requested their extradition under the terms of the European Extradition Convention of 1957 and a 1977 European convention to combat terrorism, and a French court had already approved the Swiss request. However, in an action clearly reflecting the anxiety of Prime Minister Edouard Balladur's conservative government, the men were released without explanation. The action drew bitter criticism from Switzerland as well as from the French press and opposition parties, who complained that it would ultimately produce more terrorist blackmail. However, comparable actions had been taken by the previous Socialist government, which in 1990 had pardoned an Iranian convicted of attempting to kill an exiled former Iranian Prime Minister, and by Gaullist and Conservative governments in the 1970s. These actions reflected both a sense of vulnerability to terrorism, for example as experienced in a wave of bombings that hit Paris in 1986, as well as a desire to maintain a favorable relationship with a large oil-producing country and potential market for French exports.[23]

Constraints have been evident in the realm of economic policy as well.[24] For example, consider the experience of France's democratic socialist government (1981–1985). After taking office in mid 1981, President François Mitterrand's government stimulated the economy in order to reduce unemployment and pay for improvements in social services. Almost at once, however, the effort encountered grave obstacles. The most serious of these was that American and global economic recovery did not materialize when expected. The initial effects of

Reaganomics, including high U.S. interest rates and a rising dollar, together with the propensity of the French economy to satisfy expanding consumer demand by rapidly pulling in imports, exacerbated a series of difficulties for France. One of these problems was capital flight, which occurred for domestic as well as international reasons. France's other economic troubles included high inflation, balance-of-payments problems, and a weakened franc. In less than a year, the government found itself with little alternative to curtailing its economic expansion and social programs, devaluing the franc, and moving toward policies of austerity. These June 1982 measures proved inadequate, and a year later even more stringent actions were adopted.

The increased value of the dollar in relation to the French franc also imposed serious costs upon the French economy.[25] In 1982 alone, these effects accounted for a 1 percent reduction in France's economic growth rate, a 3 percent to 5 percent increase in inflation, and a large increase in the foreign trade deficit.[26] The difficulty resulted from interaction between policies and problems specific to France on the one hand, and from broader features of the international economy on the other. France faced the need to bring down inflation and to adapt its industrial structure to the requirements of technological change. As long as France's major trading and monetary partners did not also embark on a path of economic expansion, the room for maneuver of the Socialist government was painfully limited. This was not only a matter of American policies. In the first year of the Mitterrand government, France's trade deficit with the Federal Republic of Germany increased 80 percent.[27] Without sustainable expansion and economic growth, the Socialist government could not generate the added revenue to pay for the social objectives of its program. In the end, it was left with no viable alternative but to jettison much of the agenda with which it had come to office and which had been endorsed by the French electorate. Somewhat poignantly Mitterrand observed, "We are not masters of the international crisis that is hitting us."[28]

During the latter half of the 1980s, France's economic performance improved significantly, but it did so within the confines of an international economic environment in which French governments, both conservative and socialist, accepted prevailing constraints.

Subsequently, however, France again found its domestic economy disrupted by external causes. As analyzed at length in Chapter 13, the huge costs of Germany's October 1990 unification eventually led the Bundesbank to raise interest rates. Germany's partners in the European Community had little choice but to raise their own rates in response. The resultant recession hit the French economy, where unemployment soared to 12 percent, its highest level in a generation. As the French franc came under increasing pressure on foreign exchange markets, the Bank of France spent vast sums in an unsuccessful attempt to defend the currency, and in August 1993 a currency crisis caused the Exchange Rate Mechanism to be abandoned in all but name. In this case, a series of difficulties—high interest rates, recession, a weakened franc, unemployment—had their origins in circumstances outside the boundaries of France and over which the French state had little influence.

The French case illustrates how the industrial democracies experience a very real problem of limits on national policy. They are thus faced with a need to manage cooperation. The experiences of France and the other European countries show that it remains difficult for them to pursue individual policies that vary significantly from the directions being followed by their major partners.

CONSTRAINTS ON NATIONAL POLICY: THE UNITED STATES

Until well into the 1960s, the United States was relatively less affected by economic interdependence than other industrial democracies. (Among other major countries, the Soviet Union remained far more closed, or autarkic, which was characteristic of its Marxist-Leninist political system and the legacy of Stalin.) America's principal industries enjoyed positions of international dominance, and the domestic United States market was not deeply penetrated by exports from abroad. Since that time, however, American preeminence has been challenged.

The impact of change is evident in some key statistics. In a single decade, from 1965 to 1975, the importance of international trade doubled in proportion to the American economy. During that period, imports plus exports as a percentage of gross national product grew from 7 percent to 14 percent.[29] Although in the late 1940s America produced nearly half the world's goods, this share declined sharply over the following 40 years. Moreover, during the 1950s, just one-fourth of United States goods were subject to international competition; some 30 years later the figure had grown to three-fourths.

As a result of changes such as these, the United States has become substantially more integrated into the world economy. Not that the United States had previously been uninvolved, but the domestic impact of the international economy is now felt within the United States with previously unknown intensity. In some important sectors, American industries have been overtaken by their competitors, and evidence of basic economic distress is considerable. For example, significant numbers of workers have been displaced by international competition and the spread of new technologies, and entire communities have been disrupted by plant closings in industries such as steel, automobiles, mining, and food processing.

Many of the above examples concern the impact of trade, but monetary interdependence has also had a pervasive impact. Indeed, it has magnified the effects of international competition. From 1981 to 1985, as a consequence largely of high real interest rates at home, the value of the dollar rose in spectacular fashion. By some calculations the dollar was overvalued by as much as 50 percent or more, in terms of the amount of foreign currency (Japanese yen, French francs, German marks) for which it could be exchanged. While this was advantageous for Americans as tourists and as consumers of foreign goods, American industries reeled under the shock of foreign competition. The United States' firms not only found their home markets invaded by products with which they had difficulty competing on the basis of price, but many of their traditional export markets (e.g., for heavy machinery, agricultural commodities, paper products) were lost because the inflated value of the dollar made their goods uncompetitive.

By one estimate, each $1 billion of the trade deficit resulted in a loss of 25,000 jobs within the United States. With a trade deficit of some $170 billion in 1986, the impact on American unemployment could thus be roughly estimated at some 4.25 million persons. However, after the exchange rate of the dollar peaked in early 1985, it underwent a substantial decline. This helped to improve the competitiveness of American exports and reduce the trade deficit to an estimated $114 billion in 1990. The change contributed to a reduction in unemployment from 7.0 percent in 1986 to a low point of 5.2 percent in 1989.[30]

With the huge expansion of trade and financial flows, currency exchange rates have become a key component of a country's competitiveness. The term has implications that are not only narrowly economic but affect a country's long-term prosperity, economic strength, and even political and military standing. As defined by Joan Spero, competitiveness is:

> The ability of an entity to operate efficiently and productively in relation to other similar entities. Competitiveness has been used most recently to describe the overall economic performance of a nation, particularly its level of productivity, its ability to export goods and services and its maintenance of a high standard of living for its citizens.[31]

Although other factors such as technology, education and training, and worker productivity are also significant, and are much more subject to domestic determination, exchange rates are often more visible and more readily altered.

For example, even after the American dollar began to decline from its peak rates of the mid 1980s against the Japanese yen, many observers continued to consider it overvalued. During the early 1990s, a combination of factors, including interest rates, the continuing American balance-of-payments deficit, and government policies caused the dollar to decline further against the yen. By the summer of 1994, one dollar was worth approximately 100 yen—a level less than half of what it had been a decade earlier. This change helped to make American-manufactured automobiles less expensive in comparison to comparable Japanese cars, and thus more competitive in the marketplace. As a group, the large U.S. companies began to regain some of the market share they had lost to Japanese imports during the previous two decades. Other factors also contributed to this result, including improved technology and quality control, better worker productivity, and a greater willingness on the part of industry leaders to restore competitiveness. However, the distinction between domestic and imported automobiles was becoming blurred. For example, one of the best-selling Japanese cars, the Honda Accord, was actually manufactured in Ohio, and other Japanese and German firms were also turning to greater use of assembly plants in states such as Tennessee and Kentucky. Meanwhile, among a number of imported models selling under American names, the Ford Crown Victoria was assembled in Canada, the General Motors Geo Prizm was actually a Toyota Corolla manufactured in Fremont California, and Chevrolet's Geo Metro was made by Suzuki and Isuzu.[32]

From these examples, it is evident that interdependence is no mere abstraction, but something which has an immediate impact on the lives of many Americans. To understand how this change took place, it is necessary to begin by examining the remarkable leadership role the United States played in the post-1945 world.

AMERICA'S HEGEMONIC ROLE IN THE POST–WORLD WAR II WORLD

The United States emerged from World War II as the preeminent military and economic power in the non-Communist world. Contemporary scholarship on international relations has increasingly adopted the term *hegemony* to describe the United States' position during this immediate postwar period, although other students of the subject have preferred the concept of *leadership*, because of its less pejorative connotations.[33] American leadership provided the basis for establishing a series of major institutional arrangements and "regimes" (rules of the game)[34] for international cooperation. The most important of these included the Atlantic alliance, the General Agreement on Tariffs and Trade (GATT), the International Monetary Fund, and the World Bank.

American Hegemony and the Diffusion of Power

The United States emerged from World War II as the world's preeminent economic and military power. However, America's international position resulted from a combination of factors, many of them external. For example, in the military realm the United States in 1945 held a paramount role. It had more men under arms than any country on earth. It possessed a nuclear monopoly. Its World War II adversaries, Germany and Japan, were prostrate, while its principal allies (Britain and the Soviet Union) were either exhausted or devastated by six years of war. By the late 1960s, however, the Soviet Union had attained strategic nuclear parity with the United States, and had developed massive conventional forces. Meanwhile, France, Britain, and China acquired nuclear weapons, and a series of important regional actors emerged (India, Nigeria, Iran, Egypt, and Brazil, among others), each with real or potential power of its own.

Comparable shifts took place in the economic realm. After 1945, the United States accounted for nearly half the world's manufacturing production. Indeed, as late as 1953, America accounted for 44.8 percent of the world total. By the late 1950s, however, Western Europe and Japan had recovered from the ravages of war and had begun the process that would make them formidable economic competitors of the United States. Ironically, this development represented a success for American postwar policies, which sought to promote economic recovery abroad by means of Marshall Plan aid, containment of the Soviet Union, and the creation of international mechanisms for trade, money, and investment. As a con-

Table 14.2 PERCENTAGE SHARE OF WORLD MANUFACTURING PRODUCTION

Year	USA	Britain	Japan	Developed Countries	Third World
1953	44.7%	8.4%	2.9%	93.5%	6.5%
1963	35.1	6.4	5.1	91.5	8.2
1973	33.0	4.9	8.8	90.1	9.9
1980	31.5	4.0	9.1	88.0	12.0

Source: Adapted from Paul Bairoch, "International Industrialization Levels from 1750 to 1980," *Journal of European Economic History* 11 (Fall 1982): 304.

sequence, the U.S. share of world industrial production declined to 35.1 percent in 1963, 32.6 percent in 1973, and 31.2 percent in 1980.[35] (See Table 14.2.)

Other indicators showed comparable changes in the relative economic position of the United States. They include the percentage of gross world product, share of world trade, and amount of gold and hard currency reserves, among other indicators.[36]

The change in America's economic position was not solely a consequence of European and Japanese recovery. In fact, the diffusion of economic power has been global. Many of the newly industrializing countries (Taiwan, South Korea, Singapore, etc.) have emerged as fierce economic competitors in their own right, rapidly moving from primary products into semimanufactured goods such as textiles, then into basic industries such as steel, and subsequently into more sophisticated products such as ships, automobiles, consumer electronics, and computers.

The diffusion of power has also encompassed raw materials. America became a net importer of oil as early as 1948 and became increasingly dependent and then vulnerable as a result of its increased oil imports.

The impact of these changes meant that the United States no longer possessed the same relative position as at the end of World War II, even though America continued to be the one country that was simultaneously an economic superpower (unlike the Soviet Union and China) and a military one (in contrast to Western Europe and Japan).

These developments gave rise to a debate about whether the United States was entering a cycle of imperial decline, reminiscent of the fate of world powers in previous historical epochs. British historian Paul Kennedy, in *The Rise and Fall of The Great Powers*,[37] drew comparisons with the cases of Spain after the seventeenth century and Great Britain in the early and mid twentieth century. For Kennedy, the United States appeared to exhibit the problem of imperial overstretch, in which an excess of commitments over resources led to a precipitous decline in the basis of a country's power.

Other interpretations have suggested a more complex picture. In explaining the long-term causes of hegemonic decline, Robert Gilpin has drawn comparisons from the historical experiences of Athens, Rome, Holland, Britain, and the United States. Gilpin formulates propositions to explain these cycles of decline.[38] In particular, he finds the causes to lie in three key areas: external burdens of leadership, internal tendencies toward rising domestic consumption, and the international diffusion of technology. Together, these factors work to weaken the foundations of hegemonic power.

Gilpin's criteria can be applied to the experience of the United States. First, the initial costs of containment of the Soviet Union, and then the globalization of containment (with the ultimate overextension in Vietnam), coupled with the demands of alliance leadership, placed a disproportionate burden on the United States. Illustratively, during the 1960s and 1970s, the United States spent an average of 7.4 percent of GDP on defense, in contrast with West Germany's 3.9 percent and Japan's 0.9 percent.[39] Moreover, defense spending remained relatively high, with a military buildup beginning at the end of the Carter administration and expanding under the Reagan administration. In 1985, for example, the U.S. figure of 6.5 percent was more than double that of Germany (3.2 percent) and more than six times that of Japan (1.0 percent) Expenditure declined after the end of the Cold War. In 1992 it was still 5.3 percent,[40] though both the Bush and Clinton administrations undertook significant force reductions, with the consequence that spending was to be reduced below 4 percent by the mid 1990s.

Second, a pattern of increasing domestic consumption is also evident. During the 1960s and 1970s, America's annual rate of government and private consumption averaged 73.9 percent of GNP, compared with 68.8 percent for West Germany and 63.1 percent for Japan. At the same time, investment (as measured by fixed capital formation) grew by 17.6 percent in the United States, in contrast with 24.1 percent in Germany and 32.7 percent in Japan. Moreover, the pattern of increasing consumption in relation to investment tended to accelerate during the first half of the 1980s, with some 3 percent of GDP represented by international borrowing to finance domestic consumption.

As a consequence of those trends, between 1970 and 1989 real productivity in Japan increased by almost 100 percent and in Western Europe by 50 percent, but productivity in the United States rose by less than 20 percent.[41]

Third, the diffusion of American technology has proceeded on a global basis. In the military realm, American advances in nuclear weapons, missiles, aircraft, armour, electronics, and other areas were—after a lag of years—often matched by the Soviets (whether through their own development efforts or through covert means). While the subsequent collapse of the USSR left Russia a far less formidable competitor in the most technologically advanced weapons, the United States remains vulnerable to Moscow's strategic nuclear arsenal. Elsewhere, weapons capabilities have spread widely among allies and potential adversaries. Missile and chemical weapons technologies have become widely dispersed, and countries such as China, North Korea, and Iran have either acquired advanced military technologies or in some cases are actually exporting them to other countries. It remains true, however, that mere possession of advanced weapons does not necessarily bring with it the capability to use them effectively. As Operation Desert Storm demonstrated, the United States retains a considerable edge both in technology and in the training, personnel, and organizational skills needed to use modern weapons decisively. Nonetheless, even the diffusion of technology that is less than state of the art, and its use under less than optimal conditions, can still have a deterrent effect by making it more costly for outside actors such as the United States to intervene at a relatively low human and material cost.

In civilian sectors, an even more rapid spread of technology has taken place, owing to the operation of multinational corporations, licensing agreements, and the development of a global scientific community. American science continues to play a leading role in many of the most important areas of basic research (as evident in the winning of Nobel prizes, for example), but the spread and implementation of these advances has nonetheless proceeded at a rapid rate. Indeed, it has not been at all unusual for foreign firms (often effectively managed, adept at quality control, and attentive to consumer tastes) to take the lead in marketing a commercially viable technology that had its origin in the United States.

Despite these changes, it is important not to overstate the implications for America's international position. For one thing, Gilpin's criteria leave open the matter of timing. That is, even if a decline process is at work, the process may take varying periods—decades or even generations. Moreover, Gilpin sees existing international systems or configurations of power continuing in their existing patterns until such time as the rising power of others, and war, bring about a new distribution of power. But whatever the change in America's relative situation, no alternative claimant to comparable status has yet emerged, and the risks of war in a nuclear age are so terrible that the prospect of system change resulting from war remains remote.

Moreover, other authors have suggested more basic conceptual problems with the entire "decline" debate. As Joseph Nye observes, the use of a 1945 baseline from which to measure the American role is misleading because it represents a temporary peak based on the unique circumstances prevailing at the end of World War II. Nye and other authors reject the comparison with Great Britain and note that since the late 1960s the United States has—by various measurements—continued to account for more than one-fifth of global economic product and a comparable proportion of world military expenditures.[42] While acknowledging important changes in world politics, as well as significant problems in domestic economic policies, Nye argues that it is not clear the remedy is American withdrawal from international commitments, as opposed to changes in national policies on taxation, the budget deficit, education, and other matters.

Implications for International Cooperation

Studies of British preeminence during the nineteenth century and of America's leadership after 1945 have emphasized the role of a global power in providing the basis for international stability and cooperation. In the words of Robert Gilpin:

> The Pax Britannica and Pax Americana, like the Pax Romana, ensured an international system of relative peace and security. Great Britain and the United States created and enforced the rules of a liberal international economic order. British and American policies fostered free trade and freedom of capital movements . . . supplied the key currency and managed the international monetary system. . . . The benefits to them of a secure status quo, free trade, foreign investment, and a well-functioning international monetary system were greater than the associated costs.[43]

By contrast, the Depression of 1929 and its aftermath were disastrous because Britain was unable and the United States unwilling to assume the responsibilities of a global stabilizer. Had they been responsibly exercised, the obligations of the leader would have included furnishing an outlet for goods, maintaining capital flow to borrowers, serving as the lender of last resort in times of financial crisis, maintaining the structure of exchange rates, and coordinating macroeconomic policies.[44]

These analyses have given rise to a *theory of hegemonic stability*. Its two main propositions are that "order in world politics is typically created by a single dominant power" (in essence, the establishment of regimes usually depends on hegemony), and that "the maintenance of order requires continued hegemony."[45] In light of the partial erosion of American hegemony and the accompanying diffusion of power, international cooperation may become more difficult—even while the need for it remains at least as great as before.

One group of analysts (realists) suggests that international cooperation will become more difficult. Their argument rests on the assumption that the diffusion of power undermines the ability of anyone to create order and pay the necessary costs of doing so. A second group (globalists or institutionalists) suggests that the greater need for policy coordination created by increased interdependence should lead to enhanced cooperation.

In evaluating the positions of realists and globalists, modifications to the theory of hegemonic stability have been suggested. Robert Keohane argues that while cooperation initially may be fostered by hegemony, the existence of hegemonic stability is neither a necessary nor sufficient condition for order. Instead, he suggests that cooperation can take place in world politics despite the absence of hegemony. This possibility results from shared interests, expectations, and practices, as well as from the momentum created by the existing international institutions and regimes.[46]

This approach, and that of a number of other authors, has been characterized as *neoliberal institutionalism*.[47] Whereas realists tend to hold a less optimistic view concerning opportunities for cooperation and the role of international institutions, neoliberal institutionalists consider that these organizations can foster cooperation among states. Although they do accept a number of realist arguments, including a recognition of anarchy as an obstacle to cooperation, they hold that realism tends to exaggerate conflict and that it fails to recognize the independent role of international institutions in enlarging cooperation.

The concepts of hegemonic stability and international regime have influenced the terms of discussion among scholars of interdependence. These ideas possess important heuristic value, inasmuch as they stimulate thought about the conditions for achieving and maintaining international cooperation. Even so, a number of criticisms of the concepts have been made.[48] These focus on problems of definition (e.g., how do we know when and whether a regime exists?). A number of studies have suggested modifications of some initial assumptions about Britain's role in the nineteenth century. Moreover, events of the 1960s and 1970s present a sometimes contradictory picture. For example, GATT and the international trading regime encountered serious problems at the height of American hegemony in the 1960s (as Keohane acknowledges).

Another case in point concerns the creation of the International Energy Agency in 1974, which reestablished an energy regime among the Western countries and Japan. This regime creation did not occur because of institutional momentum or the perceived need for cooperation among the players acting in their own interests in the absence of hegemony.[49] Instead, as accounts of the period, including Secretary of State Henry Kissinger's memoirs, make clear,[50] the United States used its economic and military predominance—in short, its hegemony—in pressuring the allies into agreement.

INTERDEPENDENCE: DIVERGENT VIEWS

Much thinking about interdependence was shaped by events of the early and mid 1970s. During that period, America's détente with the Soviet Union, recognition of China, and withdrawal from Vietnam reflected a series of changes in superpower relations. Along with these phenomena, the rise in importance of matters such as trade, debt, and the role of OPEC caused many observers to question basic understandings about contemporary world politics. Specifically, they began to ask whether prevailing assumptions about power politics, East-West conflict, and related matters would be superseded by North-South issues and an expanding agenda in which interdependence increasingly dominated. However, the subsequent decline of détente, reduction in the power of OPEC, eruption of conflicts such as the Iran-Iraq war, and intensified problems of economic development caused some of the initial assumptions about interdependence to be reexamined.

At the outset of the 1990s, however, in light of revolutionary changes in Eastern Europe, the end of the Cold War, and the increasing importance of trade, questions of interdependence gained renewed prominence.

What, then, is the connection between interdependence and international order? Some interpretations identify enhanced cooperation as a virtually inevitable outcome of increased interdependence. Others regard the basic elements of state primacy and the obstacles as almost unchanged since the time of Thucydides.

The Globalist or "Institutionalist" Perspective

Several observers have concluded that interdependence leads, almost ineluctably, to cooperation. These approaches suggest that modernization, industrialization, mass consumption, the communications revolution, and a broad increase in the importance of economic issues mean that international relations no longer conform to models of power politics and of anarchy in the interactions among states.

For example, we are told that "The emerging international system may, however, reflect far more than the breakdown in old social values. In many ways it reflects a growing international consensus concerning fundamental human and political values."[51] Others hold that common economic interests create a demand for international institutions and rules.[52] Another scholar argues that an intellectual consensus of some three centuries' duration (i.e., since the Peace of Westphalia) has broken down in the past decade, and with it the predominance of a realist and state-centric tradition of examining world politics.[53]

Modifications of Interdependence

Another group of approaches represents a view of interdependence tempered by recognition of the more enduring aspects of realism and of power politics. Richard Rosecrance, for example, observes:

> ... after 1945 ... The risks of trying to take new territory through military invasion mounted while the alternative of development through economic processes and trade heralded new rewards for a peaceful strategy. The shift toward an international trading world gained momentum and adherents while raising important questions about the traditional military and territorial orientation of Western and industrial states.[54]

The author goes on to describe this as a *partial* shift, in acknowledging that the dominant orientation of the international system still remains "military-political and territorial in character."

Keohane and Nye developed the term *complex interdependence* to reflect their dissatisfaction with more simple conceptions of interdependence. They define complex interdependence as a model, or ideal type, of an international system designed to contrast with another ideal type, the realist model, which they see as often inadequate for analyzing the politics of interdependence.[55] They identify realism as resting on three assumptions. First, "states as coherent units are the dominant actors in world politics." Second, "force is a usable and effective instrument of policy." Third, there is "a hierarchy of issues in world politics, headed by questions of military security: the 'high politics' of military security dominates the 'low politics' of economic and social affairs."[56]

To this realist model, Keohane and Nye contrast the notion of complex interdependence. Its three main characteristics are as follows: First, "multiple channels connect societies." These include not only formal governmental arrangements, but informal links among both governmental and nongovernmental elites, transnational organizations such as multinational corporations, and an array of other channels. Second, there is an "absence of hierarchy among issues." This means that matters of military security do not consistently predominate on the agenda. Instead, different issues arise at different times, many from domestic sources, and the separations between domestic and foreign policy matters become blurred. Third, "military force is not used by governments toward other governments within the region, or on issues, when complex interdependence prevails." However, force may still be important under other circumstances, even though it may be irrelevant to disagreements over economic issues.[57]

It is important to note, however, that Keohane and Nye do not argue that complex interdependence faithfully reflects world political reality. Indeed, in the words of the authors, "Quite the contrary: both it and the realist portrait are ideal types. Most situations will fall somewhere between these two extremes. Sometimes, realist assumptions will be accurate, or largely accurate but frequently, complex interdependence will provide a better portrayal of reality."[58]

Marxist and Neo-Marxist Conceptions

While a multitude of different interpretations and revisions of Marxism exist, most of these views hold that economics fundamentally determines politics, rather than vice versa. These perspectives reverse those of realism, which posits politics and state interests as shaping economics.

For Marxist analysts, interdependence is taken as a given in international relations. Economic factors play roles of great intrinsic importance, often overshadowing state autonomy. International relationships are typically viewed in class terms, and rather than assuming that harmony and corporation grows out of interdependence, Marxists tend to see conflict as the intrinsic result of this process. In common with realists, Marxists thus adopt a premise of conflict. Unlike realists, many of them do not focus on the state as the key actor.[59]

As discussed in Chapter 5, Marxist approaches were often associated with dependency theory and the idea that the poverty of the developing world was a consequence of external causes, particularly the operation of the international capitalist system. However, the demise of the Marxist-Leninist systems in Eastern Europe and the Soviet Union, and the extraordinary economic success of a some developing countries, particularly in East Asia, are difficult to explain within Marxist and *dependencia* frameworks.[60]

Realist and Neorealist Interpretations

The most persuasive case for realism is that of Kenneth Waltz. His interpretation has been described as *structural realism* or *neorealism,* in that Waltz has sought systematically to adapt the realism of Morgenthau and Herz to a rigorous theory of international relations.[61]

For Waltz, international relations take place in an anarchic system that shapes state behavior. States are unitary actors, who at a minimum seek their own survival but may aspire to greater power. For Waltz, military power continues to be both important and useful. Indeed, concerning the 45-year period after World War II, he observes that, "The longest peace yet known rested on two pillars: bipolarity and nuclear weapons."[62] During the Cold War, Waltz held that interdependence was relatively low, and he rejected the notion that states were no longer the most important of actors. In his view, real interdependence required that states experience *mutual* vulnerability.[63] Waltz, however, found an immense discrepancy between the homogeneity implied by "interdependence" and the actual heterogeneity among states in the contemporary world. As he put it, "A world composed of greatly unequal units is scarcely an interdependent one. A world in which the Soviet Union and China pursue exclusionary policies is scarcely an interdependent one. A world of bristling nationalisms is scarcely an interdependent one."[64]

In the post–Cold War environment, despite significant changes and the weakened condition of Russia, Waltz finds that bipolarity endures, though in an altered state. As he explains, "Bipolarity continues because militarily Russia can take care of itself and because no other great powers have yet emerged,"[65] though he adds that the United States is no longer held in check by any other country or group. Based on balance-of-power theory, he anticipates that eventually the emerging structure of the international system will involve four or five great powers.

Even though the post–Cold War era brings a reduced concern for military security, Waltz does not believe that there will be a corresponding reduction in concern over competing national economic positions. In his view, there are four strong reasons for this. First, the basic structure of international politics remains anarchic and the leaders and peoples of states are concerned for their relative standing or competitive position. Second, concern over relative gains continues to take precedence over absolute ones. Economic competition ultimately can be more important than military competition, in that technological and economic advantage accumulate. Third, with the use of military force for serious advantage negated, at least among the nuclear powers, countries that are more advanced technologically and more productive have more ways to influence international outcomes. Fourth, uncertainty is a fact of life, especially in international politics. As Waltz puts it, "Anarchy places a premium on foresight. If one cannot know what is coming, developing a resource base for future use takes precedence over present prosperity."[66]

THE LIMITS OF INTERDEPENDENCE

Interdependence remains a vital fact of international relations, even though its consequences are often very uneven among states and geographic regions. Trade, monetary flows, technology, communications, and the role of multinational enterprises as well as other nonstate actors have all gained increased importance in recent decades. Capabilities—economic and in some cases military—have also burgeoned among actors other than the traditional players in Europe and North America.[67] At the same time, both a diffusion of power and increases in practical cooperation (particularly among the industrial democracies) have accompanied the expansion in international economic exchange and contact.

In most smaller and medium-sized states there has also been a diminution in national autonomy. These actors, other things being equal, encounter more tenacious constraints on their economic behavior than are often acknowledged. The few exceptions are those states that have isolated themselves from the international environment. The most autarkic states are either those dominated by brutal and often totalitarian regimes (such as North Korea), or those whose domestic society has been plunged into an anarchy of civil breakdown or spasmodic internal warfare (such as Zaire).

The largest and most powerful states remain generally less constrained in their interactions than smaller actors. While one observer has described the contemporary system as qualitatively different, so that, "it is now the national economies which must be looked upon as the extension of a global and integrated system with a logic of its own,"[68] the judgment actually applies even more to smaller and medium-sized states than to the largest actors. Even so, a country as large and powerful as the United States is significantly affected as well.

Insofar as interdependence is concerned, major realms of international relations thus exist in which the Hobbesian anarchy model has only limited application. Here the concepts of realism and power politics are insufficient for describing relationships in which extensive cooperation takes place on a systematic basis. Moreover, for states most open to the international environment, in both economic terms and in the freedom of their people to interact with the outside world, concepts concerning cooperation may have added relevance as opposed to those models based on conflict.

In this regard, Stanley Hoffmann has noted that, in the economic arena, there are significant restraints arising from "the shackles of interdependence." This occurs because "very few states, including the biggest ones, are capable of reaching their economic objectives by what has been the basic principle of international affairs: self-help."[69]

Historically, however, interdependence has waxed and waned. Economic issues have held top positions on international agendas in the past, and extensive trade, exchange, and cultural contacts did not prevent World War I from destroying many of the most civilized forms of interdependence. Interdependence is also asymmetrical, in that one side may be much more vulnerable to changes in a mutual relationship. The ability to manipulate this unequal relationship provides a source of power to the party that is less dependent and less vulnerable.[70]

On occasion, interdependence can also have negative effects. Inflationary pressures created by the twin oil shocks of the 1970s proved harmful throughout much of the world; and problems of unemployment, monetary instability, and collapsing agricultural prices as a result of excessive subsidies all illustrate damaging effects that can easily extend beyond national borders.

In vital areas, much of international relations remains subject to the basic existential problem this book has been concerned with: states exist in an international system without a single, accepted overall authority; this "self-help" system creates imperatives that shape foreign policy behavior, especially in security matters, and sometimes in other realms. Moreover, even though relations among states with market economies and democratic polities appear to offer opportunities for cooperation greater than those that have existed at any time in the post–World War II era, there remain regional areas (the Middle East, portions of South and Southeast Asia and of sub-Saharan Africa) where the perils of conflict and war often seem at least as immediate as the prospects for cooperation. In short, both real interdependence and Hobbesian power politics exist as intrinsic characteristics of contemporary international relations.

NOTES

1. *The Rise of the Trading State: Commerce and Conquest in the Modern World* (New York: Basic Books, 1986), pp. x–xi.
2. *Theory of International Politics* (Reading, MA: Addison-Wesley, 1979), p. 159.
3. "What Should We Do in the World?" *The Atlantic Monthly*, (October 1989): 84.

4. See, for example, Joanne Gowa, *Closing the Gold Window: Domestic Politics and the End of Bretton Woods* (Ithaca, NY: Cornell University Press, 1983).

5. *U.S. Power and the Multinational Corporation: The Political Economy of Direct Foreign Investment* (New York: Basic Books, 1975), pp. 4–5. Also see Gilpin, *The Political Economy of International Relations* (Princeton: Princeton University Press, 1987), Chapter 1, and Martin Staniland, *What Is Political Economy?* (New Haven: Yale University Press, 1985).

6. For elaboration of this point, see Lieber, *The Oil Decade* (New York: Praeger, 1983, and Lanham, MD: University Press of America, 1986), p. 3.

7. Important thinking about international economic matters can also be identified in still earlier periods. On sixteenth- and seventeenth-century mercantilist thought, for example, see Eli Hecksher, *Mercantilism* (London: Allen & Unwin, 1935); also Jacob Viner, "Power versus Plenty as Objectives of Foreign Policy in the Seventeenth and Eighteenth Centuries," *World Politics* 1 (October 1948):1–29.

8. Waltz, *Theory of International Politics,* p. 212.

9. For important statements of the consequences for national sovereignty of interdependence and the spread of multinational corporations, see Raymond Vernon, *Sovereignty at Bay: The Multinational Spread of U.S. Enterprises* (New York: Basic Books, 1971), and Charles P. Kindleberger, *American Business Abroad* (New Haven: Yale University Press, 1969). For a more radical treatment, see, for example, Immanuel Wallerstein, *The Capitalist World Economy* (New York: Cambridge University Press, 1979).

10. The term is that of Albert Bressand, in "Mastering the 'Worldeconomy,'" *Foreign Affairs* 61 (Spring 1983):745–746.

11. The World Bank, *World Development Report 1986* (New York: Oxford University Press, 1986), pp. 24 and 158; 1989 edition, pp. 165 and 191, 1993 edition, p. 239.

12. Data from World Bank, *World Development Report 1993* (New York: Oxford University Press, 1993), pp. 239 and 265.

13. Data from IMF and OECD, as reported in the *Economist,* 1 November 1986, p. 105. Note that calculations of trade percentages vary among sources. Part of the discrepancy depends on whether the reference is to gross *domestic* product or gross *national* product. In addition, some sources use the figure for exports alone, while others (as in the data cited here) employ the average of imports and exports.

14. See William Cline, *International Debt and the Stability of the World Economy* (Washington, DC: Institute for International Economics, 1983).

15. See, in particular, the skillful analysis by Benjamin J. Cohen, *In Whose Interest? International Banking and American Foreign Policy* (New Haven: Yale University Press, 1986).

16. For useful treatments of these institutions, see Joan Edelman Spero, *The Politics of International Economic Relations,* 4th ed. (New York: St. Martin's, 1990); and Robert S. Walters and David H. Blake, *The Politics of Global Economic Relations,* 4th ed. (Englewood Cliffs, NJ: Prentice-Hall, 1992).

17. Figures are from Helmut Schmidt, *A Grand Strategy for the West* (New Haven: Yale University Press, 1985), p. 110. Also see *The Economist,* 7 March 1992, p. 111.

18. Schmidt, p. 112.

19. *The Economist,* 12 December 1992, Survey p. 3.

20. The first four of these general changes are set out in Robert J. Lieber, "British Foreign Policy: The Limits of Maneuver," in Roy C. Macridis, ed., *Foreign Policy in World Politics,* 5th ed. (Englewood Cliffs, NJ: Prentice-Hall, 1985), pp. 1–2.

21. Robert O. Keohane and Joseph S. Nye make a similar point: "States that are better placed to maintain their coherence (because of a centralized political tradition such as France's) will be better able to manipulate uneven interdependence than fragmented

states that at first glance seem to have more resources in an issue area." *Power and Interdependence: World Politics in Transition* (Boston: Little, Brown, 1977), p. 35.

22. Calculations by Daniel Yergin and Cambridge Energy Research Associates, *International Herald Tribune*, 24 September 1984.

23. For detailed accounts see Sharon Waxman, "France's Release of Iranians Triggers Swiss Complaint," *Washington Post*, 1 January 1994, p. A15; and Alan Riding, "France Sends 2 Murder Suspects Back to Iran, Stirring Wide Protest," *New York Times*, 4 January 1994, p. A5.

24. Note that states such as France and Britain have responded to economic challenges in very different ways. For a lucid comparison of these two countries, see Peter Hall, *Governing the Economy: The Politics of State Intervention in Britain and France* (New York: Oxford University Press, 1986).

25. The dollar bought 5.35 French francs in April 1981. It peaked at almost 10 francs in March 1985, then declined to less than 7 francs a year later. The decline in the exchange rate of the franc did make French exports competitive internationally, but this effect was offset by other negative consequences discussed here.

26. Peter Hall, "Socialism in One Country: Mitterrand and the Struggle to Define a New Economic Policy for France," in Philip G. Cerny and Martin A. Schainw, eds., *Socialism, the State and Public Policy in France* (New York: Methuen, 1985), pp. 82 and 86, based on *Le Monde*, 24 March 1983, p. 40.

27. *Economist*, 19 June 1982.

28. Quoted, *New York Times*, 22 April 1984. Also see Mark Kesselman, "Socialist Possibilities and Capitalist Realities: All's Quiet on the French Leftist Front," *Research in Political Economy* 6 (1983): 277–303.

29. Data from Council on International Economic Policy, *International Economic Report of the President* (Washington, DC: U.S. Government Printing Office, January 1977), as summarized in Waltz, *Theory of International Politics*, Table 1, p. 212.

30. Data from *OECD Economic Outlook*, December 1987, p. vi, and December 1989, pp. vi and 140.

31. Spero, *The Politics of International Economic Relations*, 4th ed., (1990), p. 358.

32. See for example, the list of these arrangements in, "What is an American Auto?" *Washington Post*, 31 January 1992.

33. For use of the term "hegemonic stability," see Robert Keohane, "The Theory of Hegemonic Stability and Changes in International Economic Regimes, 1967–77," in Ole Holsti, R. Siverson, and A. George, eds., *Change in the International System* (Boulder: Westview, 1980). Also see the theoretical treatments by Stephen D. Krasner, "State Power and the Structure of International Trade," *World Politics* 28 (April 1976): 317–347, and by Keohane, *After Hegemony*, especially Chap. 1. On leadership, see especially the lucid argument of Charles P. Kindleberger, "Hierarchy Versus Inertial Cooperation," *International Organization* 40 (Autumn 1986): 841–842.

34. International regimes may be formal, through established international institutions, or informal. These regimes have been defined as, "principles, norms, rules and decision-making procedures around which actor expectations converge in a given issue area." See Stephen D. Krasner, "Structural Causes and Regime Consequences: Regimes as Intervening Variables," in Krasner, ed., *International Regimes* (Ithaca, NY: Cornell University Press, 1983), p. 1.

35. Data from Paul Bairoch, "International Industrialization Levels from 1750 to 1980," *Journal of European Economic History* 11 (Fall 1982): 269–333, at p. 275.

36. See, for example, Kenneth A. Oye, "Constrained Confidence and the Evolution of Reagan Foreign Policy," in Oye, Lieber, and Rothchild, eds., *Eagle Resurgent? The Reagan Era in American Foreign Policy* (Boston: Little, Brown, 1987) pp. 8–13.

37. New York: Random House, 1987.
38. Robert Gilpin, *War and Change in World Politics* (New York: Cambridge University Press, 1981).
39. Data from Council on Economic Priorities, as presented in Oye, pp. 10–11. Oye provides a systematic application of Gilpin's propostions to the American experience.
40. Data from International Institute for Strategic Studies, *The Military Balance, 1993–94* (London: Brassey's, October 1993), pp. 224 and 226.
41. Productivity figures from Kenneth Oye, "Beyond Postwar Order and New World Order: American Foreign Policy in Transition," in Oye, Lieber, and Donald Rothchild, eds., *Eagle in a New World: American Grand Strategy in the Post–Cold War Era* (New York: HarperCollins, 1992), p. 12.
42. See Nye, "Understating U.S. Strength," *Foreign Policy,* No. 72 (Fall 1988): 105–129; and *Bound to Lead: The Changing Nature of American Power* (New York: Basic Books, 1990). Nye notes that the United States held a 23 percent share of world product in 1975 as well as in 1990. Also see Samuel Huntington, "The U.S.—Decline or Renewal?" *Foreign Affairs,* Vol. 67, No. 2 (Winter 1988/89): 76–96. Susan Strange not only argues against the "myth" of America's lost hegemony, but concludes that "the United States' structural power has, on balance, increased." "The Persistent Myth of Lost Hegemony," *International Organization,* Vol. 41, No. 4 (Autumn 1987): 551–574, at p. 552. In another approach, which challenges those who focus on material power and wealth, Henry Nau argues that America's position depends far more on how it defines national purpose and on the efficiency of its economic policies. See, *The Myth of America's Decline: Leading the World Economy into the 1990s* (New York: Oxford University Press, 1990).
43. Gilpin, *War and Change in International Politics,* p. 145.
44. The first three of these criteria appear in Charles Kindleberger, *The World in Depression: 1929–39* (Berkeley: University of California Press, 1973). The last two were added later for a revised edition. See also his "Hierarchy versus Inertial Cooperation," p. 841. On the 1930s, see also Kenneth A. Oye, *Economic Discrimination and Political Exchange: World Political Economy in the 1930s and 1980s* (Princeton University Press, 1992).
45. Robert O. Keohane, *After Hegemony: Cooperation and Discord in the World Political Economy* (Princeton: Princeton University Press, 1984), p. 31.
46. *After Hegemony,* pp. 7–9 and 46.
47. Also see Robert Axelrod, *The Evolution of Cooperation* (New York: Basic Books, 1984); Charles Lipson, "International Cooperation in Economic and Security Affairs," *World Politics,* Vol. 38 (October 1985): 226–254; as well as Keohane's work, cited above. For a lucid analysis and critique, see Joseph M. Grieco, "Anarchy and the Limits of Cooperation: A Realist Critique of the Newest Liberal Institutionalism," *International Organization,* Vol. 42, No. 3 (Summer 1988): 485–507. Grieco makes the point that neoliberal institutionalism represents the fourth in a series of liberal institutionalist approaches. He identifies (p. 486) the earlier versions as functionalist integration theory in the 1940s, neofuntionalist regional integration theory in the 1950s and 1960s, and interdependence theory in the 1970s. Also see Grieco, *Cooperation Among Nations* (Ithaca: Cornell University Press, 1993).
48. See, for example, Susan Strange, *"Cave! hic dragones:* A critique of regime analysis," in Krasner, ed., *International Regimes,* pp. 337–354. Also see James N. Rosenau, "Before Cooperation: Hegemons, Regimes, and Habit-driven Actors in World Politics," in *International Organization* 40 (Autumn 1986): 849–894. Rosenau describes *After Hegemony* as "a daring and grandiose book," but also as "contradictory, ambivalent, and outrageous" (p. 850).

49. Cf. Keohane in regard to the International Energy Agency, "As hegemony erodes, the demand for international regimes may even increase, as the . . . institution of one in 1974 suggest[s]." *After Hegemony,* p. 244.

50. Henry A. Kissinger, *Years of Upheaval* (Boston: Little, Brown, 1982), pp. 915–916. For an account of this episode, see Lieber, *The Oil Decade,* pp. 19–21.

51. Edward L. Morse, *Modernization and the Transformation of International Relations.* (New York: Free Press, 1976), p. 150. Elsewhere, Morse adopts a less optimistic view: "interdependence in a world of nation-states is far more destabilizing than its earlier proponents or current detractors would admit. It leads to breakdowns in both domestic and international mechanisms of control and does not guarantee the development of new instruments to maintain political order" (p. 116).

52. Keohane cites this position of David Mitrany, as exemplifying what he terms an "institutionalist" view. See Mitrany, *The Functional Theory of Politics* (London: St. Martin's, 1975). Keohane adds that some of the institutionalist approaches "run . . . the risk of being naive about power and conflict." *After Hegemony,* pp. 7–8. For a different globalist perspective, see, for example, Chadwick F. Alger, "The Quest for Peace," *Quarterly Report,* Columbus, Ohio, The Mershon Center, Ohio State University, Vol. 11, No. 2 (Autumn 1986).

53. K. J. Holsti, *The Dividing Discipline: Hegemony and Diversity in International Theory* (Boston: Allen & Unwin, 1985), pp. vii and 1–2. (In reality, the anarchy paradigm has never been so pervasive as the author suggests. Certainly the realist conceptions of E. H. Carr and Hans Morgenthau, set out just before and immediately after World War II, were a reaction against a widely held outlook which was anything but anarchic in its assumptions.)

54. Rosecrance, *The Rise of the Trading State,* p. x.

55. *Power and Interdependence* 2nd ed. (Glenview, IL: Scott Foresman, 1989), pp. 22 and 249.

56. *Ibid.,* pp. 23–24.

57. *Ibid.,* pp. 24–25.

58. *Ibid.,* p. 24.

59. See, for example, Andre Gunder Frank, *Dependent Accumulation and Underdevelopment* (London: Macmillan, 1978); Harry Magdoff, *The Age of Imperialism* (New York: Monthly Review Press, 1969); Johan Galtung, *Europe: A Superpower in the Making* (London: Allen & Unwin, 1973); Immanuel Wallerstein, *The Capitalist World Economy* (New York: Cambridge University Press, 1979); Samir Amin, *Imperialism and Unequal Development* (New York: Monthly Review Press, 1977); and Anthony Brewer, *Marxist Theories of Imperialism: A Critical Survey* (London & Boston: Routledge & Kegan Paul, 1980).

60. See, for example, the critique by Stephen Krasner, who notes, "As variation in the performance of Third World states increased over time, dependency theory, with its focus on the world capitalist system as opposed to the indigenous characteristics of individual states, became more problematic." Krasner's essay, "International Political Economy," appears in Joel Krieger, ed., *The Oxford Companion to Politics of the World* (New York: Oxford University Press, 1993), pp. 453–455.

61. Keohane, ed., *Neorealism and Its Critics* (New York: Columbia University Press, 1986), p. 15.

62. Kenneth N. Waltz, "The Emerging Structure of International Politics," *International Security,* Vol. 18, No. 2 (Fall 1993): 44.

63. *Theory of International Politics,* pp. 138–139.

64. *Theory of International Politics,* p. 159.

65. "The Emerging Structure of International Politics," p. 52.

66. "The Emerging Structure of International Politics," p. 60. (Waltz summarizes the four reasons at pp. 59–60.)
67. See, for example, the analysis of Robert L. Paarlberg, "A More Capable Third World: Consequences for U.S. Security Policy," Working Paper No. 78, Woodrow Wilson International Center for Scholars, International Security Studies Program, Washington, DC, June 1985.
68. Bressand, "Mastering the 'Worldeconomy,'" *Foreign Affairs* 61 (Spring 1983): 746.
69. Stanley Hoffmann, "What Should We Do in the World?" *Atlantic Monthly* (October 1989): 86.
70. Waltz assesses the elements of sensitivity and mutual vulnerability as components of interdependence in *Theory of International Politics,* pp. 140–146. The idea of asymmetrical interdependence is discussed in Keohane and Nye, "World Politics and the International Economic System," in C. Fred Bergsten, ed., *The Future of the International Economic Order: An Agenda for Research* (Lexington, MA: Lexington Books, 1973), pp. 118–122; the authors elaborate on sensitivity versus vulnerability in *Power and Interdependence* (Boston: Little, Brown, 1977), pp. 12ff.

PART 5

Conclusion: Anarchy, Order, and Constraint

chapter 15

Conclusion

To be prepared for war is one of the most effectual means of preserving peace.
—GEORGE WASHINGTON[1]

Political realism does not require, nor does it condone, indifference to political ideals and moral principles, but it requires indeed a sharp distinction between the desirable and the possible.
—HANS J. MORGENTHAU[2]

Some argue that the end of the Cold War means the end of history as we have known it. Unfortunately, every day's newspaper contains dramatic and tragic evidence that the end of the Cold War means the return to history as we used to know it.
—SAMUEL P. HUNTINGTON[3]

Major changes have taken place in contemporary international relations—among them the end of the cold war and the bipolar distribution of power, globalization of the international economy, and the growing importance of regional actors and ethnic conflict. Despite these developments, a number of intrinsic characteristics of the international system remain relatively durable. Change has been much more common within states than in the nature of relations among states. At the level of the individual state, constraints on behavior have—if anything—intensified and strongly affect national conduct in world affairs. On the systemic level, the phenomena of both anarchy and order remain fundamental.

This chapter reviews these three enduring features of international relations—anarchy, order, and constraints on state behavior—and then reexamines realism as well as the strengths and weaknesses of the realist perspective. Finally, it assesses a series of moral imperatives and the relation of understanding to action in the international realm.

THE ENDURING FEATURES OF INTERNATIONAL RELATIONS: ANARCHY

Prediction of human affairs is a perilous and uncertain business. However, certain regularities can be identified. One of them is that the world remains divided among independent states. This reality has decisive implications for international relations. Its consequence is that states continue to feel compelled to provide for their own security. In doing so, they seek power and the means to preserve their security as they understand it. Other things being equal (and this is not always the case), their actions tend to make other states more anxious about their own security, and hence inclined to intensify their defensive efforts. The quest for power among states is thus shaped more by the security dilemma (as John H. Herz has noted), than by an inherent human urge for power (the view of Morgenthau) or the original sin of human pride (Reinhold Niebuhr).[4]

It is these basic elements—independent states existing in an international realm without any effective overall authority for resolving disputes among themselves, coupled with the security dilemma and the struggle for power to which this situation gives rise—that comprise the quasi-anarchic environment. This is the problem long ago identified by Thucydides and Hobbes. However, certain new features give this environment a nature far different from that of the Greek city-states some 2,500 years ago or even from Europe of the nineteenth century. One of the most important of these is the existence of nuclear weapons. Anarchy remains a fundamental fact of international life, but the nuclear component not only represents a potential penetration of the state; it also raises the risks of conflict in a way that threatens the very existence of international relations. As we have seen (in Chapter 6), the impact of nuclear weapons on the behavior of the United States and Russia—and quite possibly on the other overtly nuclear powers

(Britain, France, China)—was to make them more cautious in their behavior and in their willingness to risk major war.

Whether the nuclear constraint will also characterize the behavior of states in the developing world who are at—or even across—the nuclear threshold is less certain. Erich Weede has argued that general nuclear deterrence prevented war between East and West, but that stability is likely to be more precarious elsewhere:

> The end of the Soviet Union and her bloc implies the abolition of extended deterrence without its replacement by another pacifying condition. Moreover, some nuclear proliferation to developing countries is to be expected. Unfortunately, the combination of precarious balances of terror with domestic instability among poor countries seems unlikely to make nuclear deterrence work as well in future as it did in the Cold War past.[5]

Interdependence and the impact of nonstate actors (movements, ideologies, belief systems, organizations) that operate across national boundaries also have a major impact on the traditional international system. They do not reshape it altogether, but they constitute modifications of the system as classically understood. We are thus left with a paradox. On the one hand, there exists a formally anarchic structure of international relations. On the other, orderly behavior among states is a common characteristic of international society. The system, therefore, can best be described as one of *mitigated anarchy*.

THE ENDURING FEATURES OF INTERNATIONAL RELATIONS: ORDER AND THE MITIGATION OF ANARCHY

International relations is no simple, anarchic, Hobbesian war of all against all. As described earlier (in Chapter 12), efforts to establish rudimentary forms of international law and international organization have almost as long a history as those of conflict and warfare. Indeed, many of the most ambitious efforts at order have taken shape in the aftermath of crisis and war. However, impulses toward cooperation stem from more than a series of haphazard efforts to establish formal international and regional order. Important forms of cooperation under conditions of quasi-anarchy do take place. Chief among the means of cooperation are alliances, power balances, diplomacy and negotiation, and economic interdependence. Each of these deserves attention.

Alliances

As a fact of life, states are unequal in actual or potential power. Consequently, in seeking to cope with the security dilemma, they have often sought to improve their security not only through their own individual efforts, but also by means of alliances. This is hardly a novel phenomenon: it can be found in the city-state systems of classical Greece and Renaissance Italy. What is fundamental about both past and present patterns is that the criteria for alliance behavior have typically been shaped at least as much by power and geopolitics as by ideology. Moreover, as Waltz observes, neorealist or structural realist theory leads to the belief that "the placement of states in the international system accounts for a good deal of their behavior."[6] Thus the ancient maxim that "my enemy's enemy is my friend" finds applicability in very diverse settings. Consider several illustrations of this principle:

> Great Britain's and the United States' alliance with Stalin's Russia against Nazi Germany in World War II.

> American rapprochement with China vis-à-vis the Soviet Union.

> Brazil's tacit cooperation with Britain during the latter's war with Argentina in the Falkland Islands.

> Syria's support for Iran during the Iran-Iraq War and for the American-led coalition against Iraq in the Gulf conflict.

These examples, as well as an extensive historical list of cases, demonstrate that alliances have long provided a means for states to mitigate the degree of anarchy in their environment. Indeed, an even better example can be found in the experience of Western Europe after World War II. There, the ravages of war, the threat posed by the Soviet Union, the division of Europe, and the alliance hegemony (or leadership) exercised by the United States caused the creation of a security community. Both the role of American authority and the growth of a wide network of institutions (NATO, European Community, and others) made the anarchy model largely inapplicable as a description of relations among the countries of Western Europe. This did not preclude conflict or even war at the margins, as in the case of rivalry between Greece and Turkey in the Aegean Sea and eastern Mediterranean. Nor did it rule out involvement in conflict elsewhere, as in the case of Britain in the Falklands, or eliminate the need for deterrence of the Soviet Union in Central Europe. Nonetheless, at least as far as the major actors (Britain, France, Germany, Italy, Holland, Spain) were concerned, an epoch of three centuries of conflict and war was superseded.

The European example is instructive in that it demonstrates that systemic anarchy can be overcome despite a long and bloody history of warfare. On the other hand, the example is nearly *sui generis* in that it is based on a limited geographic area and unique historical circumstances.

Power Balances

The structure of the international system creates a propensity for states to seek to enhance their own power. They do this either through their own efforts or in combination with other states by means of alliances. Concern with power can bring about an equilibrium when roughly comparable alignments emerge. The balance of power—understood in this sense of approximate parity—has been associated with stability and restraint for lengthy periods of time.

As Kenneth Waltz has noted, balance-of-power logic suggests that tendencies toward the concentration of international power are offset by the opposite tendency toward formation of countervailing coalitions. The rise of a powerful, aggressive state creates an incentive for others to align against it. The past four centuries of Western history support the notion that, in the terms of Waltz, Stephen Van Evera, Kenneth Oye, and others, *balancing* dominates *bandwagoning*.[7] That is, rising powers such as Louis XIV, Napoleon, Kaiser Wilhelm, Hitler, and even the Soviet Union at times during the postwar era, sought hegemony but wound up galvanizing the creation of powerful coalitions against themselves.

Historically, the peace in Europe was twice maintained for a century or more as a result of a balance of power among the principal actors. This correspondence of peace and power balance can be identified as beginning in 1648 with the Treaty of Westphalia, which ended the wars of religion and ushered in the era of territorial states as the basis of the modern state system. The resultant stability in Europe lasted until 1772. Following the Napoleonic Wars, there again emerged a long period of *relative* stability (i.e., of no major general war, though there were sporadic lesser conflicts). This period lasted from 1815 to the outbreak of World War I in 1914. More recently, the bipolar confrontation between the United States and the Soviet Union saw an evolving but durable balance between the two superpowers. Despite numerous regional conflicts, this balance helped to prevent a major war between the blocs or between the Americans and Soviets directly.

From this experience it is evident that a stable balance-of-power situation can be conducive to order.[8] It may prevent domination by a single imperial power, afford protection to weaker states, cause the major actors to conduct themselves with greater restraint, and forestall the onset of war. Ironically, the accumulation of power, armament, and alliances can at times lead to a diminution of anarchy rather than an intensification of it. Conversely, the absence of a power balance can be destabilizing. Thus Iraq's August 1990 invasion of Kuwait resulted not only from the ruthlessness of Saddam Hussein, but also because the severe weakening of Iran in the Iran-Iraq war left the Persian Gulf region without a counterbalance to Iraqi power.

The balance of power is not, however, a panacea for promoting order in an otherwise anarchic world. The conditions for its successful operation are by no means universal, and when it does break down, the consequences (as in World Wars I and II) can be catastrophic. The lessons of seventeenth-through nineteenth-century Europe suggest a series of prerequisites if the balance of power is to operate effectively in a multipolar system. These include the following:

1. The principal states involved should be roughly similar in size and power.
2. They should be in general agreement on the rules of conduct.
3. No state should seek to destroy another nor the existing system itself.
4. Every state should be a potential ally for the others, and any state defeated in war (as in the case of France in 1815) should be rapidly readmitted to the system.
5. Differences of value or ideology among states should not be so great as to make the system and the above rules unworkable.[9]

Limits to the Applicability of Power in Mitigating Anarchy

From the above list it is clear that mitigation of anarchy through a balance of power can apply only in special circumstances.[10]

1. Europe during the more than two and a half centuries from 1648 to 1914 exhibited more of a consensus on basic values than has subsequently been the case for the twentieth-century world; moreover, until the early twentieth century, Britain was unique in acting as a balancer, throwing its weight against whichever European power seemed likely to achieve continental predominance.

2. The closing of colonial frontiers after 1900 (with the division of Africa completed) meant that adjustments among the powers would be less flexible in the future, in that a gain for one actor could only come at the direct expense of another.

3. In a modern era it is much harder to conduct an adroit and often cynical realpolitik, especially in a democratic society with its press, attentive public, legislative bodies, and pressure groups.

4. The spread and intensification of powerful ideological, religious, and ethnic rivalries may make conflicts more bitter and less restrained, while compromises and alliances become harder to achieve.

5. The intensity of modern warfare, culminating in the nuclear era, makes the fighting of major wars among the principal players more and more untenable as a means of resolving disputes.

Conceptual questions also exist in identifying the balance of power as an effective, nonutopian means of providing international stability. More than a generation ago, Ernst Haas and others noted serious problems in defining what the term *balance of power* actually means.[11] For example, is the balance of power a quasi-automatic process characteristic of relations between states, or is it something that can only be achieved by skilled and subtle diplomatic maneuver? Is it correct to assume that the nineteenth-century European experience demonstrates the need for at least five major actors in a multipolar system (so that there exists sufficient room for maneuver and bargaining), or is it the case instead that a bipolar alignment (as in the Soviet-American confrontation during the Cold War) may actually make for more durable stability?*

Finally, is peace more likely when power is evenly balanced or, instead, when one side predominates? The body of theorizing on hegemonic stability, as well as the historical experience of the Pax Romana (which brought nearly a thousand years of stability and progress—though by no means justice or complete peace—to much of Europe, North Africa, and the Middle East) makes this an intriguing question. Waltz notes an important distinction between peace and stability. Although major wars are often identified with the instability of a system, those systems that survive such wars demonstrate their stability. In this sense, "The multi-

---

*The stability of bipolar versus multipolar systems is considered in Chapter 11.

polar world was highly stable, but all too war-prone. The bipolar world has been highly peaceful, but unfortunately less stable than its predecessor.[12]

Without minimizing the weight of these historical and conceptual difficulties, thinking in terms of power realities does provide a corrective to simplistic, one-dimensional modes of analysis. Indeed, power considerations continue to make themselves felt, even in the presence of strong ideological and religious imperatives. Consider, for example, that at the height of the Cold War the United States provided major military aid to Marshall Tito's Yugoslavia. The Balkan country remained a Marxist-Leninist dictatorship, yet Tito's defection from Stalin's Soviet bloc provided ample motivation for strong American support of a maverick Communist leader.

American rapprochement with China in the early 1970s provides another case in point. Although the People's Republic of China was still ruled by its original revolutionary leaders (Mao Zedong and Zhao Enlai), and was even in the midst of the Cultural Revolution, it was President Richard Nixon (one of the staunchest anti-Communist figures of the early Cold War period) who presided over this policy of rapprochement. In doing so, Nixon was motivated by the desire to counterbalance Soviet power at a time when the United States was undertaking its own agonizing withdrawal from Vietnam.

In yet another example, the radical Islamic fundamentalist regime of the Ayatollah Khomeini in Iran received support from three unlikely sources during the early and mid 1980s: Syria, which, though Arab and secular rather than Persian and fundamentalist, supported Iran because of bitter political differences with Iraq; Israel, which sold arms to the fanatically anti-Zionist ayatollah in order to weaken the closer and more threatening Iraq, which had fought in each of the previous Arab-Israeli wars; and the United States, which, despite staunch opposition to terrorism, covertly arranged major arms shipments in the hope of maintaining an opening to Iran for an eventual post-Khomeini era, but especially in a bungled effort to secure the release of hostages held by pro-Iranian groups in Lebanon.

In another Middle East case, the Syrian regime of President Hafez al-Assad sided with the American-led coalition against Saddam Hussein and Iraq during the 1990–1991 Gulf crisis and war. Although the Syrian and Iraqi regimes exhibited important domestic similarities (brutally authoritarian, secular, Arab-nationalist, anti-Israel), the intense power rivalries between the two countries and their leaders, along with the demise of the Soviet Union as Syria's patron, proved to be a stronger determinant of Syria's external behavior.

Diplomacy and Negotiation

International relations has long seen the formal exchange of emissaries charged with tasks of representation, communication, and negotiation. Indeed, practices such as diplomatic immunity can be found in ancient history. The realm of diplomacy and negotiation thus provides yet another means by which the elements of international anarchy are regularly mitigated.

Though modern students of realism typically emphasize the role of power and force in international relations, it is vital to recognize that realism makes considerable room for diplomacy. Morgenthau, for example, emphasized the importance of prudence in pursuing national objectives and viewed diplomacy as the best available means for preserving peace, even while acknowledging grave obstacles to its success.

Negotiation as a means of adjustment and flexibility in the relations among states is a component of contemporary international relations that deserves attention. For example, in the last three decades of the Cold War, the superpowers had conducted arms control negotiations concerning strategic nuclear weapons and conventional forces. Note that these negotiations, as in the case of the limited nuclear test ban treaty of 1963, signed by President Kennedy and Nikita Khrushchev, as well as the subsequent SALT I and II and start negotiations, did not at the time represent an end to the military competition between the United States and USSR. They did, however, help to channel an adversarial relationship in ways manageable by both sides, thus reducing the risks that their confrontation might escalate out of control, either inadvertently or in response to a regional crisis.

Diplomacy and negotiations do not eliminate conflict or warfare, but they often alleviate the anarchy problem as well as divert inevitable rivalries and competition so that these can be better managed by the parties involved.

Economic Interdependence

A vast amount of economic interchange takes place across national borders. While these exchanges are not always harmonious, they provide another compelling example that international relations does not conform to a narrow definition of the anarchy model. As Stanley Hoffmann has observed, the logic of the global economic arena is not a zero-sum game. Instead, countries have an interest in the prosperity of the global economy and in that of the other players.[13]

The globalization of the international economy thus has had a major impact on peoples and their governments. This is evident in the vast expansion of world trade and investment, as exemplified in the remarkable economic growth of East Asia and the integration of China into the world economy despite the continuation of its Communist regime. Other examples include the growing economic integration of Western Europe; establishment of the North American Free Trade Agreement to include Mexico as well as Canada and the United States; major reductions in trade barriers by means of the January 1994 GATT agreement; and the way in which international economic imperatives have shaped a movement toward market economies, privatization, and democratization in Latin America and Eastern Europe.

The established international regimes, or rules of the game, for trade, money, investment, technology, energy, communications, travel, tourism, and a host of other issue areas demonstrate that these are not exclusively "low politics" side shows on a world stage mainly preoccupied with the big issues of war and peace. To be sure, in one-to-one confrontations, political and security considerations often override those of economics or interdependence, and it is vital to understand that economic relationships can experience conflict. Thus Stanley Hoffmann identifies the workings of the global economy, including poverty, overpopulation, migrations, and inequality among states as especially important sources of international insecurity (along with nationalism) in the post–Cold War world.[14] Nonetheless, the mitigation of anarchy is a fact of international life.

In sum, while anarchy is unquestionably an enduring feature of international relations, order and the mitigation of anarchy are fundamental as well. Competition and sometimes conflict invariably accompany relations among states, but the competition can be and is channeled into a variety of avenues. In turn, conflict does not by any means always entail war. It may be redirected into nonmilitary pursuits (economic, cultural, and even sporting rivalries), and as a practical matter is frequently expressed through membership in alliances, in power balances among competing states, and in diplomacy and negotiations. Order, the maintenance of peace, and even active cooperation occur regularly and necessarily in international relations, and not merely as occasional chance expressions of idealistic but doomed impulses. "Cooperation under anarchy" thus takes many forms.

THE ENDURING FEATURES OF INTERNATIONAL RELATIONS: CONSTRAINTS ON STATE BEHAVIOR

Anarchy and order are fundamental characteristics of the international system. State behavior within this system is shaped by these and other conditions of the international environment. Peter Gourevitch has used the phrase "second-image-reversed" to describe this phenomenon.[15] While states continue to exercise important matters of choice in their external conduct, they nonetheless remain more subject to constraints than is often appreciated. This problem of constraint has been treated at length (in Chapter 14), but several key features are worth highlighting here because of their enduring importance.

The sources of constraint are not only external. Democratic states typically find that their foreign policies require domestic support if they are to succeed. This means not only popular acceptance, but often legislative support and the backing of influential pressure groups. Constraints shape not only international behavior; policies thought of as primarily domestic in scope are often significantly affected by a state's position in the international environment. Thus domestic politics and foreign policy frequently become intertwined, as do issues otherwise considered economic or political in nature. To be sure, constraints are far more pronounced for small states than for larger and more powerful ones, yet even the superpowers can be significantly affected.

In the case of the United States, in addition to obvious areas such as national security and strategic nuclear deterrence, such important matters as economic growth, unemployment, the balance of trade, exchange rates, energy prices, the environment, and immigration are deeply affected by external circumstances. Another external influence, the end of the Soviet threat, has also had a major impact on American policy. As a result, the public and Congress have given a much lower priority to foreign affairs,[16] and they are far less willing to support foreign expenditures or the commitment of American forces in conflicts abroad.

Even the Soviet Union, during the 1970s and increasingly in the 1980s, despite a far greater degree of economic and political closure toward the external world and dictatorship by the Communist Party, was unable to act without significant constraints on its behavior. Many of these constraints were economic and technological. The USSR maintained an overall military budget at least as great as that of the United States, yet it did so with a gross national product less than one-half that of the United States, and with technology that lagged significantly behind the West and Japan. The increasing costs of foreign military and political commitments became a huge drain on the Soviets' limited economic base. Major competing demands also came from other sectors: seriously inadequate housing and agriculture, energy exploration and development to arrest a decline in oil production and deal with difficulties in civilian nuclear power, public health (e.g. in response to declining life expectancy), demands for the modernization of domestic industry and technology, and efforts to cope with an inadequate supply of modern consumer goods.

A decline in world prices for exports of energy and of gold in the mid 1980s proved costly to the Soviets. So did expenditures for pro-Soviet regimes in Cuba, Ethiopia, Angola, Nicaragua, and the long war in Afghanistan. Indeed, the Soviets, by their power and size as well as their efforts to exert hegemony around their periphery, mobilized a remarkably broad and diverse array of opposition against themselves. This ranged from endemic discontent in Poland and most of Eastern Europe, to Asian and Middle Eastern opposition to the Soviet invasion of Afghanistan, to opposition by China and Japan in the Far East. Ultimately, while external constraints did not by themselves determine the transformation in Soviet policies undertaken by Gorbachev and the subsequent collapse of the USSR, they undoubtedly had a major impact in shaping the dramatic choices he made, as well as those of his successor, Boris Yeltsin.

THE NEOREALIST IMPERATIVE

Realism is an elusive concept. It is variously identified as a means of understanding and explaining international relations, as a prescription for how to conduct policy, and as a specific mode of analysis identified with Hans Morgenthau and subsequently modified by Kenneth Waltz and others in a number of divergent approaches loosely termed *structural realist* or *neorealist.**

Few observers or practitioners would care to categorize themselves as "unrealistic" in their approach to world affairs. But if realism has become pervasive, it is important to be reminded of what it is and is not. Understood in any of its above variations, realism implies rejection of modes of thought that are utopian or narrowly legalistic. However, realism's dismissal of international idealism (particu-

---

*Approaches to neorealism are considered in Chapter 14.

larly of the kind that failed in the years prior to World War II) was also accompanied by aversion to an opposite tendency. The latter involved a zealous or ideological mindset in approaching foreign policy and was periodically evident during the Cold War.

The neorealist concern with power and national interest should not be confused with a simple and unqualified emphasis on anarchy and force as both the overriding explanatory tools and the chief criteria by which foreign policy is conducted. Although the anarchy problem indelibly shapes the international environment, neorealism also takes into account order and constraint as intrinsic to international relations. No mode of analysis, nor any guidelines for policy that overlook these realities, is worthy of being labeled "realist." In short, it remains vital to appreciate the distinction between "Rambo" and reality.[17]

In practical terms, both the understanding of world affairs and precepts for the conduct of foreign policy must be conditioned on an appreciation of prevailing power realities and of the need for prudence. For example, Morgenthau was critical of American policy in Vietnam, not because he entertained any illusions about Ho Chi Minh and the North Vietnamese, but because the policy established goals unattainable at a price that the United States could afford,[18] and because it imposed costs that were damaging to more fundamental American interests. Realism also cautions against strategies that assume benign invincibility (the notion that one's own intentions are self-evidently pure and that it is possible to prevail in *any* task, no matter how unlimited the objective, provided only that the effort is made).

In the post–Cold War international evironment, neorealism provides a useful perspective on the failure of the international community to deal effectively with military dictatorship and oppression in Haiti, instability and warlordism in Somalia, and war and appalling human rights abuses in Bosnia. It does so by reminding us of the lack of real authority at the international system level and the inadequacy of words, resolutions, and good intentions unsupported by power.

In a sense, it seems appropriate to use the term *existential realism* to convey the basic meaning of the concept. Borrowing from the literature of deterrence, there is a valuable antecedent for this terminology. In the early 1980s, Robert Jervis in writing about strategic nuclear deterrence observed that mutual assured destruction "exists as a fact, irrespective of policy,"[19] and he citd what has been termed "existential deterrence."[20] Adopting that language, it can be said that realism is *existential,* in the sense that the concept designates a series of realities about the international system in which states exist.[21]

Moral Imperatives

To an important degree, state behavior is shaped by the conditions of the international environment and the tenacious constraints these impose. This does not mean, however, that all political systems should be regarded as somehow comparable, or that we can or should turn a blind eye to matters of human rights, morality, and common decency.

Profound differences remain between societies in which governments operate with the consent of the governed and where minority rights are protected, and those that oppress their people—regardless of whether the rationale is ideological, ethnic, or merely to protect the privileges of a narrowly based ruling elite. Societies that respect political liberties and human rights are much more likely to remain viable over the long run than those that do not. Other things being equal, democratic societies—however imperfect—are often more prudent in their behavior than dictatorships. Democracies are not necessarily more likely to avoid war, but war *between* democracies has rarely if ever taken place. Moreover, international agreements, for example, in the form of international law, the United Nations Charter, the Universal Declaration of Human Rights, and the Helsinki Accords of 1975, have typically included specific undertakings in regard to human rights and acceptable norms of international behavior.

The Relationship of Understanding to Action

There are bona fide human and moral reasons for seeking to better the conditions in which people live. Nothing here can or should be understood as ruling out value judgments, nor dictating "benign neglect" of pressing human problems and abuses of human rights. Indeed, to act otherwise is often neither "realistic" nor good politics. Some types of political systems and international behavior can and should be condemned, and national policies can often be framed with these criteria in mind. Illustratively, during the Cold War long-term support for "friendly" dictatorial regimes, on the grounds that this was required by the harsh realities of world politics, often proved counterproductive. American experience with the dictatorships of Batista in Cuba, the Shah in Iran, and Somosa in Nicaragua suggested that the longer such regimes endured, the more radical and anti-American were the successor regimes that captured power after their demise.[22] By contrast, U.S. support for human rights in Argentina and the Philippines may have contributed to much more moderate outcomes in those societies.

A sense of proportion does require that broader concerns be linked to a recognition of real and sometimes painful limits. In addressing a wide range of world issues, it is vital to appreciate that the consequences of political action almost invariably involve a degree of uncertainty. Not infrequently, outcomes differ from what policymakers or advocates of policy originally intend. Theologians such as Reinhold Niebuhr have observed that the realms of politics and morals must be differentiated. We can seek to act morally and responsibly in international affairs, but politics frequently imposes choices of lesser evils. To address basic questions of international relations, or domestic politics for that matter, as though all issues could be reduced to simple questions of right or wrong, as though tradeoffs and competing values were not often at stake, is to impose a degree of certainty and simplicity that bears little relation to reality.

In a nuclear age, harsh realities cannot be avoided—indeed, overlooking them creates major dangers. We cannot wish away the existence of nuclear weapons; they will not disappear, nor will states soon come to coalesce into any identifiable form of acceptable international order or authority. Regularities in both human and international behavior are identifiable from past eras, but the existence of nuclear weapons does make world affairs of the last half of the twentieth century unique. To state this irreducible fact does not by itself dictate a particular course of action; it does, however, remind us that there exists an issue hierarchy that we ignore at our peril.

In sum, it is important to approach international relations with an appreciation of its most durable features. These include realities of power and anarchy, the enduring rudiments of order and constraint, moral imperatives, value tradeoffs and the limits of certainty in political action, and the ultimate risks of catastrophe. The difficulty of this task brings to mind the observation of Albert Einstein. He was once asked, "Why is it that when the mind of man has stretched so far as to discover the structure of the atom we have been unable to devise the political means to keep the atom from destroying us?" He is said to have replied, "That is simple, my friend, it is because politics is more difficult than physics."[23]

To pose the problem at this level is not a counsel of inaction, but instead a reminder of the need to avoid oversimplification. The key to both understanding and action is a reliable grasp of the realities that characterize international relations. To bear in mind the above stipulations, while at the same time aspiring toward some viable form of international society, is a fundamental task.

NOTES

1. *First Annual Address, to both Houses of Congress,* 8 January 1790. The widely quoted Latin antecedent is, "Qui desiderat pacem praeparet bellum" (Who would desire peace should be prepared for war). Vegetius, *Rei Militari* 3, Prolog.

2. Morgenthau, *Politics Among Nations,* 5th ed., p. 7.

3. Samuel P. Huntington, "Why International Primacy Matters," *International Security,* Vol. 17, No. 4 (Spring 1993): 68–83 at p. 71.

4. John H. Herz, "From Geneva 1935 to Geneva 1985: Roots of My Views on World Affairs," *International Studies Notes* 12 (Spring 1986): 28.

5. Erich Weede, "Conflict Patterns During the Cold War Period and Thereafter," paper presented at Conference on The Impact of Global Political Change on the Middle East, Haifa University, May 4–6, 1993, p. 1.

6. Kenneth N. Waltz, "The Emerging Structure of International Politics," *International Security,* Vol, 18, No. 2 (Fall 1993): 45. Waltz goes on to identify what he considers to be striking similarities in the external behavior of the United States and the Soviet Union during the Cold War. Also see *Theory of International Politics* (New York: McGraw-Hill, 1979).

7. See Kenneth N. Waltz, *Theory of International Politics* (New York: Random House, 1979), pp. 125–126. The term "bandwagoning" originates with Stephen Van Evera. Also see Kenneth Oye's lucid discussion and application of the concepts in "Constrained Confidence and the Evolution of Reagan Foreign Policy," in Oye, Lieber, and Donald Rothchild, eds., *Eagle Resurgent? The Reagan Era in American Foreign Policy* (Boston: Little, Brown, 1987), p. 21. See also Stephen M. Walt, *The Origins of Alliances* (Ithaca, NY: Cornell University Press, 1987).

8. This point was also made by Hedley Bull in *The Anarchical Society* (New York: Columbia University Press, 1977).

9. The restraint engendered by a moral consensus is discussed in Morgenthau, *Politics Among Nations,* 5th ed. (1978), pp. 221–228.

10. The historical limits of the balance of power model have been widely analyzed by historians and by such leading realist figures as Morgenthau and Henry Kissinger, among others.

11. Ernst Haas, "The Balance of Power: Prescription, Concept or Propoganda?" *World Politics* 5 (July 1953): 442-476.

12. "The Emerging Structure of International Politics," p. 45.

13. "What Should We Do in the World?" *Atlantic Monthly* (October 1989): p. 84.

14. Stanley Hoffmann, "Delusions of World Order," *New York Review of Books,* 9 April 1992, p. 37.

15. See Peter Gourevitch, *Politics in Hard Times: Comparative Responses to International Economic Crises* (Ithaca, NY: Cornell University Press, 1986).

16. Illustratively, exit polls of voters in the November 1992 presidential election found that only 9 percent of Americans cited foreign policy as among the two top issues influencing their vote. Source: Voter Research & Surveys. Election day poll conducted by a consortium of CBS, NBC, ABC and CNN, November 3, 1992.

17. For the phrase, I am indebted to the title of William Schneider's thoughtful essay, "'Rambo' and Reality: Having it Both Ways," in Oye, Lieber, and Rothchild, eds. *Eagle Resurgent? The Reagan Era in American Foreign Policy,* pp. 41–73.

18. Hoffmann emphasizes this point in "Realism and Its Discontents," p. 134. Morgenthau criticized the impulse toward "nationalistic univeralism," which claims for a single nation the right to impose its world view on all others. See *Politics Among Nations,* 5th ed., p. 339. Also see Stephen M. Walt, "The Case for Finite Containment: Analyzing U.S. Grand Strategy," *International Security* 14:1 (Summer 1989): 5–49.

19. Jervis, *The Illogic of American Nuclear Strategy* (Ithaca, NY: Cornell University Press, 1984), p. 184.

20. Ibid., p. 155, quoting McGeorge Bundy, "The Bishops and the Bomb," *New York Review of Books,* 16 June 1983, pp. 3–8.

21. This argument is developed in Lieber, "Existential Realism After the Cold War," *The Washington Quarterly,* Vol. 16, No. 1 (Winter 1993): 155–168, at p. 156.

22. See Robert A. Pastor, "Preempting Revolutions: The Boundaries of U.S. Influence," *International Security,* Vol. 15, No. 4 (Spring 1991): 54–86.

23. Quoted in John H. Herz, *International Politics in the Atomic Age* (New York: Columbia University Press, 1962), p. 214n.

INDEX